12038923

26

Preface

This is the seventh volume in the Commission's series of *Guides to sources for British history*. Like its predecessors, it is based on the resources of the National Register of Archives. However, as the introduction explains and as the text bears witness, the volume also embodies the results of considerable additional research, in order to check, amplify or supplement information already in the Register. This work could not have been carried out without the generous help of many individuals, and the Commissioners wish to express their warm gratitude to all those owners and custodians of manuscripts, librarians, archivists and historians who so readily responded to requests for information and assistance.

The guide has been compiled by a research and editorial team consisting of Dr NW James, Dr SG Roberts and Mr RJ Sargent and led by Dr RJ Olney.

BS SMITH
Secretary
18 November 1988

Quality House, Quality Court,
Chancery Lane, London WC2A 1HP

Preface

Contents

Introduction

This guide describes the papers of men and women who were active in British political life between 1782 and 1900, excluding those whose papers have already been dealt with in the first volume of the series, *Papers of British cabinet ministers 1782-1900* (1982). Its main focus is on members of the House of Commons and House of Lords, both those who held office outside the Cabinet and back-benchers. Also included are private secretaries of senior politicians (where their papers can be separately described), political hostesses, party managers, national agents, political journalists, local politicians and those engaged in extra-parliamentary movements. Pamphleteers, political economists, philanthropists and holders of non-political offices have been excluded unless they can also be described as active politicians; and paid local agents have also been omitted.

Within the category of active politician as thus defined, the guide includes all those individuals known to the Commission who left a significant quantity of political papers relating to the period 1782-1900. As in previous volumes in the series, the guide is concerned in each case with the papers remaining in the hands of an individual at his or her death, including letters subsequently returned to their senders. Non-political as well as political papers are described, although miscellaneous printed items and formal documents such as patents or commissions are normally excluded. Legal and estate papers are excluded unless they are clearly part of the individual's personal papers, but political papers forming part of large family collections have been attributed where possible to individual members of the family. Family letters, particularly from a politician to his wife, are described where they are intermingled with his own papers and are of political importance.

The covering dates of the volume were chosen to conform with those for the volumes on Cabinet ministers, diplomats and colonial governors already published in the series. In geographical terms the guide covers Ireland, which for most of the period had no separate legislature, as well as Great Britain. The Commission has always concerned itself with pre-1922 Irish records; and in the period under consideration the Irish question was seldom far from the forefront of British politics.

The starting point of this guide, as of its predecessors in the series, was the Commission's National Register of Archives. An initial trawl of its resources produced some 600 names, but this list was modified and amplified during subsequent research and investigation. Eventually about 1,350 politicians were identified as having left papers of some description, and of these 705 were chosen for inclusion in the guide. Of those 705, the entries relating to 85 are based on, or incorporate, knowledge acquired through the personal inspection of manuscripts during research for the volume.

The subjects of the guide range from the anti-Catholic Duke of Cumberland, later King of Hanover, to the radical tailor Francis Place, and from Viscount Pery, born in 1719, to Viscount Samuel, who died in 1963. Among the senior office-holders lords lieutenant of Ireland are most fully represented, whilst there are two presidents of the Board of Control and seven out of a possible nine Speakers of the House of Commons. Among the most important collections, however, are those of Edmund Burke, who held only minor government office, and those of Richard Cobden, Daniel O'Connell and Samuel Whitbread, who held no office at all. Other collections, varying from the substantial to the fragmentary, relate to politicians who did not enter Parliament—abolitionists, Chartists, Anti-Corn Law Leaguers, United Irishmen, advocates of women's suffrage and others.

As with the guide to the *Papers of British cabinet ministers*, this volume also includes a large number of individuals whose interests extended far beyond party politics, and who left correspondingly rich and varied collections. In a period, for instance, when politics and religion were so closely connected it is not surprising that a number of politicians should have left papers relating to their positions as leading catholic or protestant laymen. The entries for such figures as Henry Drummond, CN Newdegate, the seventh Earl of Shaftesbury and William Wilberforce could in fact be regarded as a supplement to the immediately preceding volume in this series, *Papers of British churchmen 1780-1940*.

For the 705 individuals in the guide a total of 1,276 groups of papers have been identified, varying considerably in type of document as well as size. Office-holders sometimes left semi-official papers of a kind familiar from the papers of Cabinet ministers, diplomats or colonial governors. Characteristic, for instance, of the papers of lords lieutenant of Ireland are letter books, audience books, memorials, petitions and accounts relating to their official establishments. Papers of parliamentarians contain Speakers' diaries, parliamentary journals and diaries, and records relating to commissions and select committees, including (in Thomas Greene's papers) material relating to the rebuilding of the Palace of Westminster itself. Diaries such as those of Charles Greville and Sir Edward Hamilton have long been well-known; less so are the political reports written to relatives such as those to be found in the papers of RB Haldane, RC Munro-Ferguson and Sir Richard Temple.

Not surprisingly, papers relating to parliamentary and other elections and to constituency and local politics are prominent in many of these collections. As well as correspondence they may include freeholders' books and rolls, copies of registers, legal records of burgage properties conferring the vote in certain boroughs, canvass and poll books, election squibs and other printed material, minutes of election committees, and papers relating to disputed returns. In some cases records of political associations have survived among the papers of individuals—those, for instance, of the Central Agricultural Society 1836-40 among the papers of Sir Charles Broke Vere, those of the Northern Reform Union 1857-60 among Joseph Cowen's papers, and those of the Reform League 1865-9 in the Howell collection. Towards the end of the nineteenth century the increasingly rapid growth in political organisation is reflected in the changing character of politicians' papers, and nowhere is this more clearly seen than in the large accumulations of Irish politicians such as Michael Davitt, John Dillon, Timothy Harrington, William O'Brien and John Redmond.

The papers in the guide are to be found in 208 repositories and 156 private collections, making a total of 363 known locations for the 1,276 groups. Of the 208 repositories, 157 are in Great Britain and Northern Ireland and a further 51 in the

Republic of Ireland, the United States of America and elsewhere in the world. Of the 156 private collections, all are in Great Britain or Ireland. In a few cases large collections have been dismembered through sale at auction, notably the papers of JW Croker and JS Mill in the 1920s and the Sheffield Park papers, including the papers of the 1st Earl of Sheffield and Lord Glenbervie, in 1981. The Croker papers are now in eleven known locations, the Mill and Sheffield papers in ten. By contrast many collections have been preserved intact, either in private hands or in a library or record office; but it is noteworthy that the historian seeking the complete papers of an individual is more likely than not to find them in two or more physically separated groups.

In 27 cases the Commission has noted the passage of groups of papers through the sale room but has not yet discovered their present whereabouts. In this and other ways the guide cannot claim to be exhaustive, and the Commission is always very glad to receive fresh information from owners, custodians and scholars.

A few of the individuals in this guide have also appeared in previous volumes in the series. In such cases only their political papers are described here, and where necessary a cross-reference is given in the form 'See also *Diplomats*' or 'See also *Colonial Governors*'.

Access to privately owned papers

Privately owned collections of papers deposited on loan in libraries, record offices and other public institutions are normally available for research without restriction. Special conditions, however, may sometimes apply to their use, particularly if they are to be cited in published works. Advice on such matters should be sought from the institutions concerned.

Permission to see a collection that remains in private custody should be sought from its owner in writing, either direct, or, where indicated, through an intermediary. Applicants are reminded that such papers can normally be made available for study only at considerable inconvenience to their owners, and that access for the purposes of research is a privilege and not a right. The conditions of access cited in the guide are those that prevailed in September 1988. Details of the present location of collections whose ownership or whereabouts is not specified in the guide may, where appropriate, be obtained from the Commission.[1]

Those wishing to consult papers in private hands are also advised to consult catalogues or other finding aids available in the Commission's search room or elsewhere before approaching owners or custodians. The Commission's published reports are cited by the initials HMC. Lists available for consultation in the National Register of Archives are cited by their NRA number.

1. Enquiries to the Commission should be addressed to the Secretary, The Royal Commission on Historical Manuscripts, Quality House, Quality Court, Chancery Lane, London WC2A 1HP. Where indicated, enquiries about Scottish collections should be addressed to the Secretary, National Register of Archives (Scotland), West Register House, Charlotte Square, Edinburgh EH2 4DF. For addresses of repositories generally see the Commission's *Record Repositories in Great Britain, a geographical directory*, eighth edition, HMSO 1987.

Papers of British politicians 1782-1900

[1] **ABBOT, Charles** (1757-1829), 1st Baron Colchester 1817

MP Helston 1795-1802, New Woodstock 1802-6, Oxford University 1806-17; chief secretary for Ireland 1801-2; Speaker of the House of Commons 1802-17

Corresp and papers as chief secretary 1801-2 (69 folders); papers as Speaker 1802-17 (3 boxes); speeches mainly as Speaker (1 vol); political and misc corresp 1802-29 (c7 boxes, 4 bundles); journals incl bound-in corresp 1757-1829 (7 vols); memoranda rel to audiences, etc, with some autobiographical notes (2 folders); family corresp 1812-28 (5 folders); accounts 1778-1826 (9 vols); travel journals 1778-1822 (19 vols); misc political, literary, travel and other papers 1794-1828 (c23 vols, folders and bundles).
Public Record Office (PRO 30/9). Presented by Lady Colchester 1923. NRA 8652.

Address from the Committee of London Protestants 1813.
House of Lords Record Office. See *List of accessions to repositories [1956]*, 1957, p41.

Legal MSS and notebooks (31 vols).
Lincoln's Inn Library, London (Misc 102-32). Presented 1848.

Travel journals 1815, 1827 (2 vols).
Untraced. Sold at Lawrence's of Crewkerne 24 June 1982, lot 247.

ABERCROMBY, see Duff.

[2] **ACHESON, Arthur** (c1742-1807), 2nd Viscount Gosford 1790, 1st Earl of Gosford 1806

MP Old Leighlin 1783-90

Political and personal corresp c1776-1805 (c145 items), incl letters rel to co Armagh elections and county affairs.
Public Record Office of Northern Ireland (D 1606/1/1). Deposited by the 6th Earl of Gosford 1963. NRA 29999.

Corresp 1785-1802, nd (c40 items).
National Library of Ireland (MS 8018). NRA 29999.

[3] **ACLAND, Sir Thomas Dyke** (1787-1871), 10th Bt

MP Devon 1812-18, 1820-31, N Devon 1837-57

Election corresp and papers 1813-52 (c15 bundles); letters to him rel to personal, political and religious affairs, etc 1806-68 (c500 items); misc political papers 1812-85, incl some of his son the 11th Bt (35 bundles); corresp and papers rel to religious affairs 1815-50 (5 bundles); to education c1820-63 (c10 bundles); to local affairs 1809-c1850 (c5 bundles); to European tours 1807-51 (10 bundles); misc corresp rel to Africa, America, Australia and New Zealand, and to overseas tours and cruises 1809-54 (c17 bundles); family and personal corresp 1805-63 (c35 bundles); diaries rel to the Congress of Vienna 1814-15 (2 vols).
Devon Record Office (1148 M). Deposited 1962. NRA 14687.

Letters from his son Sir Henry Acland 1822-71 (2 vols).
Bodleian Library, Oxford (MSS Acland d. 30-1). Presented 1926-7. NRA 22893.

[4] **ACLAND, Sir Thomas Dyke** (1809-1898), 11th Bt

MP W Somerset 1837-47, N Devon 1865-85, Somerset (Wellington division) 1885-6

Political corresp and papers c1834-84 (c6 bundles), incl letters from WE Gladstone and his wife 1839-55 (1 bundle); election corresp and papers c1837-68 (c8 bundles); corresp and papers rel to Australia and New Zealand c1844-87 (c2 bundles); to religious affairs c1845-74 (c1 bundle); to education 1871 (1 bundle); to local charities 1890 (1 bundle); misc letters to him rel to estate matters, trusts, etc 1837-90 (c150 items); family corresp and papers 1841-98 (24 bundles).
Devon Record Office (1148 M). Deposited 1962. NRA 14687.

Corresp rel to New Zealand, family affairs, etc c1840-98 (c150 items).
Devon Record Office (51/12). Presented to Exeter City Library by the British Records Association 1951. NRA 6749.

Letters to him and his wife from their daughter Agnes and her husband Frederick Anson 1885-92 (1 bundle).

Devon Record Office (2862 M). Deposited by Sir Richard Acland, Bt. NRA 22118.

Letters to him and his family from politicians and others 1811-1901 (1 vol); letters to WE Gladstone 1829-89, with notes and memoranda on Home Rule 1885 (1 vol).
Bodleian Library, Oxford (MSS Eng. lett.d.81-2). Purchased 1940. NRA 10087.

Misc corresp and papers 1859-98 (61 items), mainly letters from his son Arthur (later 13th Bt) rel to the political career of Charles Acland (later 12th Bt), etc.
William R Perkins Library, Duke University, Durham, North Carolina. Purchased 1970. *Guide to the cataloged collections,* 1980, p2.

[5] **A'COURT, William** (1779-1860), 1st Baron Heytesbury 1828

Lord lieutenant of Ireland 1844-6

Misc corresp, memoranda, etc as lord lieutenant 1844-6 (15 items); corresp and papers rel to Heytesbury borough elections 1817-31 (c35 items). *Wiltshire Record Office* (WRO 635). Deposited by the 6th Baron Heytesbury 1975. NRA 671.

See also *Diplomats.*

[6] **ADAIR, James** (c1743-1798)

MP Cockermouth 1775-80, Higham Ferrers 1793-8

Corresp with John Forbes 1780-97 (1 vol) and Stephen Popham 1773-86 (2 vols); general corresp 1771-98 (3 vols); family corresp 1746-94 (2 vols); letter book 1758-9 (1 vol); political and private papers (2 vols); financial papers 1782-98 (1 vol). *British Library* (Add MSS 50829-30, 53800-8, 53815). Presented by the British Records Association 1961, 1966.

[7] **ADAM, Admiral Sir Charles** (1780-1853)

MP Kinross-shire 1831-2, Clackmannan and Kinross-shire 1832-41; first naval lord of the Admiralty 1835-41, 1846-7

Naval, Admiralty, political, business and estate corresp and papers 1795-1853 (several thousand items), incl misc political and local corresp 1825-53 (c140 items), corresp with Lord Auckland 1834-8 (1 bundle), and notebooks 1836-41 (7 vols). *KR Adam Esq.* Enquiries to NRA (Scotland) (NRA(S) 0063, 1454). NRA 9954.

[8] **ADAM, William** (1751-1839)

MP Gatton 1774-80, Wigtown burghs 1780-4, Elgin burghs 1784-90, Ross 1790-4, Kincardineshire 1806-12; treasurer of the Ordnance 1780-2, 1783; solicitor-general 1802-5 and attorney-general 1805-6 to the Prince of Wales

Corresp and misc papers 1769-1839 (c138 boxes), rel to national politics, Scottish elections and local affairs, the financial affairs of the Prince of Wales and the royal dukes, patronage, legal and estate business, and family affairs.
KR Adam Esq. Enquiries to NRA (Scotland) (NRA(S) 0063, 1454). NRA 9954.

[9] **ADAM, William Patrick** (1823-1881)

MP Clackmannan and Kinross-shire 1859-80; first commissioner of Works and paymaster-general 1873-4, 1880; Liberal whip 1874-80

Political corresp and papers mainly as Liberal whip 1874-80 (c22 vols and bundles), incl letters from WE Gladstone, Lord Granville, Lord Hartington and Scottish Liberal politicians, corresp with Liberal MPs rel to the choice of a leader 1875, papers rel to management of the election campaigns of 1874 and 1880, and pocket books containing notes of divisions nd; corresp and papers rel to personal and business affairs c1846-80 and as governor of Madras 1880-1 (c40 vols and bundles). *KR Adam Esq.* Enquiries to NRA (Scotland) (NRA(S) 1454). NRA 9954.

ADAMS, George, see Anson, George.

ADAMS, WH, see Hyett.

[10] **ADDERLEY, Charles Bowyer** (1814-1905), 1st Baron Norton 1878

MP N Staffordshire 1841-78; vice-president of the Committee of Council for Education 1858-9; under-secretary for the colonies 1866-8; president of the Board of Trade 1874-8

Letters from AJ Balfour, John Bright, Joseph Chamberlain, Lords Derby, Lytton, Salisbury and Shaftesbury and others (40 items); brief diaries 1838-86.
In private possession.

Letters to him mainly rel to legal and estate affairs 1837-c1900 (11 bundles); minutes of the council of the Society for the Reform of Colonial Government 1850-1 (1 vol); misc printed papers.
Birmingham Central Libraries Archives Department (Dep 2041A). Deposited by the 2nd Baron Norton 1922. NRA 8588.

[11] **AGAR, Charles** (1736-1809), 1st Baron Somerton 1795, 1st Viscount Somerton 1800, 1st Earl of Normanton 1806

Archbishop of Cashel 1779-1801, of Dublin 1801-9

Political, ecclesiastical and personal corresp and papers 1765-1809 (c14 boxes), incl letters to him 1767-1809 (c1,200 items), minutes of the secret committee of the Irish House of Lords 1793, 1797-8 (4 vols), annotated summonses to Cabinet meetings

1798-1800 (52 items), and notes rel to the Union, the Catholic question, etc (several bundles).
Hampshire Record Office (21M57). Deposited by the 5th Earl of Normanton 1957. NRA 8798.

[12] **AGAR-ELLIS**, George James Welbore (1797-1833), 1st Baron Dover 1831

MP Heytesbury 1818-20, Seaford 1820-6, Ludgershall 1826-30, Okehampton 1830-1; first commissioner of Woods and Forests 1830-1

Political and general corresp 1820-32 (18 bundles), incl corresp rel to Ireland 1821-31; indexes to corresp 1817-31 (14 bundles); drafts and notes for political speeches, articles and pamphlets, a report on the Office of Works 1831, and misc papers rel to tithes and politics in co Kilkenny, Catholic emancipation, parliamentary reform, etc 1816-31 (*c*33 bundles); diaries 1814-33 (57 vols); literary and historical MSS 1811-33 (*c*98 vols and bundles).
Northamptonshire Record Office (Annaly (Holdenby) Collection). Deposited by his great-grandson the 4th Baron Annaly 1945. NRA 26235.

Diaries 1814, 1833 (2 vols).
In private possession. NRA 26235.

Letters from Ralph Sneyd rel to political and social affairs 1815-32 (179 items).
Keele University Library (SC 9). NRA 1248.

Letters to him 1813-17 (6 items).
Department of Special Collections, University of Chicago Library, Illinois. Purchased 1929. *National union catalog*, MS 64-810.

[13] **AGG-GARDNER**, Sir James Tynte (1846-1928)

MP Cheltenham 1874-80, 1885-95, 1900-6, 1911-28

Parliamentary notebooks *c*1887 (3 vols); misc manuscript and printed papers mainly rel to Cheltenham elections and local government 1866-1926 (*c*25 items).
Gloucestershire Record Office (D 3893). Transferred from Cheltenham Art Gallery and Museum 1979. NRA 23475.

[14] **ALDAM**, William (1813-1890)

MP Leeds 1841-7

Corresp rel to political and philanthropic affairs *c*1830-80, incl letters rel to constituency and parliamentary business 1841-7 (40 items); diaries 1848-90 (*c*40 vols), incl references to his political and social activities; memorandum books and papers, mainly rel to Doncaster and West Riding affairs, incl drafts and texts of political speeches 1841-3 (18 items), the report of a committee on electoral registration 1841, with related memoranda (3 items), and notebooks as chairman of a select committee on Welsh railways bills *c*1846 (2 vols); printed pamphlets and parliamentary papers.
Doncaster Archives Department (DD WA). *Guide to the Archives Department*, 1981, pp 46-7.

Papers rel to Yorkshire and business affairs (2 boxes), incl political corresp and papers 1832-52, 1874, 1880, mainly as MP for Leeds (1 bundle).
Wakefield Libraries Department of Local Studies (Goodchild Loan MSS: Aldam MSS). NRA 23091.

[15] **ALEXANDER**, Du Pré (1777-1839), 2nd Earl of Caledon 1802

MP Newtownards 1800; Irish representative peer 1804-39

Corresp rel to political and local affairs 1798-1838 (*c*510 items), incl letters rel to his candidature for the representative peerage 1804 (73 items) and to Old Sarum 1802-27 (67 items); letter books as lord lieutenant of co Tyrone 1831-9 (2 vols); corresp and papers rel to Cape Colony 1795-1830 (90 vols and bundles, *c*300 items); family and business corresp 1804-39 (*c*450 items); minutes and papers of the Irish Distress Committee 1831-5 (9 vols, 54 items).
Public Record Office of Northern Ireland (D 2431, D 2433). Deposited by the trustees of the Caledon Estates 1969. NRA 13276.

See also *Colonial Governors*.

[16] **ALLEN**, John (1771-1843)

Political writer; member of the Holland House circle

Political, literary and general corresp and papers 1799-1843 (76 vols), incl corresp with Lord Brougham 1799-1842 (3 vols), Lord and Lady Holland 1807-32 (2 vols), Lord Jeffrey 1806-42 (1 vol) and Sir Francis Palgrave *c*1830-1840 (2 vols), and political journals 1806-41 (1 composite vol).
British Library (Add MSS 52172-247). Purchased from the trustees of the 5th Earl of Ilchester 1960.

Corresp and papers rel to his proposed edition of Lord Holland's biography of CJ Fox 1840-2 (4 vols).
British Library (Add MSS 47594-7). Presented by Professor GM Trevelyan 1951.

Corresp and papers 1824-37 (3 boxes), mainly rel to the Record Commission, incl letters from CP Cooper and Sir Francis Palgrave.
Public Record Office (PRO 30/26/109-11). Presented by the 6th Earl of Ilchester 1933. NRA 23347.

Letters from Francis Horner 1802-13 (31 items).
British Library of Political and Economic Science, London (R(SR)1054). Returned after Horner's death in 1817. NRA 7527.

Journal of a tour in France *c*1825.
Glasgow University Library. See *Accessions to repositories 1974*, 1975, p4.

[17] ALLSOP, Thomas (1795-1880)

Radical reformer

Letters from Richard Oastler, JB O'Brien and Feargus O'Connor 1839-61 (4 folders).
British Library of Political and Economic Science, London (Coll Misc 525). Purchased from Francis Edwards Ltd 1968. NRA 28876.

Letters from Charles Voysey 1869-71 (28 items).
Manchester College, Oxford. P Morgan, *Oxford libraries outside the Bodleian*, 1980, p214.

[18] ANSON (formerly **ADAMS**), **George** (1731-1789)

MP Saltash 1761-8, Lichfield 1770-89

Corresp and papers 1762-89 (several vols and bundles), incl letters from the Duke of Portland rel to parliamentary matters 1786-8 (1 bundle), letters to him and his son from CJ Fox 1783-1806 (1 bundle), corresp rel to Norfolk politics 1778-c1789, Lichfield canvass book 1774, and personal and household accounts 1762-89.
Staffordshire Record Office (D 615 P, E(H)). Deposited by the trustees of the Estate of the Earl of Lichfield 1963. NRA 7282.

[19] ANSON, Thomas (1767-1818), 1st Viscount Anson 1806

MP Lichfield 1789-1806

Corresp, accounts, etc rel to Lichfield elections 1799-1812 (2 vols, c3 bundles); corresp rel to Norfolk elections and local affairs 1778-1806 (2 bundles) and papers rel to bribery at Great Yarmouth 1806 (1 bundle); misc political corresp c1783-1817 (2 bundles, 4 items); personal corresp 1795-1815, nd (3 bundles).
Staffordshire Record Office (D 615 P). Deposited by the trustees of the Estate of the Earl of Lichfield 1963. NRA 7282.

[20] ANSON, Thomas George (1825-1892), 2nd Earl of Lichfield 1854

MP Lichfield 1847-54

Political and election corresp and papers 1846-81 (c7 bundles, c25 items); corresp and papers rel to friendly societies and related organisations 1857-78 (12 vols, bundles and items); papers rel to Staffordshire lieutenancy business 1854-71 (6 bundles); to charities, church patronage and other local affairs 1853-92 (c55 bundles and items); personal corresp and papers 1851-80 (7 bundles, 4 items); bank books 1869-78 (2 vols).
Staffordshire Record Office (D 615 P). Deposited by the trustees of the Estate of the Earl of Lichfield 1963. NRA 7282.

[21] ANSON, Thomas William (1795-1854), 2nd Viscount Anson 1818, 1st Earl of Lichfield 1831

MP Great Yarmouth 1818; master of the Buckhounds 1830-4; postmaster-general 1835-41

Political and Post Office corresp and papers 1826-47 (10 bundles and items), incl letters from Lord Melbourne 1831-5 (1 bundle); Lichfield election corresp and papers 1820-48 (5 vols, c9 bundles); letters rel to his earldom 1831 (1 bundle); corresp and papers rel to his personal affairs 1831-42 (2 bundles, 15 items); to hunting and racing 1820-43 (c12 bundles and items); to the Staffordshire Yeomanry 1829-51 (8 bundles and items); to Colwich charities c1801-34 (2 bundles).
Staffordshire Record Office (D 615 P). Deposited by the trustees of the Estate of the Earl of Lichfield 1963. NRA 7282.

[22] ANSTRUTHER, Sir John (1753-1811), 1st Bt

MP Anstruther Easter burghs 1783-90, 1796-7, 1806-11, Cockermouth 1790-6; solicitor-general to the Prince of Wales 1793-5

Corresp and papers rel to the Prince of Wales's debts 1789-95 (10 bundles); papers rel to the bullion question c1797-1817 (1 box); corresp and papers mainly as chief justice of Bengal 18th cent-1808 (2 boxes, 2 bundles).
Scottish Record Office (GD 147). Deposited by Miss Lavinia Baird 1961.

[23] ARBUTHNOT, Charles (1767-1850)

MP East Looe 1795-6, Eye 1809-12, Orford 1812-18, St Germans 1818-27, St Ives 1828-30, Ashburton 1830-1; under-secretary for foreign affairs 1803-4; joint secretary to the Treasury 1809-23; first commissioner of Woods and Forests 1823-7, 1828; chancellor of the Duchy of Lancaster 1828-30

Family and misc corresp 1802-50 (c1,150 items), incl letters from him to his son CGJ Arbuthnot rel to politics, etc 1816-50 (760 items); misc papers 1804-49 (7 items), incl political memoranda 1830-1 and an autobiographical sketch written 1847-9.
Aberdeen University Library (MSS 3029). Deposited by Sir John Arbuthnot, Bt 1980. NRA 25353.

Letters to him and his second wife from the Duke of Wellington 1819-34 (632 items).
The Duke of Wellington. Returned to Wellington by CGJ Arbuthnot after his father's death. See *Wellington and his friends*, ed Duke of Wellington, 1965. Closed to research.

Letters to him and CGJ Arbuthnot from Wellington 1822-51 (82 items); letters to him from CGJ Arbuthnot and others 1841-50 (16 items).
Untraced. Sold by Miss Marcia Arbuthnot at Sotheby's 17 Dec 1951, lots 208-9.

Letters from the Duke of Bedford 1846-50 (73 items, originals and typescript copies).

Trustees of the Bedford Estates. Enquiries to the Archivist, Bedford Office, 29A Montague Street, London WC1. NRA 26179.

Letters mainly from Lord and Lady Clanwilliam 1848-50 (16 items).
Public Record Office of Northern Ireland (D 3044/G/1/72-87). Returned to Lady Clanwilliam by CGJ Arbuthnot 1851, and deposited by the 6th Earl of Clanwilliam 1973. NRA 21971.

[24] **ARMOUR, James Brown** (1841-1928)

Ulster Presbyterian minister and Home Ruler

Political, personal and family corresp and papers c1860-c1930 (c1,300 items), incl letters from Sir James Dougherty rel to political and educational affairs 1878-1928 (26 items) and from Ulster Home Rulers on the Home Rule Bill 1893 (31 items), political and misc letters to him 1876-1928 (59 items), collected corresp rel to political and other affairs 1859-1928 (38 items), and drafts of political speeches, etc.
Public Record Office of Northern Ireland (D 1792). Deposited by JKC Armour 1964 and JSS Armour 1979. JRB McMinn, *Against the tide. A calendar of the papers of Rev JB Armour*, 1985.

[25] **ASHBURNHAM, George** (1760-1830), 3rd Earl of Ashburnham 1812

A lord of the Bedchamber to the Prince of Wales 1784-95

Corresp rel to Sussex elections 1801, 1807-20 (7 bundles, 23 items); to the East Sussex Conservative Association 1827-35 (5 items); diary of European tour 1781-3 (1 vol); misc personal and family corresp and papers.
East Sussex Record Office (Ashburnham Archives). Deposited 1954 by the Revd JD Bickersteth, a descendant of Margaret, second daughter of the 4th Earl of Ashburnham. *The Ashburnham archives: a catalogue*, 1958, pp33-4 *et passim*.

[26] **ASHLEY, Hon Anthony Evelyn Melbourne** (1836-1907)

Private secretary to Lord Palmerston 1858-65; MP Poole 1874-80, Isle of Wight 1880-5; secretary to the Board of Trade 1880-2; under-secretary for the colonies 1882-5

Corresp 1849-1907 (1 box); diaries 1860-1904 (2 boxes); family and misc papers 1821-1922 (2 boxes).
Southampton University Library (Broadlands Papers). Deposited by the Broadlands Archives Trust 1987.

[27] **ASHLEY-COOPER, Anthony** (1801-1885), 7th Earl of Shaftesbury 1851

MP Woodstock 1826-30, Dorchester 1830-1, Dorset 1831-46, Bath 1847-51

Dorset election corresp and papers 1831 (2 bundles); political, religious and philanthropic corresp 1827-85 (c1,700 items), incl corresp with WE Gladstone 1868-82 (29 items) and Lord Palmerston 1855, 1861-2 (29 items), and corresp rel to the Dorchester election 1831, foreign affairs, ritualism, factory reform, the Ragged Schools, etc; local and personal corresp 1836-85 (c210 items); diaries and notes of tours 1833-66 (4 vols, 1 file); philosophical and other notes 1826-31 (2 vols); manuscript speeches, notes, etc 1836-81, nd (7 vols, c70 items); printed speeches, press cuttings, etc, with some manuscript items (c40 vols, c120 items); original letters from him to the Revd Alexander McCaul 1838-48 (23 items); addresses, petitions, etc 1850-85 (17 items); accounts 1869-79 (1 vol).
The Earl of Shaftesbury.

Corresp with politicians, churchmen and others 1830-85 (112 items), incl letters from Lord Palmerston 1830, 1863-5 (9 items); diaries, journals and political and religious notes and reflections 1825-85 (17 vols); legal and estate papers 1817-82 (3 vols, 1 bundle, 6 items); misc papers, mainly printed, 1831-c1885 (c70 items).
Southampton University Library (Broadlands Papers SHA). Deposited by the Broadlands Archives Trust 1985. NRA 25761.

Letters from his wife 1831-2 (22 items) and from Lady Cowper 1830, nd (11 items); letters rel to his financial difficulties 1863-4 (19 items), incl letters from Samuel Morley; corresp 1870 (1 file); misc letters mainly from him.
Southampton University Library (Broadlands Papers). Deposited by the Broadlands Archives Trust 1987.

[28] **ASHLEY-COOPER, Anthony** (1831-1886), 8th Earl of Shaftesbury 1885

MP Hull 1857-9, Cricklade 1859-65

Corresp and papers rel to Hull and Cricklade elections, etc 1857-60 (114 items); commonplace book 1885 (1 vol).
The Earl of Shaftesbury.

[29] **ASHWORTH, Henry** (1794-1880)

A founder of the Anti-Corn Law League

Personal corresp and papers c1812-1880 (c30 vols, bundles and items), incl letters from Quakers 1812-78 (1 folder), letters from the United States 1857-76 (1 folder), his account of a visit by Lord John Manners and friends to the manufacturing districts 1841 (55pp), notes and printed papers rel to India 1857-66 (2 vols, 2 bundles, 1 folder), and notes on the United States and colonies c1861 (1 folder).
Lancashire Record Office (DDAs). Deposited by Robert Walch 1973, 1976. NRA 30812.

Scrapbooks concerning the Preston mill-workers' strike 1854 (3 vols).
Lancashire Record Office (DDPr 138/87a).

Political and personal notebooks; family corresp.
Sir Rhodes Boyson, MP.

Corresp with Richard Cobden 1841-65 (2 vols).
British Library (Add MSS 43653-4). Presented by
Mrs EJC Cobden Unwin 1933.

Business and personal diaries 1849-53 (6 vols);
memoirs 1873 (1 vol); game books 1819-26, 1841-56
(2 vols); misc letters and pamphlets 1829-78 (3
vols, 4 items).
Staffordshire Record Office (D 3016). Deposited by
the executors of Sir John Ashworth. NRA 21616.

Letters mainly from correspondents in the United
States 1856-67 (17 items); personal accounts
1823-74.
Bolton Archive Service (ZWL 50, 69). Deposited
by the executors of Robert Walch 1981. NRA
27224.

Letters from politicians and others rel to the Corn
Laws, cotton manufacture, slavery, etc *c*1841-65
(*c*50 items).
Blackburn Museum and Art Gallery. Purchased at
Sotheby's 4 Oct 1977, lot 207 and 16 Oct 1978,
lot 19.

Notebook rel to tithes 1850.
Society of Friends Library, London.

[30] ATKINSON, James (fl 1817-36)

London agent for the Whig interest in Cumberland
and Westmorland

Corresp and misc papers 1817-36 (*c*540 items),
mainly rel to Westmorland county and borough
elections, incl letters from HP Brougham 1818-26
(41 items), James Brougham 1818-33 (103 items),
John Crosby of Kirkby Thore 1817-36 (71 items)
and John Thomson of Kendal 1818-31 (51 items),
and an annotated poll book, Westmorland 1820.
University College London (Brougham Papers).
Presented 1953 by CK Ogden, who had purchased
them from the 4th Baron Brougham and Vaux at
Sotheby's 15 May 1939, lot 215. NRA 31344.

[31] BACKHOUSE, John (1784-1845)

Secretary of the Liverpool Parliamentary Office in
London 1812-23; private secretary to George
Canning 1816-22; acting under-secretary for foreign
affairs 1822-3; permanent under-secretary 1827-42

Corresp rel to his career as a merchant, as private
secretary to Canning, as a commissioner of excise
1823-7, as permanent under-secretary and as an art
collector, with corresp and papers of his sons and
other members of his family, and extensive printed
material, 1740-1956 (7 vols, 4,473 items).
*William R Perkins Library, Duke University,
Durham, North Carolina.* Presented 1968. NRA
24155.

Letters to him 1813-30 (22 items), mainly as
secretary of the Liverpool Parliamentary Office.
Liverpool Record Office (328 PAR). Purchased from

a bookseller by the Liverpool Town Clerk's
Department 1908. NRA 17048.

Corresp and papers rel to his mission to Don Carlos
of Spain at Portsmouth 1834 (1 vol).
Public Record Office (FO 323/6). Presented to the
Foreign Office by his great-grandson the Revd FL
Sheppard 1939.

[32] BAGGE, Sir William (1810-1880), 1st Bt

MP W Norfolk 1837-57, 1865-80

Corresp rel to politics and elections; press cuttings
rel to elections, etc (1 vol).
In private possession. NRA 29872.

[33] BAINES, Sir Edward (1800-1890)

Editor and subsequently proprietor of the *Leeds
Mercury* 1818-90; MP Leeds 1859-74

Political, family and misc corresp and papers
1801-90 (34 bundles, 204 items), incl corresp rel
to the Leeds election 1874 (28 items), papers rel
to parliamentary reform and the borough franchise
1859-66 (*c*25 items), and rough notes rel to the
Schools Enquiry Commission 1865-6 (1 bundle)
and the Sunday Liquor bill 1868 (1 bundle).
West Yorkshire Archive Service, Leeds. Purchased
from Dr EF Baines 1966. NRA 17125.

Letters from politicians and others 1822-76 (81
items); misc family corresp and papers 1834-7,
1859, nd (2 bundles, 10 items).
West Yorkshire Archive Service, Leeds. Purchased at
Sotheby's 31 Oct 1961, lots 258, 262. NRA 17125.

Letters from politicians and others 1837-85 (*c*58
items).
West Yorkshire Archive Service, Leeds. Purchased at
Phillips's 13 Nov 1979, lot 101.

Political corresp 1832-80 (29 items), incl letters
from WE Gladstone and TB Macaulay.
*William R Perkins Library, Duke University,
Durham, North Carolina.* Formerly sold at
Sotheby's 31 Oct 1961, lots 261, 265-6. *Guide to
the cataloged collections,* 1980, p26.

Corresp with Richard Cobden 1842-61 (119ff).
British Library (Add MS 43664, ff129-247).
Presented among the Cobden papers by Mrs EJC
Cobden Unwin 1933.

[34] BAKER, William (1743-1824)

MP Plympton Erle 1768-74, Aldborough 1777-80,
Hertford 1780-4, Hertfordshire 1790-1802, 1805-7

Political, personal and family corresp and papers
1759-1824 (*c*63 bundles), incl political corresp with
Edmund Burke 1771-90 (9 items).
Hertfordshire Record Office (D/E Bk). Deposited by
WL Clinton Baker 1953. NRA 18350.

[35] **BAKER-HOLROYD** (formerly **HOLROYD**),
John (1735-1821), 1st Baron Sheffield 1781, 1st
Earl of Sheffield 1816

MP Coventry 1780, 1781-4, Bristol 1790-1802; a
member of the Board of Trade 1809-21

A large quantity of his papers was sold at Phillips's
on 2 July 1981, lots 264-95, with other papers of
the Holroyd, North and Douglas families. The
present location of some miscellaneous lots has not
been traced.

Letters from Lords Chichester, Colchester and
Egremont, Sir Henry and Sir William Clinton and
others rel to national politics, military business,
commerce, agriculture, Sussex affairs, etc
c1760-1820 (c1,500 items); drafts of letters,
memoranda, etc nd (c100 items); corresp and
papers rel to the 22nd (Sussex) Light Dragoons
1779-82 (5 vols, over 900 items), the North
Pevensey Legion 1803-11 (over 1,500 items) and
the Sussex 'Loyal Declaration' 1820-1.
East Sussex Record Office. Purchased at Phillips's
2 July 1981, lots 265-6, 270, 293.

Letters mainly from members of the Foster, North
and Pelham families rel to British politics, Irish
Union, Catholic emancipation, Sussex elections and
patronage, foreign affairs, etc 1774-1820 (471
items).
East Sussex Record Office (Add MS 5440).
Deposited by the 6th Viscount Gage 1954. NRA
26493.

Political, personal and family corresp and misc
papers 1763-1821 (3 vols, 14 bundles), incl letters
from Lord Auckland 1790-1814 (1 bundle), John
Foster 1773-1816 (1 bundle) and JT Stanley 1798
(1 bundle), corresp rel to the Sussex election 1820
(1 bundle) and journal of his travels in Holland
and Prussia 1763-5 (1 vol).
Cheshire Record Office (DSA 13-33). Deposited by
Lady Kathleen Stanley 1953. NRA 17206.

Corresp, memoranda, voters' lists, addresses, bills
and receipts, etc mainly rel to Coventry politics
and elections 1780-4 (c2 vols, 9 bundles, 350 items).
Coventry City Record Office (Acc 854). Purchased
at Phillips's 2 July 1981, lot 279. NRA 25071.

Letters from British and Irish correspondents rel
to parliamentary business, elections, commerce,
patronage, the Napoleonic wars, etc 1801-19 (3
vols).
*William L Clements Library, University of Michigan,
Ann Arbor.* Purchased 1939. *Guide to the manuscript
collections,* 1942, pp218-19.

Corresp and papers rel to Irish affairs 1772-1820
(117 items), incl letters from Sir William Clinton
1798, 1804-6 (13 items), William Downes
1773-1820 (15 items), John Foster 1772-1803 (16
items) and Thomas Pelham 1794-8 (10 items).
Public Record Office of Northern Ireland (D 3541).
Purchased at Phillips's 2 July 1981, lot 286.

Letters from Lord Auckland 1781-c1814 (2 vols).
British Library (Add MSS 45728-9). Presented
1941 by Miss VM Dickinson, a descendant of
Auckland.

Letters from Lord Auckland, William Hayley,
Lord North and others 1783-1804, and corresp and
papers rel to British North American commerce
1805-11 (1 vol); letters mainly to him and his wife
from the 5th Earl of Guilford 1789-1827 (3 vols);
journal of his travels in France, Switzerland and
Italy 1763-4 (1 vol).
British Library (Add MSS 61979-83). Purchased at
Phillips's 2 July 1981, lots 271, 272, 276, 284, 288,
298.

Letters to him and others from Edward Gibbon
1750-94 (3 vols); letters from French émigrés
1792-3, corresp and papers rel to his publication
of Gibbon's *Miscellaneous Works* 1794-1819, etc (1
vol).
British Library (Add MSS 34883-5, 34887).
Purchased from the 3rd Earl of Sheffield 1896.

Returns, accounts, muster rolls, etc as a captain in
the 21st Light Dragoons 1761-3 (5 vols, 28 items).
National Army Museum (8107-19). Purchased at
Phillips's 2 July 1981, lot 264. NRA 24935.

Letters from Sir Joseph Banks 1786-1819 (46
items).
*Beinecke Library, Yale University, New Haven,
Connecticut* (Osborn Collection). Purchased at
Phillips's 2 July 1981, lot 274.

Letters from Colonel Joseph Hardy 1816, Sir John
Sinclair 1793-4 and Sir Benjamin Thompson 1791,
1796 (7 items); tables showing the value of British
and Irish trade 1698-1765, and tables of Ireland's
imports and exports 1764-83 (2 vols).
London University Library (MSS 124, 126, 423; AL
55, 115-16). Purchased 1910, 1912, 1955, nd.

Letters from JJ Oddy and others 1797-1811 (8
items); notebooks of him or Lord Glenbervie rel
to the management of Frederick North's affairs in
England 1798-1804 (3 vols).
Kent Archives Office (U 471/A112, C134).
Deposited by the 9th Earl of Guilford 1954. NRA
5392.

[36] **BALFOUR, Gerald William** (1853-1945), 2nd
Earl of Balfour 1930

MP Leeds (Central division) 1885-1906; private
secretary to AJ Balfour 1885-6; chief secretary for
Ireland 1895-1900; president of the Board of Trade
1900-5; president of the Local Government Board
1905-6

Semi-official papers 1895-1906 (41 boxes), incl
papers as chief secretary 1895-1900 (22 boxes) and
Cabinet papers, memoranda, etc mainly rel to the
Board of Trade and to imperial defence 1897-1906
(19 boxes).
Public Record Office (PRO 30/60). The Irish papers
are closed for 100 years. NRA 23635.

Political and personal corresp and papers 1887-1944
(3 vols, c47 bundles), incl letters on Irish affairs
from John Atkinson, Lord Cadogan, Sir Horace
Plunkett, Sir Henry Robinson and others
1895-1909 (7 bundles), and papers rel to the Board

of Trade and tariff reform 1900-6 (several bundles).
Scottish Record Office (GD 433). Deposited by the
4th Earl of Balfour 1987. NRA 10026.

[37] **BALFOUR, John** (1750-1842)

MP Orkney and Shetland 1790-6, 1820-6

Personal, political, business and family corresp and
papers 1774-1841 (*c*46 bundles), incl corresp and
papers rel to Orkney and Shetland politics and
elections 1790-1841 (*c*13 bundles) and to India
*c*1780-1821 (*c*12 bundles).
Orkney Archives (Balfour of Balfour and Trenabie
Papers). NRA 16075.

[38] **BALFOUR, John Blair** (1837-1905), 1st
Baron Kinross 1902

MP Clackmannan and Kinross-shire 1880-99;
solicitor-general (Scotland) 1880-1; lord advocate
1881-5, 1886, 1892-5

Political, legal and general corresp 1862-1904 (1
box); letters of congratulation 1899, 1902 (5 boxes);
addresses, genealogical papers, etc mainly 19th cent
(1 box).
National Library of Scotland (Acc 7638). Purchased
1980. NRA 29191.

[39] **BALFOUR, Thomas** (1810-1838)

MP Orkney and Shetland 1835-7

Political and misc corresp and papers *c*1831-7 (1
vol, *c*21 bundles), incl constituency corresp, notes
rel to the select committee on land revenues
(Scotland) 1834 and corresp rel to the Scottish
Prisons Bill 1837.
Orkney Archives (Balfour of Balfour and Trenabie
Papers). NRA 16075.

[40] **BANKES, Henry** (*c*1757-1834)

MP Corfe Castle 1780-1826, Dorset 1826-31

Political corresp and papers 1781-1831 (*c*100 items),
incl letters from George Canning (22 items);
personal corresp (2 boxes); notebooks on
contemporary affairs, classical history, etc (2
boxes); narrative history of his own times (177 thin
vols); printed election papers 1806-7.
Dorset Record Office (D/BKL). Deposited by the
National Trust 1982.

[41] **BARHAM, John Foster** (1799-1838)

MP Stockbridge 1820-6, 1831-2, Kendal 1834-7

Corresp and papers rel to Kendal elections 1832,
1834 (10 bundles), incl letters from Lord
Brougham; business, estate, personal and family
corresp, with that of his father Joseph Foster
Barham.

Bodleian Library, Oxford (MSS Clar. dep. b.33-8,
c.357-91, c.428-32). Deposited by the 7th Earl of
Clarendon 1959. NRA 6302.

[42] **BARHAM, Joseph Foster** (1759-1832)

MP Stockbridge 1793-9, 1802-6, 1807-22,
Okehampton 1806-7

Corresp and papers rel to the abolition of the slave
trade 1814-15 (2 bundles); corresp rel to missionary
affairs nd (2 bundles); papers rel to the Catholic
question 1813, 1818-28 (3 bundles); misc political
papers *c*1786-1832 (2 bundles); letter book
1789-1831 (1 vol); misc business, estate, personal
and family corresp and papers *c*1730-1836 (*c*10
vols, *c*200 bundles and folders), incl accounts and
papers rel to his West Indian estates.
Bodleian Library, Oxford (MSS Clar. dep. b.33-8,
c.357-91, c.428-32). Deposited by the 7th Earl of
Clarendon 1959. NRA 6302.

[43] **BARING, Sir Francis** (1740-1810), 1st Bt

MP Grampound 1784-90, Chipping Wycombe
1794-6, 1802-6, Calne 1796-1802

Financial, commercial, Indian and other corresp
and papers *c*1763-1810 (4 boxes), incl political and
personal letters from the 1st, 2nd and 3rd
Marquesses of Lansdowne 1782-1810 (over 200
items), and letters rel to India from Henry Dundas
1785-*c*1800 (1 bundle) and William Pitt 1785-6 (10
items); copies of corresp with Dundas, Lansdowne,
Pitt and others 1782-1801 (3 vols).
Baring Brothers & Co Ltd (Northbrook Papers,
boxes A-D, N4). Enquiries to the Archivist, Baring
Brothers & Co Ltd, 8 Bishopsgate, London EC2N
4AE.

Letters to him rel to estate business 1806 and
enclosure 1809 (16 items).
Lewisham Local History Centre (A 62/6). Deposited
by the British Records Association 1962.
NRA 8913.

[44] **BARING, Harriet Mary** (1805-1857), Lady
Ashburton

Political hostess

Letters from her husband 1823-57 (*c*90 items);
political, literary, social and family corresp
*c*1827-57 (*c*580 items), incl letters to her from the
4th Earl of Clarendon, Edward Ellice the elder and
the younger, the 3rd Marquess of Lansdowne and
Lord Stanley, and some corresp of her husband
and his second wife Louisa; misc letters from
political and literary figures to the 1st and 2nd
Barons Ashburton and their wives from 1818 (*c*55
items).
The Marquess of Northampton. Access through the
Historical Manuscripts Commission. NRA 24219.

[45] **BARING, William Bingham** (1799-1864), 2nd Baron Ashburton 1848

MP Thetford 1826-30, 1841-8, Callington 1830-1, Winchester 1832-7, N Staffordshire 1837-41; joint secretary of the Board of Control 1841-5; paymaster-general 1845-6

Corresp as MP for Winchester 1832-7 (14 items); letters from Edward Ellice the elder 1847, nd (c25 items); corresp and printed papers rel to his arbitration in an engineers' strike 1852 (19 items); corresp rel to educational affairs 1855-9 (c30 items); misc personal corresp 1826-64 (c220 items); papers 1827-64 (2 vols, 14 bundles and loose items), incl notes of proceedings in the House of Commons Feb 1827, Feb 1828 and June 1831, political notes 1850s and notes for speeches on education, etc with other misc personal and estate papers c1848-64.
The Marquess of Northampton (his great-grandson). Access through the Historical Manuscripts Commission. NRA 24219.

[46] **BARRETT LENNARD, Sir Thomas** (1762-1857), 1st Bt

MP S Essex 1832-5

Essex election papers 1830-4 (4 vols, 2 bundles); family corresp c1800-50 (7 bundles), incl corresp rel to local and national politics; diaries 1830-48 (4 vols).
Essex Record Office, Chelmsford (D/DL). Deposited by Sir Richard Barrett Lennard, Bt 1945, 1973; converted to a gift 1974. NRA 8987.

[47] **BARRETT LENNARD, Thomas** (1788-1856)

MP Ipswich 1820-6, Maldon 1826-37, 1847-52

Corresp and papers rel to the Ipswich election 1820-1 (1 vol, 5 items); papers rel to his candidature for co Monaghan 1813 (20 items), and to Maldon elections 1826-52 (4 vols, 24 items); misc political corresp and papers 1814-40 (47 items); journals and notebooks c1832-56 (13 vols), incl draft speeches and notes of Commons debates.
Essex Record Office, Chelmsford (D/DL). Deposited by Sir Richard Barrett Lennard, Bt 1945, 1973; converted to a gift 1974. NRA 8987.

[48] **BARRINGTON, George William** (1824-1886), 7th Viscount Barrington 1867

MP Eye 1866-80; private secretary to Lord Derby 1866-8; vice-chamberlain 1874-80

Personal and family corresp and papers 1822-1901 (463 items), incl many letters, memoranda, etc c1865-86 rel to politics, parliamentary elections and reform, the House of Lords, and relations with Russia and Turkey.
William R Perkins Library, Duke University, Durham, North Carolina. Acquired as part of the WB Hamilton collection 1966. NRA 30671.

Misc personal corresp and papers 1868-82, mainly rel to genealogical matters (c12 items).

Suffolk Record Office, Ipswich (HA 174). Deposited 1965. NRA 30623.

[49] **BARTLETT, William Walter** (fl 1887-1942)

Socialist

Corresp and papers 1887-1942 (2 boxes), incl letters from EB Aveling, ER Pease and SJ Webb, and papers rel to local government elections in London and Brighton 1889-1927.
Sussex University Library (Sx Ms 20). NRA 19480.

[50] **BEACH, William Wither Bramston** (1826-1901)

MP N Hampshire 1857-85, Hampshire (Andover division) 1885-1901

Election papers from 1857 (1 box, 1 bundle); personal corresp of him and his wife c1850-1910 (1 box); executorship corresp 1893 (1 box); printed papers c1900 (1 box).
Gloucestershire Record Office (D 2440, D 2445). Deposited by his kinsman the 2nd Earl St Aldwyn 1969, 1975. NRA 3526.

[51] **BECKER, Lydia Ernestine** (1827-1890)

Advocate of women's suffrage

Corresp 1867-90 (c65 items) and letter book nd (1 vol) as secretary of the Manchester Society for Women's Suffrage.
Manchester Central Library (M 50/1). Presented by Miss Margaret Ashton, formerly chairman of the Society. NRA 20885.

Misc corresp with politicians and others 1836-90 (60 items); notebook 1848-63, 'family diary' 1873 and draft of an unpublished work on 'Stargazing for Novices' nd.
Fawcett Library, London (LEB/1: Autograph Collection vol 28 part A). Deposited by WTL Becker 1969. NRA 20625.

[52] **BENFIELD, Paul** (1741-1810)

MP Cricklade 1780-4, Malmesbury 1790-2, Shaftesbury 1793-1802

Political, Indian and financial corresp 1775-1804 (5 vols), incl letters from NW Wraxall 1781-90 and misc Cricklade election papers 1781-4 (2 vols).
India Office Library and Records (MSS Eur C 307). Purchased 1979. NRA 27439.

[53] **BENNET, Charles** (1743-1822), 4th Earl of Tankerville 1767

Joint postmaster-general 1782-3, 1784-6

Corresp and papers rel to the Post Office 1784-7 (2 bundles), incl papers rel to his dismissal; misc family, estate and legal corresp and papers.
Northumberland Record Office (NRO 424). Access restricted. NRA 26604.

BENTINCK, see Cavendish Bentinck.

[54] BERESFORD, General William Carr
(1768-1854), Baron Beresford 1814, Viscount
Beresford 1823

MP co Waterford 1811-14; master-general of the
Ordnance 1828-30

Letters from Lord Wellington, with some originals
and copies of replies, 1810-11 (2 vols).
British Library (Add MSS 21504, 36306). Purchased
1856, 1900.

Letters from Wellington 1810-13 (11 items); letters
to Sir John Beresford mainly from Lord Beresford
1808-42 (c120 items).
North Yorkshire County Record Office (ZBA 21/
10-11). Deposited by Sir Henry Beresford-Peirse,
Bt 1956.

Letters mainly from Lords Liverpool and
Wellington 1809-12, 1823 (67 items).
Huntington Library, San Marino, California
(Wellesley-Beresford Collection). Purchased c1924.
Guide to British historical manuscripts, 1982, p363.

Letters to him and to Archbishop Beresford rel to
the Londonderry county election 1829 and other
elections 1829-30 (26 items).
National Library of Ireland (MS 21767). *Manuscript
sources for the history of Irish civlisation, Supplement*,
1979, i, 47.

[55] BERNARD MORLAND (formerly
BERNARD), **Sir Scrope** (1758-1830), 4th Bt

MP Aylesbury 1789-1802, St Mawes 1806-8,
1809-30; private secretary to the lord lieutenant of
Ireland 1782-3, 1787-9; under-secretary for home
affairs 1789-92

Irish corresp 1782-1830 (14 bundles), incl letters
from Edward Cooke, Sackville Hamilton and Lord
Hobart; corresp and papers mainly rel to Home
Office business 1789-92 (13 bundles), incl letters
from Lord Buckingham, Henry Dundas and Lord
Grenville; corresp and papers rel to elections at
Lincoln, Aylesbury and St Mawes 1784-1821 (5
bundles), and to parliamentary business 1786-1830
(3 bundles); corresp with the clerk of the peace for
Buckinghamshire 1786-1812 (1 bundle), and papers
rel to the Aylesbury Infantry Volunteers 1788-1813
(1 bundle); corresp with clients as banker and
barrister 1780-1830 (11 bundles); personal corresp
1775-1818 (c22 bundles); personal accounts
1781-1831 (2 bundles).
Buckinghamshire Record Office (D/SB). Deposited
by Mrs EP Spencer Bernard 1980. NRA 7343.

BIDDULPH, see Myddelton-Biddulph.

[56] BILL, Charles (1843-1915)

MP Staffordshire (Leek division) 1892-1906

Political and personal corresp and papers 1879-1915
(c390 items), incl papers rel to Staffordshire

elections; notes as a magistrate 1870s, nd (25 items);
misc personal and financial corresp and papers
c1860-1912 (1 vol, c250 items).
Staffordshire Record Office (D 554). Deposited by
his granddaughter Mrs Pamela Clifford 1958. NRA
6841.

BLACKWOOD, FT, see Hamilton-Temple-
Blackwood.

[57] BLACKWOOD, James Stevenson
(1755-1836), 2nd Baron Dufferin 1807

MP Killyleagh 1788-1800, Helston 1807-12,
Aldeburgh 1812-18; Irish representative peer
1820-36

Corresp rel to co Down politics and county affairs
1825-36 (3 bundles), incl letters from Lord
Downshire and William Sharman Crawford;
corresp with the Duke of Clarence rel to his proxy
1827-30 (1 bundle); legal, financial, estate and
family corresp and papers 1767-1836 (c26 bundles).
Public Record Office of Northern Ireland (D 1071).
Deposited by the Marchioness of Dufferin and Ava
1957. NRA 5700.

[58] BLAKE, Edward (1833-1912)

MP co Longford (S division) 1892-1907

Political, legal, personal and family corresp, papers
and printed material 1749-1917 (53 feet), mainly
rel to Canada but incl corresp with James Bryce,
Michael Davitt, John Dillon, WE Gladstone, JE
Redmond and other British and Irish politicians
1892-1910 and misc Irish political papers
1777-1907.
Archives of Ontario, Toronto. See *Guide to the
holdings of the Archives of Ontario*, 1985, i, 225-6.

[59] BLAKE, Martin Joseph (1790-1861)

MP Galway 1833-57

Galway election corresp and papers 1812-59 (9 vols,
3 bundles, c175 items), incl voters' lists, canvass
books, poll books, papers rel to expenses, case
papers and printed items; personal, local and
political corresp 1807-60 (c19,350 items); letter
book 1834-5; copies of out-letters 1833-60 (c1,640
items); indexes to corresp 1836-8 (2 vols).
Public Record Office of Ireland (M 6935-6).
Presented by AJ Blake 1964.

[60] BLIGH, Edward (1795-1835), 5th Earl of
Darnley 1831

MP Canterbury 1818-30

Corresp and papers rel to his election 1818 (1 vol,
8 items), incl the minute book of his committee
1817-18; bank books 1815-30 (2 vols).
Kent Archives Office (U 565/F10, O13-15).
Deposited by the 10th Earl of Darnley 1956-7.
NRA 1179.

[61] **BLUNT, Wilfred Scawen** (1840-1922)

Stood for Camberwell (N division) 1885, Kidderminster 1886, Deptford 1888

Corresp and misc papers 1857-1922 (74 boxes, 9 vols), incl letters from Arabi Pasha and his family 1882-1911, nd (48 items), Lord Cromer 1883-99, nd (22 items), John Dillon 1886-1911 (c160 items), WJ Evelyn 1885-1908 (68 items), the 2nd Viscount Hampden 1877-1906, nd (28 items) and HD Labouchere 1883-93, nd (19 items), papers rel to Irish affairs 1880-1921 and to his candidature at Deptford (1 box), and papers rel to Egyptian and other affairs 1878-1918, nd (1 box).
West Sussex Record Office (Blunt MSS). Deposited 1980 by his great-grandson Lord Knebworth.

Corresp and telegrams (c3,500 items), incl letters and telegrams from Margot Asquith 1892-1922, nd (80 items) and WLS Churchill 1904-22, nd (33 items), and letters from HBW Brand 1876-7 (12 items) and Lord Randolph Churchill 1883-93, nd (20 items); autograph diaries 1863-1922, draft fragments of diaries 1860-80, journal in Paris 1870 and transcripts of diaries and memoirs 1840-1918; memoirs, etc 1888-1918 (38 vols), incl memoirs rel to Egypt (4 vols), India 1883-5 (4 vols) and Ireland 1886-7 (1 vol); notebooks and literary and misc papers, incl papers rel to Egyptian independence and an account of his imprisonment in Galway Gaol 1888.
Fitzwilliam Museum, Cambridge. Deposited by his literary executors.

Corresp with his wife 1867-1917 (9 vols); Arabian travel journals (1878-9), sketches, notebooks, etc (11 vols); autobiographical accounts of his youth to 1857, dictated to his wife (1 vol); other family papers.
British Library (Add MSS 53817-54155 *passim*). Bequeathed by his daughter Baroness Wentworth and deposited 1967.

Letters from William Morris 1885-96 (20 items). *Victoria and Albert Museum Library.* See *Catalogue of English non-illuminated manuscripts*, 1975, p69.

[62] **BOND, Nathaniel** (1754-1823)

MP Corfe Castle 1801-7; a lord of the Treasury 1801-3; vice-president of the Board of Trade 1806; judge advocate-general 1806-7

Political and election papers 1715-1807 (5 bundles), mainly printed; letters and verses from Joseph Jekyll rel to social, political and legal affairs 1785-1823, nd (1 vol, 356 items); corresp 1789-1806 (40 items), mainly personal, incl letters from Lord Sidmouth 1801-5 (19 items).
Dorset Record Office (D367). Deposited by M Bond 1970, 1972. NRA 24118.

[63] **BONHAM, Francis Robert** (1785-1863)

MP Rye 1830-1, Harwich 1835-7; principal storekeeper of the Ordnance 1834-5, 1841-5; Conservative party agent

His papers were purchased from his sister in 1863 by the Peel trustees, Edward Cardwell and Lord Stanhope. Stanhope destroyed most of the 'very voluminous' correspondence as being of no interest, but retained his own letters to Bonham and selected letters from other politicians (Norman Gash, 'Bonham and the Conservative party 1830-1857', *Pillars of Government*, 1986, p109).

Corresp with Sir Robert Peel 1829-50 (c1,160ff); letters from Sir James Graham 1837-57 (1 vol), and from Lord Ellenborough, the 7th Earl of Shaftesbury and others 1832-59 (1 vol).

British Library (Add MSS 40399-40429 *passim*, 40485-40603 *passim*, 40616-17). Presented in 1917 by the Hon George Peel on behalf of the Peel trustees.

Letters from Lord Stanhope 1836-63 (2 bundles). *Kent Archives Office* (U 1590/C330/1-2). Deposited by the administrative trustees of the Chevening Estate 1971. NRA 25095.

BONTINE, see Cunninghame Graham.

[64] **BOOTLE-WILBRAHAM** (formerly **WILBRAHAM-BOOTLE**), **Edward** (1771-1853), 1st Baron Skelmersdale 1828

MP Westbury 1795-6, Newcastle-under-Lyme 1796-1812, Clitheroe 1812-18, Dover 1818-28

Parliamentary diaries 1806-7 (7 vols).
Wiltshire Record Office (WRO 1946). Deposited by the 8th Earl of Radnor, whose great-aunt married Skelmersdale's great-grandson.

Letters from George Canning rel to political and personal affairs 1792-1827 (1 vol).
British Library (Add MS 46841). Presented 1949 by his great-granddaughter Lady Barbara Ann Seymour.

[65] **BOWES, John** (1811-1885)

MP S Durham 1832-47

Election and registration corresp and papers 1832-46, mainly rel to the S Durham elections of 1832 (212 items) and 1841 (255 items); general corresp 1831-85 rel to estate and business matters, the Bowes Museum, etc.
Durham County Record Office (D/St/C 1/16, and Appendix I). Deposited by the 16th Earl of Strathmore 1963.

Corresp and papers rel to the foundation and building of the Bowes Museum 1864-87 (29 bundles, 14 items).
Durham County Record Office (D/Bo/E 1-33). Transferred from the Bowes Museum 1963. NRA 23425.

[66] **BOWES-LYON** (formerly **LYON-BOWES**),
Claude (1824-1904), 13th Earl of Strathmore 1865

Scottish representative peer 1870-87

Personal and political corresp and papers
c1840-1903 (c21 bundles), incl patronage corresp
1874-80 (1 bundle), corresp rel to Forfarshire
elections 1868, 1893 (2 bundles), and corresp rel
to the Barnard Castle Conservative Association
1893-1901 (c3 bundles); diaries 1867-1904, incl
references to House of Lords business (38 vols).
The Earl of Strathmore. Enquiries to NRA
(Scotland) (NRA(S) 0885). NRA 381.

[67] **BOWRING, Sir John** (1792-1872)

MP Clyde burghs 1835-7, Bolton 1841-9

Letters from politicians and others 1816-65, incl
George Canning and Lords Clarendon, Holland
and Palmerston (119 items); literary corresp and
papers (1 vol, 39 items).
*Houghton Library, Harvard University, Cambridge,
Massachusetts* (b MS Eng 1247). Acquired 1966-71.
NRA 20033.

Misc corresp 1795-1908 (176 items), mainly
political and literary, but incl letters from Roman
Catholic bishops to members of his family after his
death.
Huntington Library, San Marino, California.
Purchased from Francis Edwards Ltd 1967.
National union catalog, MS 71-1046.

Autograph collection c1691-c1910, mainly letters to
him c1814-69 (c250 items).
University College London (MS Ogden 62).
Purchased from CK Ogden 1953.

See also *Diplomats.*

[68] **BOYLE, David** (1772-1853), Lord Boyle

MP Ayrshire 1807-11; solicitor-general (Scotland)
1807-11

Corresp and papers rel to Ayrshire politics 1807-28
(3 bundles), incl letters from the 1st Viscount
Melville; patronage corresp 1808-23 (1 bundle);
corresp with politicians rel to the death penalty
1814-41 (1 bundle); letters of congratulation on his
appointments 1811-41 (1 bundle); misc political,
legal and personal corresp and papers 1789-1853
(c43 bundles).
The Earl of Glasgow. Enquiries to NRA (Scotland)
(NRA(S) 0094). NRA 10152.

Justiciary notebooks 1811-48 (26 vols).
National Library of Scotland (Adv MSS
36.3.1-36.4.10).

[69] **BOYLE, Henry** (1771-1842), 3rd Earl of
Shannon 1807

MP Cloghnikelty 1794-7, co Cork 1797-1807,
Bandon 1807

Political and patronage corresp 1793-1829 (48
items); corresp rel to the borough of Youghal

c1812-22 (108 items); letters from his father
c1790-1802 (115 items); corresp and papers rel to
the militia and yeomanry 1796-1805 (54 items);
family and misc corresp and papers c1797-1829
(107 items).
Public Record Office of Northern Ireland (D 2707).
Deposited by the 9th Earl of Shannon 1971. NRA
18812.

Political and family corresp 1790-1829 (c120 items),
mainly letters from his father.
National Library of Ireland (MSS 13303-6). NRA
18812.

[70] **BOYLE, Richard** (1728-1807), 2nd Earl of
Shannon 1764

Joint vice-treasurer (Ireland) 1781-9; a lord of the
Treasury (Ireland) 1793-1804

Corresp and papers rel to politics and patronage
1765-1807 (125 items); family, business and misc
corresp and papers 1760-1807 (164 items).
Public Record Office of Northern Ireland (D 2707).
Deposited by the 9th Earl of Shannon 1971. NRA
18812.

Further political and family corresp 1768-1807
(c150 items).
National Library of Ireland (MSS 13300-4). NRA
18812.

[71] **BRABAZON, John Chambre** (1772-1851),
10th Earl of Meath 1797

Lord lieutenant of co Dublin 1831-51

Corresp and papers rel to the borough of
Leominster 1806-18, Lord Brabazon's contests for
co Dublin 1830, 1832, the Irish representative
peerage 1804, 1825-6, and Irish politics and local
affairs 1797-1839 (3 bundles, 4 envelopes);
personal, family and estate corresp and papers
1801-50 (1 vol, 15 bundles, 1 envelope), incl letters
from the Duke of Bedford 1846-50 (1 bundle).
The Earl of Meath. NRA 4528.

[72] **BRADLAUGH, Charles** (1833-1891)

MP Northampton 1880-91

Personal and family corresp and papers 1824-1948
(2 boxes, 4 vols, 7 bundles, c3,500 items), incl
corresp and papers rel to his campaign to take his
seat in Parliament 1880-6, to Indian affairs and to
free thought, etc, letters from EB Aveling 1879-89,
nd and from Prince Jerome Napoleon 1872-80, and
letters to his daughters Alice and Hypatia 1872-91.
Bishopsgate Institute, London. Deposited by the
National Secular Society. Mainly listed in Edward
Royle, *The Bradlaugh papers: a descriptive index*,
1975.

Letters to or about him from politicians and others
1859-88 (42 items).
Bodleian Library, Oxford (MS Eng. lett. d. 180,
ff104-77). Acquired 1961.

Addresses presented during his Indian tour 1889
(5 items); misc pamphlets, photographs, etc
1870-91.
Hackney Archives Department (D/F/BRA).
Deposited by the National Secular Society 1985.
NRA 21875.

[73] **BRADY, Sir Maziere** (1796-1871), Bt

Solicitor-general (Ireland) 1837-9; attorney-general
(Ireland) 1839-40; lord chancellor (Ireland)
1846-52, 1853-8, 1859-66

Corresp 1840-66 (78 items), mainly rel to the Irish
magistracy and patronage.
Trinity College Library, Dublin (MS 7636).
Purchased 1977. NRA 21055.

[74] **BRAND, Henry Bouverie William**
(1814-1892), 1st Viscount Hampden 1884

MP Lewes 1852-68, Cambridgeshire 1868-84;
patronage secretary to the Treasury and chief whip
1859-66; Speaker of the House of Commons
1872-84

Political and misc corresp and memoranda 1855-92,
nd (c400 items), incl letters from Charles
Bradlaugh, WE Gladstone, Sir George Grey, Lord
Iddesleigh, Sir Erskine May, Lord Palmerston and
Lord Russell; parliamentary diaries 1872-84 (13
vols), incl notes of his rulings as Speaker.
House of Lords Record Office (Historical Collection
95). Deposited 1965. NRA 6114.

[75] **BRETT, Reginald Baliol** (1852-1930), 2nd
Viscount Esher 1899

MP Penryn and Falmouth 1880-5; private secretary
to Lord Hartington 1878-85

Royal corresp 1878-1929 (9 vols); corresp rel to
India with Lords Binning, Hartington, Rosebery
and others 1861-1907 (18 vols), and to army reform
mainly 1901-12 (36 vols); 'letters and memoranda'
1898-1919 (11 vols); general corresp 1867-77,
1882-1930 (61 vols); papers (many printed) rel to
Indian and colonial affairs 1877-85, 1902-10 (13
vols), military affairs and army reform 1896-1919
(32 vols), and the Office of Works, Honours
Committee and royal occasions 1885-1911 (13 vols);
journals (mainly typescript copies) 1870-1922 (25
vols); literary MSS and related corresp 1868-1920
(42 vols); personal and family corresp 1853-1929
(111 vols); misc corresp and papers 1873-1929 (19
vols).
Churchill College, Cambridge (ESHR). Deposited
by the 4th Viscount Esher 1968. NRA 13626.

Papers rel to the South African War Commission
c1902-4 and the Imperial Defence Committee
1906-7 (3 vols).
Imperial War Museum.

Letters from politicians and others mainly
1880-1907 (c60 items).
Liverpool University Library (MS 2.89). Purchased
from Edward Hall, dealer, 1960. NRA 30047.

[76] **BRIDGEMAN, Orlando George Charles**
(1819-1898), 3rd Earl of Bradford 1865

MP S Shropshire 1842-65; lord chamberlain
1866-8; master of the Horse 1874-80, 1885-6

Political, general and family corresp 1840-91, incl
letters from the 7th Duke of Bedford, Joseph
Chamberlain, the 14th and 15th Earls of Derby,
Lord Lansdowne and Lord Shaftesbury; election
papers 1842; corresp and papers as lord
chamberlain and master of the Horse; business and
estate corresp 1848-93; letters to his wife rel to
politics and personal affairs from Lord Beaconsfield
1873-81 (c1,080 items) and the 7th Duke of Rutland
1839-94.
Staffordshire Record Office (D 1287).

[77] **BROADHURST, Henry** (1840-1911)

Secretary of the TUC parliamentary committee
1875-90; MP Stoke-on-Trent 1880-5, Birmingham
(Bordesley division) 1885-6, Nottingham (W
division) 1886-92, Leicester 1894-1906; under-
secretary for home affairs 1886

Letters from WE Gladstone, Sir William Harcourt,
Lord James of Hereford, Sir Wilfrid Lawson, Lord
Rosebery, Sir James Stephen and other politicians,
churchmen, trade union leaders and social
reformers 1873-1911 (6 vols); press cuttings and
other printed matter 1882-1905 (1 box).
*British Library of Political and Economic Science,
London* (Coll L). NRA 7521.

[78] **BRODRICK, William St John Fremantle**
(1856-1942), 9th Viscount Midleton 1907, 1st Earl
of Midleton 1920

MP W Surrey 1880-5, Surrey (Guildford division)
1885-1906; financial secretary to the War Office
1886-92; under-secretary for war 1895-8, for
foreign affairs 1898-1900; secretary for war 1900-3,
for India 1903-5

Corresp and misc papers 1885-1933 (mainly
1895-1905) (1,436ff) rel to politics, the South
African war, the Boxer rebellion, War Office
reform and India, incl letters from Sir Michael
Hicks Beach, Lord Kitchener, Sir Francis Knollys,
Lords Lansdowne, Milner, Morley of Blackburn
and Roberts, and the 3rd Marquess of Salisbury;
corresp and papers rel to Irish affairs 1893-1941
(1,900ff), incl Home Rule, the Irish Convention
1917-18 and the creation of the Irish Free State.
Public Record Office (PRO 30/67). Deposited by
his daughter Lady Moyra Loyd 1967. NRA 23461.

Corresp with Lord Curzon 1903-6 (6 vols).
British Library (Add MSS 50072-7). Acquired 1959.

Letters to him and his wife from politicians and
others 1890-1933 (1 vol).
*William R Perkins Library, Duke University,
Durham, North Carolina.* Purchased 1969. *Guide to
the cataloged collections,* 1980, pp62-3.

Letters from Lord Kitchener 1900-4 (*c*93 items).
Public Record Office (PRO 30/57/22). Presented by
his widow to the 3rd Earl Kitchener, and deposited
among the Kitchener papers 1959. NRA 7283.

Letters to him 1897-1902 (13 items), mainly rel to
the South African war.
Brenthurst Library, Houghton, South Africa (MS 73).
Purchased at Sotheby's 1 July 1968, lot 377. The
present location of further letters (lots 378-81) has
not been traced.

[79] **BROGDEN, James** (*c*1765-1842)

MP Launceston 1796-1832; a lord of the Treasury
1812-13; chairman of the Committee of Ways and
Means 1813-26

Corresp and papers rel to politics, foreign affairs,
patronage, commerce, etc *c*1750-1842 (*c*20
bundles), incl political letters from the Duke of
Northumberland 1799-1813 (1 bundle) and letters
from Daniel Bayley rel to Russian affairs 1813-16
(1 bundle), other political and patronage corresp,
etc *c*1774-1842 (*c*5 bundles), estate and business
corresp 1827-42 (*c*4 bundles), and misc financial
papers 1805-38 (3 bundles).
Essex Record Office, Chelmsford (D/DSe).

[80] **BROKE VERE** (formerly **BROKE**), **Major-
General Sir Charles** (1779-1843)

MP E Suffolk 1835-43

Minutes, accounts, corresp and papers of the
Central Agricultural Society 1836-40 (113 vols,
bundles and items); misc military and other corresp
and papers 1812-37 (*c*24 items); diary, France 1814
(1 vol); engagement diaries 1824-42 (20 vols);
address book nd (1 vol); order book as deputy
quartermaster-general to the British army in
Portugal 1826-8 (1 vol); mathematical notebooks
1795-6, 1803 (3 vols).
Suffolk Record Office, Ipswich (HA 93). Deposited
by his great-great-nephew the 5th Baron de
Saumarez 1961-4. NRA 19292.

[81] **BROMLEY-DAVENPORT, Brigadier-
General Sir William** (1862-1949)

MP Cheshire (Macclesfield division) 1886-1906;
financial secretary to the War Office 1903-5

Political and constituency corresp and papers
*c*1890-1910 (1 box); War Office papers 1903-5 (1
box); press cuttings (16 vols); corresp and papers
rel to the Penrhyn quarries dispute 1897-1911, the
South African war *c*1900-1 and to business and
estate matters.
John Rylands University Library of Manchester
(Bromley Davenport Muniments). Deposited by
Sir Walter Bromley-Davenport 1948-70. NRA 592.

[82] **BROUGHAM, James** (1780-1833)

MP Tregony 1826-30, Downton 1830-1,
Winchelsea 1831-2, Kendal 1832-3

Letters to him rel to Westmorland politics, estate
business, family affairs, etc 1796-1833 (*c*l,500
items), incl letters from James Abercromby 1828-33
(35 items), JF Barham 1829-33 (20 items), William
Brougham *c*1819-30 (26 items), Sir George
Strickland 1818-33 (43 items) and the 9th and 11th
Earls of Thanet 1814-33 (31 items); drafts and
copies of letters from him *c*1818-33 (*c*50 items),
some to Queen Caroline 1818-21; memoranda and
misc papers 1819-32 (*c*45 items), incl notes about
the Queen's trial 1820.
University College London (Brougham Papers).
Presented 1953 by CK Ogden, who had purchased
them from the 4th Baron Brougham and Vaux at
Sotheby's 15 May 1939, lot 215. NRA 31344.

[83] **BROWNE, Howe Peter** (1788-1845), 2nd
Marquess of Sligo 1809

Lord lieutenant of co Mayo 1831-4, 1842-5

Political, family and estate corresp 1815-39, nd
(251 items), incl letters from EG Stanley as chief
secretary for Ireland 1831-4 (12 items).
Trinity College Library, Dublin (MS 6403).
Purchased 1974. NRA 25244.

Letters from Lord Grey, Lord Melbourne and
others; family corresp, incl letters from him to his
mother and others rel to his continental travels
*c*1810-15.
Untraced. Sold at Christie's, 6 Oct 1958, lots 88-90,
121. For Jamaican papers from the same sale see
Colonial Governors.

[84] **BROWNING, Oscar** (1837-1923)

Stood for Lambeth (Norwood division) 1886,
Worcestershire (E division) 1892 and Liverpool
(West Derby division) 1895

Political, educational, literary and personal corresp
1860-1913 (1,853 files), incl letters from AJ Balfour
(17 items), Sir Henry Campbell-Bannerman (18
items), Lord Curzon (*c*170 items), John Morley (23
items), HL Samuel (16 items), Francis Schnadhorst
(29 items), Sir George Trevelyan (26 items) and
the East Worcestershire Liberal Association (42
items); misc corresp 1869-1913 (137 files); corresp
and papers arranged by subject 1853-1912 (2 vols,
16 files); literary MSS (11 vols).
King's College, Cambridge. Transferred in 1986
from the Brassey Institute, Hastings, to which they
had been presented by Browning in 1916. NRA
21235.

[85] **BRUCE, Hon Robert Preston** (1851-1893)

MP Fife 1880-5, Fife (W division) 1885-9

Political and personal corresp and papers 1868-91
(*c*100 vols, bundles and items), incl political and
election corresp 1878-91 (*c*7 bundles), papers rel

to election expenses 1880-2 (1 bundle), letters, reports, etc rel to the Scottish Liberal Association 1885-7, 1890 (3 bundles, 1 item), and misc political papers, notes for speeches and press cuttings.
The Earl of Elgin. Access restricted. NRA 26223.

[86] **BRUCE, Thomas** (1766-1841), 7th Earl of Elgin 1771

Scottish representative peer 1790-1807, 1820-41

Personal, political, general and family corresp and papers 1770-1837 (*c*200 vols, bundles and items), incl papers rel to the Scottish representative peerage *c*1787-94 (*c*4 bundles); diplomatic corresp and papers 1789-1803 (*c*1,200 vols, bundles and items); corresp and papers rel to his imprisonment in France 1803-6 (36 bundles and items); to the Elgin marbles and other works of art 1793-1837 (2 boxes, 8 vols, 33 bundles and items); to the Elgin Fencibles 1794-7 (29 bundles and items).
The Earl of Elgin. Access restricted. NRA 26223 (partial list).

See also *Diplomats.*

[87] **BRUCE, Victor Alexander** (1849-1917), 9th Earl of Elgin 1863

First commissioner of Works 1886; viceroy of India 1894-9; secretary for the colonies 1905-8

Corresp and papers 1858-1912 (over 100 bundles and items), incl corresp and papers rel to politics and official business 1886 (2 bundles, *c*50 items), to general and local political affairs 1886-97 (2 bundles), to India and the colonies, and to local, personal and family affairs.
The Earl of Elgin. Access restricted. NRA 26223 (partial list).

Corresp and papers as viceroy of India 1894-9 (151 vols and bundles).
India Office Library and Records (MS Eur F 84). Deposited by the 10th Earl of Elgin 1956 and by the 11th Earl 1964. NRA 20533.

[88] **BRUNNER, Sir John Tomlinson** (1842-1919), 1st Bt

MP Cheshire (Northwich division) 1885-6, 1887-1910

Corresp and papers rel to public affairs *c*1850-1947 (6 boxes), incl letter books 1865-1908 (4 vols), letters from TE Ellis 1885-98 and corresp and papers rel to Ellis (80 items), papers rel to elections 1885-1900 (107 items), and corresp and papers rel to religious questions 1885-1908 (30 items), education 1885-1919 (95 items), the temperance question 1887-95 (71 items) and local politics 1887-1928 (64 items); family corresp and papers *c*1835-75 (2 boxes); business papers *c*1870-1915 (2 boxes); engagement diaries 1886, 1889-90, 1892-1919 (31 vols).
Liverpool University Library (Brunner Papers). NRA 19105.

[89] **BUCHANAN, Thomas Ryburn** (1846-1911)

MP Edinburgh 1881-5, Edinburgh (W division) 1885-92, Aberdeenshire (E division) 1892-1900, Perthshire (E division) 1903-11; financial secretary to the War Office 1906-8; under-secretary for India 1908-9

Corresp and papers (30 trunks), incl political corresp, letters to his wife describing his parliamentary career, and fragments of his diary.
In private possession. C Cook, *Sources in British political history 1900-1951,* iii, 1977, pp66-7.

Fragment of his diary.
British Library (Add MS 52500). Deposited with the papers of Sir Henry Campbell-Bannerman by the 1st Baron Pentland 1923.

[90] **BULL, Sir William James** (1863-1931), 1st Bt

Member of the London County Council 1892-1901; MP Hammersmith 1900-18, Hammersmith (S division) 1918-29

Diaries and corresp 1876-1930 (95 vols), incl material rel to Hammersmith constituency and LCC politics from 1889; pocket diaries 1877-1929 (5 composite vols); personal corresp 1923-7 (8 vols); commonplace book 1887-1902; notes, drafts and press cuttings rel to his parliamentary career.
Churchill College, Cambridge (Bull Papers). Deposited by Sir George Bull and Anthony Bull 1982, 1984. NRA 26806.

Corresp and papers 1832-1929 (632 items), mainly rel to Hammersmith local affairs; registers of electors, Hammersmith 1883, 1885, 1894-1919.
Hammersmith and Fulham Archives (DD/375). NRA 23169.

Political, business and personal letter books 1885-1908 (3 vols).
Greater London Record Office. Deposited by Bull & Bull, solicitors, 1980. NRA 23555.

Papers mainly rel to proportional representation 1913-24 and House of Lords reform 1925-6 (*c*160 items).
House of Lords Record Office (HC Library MS 38). *Guide to the records of Parliament,* 1971, p292.

[91] **BULLER, James** (1766-1827)

MP Exeter 1790-6, 1802-18, East Looe 1802

Election accounts and misc printed papers 1789-90 (3 vols, 6 items); papers rel to his retirement from Parliament 1818, nd (2 items); personal, business and legal corresp 1804-23; accounts 1787-1827; travel journal, France and Italy 1788-9.
Devon Record Office (2065 M). NRA 16965.

[92] **BULLER, James Wentworth** (1798-1865)

MP Exeter 1830-5, N Devon 1857-65

Political, business, personal and family corresp and papers 1806-65, incl Exeter election accounts and papers 1830-2, nd (1 vol, 2 bundles), N Devon election corresp and papers 1839-64 (13 vols and bundles), and corresp and papers as chairman of the Bristol and Exeter railway mainly 1847-65 (25 bundles).
Devon Record Office (2065 M). NRA 16965.

[93] **BULWER, William Henry Lytton Earle** (1801-1872), Baron Dalling and Bulwer 1871

MP Wilton 1830-1, Coventry 1831-5, Marylebone 1835-7, Tamworth 1868-71

Diplomatic, literary, political and misc corresp and papers 1827-72 (423 vols and bundles), incl letters from politicians, constituents and others rel to elections, parliamentary affairs and patronage 1831-7 (212 items), political memoranda, draft speeches, etc 1830-7 (107 items), corresp and papers as parliamentary agent for the Australian colonies 1833-7 (60 items), and letters from Sir Robert Peel and other papers as MP for Tamworth 1868-70 (24 items).
Norfolk Record Office (BUL 1). Deposited by Mrs H Bulwer-Long 1968, 1982. NRA 6790.

See also *Diplomats*.

[94] **BURDETT, Sir Francis** (1770-1844), 5th Bt

MP Boroughbridge 1796-1802, Middlesex 1802-4, 1805-6, Westminster 1807-37, N Wiltshire 1837-44

Royal corresp c1791-1836 (1 vol); corresp with politicians and others 1790-1843 (4 vols); corresp and papers rel to Middlesex and Westminster elections 1802-37 (1 vol), John Horne Tooke 1802-11 (4 vols), Ireland 1798-c1835 (1 vol), his imprisonment 1810, 1819 (1 vol) and prison conditions 1798-1833 (2 vols); misc letters, speech notes, financial papers, etc 18th-19th cent (6 vols).
Bodleian Library, Oxford (MSS Autogr. c.23, Eng. hist. a.9, b.196-201, c.64-6, c.292-6, Eng. lett. d.93, 96-8). Deposited by his great-granddaughter Mrs Clara Patterson 1944. NRA 16905.

Personal and family corresp early 19th cent (1 bundle); estate and misc corresp and papers (7 boxes), incl corresp between Burdett and his steward Richard Crabtree rel to political, family and estate matters, and Burdett's personal memoranda book 1808.
Wiltshire Record Office (D/EBu/E18, F14). Transferred from Berkshire Record Office 1984. NRA 8983.

BURGES, see Lamb.

[95] **BURKE, Edmund** (1729-1797)

MP Wendover 1765-74, Bristol 1774-80, Malton 1780-94; private secretary to Lord Rockingham 1765-6; paymaster-general 1782, 1783

Political, personal, family and collected corresp 1744-97 (c3,500 items), incl corresp with Lord Fitzwilliam, Charles O'Hara, the 3rd Duke of Portland and Lord Rockingham; letters to the Committee of Correspondence at New York 1771-5 (1 vol); notes and misc papers rel to Ireland and Catholic emancipation c1760-92 (1 bundle), parliamentary and political affairs 1768-95, nd (15 bundles), American affairs (1 bundle), St Eustatius (1 bundle), the French Revolution 1792-4, nd (1 bundle), and personal, family and misc affairs (2 bundles).
Sheffield Record Office (Wentworth Woodhouse MSS). Deposited by the 9th Earl Fitzwilliam 1949. NRA 1083; TW Copeland and MS Smith, *A checklist of the correspondence of Edmund Burke*, 1955.

Personal and family corresp and papers c1760-97 (36 bundles), incl corresp and papers rel to French émigrés 1792-6 (2 bundles) and notes for political speeches 1766-94 (19 bundles).
Northamptonshire Record Office (Fitzwilliam (Milton) MSS). Deposited by WTG Wentworth-Fitzwilliam 1946. NRA 4120.

Letters from French Laurence 1788-97 (80ff).
Bodleian Library, Oxford (MS Eng.lett.d.5, ff50-129). Acquired c1930.

Corresp [1759]-1793 (37 letters, mostly from him); speech notes (13 items).
National Library of Ireland (MS 5923).

Letters from various correspondents 1778-96 (11 items, 3 fragments).
Lord Burnham. Access through the Historical Manuscripts Commission. NRA 29865.

'Observations on the conduct of the minority' nd [?1797] (1 vol).
Houghton Library, Harvard University, Cambridge, Massachusetts (fMS Eng 878). NRA 20129.

[96] **BURKE, Richard** (1758-1794)

Deputy paymaster-general 1782, 1783; MP Malton 1794

Letters from his father Edmund Burke 1773-94 (42 items); corresp with politicians, French émigrés and others 1778-94 (c65 items), incl Henry Dundas 1791-3 (12 items).
Sheffield Record Office (Wentworth Woodhouse MSS). Deposited by the 9th Earl Fitzwilliam 1949. NRA 1083.

Letters from his father 1773-93 (18 items); misc corresp with Lord Fitzwilliam and others 1781-94 (51 items).
Northamptonshire Record Office (Fitzwilliam (Milton) MSS). Deposited by WTG Wentworth-Fitzwilliam 1946. NRA 4120; WT Copeland and MS Smith, *A checklist of the correspondence of Edmund Burke*, 1955, pp117-20.

[97] **BURNS, John Elliot** (1858-1943)

MP Battersea and Clapham (Battersea division) 1892-1918; president of the Local Government Board 1905-14, of the Board of Trade 1914

Royal corresp 1902-28 (1 vol); corresp with RB Cunninghame Graham 1888-1928 (1 vol), Lord Morley of Blackburn 1894-1923 (1 vol), British and Dominion prime ministers 1889-1934 (1 vol), and rel to the London docks strike 1889 and trade union affairs 1887-1939 (3 vols); other political and general corresp 1874-1942 (18 vols); speeches and memoranda *c*1877-1933 (5 vols); diaries 1888-1920 (33 vols); photographs 1885-1910 (1 vol).
British Library (Add MSS 46281-46343, 59669). Presented by David Burns and Mrs AA Fuller 1946, except for Add MS 59669 purchased from Jarndyce Antiquarian Booksellers 1976.

For small collections of his papers in Battersea District Library, the Greater London Record Office, the Trades Union Congress Library and the library of California State University at Northidge, see C Hazlehurst and C Woodland, *Guide to the papers of British cabinet ministers 1900-1951*, Royal Historical Society 1974, pp24-5.

[98] **BURY, Charles William** (1801-1851), 2nd Earl of Charleville 1835

MP Carlow 1826-32, Penryn and Falmouth 1832-5; Irish representative peer 1838-51

Corresp and papers rel to national politics, mainly of the 2nd Earl, 1829-41 (1 bundle), incl letters from the Duke of Wellington 1838-41 (9 items); corresp and papers rel to local politics, etc 1817-48 (1 vol, *c*1 bundle); estate corresp 1825-40 (1 bundle); corresp rel to Crockford's Club and the Comte d'Orsay 1834-40 (1 bundle); travel journal and passport 1820-2 (2 items).
The Longford/Westmeath Library and in private possession. Copies are in the Public Record Office of Northern Ireland (T 3069). NRA 18806.

BUSFEILD, see Ferrand.

[99] **BUTT, Isaac** (1813-1879)

MP Harwich 1852, Youghal 1852-65, Limerick 1871-9

Political corresp and papers 1862-79 (numerous folders), incl corresp rel to the land question and Home Rule; out-letters 1855-78; personal, family, professional and financial corresp and papers *c*1855-78; misc addresses, speech notes, etc.
National Library of Ireland (MSS 8686-8713, 10415, 13257, 13740). *Manuscript sources for the history of Irish civilisation*, ed RJ Hayes, 1965, i, 450-1; *Supplement*, 1979, i, 96.

[100] **BUXTON, Sir Thomas Fowell** (1786-1845), 1st Bt

MP Weymouth and Melcombe Regis 1818-37

Corresp and papers 1804-44 (47 vols and some loose items), incl copies of letters, reports, etc rel to the abolition of the slave trade 1832-42 (10 vols), and working papers for his books on the slave trade 1828-42 (8 vols).
Rhodes House Library, Oxford (MSS Brit. Emp. s.444). Presented by his family 1975, and purchased from CR Johnson Rare Book Collection 1985 and at Sotheby's 23 July 1985, lot 380. NRA 24097.

Letters from Thomas Clarkson, Elizabeth Fry, William Wilberforce and others to Buxton and members of his family *c*1807-41 (*c*130 items).
Rhodes House Library, Oxford. Purchased at Phillips's 10 Dec 1987, lot 440.

Copies of corresp and papers rel to the abolition of the slave trade 1842-4 (1 vol).
RQ Gurney Esq. A microfilm is in Rhodes House Library (MSS Brit. Emp. s.444/20A). NRA 24097.

Letter from Lord Palmerston 1839; letter rel to Robert Jamieson's African expedition 1840; fragments of personal letters 1821-37; misc papers rel to his baronetcy 1840.
Norfolk Record Office (RQG 559-61). Deposited by RQ Gurney 1970. NRA 15293.

[101] **CALVERT, Frederick** (1806-1891)

MP Aylesbury 1850-1

Family, political and general corresp *c*1822-89 (*c*1,000 items); journals with political memoranda 1842-77, nd (2 vols).
The Claydon House Manuscripts Trust, Middle Claydon, Buckinghamshire. NRA 21959.

CALVERT, Harry, see Verney.

CAMPBELL, Archibald, see Campbell Colquhoun.

[102] **CAMPBELL, Sir Ilay** (1734-1823), 1st Bt, Lord Succoth

MP Glasgow burghs 1784-9; solicitor-general (Scotland) 1783; lord advocate 1783-9

Legal, political and personal corresp and papers 1766-1824 (*c*550 items), incl corresp with Lord Melville 1783-1808 (57 items).
Strathclyde Regional Archives (TD 219). Deposited by Sir Ilay Campbell, Bt 1973. NRA 8144.

Notes on the Douglas cause 1762-6 (2 vols); letter from Lord Carmarthen rel to the commercial treaty with France 1786.
National Library of Scotland (MSS 3078-80). Deposited by Sir George Campbell, Bt 1942.

[103] **CAMPBELL, John** (1755-1821), 1st Baron
Cawdor 1796

MP Nairnshire 1777-80, Cardigan boroughs
1780-96

Papers rel to Carmarthenshire politics 18th-19th
cent (3 boxes); to Pembrokeshire politics 1807-57
and Carmarthen borough politics 1812-80 (1 box);
political notebook 1760s; misc personal and
political corresp of him and his wife 1796-1801,
1837 (9 items); militia and yeomanry papers mainly
c1781-1822 (1 box); estate corresp and papers
1730-1820 (7 boxes), with misc papers rel to
Pembrokeshire and Carmarthenshire affairs;
accounts and financial papers c1798-1821; journals
1778-1821 (12 items).
Carmarthenshire Area Record Office (Cawdor/
Campbell MSS and Cawdor Collection II).
Deposited by the 6th Earl Cawdor 1970. NRA
21492.

Corresp and papers rel to Nairnshire politics
c1771-1831 (c35 bundles), incl papers rel to freehold
qualifications and corresp rel to elections 1777-86;
papers rel to Inverness-shire and Ross-shire politics
1756-1832 (c4 bundles); legal and personal corresp
1796-1821 (1 bundle).
Earl Cawdor. Enquiries to NRA (Scotland)
(NRA(S) 1400). NRA 8147.

[104] **CAMPBELL, John** (1762-1834), 4th Earl of
Breadalbane 1782, 1st Marquess of Breadalbane
1831

Scottish representative peer 1784-1806

Corresp and papers, incl accounts and papers rel
to Perth, Perthshire and Argyllshire politics and
elections c1740-1835 (c9 bundles).
Scottish Record Office (GD 112/46). Acquired since
1926.

General, political, family and estate corresp and
papers 1782-1831 (170 items), incl letters from his
son Lord Glenorchy on political and election
matters 1826-31.
In private possession. Enquiries to NRA (Scotland)
NRA(S) 2238). NRA 25302.

[105] **CAMPBELL COLQUHOUN** (formerly
CAMPBELL), **Archibald** (c1754-1820)

MP Elgin burghs 1807-10, Dunbartonshire
1810-20; lord advocate 1807-16

Letter book 1812-13; account book 1818-20; estate
memoranda and accounts 1799-1820 (1 vol).
National Library of Scotland (MSS 10683-5).
Purchased 1961-6.

Draft letters and legal opinions as lord advocate
1807-9 (1 vol).
London University Library (MS 532). Purchased
from Winifred A Myers (Autographs) Ltd 1961.

[106] **CAREW, Robert Shapland** (1787-1856), 1st
Baron Carew 1834

MP co Wexford 1812-30, 1831-4

Political, personal and family corresp and papers
1744-1859 (294 items), incl letters from Lord
Clarendon 1847-53 (55 items), Lord Grey 1831-6
(11 items) and Lord Melbourne 1835-41, nd
(8 items).
Trinity College Library, Dublin (MSS 4020-2).
Presented by the 6th Baron Carew 1967. NRA
24847.

[107] **CARTWRIGHT, William Cornwallis**
(1826-1915)

MP Oxfordshire 1868-85

Corresp and papers 1838-1915 (c26 boxes), incl
corresp 1854-1915, nd (9 boxes), political, election
and official papers (1 box), diaries and travel
journals 1838-1912 (2 boxes) and notebooks
(2 boxes).
Northamptonshire Record Office (Cartwright
(Aynho) Collection). Deposited by Miss Elizabeth
Cartwright (afterwards Mrs Cartwright Hignett) at
various dates since 1960. NRA 21333.

[108] **CARTWRIGHT, William Ralph**
(1771-1847)

MP Northamptonshire 1798-1831, S
Northamptonshire 1832-46

Corresp and papers c1788-1846 (c5 boxes), incl
political and election papers 1814-46, nd (2 boxes)
and official papers (1 box).
Northamptonshire Record Office (Cartwright
(Aynho) Collection). Deposited by Miss Elizabeth
Cartwright (afterwards Mrs Cartwright Hignett) at
various dates since 1960. NRA 21333.

[109] **CAULFEILD, James** (1728-1799), 4th
Viscount Charlemont 1734, 1st Earl of Charlemont
1763

Irish nationalist politician; commander-in-chief of
the Irish Volunteers 1780-3

Corresp with British and Irish politicians,
churchmen, literary figures and others 1745-99
(13 vols); letters mainly from him to AH Haliday
1774-1803 (3 vols); account of his political life
1753-83 written for his sons (1 vol); description of
his travels in Greece and Turkey 1749-51 and
literary MSS (6 vols).
Royal Irish Academy, Dublin (MSS 12 R 1-7, 9-21,
23-5). HMC *Twelfth Report App X* and *Thirteenth
Report App VIII, Manuscripts and correspondence of
James, first Earl of Charlemont,* 2 vols 1891, 1894;
Manuscript sources for the history of Irish civilisation,
ed RJ Hayes, 1965, i, 538-9.

[110] **CAVENDISH, Sir Henry** (1732-1804), 2nd
Bt

MP Lismore 1764-8, 1776-97, 1798-1800,
Lostwithiel 1768-74; a lord of the Treasury
(Ireland) 1795-1801

Irish parliamentary journal 1776-89, incl shorthand
reports of debates (45 vols) and longhand transcript
(37 vols).
Library of Congress, Washington. Purchased at
Sotheby's 22 Dec 1898. *National union catalog*, MS
62-4531; HMC *Second Report, Appendix*, 1871,
pp99-100.

British parliamentary journal 1768-74 (50 vols).
British Library (Egerton MSS 215-63, 3711).
Purchased 1833, 1954.

[111] **CAVENDISH, William George Spencer**
(1790-1858), 6th Duke of Devonshire 1811

Lord chamberlain 1827-8, 1830-4

Political, general and family corresp 1797-1858
(several thousand items), incl letters from the 7th
Duke of Bedford, Lord Brougham, George
Canning, the 7th Earl of Carlisle, WF Cowper-
Temple, the 1st Baron Dover, Lord Dunfermline,
the 5th Earl Fitzwilliam, the 2nd Earl Granville,
Harriet Lady Granville, Princess Lieven, WJ
Lockett (Derbyshire political agent) and Sir Joseph
Paxton; corresp rel to his Russian mission 1826
and to Napoleon III 1848, 1857; letters rel to the
Derbyshire militia 1855; accounts 1854-6; diary
(unbound) 1821-52.
The Trustees of the Chatsworth Settlement. Enquiries
to the Librarian and Keeper of the Devonshire
Collections, Chatsworth, Bakewell, Derbyshire
DE4 1PP. NRA 20594/3,7,16.

Further letters from Harriet Lady Granville.
In private possession. Enquiries to the Keeper of
Archives, Castle Howard, York YO6 7DA. NRA
24681.

[112] **CAVENDISH-BENTINCK, George
Augustus Frederick** (1821-1891)

MP Taunton 1859-65, Whitehaven 1865-91;
secretary to the Board of Trade 1874-5; judge
advocate-general 1875-80

Corresp and misc papers, with those of his wife,
1824-96, nd (162 items), incl letters from the Duke
of Portland 1853-79, nd (36 items).
Nottingham University Library (PwM). Deposited
by the 7th Duke of Portland 1949; accepted for
the nation in lieu of tax and allocated to the Library
1987. NRA 7628.

[113] **CAVENDISH BENTINCK, Lord William
George Frederick** (1802-1848)

MP King's Lynn 1826-48

Corresp and misc papers rel to his early military
career, politics, racing, etc 1820-48 (*c*420 items),

incl letters from AF Greville nd (8 items), Lord
Howard de Walden 1825-7 (11 items) and Lord
Titchfield 1825, nd (15 items).
Nottingham University Library (PwL). Deposited by
the 7th Duke of Portland 1949; accepted for the
nation in lieu of tax and allocated to the Library
1987. NRA 7628.

[114] **CECIL, Brownlow** (1795-1867), 2nd
Marquess of Exeter 1804

Lord chamberlain 1852; lord steward 1858-9

Stamford electoral registers 1832-60, poll books
1831-2, election accounts 1841 and other misc
political papers 1832-58 (*c*8 bundles); papers rel to
Lord Brownlow Cecil's debts 1848-53 (1 bundle);
misc corresp rel to the yeomanry, lieutenancy, etc.
Burghley House Preservation Trust, Stamford. NRA
6666.

[115] **CHALMERS, Patrick** (1802-1854)

MP Montrose burghs 1835-42

Political corresp and papers mainly 1830-41 (3
vols); corresp and papers rel to Scottish railways
1836-64 (4 vols); personal and family corresp
*c*1822-54 (*c*3 vols), incl letters from Edward Ellice
senior; letter books 1831-6 (2 vols); accounts
1830-48 (3 vols); diaries 1830, 1836 (2 vols);
antiquarian corresp and papers (8 vols).
National Library of Scotland (MSS 15448–15515
passim). Acquired 1964-78.

[116] **CHARTERIS** (formerly **CHARTERIS-
WEMYSS-DOUGLAS**), **Francis Richard**
(1818-1914), 10th Earl of Wemyss 1883

MP E Gloucestershire 1841-6, Haddingtonshire
1846-83; a lord of the Treasury 1853-5

Political, personal and family corresp 1841-1908
(*c*46 box files, 3 bundles), incl corresp as MP for
Haddingtonshire and as a lord of the Treasury,
and corresp rel to parliamentary reform and the
Adullamites 1859-67, army reform, the volunteer
movement and the National Rifle Association, the
trade unions 1867-9, the Liberty and Property
Defence League, and Sunday trading; speeches,
press cuttings and other papers 1847-1907 (*c*22 box
files); political diaries 1858, 1860 (2 vols);
manuscript memoir (9 envelopes); instructions for
his secretary 1862-4 (1 vol); printed copies of
pamphlets by him.
The Earl of Wemyss and March. Enquiries to NRA
(Scotland) (NRA(S) 0208). A microfilm is in the
Scottish Record Office. NRA 10743.

[117] **CHAYTOR, William** (1732-1819)

MP Penryn 1774-80, Hedon 1780-90

Political, militia, lieutenancy and other papers
*c*1750-1819 (*c*1,600 items), incl political letters from
the 5th Duke of Leeds and John Robinson MP

and papers rel to elections and politics in Cornwall, Cumberland, Durham, Westmorland and Yorkshire 1755-1818 (*c*600 items).
North Yorkshire County Record Office (ZQH). Acquired 1970.

Personal and estate corresp 1762-1817 (410 items), incl letters from John Robinson rel to politics, legal matters, etc 1788-1802 (*c*40 items); papers as recorder of Richmond 1801-11 (*c*30 items).
Durham County Record Office (D/Ch/C,F). Deposited by Sir William Chaytor, Bt 1963. NRA 11940.

[118] CHETWYND-TALBOT, Charles Chetwynd (1777-1849), 2nd Earl Talbot of Hensol 1793

Lord lieutenant of Ireland 1817-21

Papers as lord lieutenant of Ireland 1817-22 (8 vols), incl letter books (3 vols); letter book as lord lieutenant of Staffordshire 1822-42; misc corresp and papers 1801-41 (13 items); misc financial papers 1795-1848 (6 vols, bundles and items).
Staffordshire Record Office (D 240, D 649). NRA 8481.

[119] CHILD-VILLIERS, Sarah Sophia (1785-1867), Countess of Jersey

Political hostess

Political and social corresp 1802-66, nd (*c*370 items), incl letters from the 6th Duke of Bedford, Lord Brougham, Madame de Coigny, the 3rd Baron Holland, Sir Robert Peel, the 5th Earl Stanhope and the Duke of Wellington; royal corresp *c*1805-*c*1847 (1 vol, 6 bundles, 40 items); family corresp 1793-1847, nd (60 items); misc corresp 1817-39, nd (73 items); autograph albums (4 vols); travel journal *c*1817 (1 vol); religious papers 1809-45 (1 vol, 2 items); commonplace books *c*1783-1859 (8 vols); social, literary and misc papers *c*1814-59, nd (45 vols, bundles and items).
Greater London Record Office (Acc 510, Acc 1128). Deposited by the 9th Earl of Jersey. NRA 935 (partial list).

[120] CHRISTIE, William Dougal (1816-1874)

MP Weymouth and Melcombe Regis 1842-7

Personal and family corresp and papers *c*1835-*c*1900 (several hundred items), incl letters to him from politicians, diplomats, scholars and others, with related papers.
Untraced. Sold at Sotheby's 8 Dec 1983, lots 140, 372, 377.

Letters from JS Mill rel to parliamentary and literary affairs, Christie's diplomatic career in Brazil, etc 1864-71 (23 items).
Cornell University Libraries, Ithaca, New York. Purchased at Sotheby's 3 Nov 1969, lot 277.

Letters from Sir Arthur Helps rel to parliamentary affairs, etc 1835-72 (20 items).
John Rylands University Library of Manchester. Presented by Professor JR De Bruyn 1983 following purchase at Sotheby's 3 Nov 1969, lot 278.

Letters from Lord Houghton rel to domestic and foreign affairs 1863-4, nd (20 items).
Untraced. Sold at Sotheby's 3 Nov 1969, lot 279.

CHRISTOPHER, see Nisbet-Hamilton.

[121] CLARKE, Sir Edward George (1841-1931)

MP Southwark 1880, Plymouth 1880-1900, City of London 1906; solicitor-general 1886-92

Political, legal, personal and family corresp 1858-*c*1926 (*c*180 items), incl letters from AJ Balfour, Lord Randolph Churchill, Lord Curzon, WE Gladstone and the 3rd Marquess of Salisbury 1874-1911 (*c*18 items); reminiscences *c*1872-1929 (1 bundle and loose items); election papers 1906; engagement diary 1867 (1 vol); notebooks (2 vols); misc papers; transcripts of his political, legal and misc corresp 1873-1918 (*c*250 items), incl letters from Lord Salisbury *c*1885-9 and WH Smith 1887-90, and of his personal and family corresp 1858-*c*1926 (*c*430 items).
In private possession. NRA 30373.

[122] CLEMENTS, Henry John (1781-1843)

MP co Leitrim 1805-18, co Cavan 1840-3

Political, estate and family corresp and papers *c*1803-43, incl letters rel to the co Cavan election 1840 and a list of co Leitrim freeholders *c*1807 (1 vol).
National Library of Ireland. Deposited by Mrs M Clements 1958-9. Irish Manuscripts Commission, reports 356, 437; *Manuscript sources for the history of Irish civilisation,* ed RJ Hayes, 1965, i, 597.

[123] CLERK, Sir George (1787-1867), 6th Bt

MP Edinburghshire 1811-32, 1835-7, Stamford 1838-47, Dover 1847-52; under-secretary for home affairs 1830; joint secretary to the Treasury 1834-5, 1841-5; vice-president of the Board of Trade and master of the Mint 1845-6

Political corresp and papers mainly 1813-37 (225 items), incl corresp rel to disturbances 1830 (15 items), misc Treasury papers 1834-5 (*c*25 items) and papers rel to Edinburghshire politics; corresp and papers 1838-47 (*c*2,950 items), mainly concerning Treasury business but incl some Board of Trade and Mint papers and papers as MP for Stamford; political corresp and papers 1847-61 (*c*280 items), incl papers rel to public finance and as MP for Dover; Midlothian militia papers 1813-20 (56 items); misc personal, religious, military, family, estate and other corresp and papers 1829-66 (210 items); bank book 1851-8.
Scottish Record Office (GD 18). Deposited 1948. NRA 29182.

[124] **CLIFFORD, Lewis Henry Hugh**
(1851-1916), 9th Baron Clifford of Chudleigh 1880

Liberal Unionist

Political, personal and estate corresp 1886-1916 (1 box); corresp with Liberal Unionists and rel to tariff reform, etc 1895-1912 (c3 bundles); papers of the Mid-Devon Liberal Unionist Association under his chairmanship 1888-1905 (1 bundle); parliamentary bills introduced by him 1909, 1911 (2 items); diary attributed to him 1902 (1 vol); misc personal papers 1870-1916 (1 bundle).
Lord Clifford of Chudleigh. NRA 20060.

[125] **COBBETT, William** (1762-1835)

MP Oldham 1832-5

Corresp 1800-10 (2 vols), mainly rel to the *Political Register*.
British Library (Add MSS 22906–7). Purchased 1859.

Corresp 1806-19 (1 vol), mainly rel to the *Political Register*.
Bodleian Library, Oxford (MS Eng. hist.c.33). Purchased 1893.

Collected corresp, political papers and legal papers 1807-35, nd (3 vols), incl letters from him published in the *Political Register* 1831-5, notes for parliamentary speeches 1834, nd, letters to his publisher John Wright 1807-10 and transcripts of family and other corresp 1820-7.
British Library (Add MSS 31125–7). Purchased 1879.

Family corresp 1791-1833 (300 items); literary MSS (2 vols) and misc notes.
Nuffield College, Oxford. NRA 371.

Drafts of essays on his tour of the eastern counties 1830; English grammar 1831.
British Library (Add MS 31857). Presented by Miss Susan Cobbett 1881.

Misc corresp, accounts, fragments of lectures, etc.
Fitzwilliam Museum, Cambridge.

Accounts as a bookseller in Philadelphia 1796-1800 (1 vol).
American Antiquarian Society, Philadelphia.

[126] **COBDEN, Richard** (1804-1865)

MP Stockport 1841-7, W Riding of Yorkshire 1847-57, Rochdale 1859-65

Corresp 1836-65 (26 vols), incl original letters to John Bright 1837-65 (4 vols) and corresp with Henry Ashworth 1841-65 (2 vols), Michel Chevalier 1848-65 (2 vols), Henry Richard 1849-64 (3 vols) and Joseph Sturge 1841-58 (1 vol); misc papers, copies of letters, etc (3 vols); diaries 1836-61 (8 vols); letters mainly to his wife and brother 1845-7 (4 vols).
British Library (Add MSS 43647–78, 43807–8, 50748–51, 65136). Presented by Mrs EJC Cobden Unwin 1933-4 and Richard Cobden-Sanderson 1961, and purchased 1988.

Letters from Joseph Parkes, CP Villiers and others 1838-65 (5 bundles); misc and autograph letters 1825-65, nd (18 vols, 1 bundle); copies of corresp (124 vols); family corresp 1815-65 (8 vols, 1 bundle); papers rel to the Anti-Corn Law League, parliamentary and local government, Europe and America, business interests, etc (c270 items); addresses, freedoms, etc; accounts and financial papers 1822-63; diary of European tour 1840, and notes for American journal 1859; catalogues, lists and misc papers.
West Sussex Record Office (Cobden Papers *passim*; Add MSS 2760–8, 6009–76 *passim*). Deposited by the governors of Dunford College 1961-4, and presented by Richard Cobden-Sanderson 1961-4.
The Cobden papers: a catalogue, 1964; *The Cobden and Unwin papers: a catalogue,* 1967.

Letters from John Bright 1841-64 (2 vols).
British Library (Add MSS 43383–4). Presented with the Bright papers by JA Bright and Mrs HE Darbishire 1933.

Personal, family, business and political corresp and papers 1817-87 (c300 items), incl corresp and papers rel to the Corn Laws 1826-49, nd (17 items) and elections 1837-57, nd (15 items).
Manchester Central Library (M 87). Presented by Richard Cobden-Sanderson 1962. NRA 14284.

Letters to him 1844 (3 items).
Manchester Central Library (MISC 869/1–3).

[127] **COCHRAN-PATRICK, Robert William** (1842-1897)

MP N Ayrshire 1880-5; permanent under-secretary for Scotland 1887-92

Political and misc corresp and papers 1857-1912 (11 vols); personal, political, official and misc corresp and papers 1853-97 (c90 bundles), incl letters from Lord Lothian and other papers as under-secretary; antiquarian and numismatic papers, etc (c10 vols, c5 files); misc personal and family papers, incl journal of visit to Aix-la-Chapelle 1858.
NA Hunter Esq (his great-grandson). Enquiries to NRA (Scotland) (NRA(S) 0038, 0852). NRA 18276.

[128] **COCHRANE, Admiral Thomas** (1775-1860), 10th Earl of Dundonald 1831

MP Honiton 1806-7, Westminster 1807-18

Corresp and papers 1793-1861 (10 boxes, 22 vols), mainly rel to his naval career, service in South America and Greece, and scientific and engineering interests, but incl letters, speeches and papers 1814-18 rel to his trial for fraud and expulsion from Parliament and the navy (several bundles), papers rel to Scottish peerage elections 1847-79 (2 bundles), and misc letters from Sir Francis Burdett, Sir James Graham, Joseph Hume, Lord Palmerston and other politicians.
Scottish Record Office (GD 233). Deposited by the 14th Earl of Dundonald 1968-85. NRA 8150.

Corresp with his agent Henry Dean and papers rel to ships seized at Maranhao 1823-5.
Public Record Office (J 90/531).

[129] **COCKBURN, Henry** (1779-1854), Lord Cockburn

Solicitor-general (Scotland) 1830-4

Between 1887 and 1889 his papers were sorted by his son FJ Cockburn (see *Some letters of Lord Cockburn, with pages omitted from the 'Memorials of his Times'*, ed HA Cockburn, 1932, pp112–25), and some, including the MS of the *Memorials*, letters to Lord Jeffrey and material for his *Life* of Jeffrey, were then destroyed. Others were presented to the Advocates' Library, Edinburgh. Letters from Lord Rutherfurd *c*1831-50 and TF Kennedy 1822-54 were returned to their families (the latter group has not been traced). Further papers remained in the Cockburn family until 1975.

Letters from Lord Jeffrey 1831-8 (mainly 1831-4) (1 vol); copies of letters from Jeffrey 1831-49 (4 vols); notebook for the *Life* of Jeffrey (1 vol); legal papers 1810-38 (7 vols).
National Library of Scotland (Adv MSS 9.1.1–13).

Collected corresp *c*1806-1854 (1 box), incl letters to and from Lord Jeffrey 1827-46 (66 items), and to Sir Thomas Lauder 1820-41 (26 items); material for the *Life* of Jeffrey (1 file).
National Library of Scotland (Deposit 235). Deposited by Mrs FB Cockburn 1975. NRA 25498.

Corresp with Lord Rutherfurd 1813-54 (2 vols), incl *c*24 letters from Rutherfurd *c*1831-50 returned by FJ Cockburn.
National Library of Scotland (MSS 9687–8). Deposited among Rutherfurd's papers by the Faculty of Advocates 1969.

[130] **CODRINGTON, Sir Gerald William Henry** (1850-1929), 1st Bt

Chairman of Thornbury Division Conservative Association 1885-1904

Corresp with CEH Colston and Lord Dunsany as MPs for Gloucestershire (Thornbury division) 1886-1904 (102 items) and with Conservative local and Central Office officials 1886-1924 (453 items); corresp rel to the Primrose League 1886-1914 (56 items); papers as chairman of Chipping Sodbury board of guardians 1898-1923 (27 items); legal and estate corresp 19th-20th cent (3 vols, 9 bundles); family and misc corresp 1853-1914 (4 bundles); printed political and election papers 1886, 1898-1914 (3 bundles, 59 items).
Gloucestershire Record Office (D 1610). Purchased by Gloucestershire County Council 1981, 1984. NRA 6823.

Letters from his attorneys and others in the West Indies 1872-1913 (5 bundles, *c*220 items).

Untraced. Sold by Sir Simon Codrington, Bt at Sotheby's 15 Dec 1980, lot 142. NRA 6823.

[131] **COKE, Thomas William** (1754-1842), 1st Earl of Leicester 1837

MP Norfolk 1776-84, 1790-1807, 1807-32, Derby 1807

Political, agricultural and general corresp 1776-1840 (3 vols), incl letters from CJ Fox 1776-*c*1802 (23 items), the 2nd Earl Grey and the Duke of Sussex, and letters rel to offers of peerages; letters from Samuel Parr 1790-1824 and William Roscoe 1814-30; replies to an invitation to celebrate the centenary of the Glorious Revolution; map of political influence by Humphry Repton 1788; estate letter books; papers rel to his last years and death.
In private possession.

[132] **COLE, Sir Christopher** (1770-1836)

MP Glamorgan 1817-18, 1820-30

Poll and canvass books (20 vols) and copies of land tax assessments (10 vols), Glamorgan election 1820.
National Library of Wales (Margam and Penrice MSS 10221–50). Deposited by Lady Blythswood and Mrs OD Methuen-Campbell 1942. NRA 30000.

Naval log books 1806-8, 1813-14 (2 vols); poll books, Glamorgan election 1820 (2 vols).
West Glamorgan Area Record Office (D/DMa 197–200). NRA 7621.

Naval log book 1808-9.
National Library of Wales (MS 3430). Purchased 1943.

[133] **COLVILLE, Charles John** (1818-1903), 10th Lord Colville of Culross 1849, 1st Baron Colville of Culross 1885, 1st Viscount Colville of Culross 1902

Scottish representative peer 1852-85; master of the Buckhounds 1866-8

Political corresp, mainly as a whip, 1858-90 (5 bundles), incl letters from Lords Beaconsfield, Derby and Salisbury; royal corresp 1863-96, nd (2 bundles); letters from Lord Ellenborough, the Duke of Wellington and others rel to American, Canadian and Indian affairs 1839-49 (2 bundles); autograph album 1856-*c*1910, incl letters from the royal family and politicians.
Viscount Colville of Culross. Enquiries to NRA (Scotland) (NRA(S) 0039). NRA 10112.

[134] **COMPTON, Henry Combe** (1789-1866)

MP S Hampshire 1835-57

Election corresp and papers 1820-42 (8 bundles); poll books 1806-7, 1835; shrievalty papers 1819 (54 items); papers rel to Hampshire affairs 1830-53 (1 vol, 5 bundles); legal and misc papers 1810-55.
Hampshire Record Office (12M60). Acquired 1960. NRA 25329.

[135] **CONOLLY, Thomas** (1735-1803)

MP Malmesbury 1759-68, Chichester 1768-80,
Londonderry 1761-1800

Corresp and papers 1758-1803 (3 vols, c1,300
items), incl corresp mainly rel to politics and
patronage with Lord Buckinghamshire 1776-88 (16
items), Lord Dunlo 1797-1803 (c90 items), David
La Touche 1779-84 (14 items), Thomas Pakenham
1797-1803 (c30 items) and others.
Trinity College Library, Dublin (MSS 3963–5,
3974–84). Presented by the 6th Baron Carew 1966.
NRA 20081.

Political corresp 1761-1800 (56 items); misc corresp
1761-97 (16 items).
*The Castletown Foundation, Castletown House,
Celbridge, co Kildare.* NRA 30723.

Political and other corresp 1796-1800 (1 bundle).
In private possession. Enquiries to the Public Record
Office of Northern Ireland. NRA 30594.

[136] **CONYNGHAM, Francis Nathaniel**
(1797-1876), 2nd Marquess Conyngham 1832

MP Westbury 1818-20, co Donegal 1825-31; under-
secretary for foreign affairs 1823-5; a lord of the
Treasury 1826-30; postmaster-general 1834, 1835;
lord chamberlain 1835-9

Corresp and papers, incl corresp and papers as
postmaster-general and lord chamberlain.
In private possession. NRA 6509.

[137] **COOPER, Thomas** (1805-1892)

Chartist

Corresp with his wife 1879 (70 items); misc corresp
and papers 1832-87 (17 items); papers rel to his
trial and imprisonment 1842 (20 items); copy of
his gaol notebook; sermons and lectures 1854-88,
nd (14 items); press cuttings and autobiographical
notes (1 file).
Lincolnshire Archives Office (2 Baptist). Deposited
by the trustees of the Thomas Cooper Memorial
Church, Lincoln, 1960. NRA 7273.

Letters (10 items); notebook and lecture record
books (4 vols); MS of his *Purgatory of Suicides*
(1845).
Lincoln City Library. See Lincolnshire Archives
Committee, *Archivists' Report 24, 1972-3,* p57; *25,
1973-5,* p86.

Letters to him from WJ Fox 1847-53 (4 items) and
from him to the Revd Charles Kingsley 1856-7 (13
items).
International Institute of Social History, Amsterdam.

CORRY, see Lowry-Corry, MW.

[138] **COURTNEY, Leonard Henry** (1832-1918),
Baron Courtney of Penwith 1906

MP Liskeard 1876-85, Cornwall (Bodmin division)
1885-1900; under-secretary for home affairs 1880-1,
for the colonies 1881-2; financial secretary to the
Treasury 1882-4; deputy Speaker of the House of
Commons 1886-92

Political, personal and family corresp of Courtney
and his wife 1857-1918 (13 vols), incl letters from
LS Amery, JE Cairnes, ARD Elliot, WE
Gladstone, Lord Morley of Blackburn and CP
Scott; letter book 1899-1905 and draft letters
1900-1 (1 vol, 1 file); list of his leaders for *The
Times* 1864-80 (1 vol); misc papers, pamphlets and
speeches 1864-1918 (3 vols); travel journal 1867-9
(1 vol).
*British Library of Political and Economic Science,
London* (R (SR) 1003). Mainly presented by his
sister-in-law Lady Passfield 1937. NRA 7523.

Letters to him and his family rel to politics, colonial
administration, etc 1863-1919 (109 items).
*William R Perkins Library, Duke University,
Durham, North Carolina.* Purchased 1965. NRA
29595.

[139] **COWEN, Joseph** (1831-1900)

MP Newcastle-upon-Tyne 1874-86

Corresp and papers rel to the Northern Reform
Union and the Northern Reform League 1857-77
(1,858 items), incl letters from John Bright, JP
Cobbett, GJ Holyoake, Robert Mathison, RB
Reed, PA Taylor and Lord Teynham, and minutes
of the Northern Reform Union 1857-60 (2 vols);
to home affairs 1846-98 (410 items), incl social and
educational reform; to local affairs 1847-99 (510
items), incl papers rel to the *Northern Tribune*
1853-5 and the *Newcastle Chronicle* 1859-99; to
foreign affairs 1844-97 (976 items), incl the
Newcastle on Tyne Foreign Affairs Committee,
assistance for refugees, and the visit of Garibaldi
to England 1864; misc corresp and papers 1844-98
(106 vols and items), incl copies of out-letters
1878-86 and speech notes.
Tyne and Wear Archives Service (Cowen Collection).
Transferred from Newcastle Central Library 1976.
NRA 30700.

[140] **COWPER, Francis Thomas de Grey**
(1834-1905), 7th Earl Cowper 1856

Lord lieutenant of Ireland 1880-2

Corresp with WE Gladstone as lord lieutenant of
Ireland 1880-1 (18 items).
British Library (Add MS 56453). Lent by Lord
Cowper to John Morley for his *Life* of Gladstone,
and presented by Sir William Gladstone, Bt 1970.

Corresp and papers as lord lieutenant of
Bedfordshire 1861-9 (88 items).
Bedfordshire Record Office (DDX 95/213-16).
Deposited by his great-niece Lady Salmond in
Hertfordshire Record Office 1952 and transferred
1954. NRA 6970.

Misc letters to him among his wife's corresp 1874-1912 (1 vol, *c*55 items); lecture notes nd (1 vol).
Hertfordshire Record Office (D/EP). Deposited by Lady Salmond 1952. NRA 26283.

[141] **COWPER-TEMPLE** (formerly **COWPER**), **William Francis** (1811-1888), Baron Mount-Temple 1880

MP Hertford 1835-68, S Hampshire 1868-80; under-secretary for home affairs 1855; president of the Board of Health 1855-7, 1857-8; vice-president of the Committee of Council for Education 1857-8; vice-president of the Board of Trade and paymaster-general 1859-60; first commissioner of Works 1860-6

Letters from Lord Melbourne 1833-48 (53 items); corresp mainly as first commissioner of Works 1860-6 (357 items), incl letters from Sir Thomas Biddulph, the Duke of Cambridge, General Charles Grey, Sir Charles Phipps and other officials of the royal household, politicians, architects and painters; corresp and papers rel to Office of Works business, arranged by subject 1848-66 (14 files).
Southampton University Library (Broadlands Papers WFC, MEL/CO/1-53). Deposited by the Broadlands Archives Trust 1985. NRA 25759, 25760.

General and personal corresp 1814-88 (3 boxes), incl letters from John Ruskin; corresp and papers rel to the Broadlands conferences mainly 1874-88 (2 boxes), incl letters from Laurence Oliphant; journals, diaries and notebooks 1828-88 (2 boxes); family papers 1837-1901 (2 boxes); misc papers *c*1850-91 (1 box).
Southampton University Library (Broadlands Papers). Deposited by the Broadlands Archives Trust 1987.

Letters to him and his wife from George and Louisa Macdonald 1862-1900 (1 vol).
National Library of Scotland (MS 9745). Purchased 1960.

[142] **CREEVEY, Thomas** (1768-1838)

MP Thetford 1802-6, 1807-18, Appleby 1820-6, Downton 1831-2; secretary of the Board of Control 1806-7; treasurer of the Ordnance 1830-4

Corresp and misc papers 1792-1838 (*c*2,000 items), incl letters from Lord Brougham, the 2nd Earl Grey, William Roscoe, the 2nd Earl of Sefton, Robert Waithman, Lord Western and Samuel Whitbread, and letters from Creevey to his wife, Robert Currie, Elizabeth Ord and others; transcripts of corresp 1804-34 and related papers (39 vols and some loose items), incl corresp rel to the trial of Queen Caroline 1820 (8 vols); journals and notebooks 1809-18, nd (9 vols).
Northumberland Record Office (NRO 324 addn). Deposited by JC Blackett-Ord 1978. NRA 20648.

Letters from James Currie rel to political and social affairs 1793-1805 (45 items).
Liverpool Record Office (920 CUR 1-45). Mainly purchased at Sotheby's 22 July 1918, lot 931. NRA 16742.

[143] **CREWE-MILNES** (formerly **MILNES**), **Robert Offley Ashburton** (1858-1945), 2nd Baron Houghton 1885, Earl of Crewe 1895, Marquess of Crewe 1911

Lord lieutenant of Ireland 1892-5; lord president of the Council 1905-8, 1915-16; secretary for the colonies 1908-10; lord privy seal 1908-11, 1912-15; secretary for India 1910-11, 1911-15; president of the Board of Education 1916; secretary for war 1931

General corresp (61 boxes), incl letters from John Morley as chief secretary 1892-5 (1 box); speeches (3 boxes); misc papers (21 boxes), incl papers rel to the Irish Board of Education 1893-5, the Land Commission 1895, etc (1 box); India Office papers (21 boxes); printed papers, incl parliamentary bills, etc (*c*40 boxes); personal papers (4 boxes).
Cambridge University Library. Deposited by his widow 1958. C Hazlehurst and C Woodland, *Guide to the papers of British cabinet ministers 1900-1951*, Royal Historical Society 1974, p106.

Corresp and papers rel to his *Life* of Lord Rosebery *c*1929-36 (11 vols).
National Library of Scotland (MSS 10195-10205). Presented by Lord Primrose 1966. NRA 22490.

Reports to him as ambassador to France from his press attaché Sir Charles Mendl 1926 (1 vol).
Public Record Office (FO 800/330). NRA 23627.

Addresses to him as lord lieutenant of Ireland (1 folder), and appointments 1908-13.
In private possession.

[144] **CRICHTON, John** (1802-1885), 3rd Earl Erne 1842

Irish representative peer 1845-85

Corresp rel to co Fermanagh politics 1834, 1852-4 (24 items); to his candidature as a representative peer 1842-5 (*c*80 items); to the Repeal agitation and disturbances in co Fermanagh 1840-9 (9 items), with other corresp and papers mainly as lord lieutenant of co Fermanagh 1841-85 (1 bundle); personal and misc corresp and papers *c*1824-85.
Public Record Office of Northern Ireland (D 1939). Presented by the 6th Earl Erne. NRA 28830.

[145] **CRICHTON, John Henry** (1839-1914), 4th Earl Erne 1885

MP Enniskillen 1868-80, co Fermanagh 1880-5; a lord of the Treasury 1876-80

Letters from Sir Stafford Northcote and other politicians 1879-1902 (42 items); political and misc corresp and papers 1868-87 (*c*2 bundles, *c*10 items);

estate corresp 1885 (1 bundle); bank book 1900-3.
Public Record Office of Northern Ireland (D 1939).
Presented by the 6th Earl Erne. NRA 28830.

[146] **CRICHTON-STUART, John** (1793-1848),
2nd Marquess of Bute 1814

Lord lieutenant of Bute and Glamorgan 1815-48

Corresp and papers 1814-48 (c50 bundles), mainly
rel to estate business and Ayrshire affairs but incl
papers rel to national politics and elections 1817-48
(2 bundles) and to the Church of Scotland and
church patronage 1834-46 (1 vol, 3 bundles), and
petitions rel to university tests nd (1 bundle).
The Marquess of Bute. Enquiries to NRA (Scotland)
(NRA(S) 0631). NRA 15459 (Bundles A 1043-87,
1221, 1227-30, 1240-2).

Corresp and papers rel to Chartist agitation in
South Wales 1839-43 (166 items), to Glamorgan
quarter sessions business 1829-47 (51 items), and
to Bedfordshire and Glamorgan estate matters (c50
items), incl the Bedfordshire election 1830.
South Glamorgan County Library, Cardiff (CL/Bute/
IX/27/1-20, XX-XXII).

[147] **CROKE, Thomas William** (1823-1902)

Roman Catholic archbishop of Cashel 1875-1902;
adviser to the Irish Nationalist Party

Corresp and papers 1841-1902 (c700 items), incl
letters from Michael Davitt, WE Gladstone,
William O' Brien, CS Parnell and others, journal,
printed papers, etc.
Cashel Diocesan Archives. See Mark Tierney, 'A
short-title calendar of the papers of Archbishop
Thomas William Croke in Archbishop's House,
Thurles', *Collectanea Hibernica 13, 1970*, pp100-38,
16, 1973, pp97-124, *17, 1974-5*, pp110-44. A
microfilm is in the National Library of Ireland.

[148] **CROKER, John Wilson** (1780-1857)

MP Downpatrick 1807-12, Athlone 1812-18,
Yarmouth 1819-20, Bodmin 1820-6, Aldeburgh
1826-7, 1830-2, Dublin University 1827-30; acting
chief secretary for Ireland 1808; secretary of the
Admiralty 1809-30

Many of his papers passed into the hands of the
book and manuscript dealers J Pearson & Co, and
were sold in two dozen lots among the firm's
residual stock at Sotheby's 23-26 June 1924. The
present whereabouts of several lots has not been
traced.

Letters from the 1st Baron Ashburton, Lord
Brougham, Sir Henry Bunbury, Sir George
Cockburn, the 2nd Baron Fitzgerald and Vesey,
JG Herries, JG Lockhart, the 2nd Earl of Lonsdale,
George Rose, the 5th Duke of Rutland, Sir Herbert
Taylor and others 1803-57 (41 vols); letter books
and indexes 1811-39 (31 vols); diaries and
notebooks (20 vols).

*William L Clements Library, University of Michigan,
Ann Arbor.* Mainly purchased at Sotheby's 23 June
1924, lots 171, 187, 188, 478. *Guide to the
manuscript collections*, 1942, pp35, 66-71.

Corresp and misc papers rel to politics,
parliamentary reform, national finances, naval
affairs, religious questions, etc 1793-1861 (2,874
items), incl letters from the 2nd Viscount Melville
1811-49 (350 items), Sir George Collier, Henry
Goulburn, Sir Henry Torrens and Sir Robert
Wilmot-Horton.
*William R Perkins Library, Duke University,
Durham, North Carolina.* Purchased 1960-71. *Guide
to the cataloged collections*, pp126-7; *National union
catalog*, MS 68-1539.

Corresp, memoranda, notes and transcripts 1804-57
(28 vols), incl letters from Lord George Bentinck
1847-8 (1 vol), the 3rd Marquess of Hertford
1812-42 (4 vols), John Murray 1831-57 (3 vols),
Lord Raglan 1821-54 (1 vol) and the Duke of
Wellington c1807, 1832-52 (2 vols).
British Library (Add MSS 22630, 38078-9, 41124-9,
44895-9, 52465-72, 56367, 60286-9, 63624).
Acquired by gift and purchase 1858-1985.

Letters from eminent churchmen 1813-56 (4 vols).
Bodleian Library, Oxford (MSS Eng. lett. c. 353,
d. 366-8). Purchased 1976.

Corresp and papers rel to an article in the *Quarterly
Review* on Louis Philippe's escape from France
1848 (1 vol).
*Beinecke Library, Yale University, New Haven,
Connecticut* (Osborn Collection fd 33). NRA 18661.

Letters from Lord Ripon 1810-45 (37 items) and
TE Hook 1820-41 (116 items).
*Department of Special Collections, University of
Chicago Library, Illinois.* Formerly Sotheby's 23
June 1924, lots 392, 652. *National union catalog*,
MSS 64-59, 64-112.

Letters from Sir Robert Curtis, with a few draft
replies, 1809-15 (114 items).
Boston Public Library, Massachusetts. Purchased
from Maggs Bros Ltd 1948. *National union catalog*,
MS 65-8.

Letters from Thomas Moore 1812-46 (60 items).
St John's Seminary Library, Camarillo, California.
Presented by Mrs E Doheny 1940-58. *National
union catalog*, MS 62-457.

Letters from Sir George Sinclair 1818-57 (48 items).
National Library of Scotland (MS 9817, ff1-93).
Purchased at Sotheby's 10 Feb 1970, lot 314.

Letters from Sir George Cockburn, with a few
draft replies, 1822-46 (32 items).
National Maritime Museum. Purchased at Phillips's
17 March 1983, lot 407.

Letters from Lord Brougham 1839-57 (23 items).
University College London (Brougham Papers).
NRA 31344.

[149] **CROSBIE, John** (1752-1815), 2nd Earl of
Glandore 1781

MP Athboy 1775-6, Ardfert 1776-81; Irish
representative peer 1801-15

Political, general and family corresp 1776-1815 (553
items), incl letters from Robert Day, HA Herbert,
Thomas Orde and Sir Nathaniel Wraxall; misc
Kerry militia and other papers 1793-1800 (1 folder,
4 items).
National Library of Ireland.

Misc letters and papers 1784-1804, nd (12 items).
Trinity College Library, Dublin (MS 3821).
Presented by JB Talbot-Crosbie 1964. NRA 20236.

[150] **CULLEN, Paul** (1803-1878)

Roman Catholic archbishop of Armagh 1849-52, of
Dublin 1852-78

Corresp and papers 1820-78 (*c*100 boxes), incl
papers concerning relations with the government,
the Catholic University, etc.
Diocesan Archives, Archbishop's House, Dublin.

See also *Churchmen.*

[151] **CUNNINGHAME GRAHAM** (formerly
BONTINE), **Robert Cunninghame** (1799-1863)

Stood for Renfrewshire 1832

Corresp and papers rel to Renfrewshire politics
1832-5 (9 bundles, 2 items); family and business
corresp 1820-57 (19 bundles, *c*15 items); diaries
and notebooks 1819-24 (8 vols).
Scottish Record Office (GD 22). Deposited by Vice-
Admiral AEM Cunninghame Graham 1950-5. NRA
29364.

[152] **CUNNINGHAME GRAHAM** (formerly
BONTINE), **William Cunninghame** (*c*1772-1845)

MP Dunbartonshire 1796-7

Election corresp 1802, 1806-7 (2 bundles, 1 item);
corresp with the Duke of Montrose 1797-8, 1805-6,
rel to Dunbartonshire politics, etc (2 bundles);
political and other corresp with George Dunlop
1801-26 (1 bundle) and with Lord Keith and others
1810-11 (1 bundle); personal, family, financial and
misc corresp and papers 1796-1826 (1 vol, 10
bundles, *c*15 items).
Scottish Record Office (GD 22). Deposited by Vice-
Admiral AEM Cunninghame Graham 1950-5. NRA
29364.

[153] **CUST, John** (1779-1853), 2nd Baron
Brownlow 1807, 1st Earl Brownlow 1815

MP Clitheroe 1802-7

Corresp and papers rel to the Lincolnshire election
1816, to a registration fund for the county 1835-6,
and to various elections 1807-32 (3 bundles);
corresp and papers on Lincolnshire county, local

and estate affairs *c*1803-52 (16 boxes, 11 bundles),
mainly as lord lieutenant; personal papers 1822-3
(1 bundle).
Lincolnshire Archives Office (2 BNL, 4 BNL).
Deposited by the 6th Baron Brownlow 1958, 1972.
NRA 6799.

Corresp and accounts rel to Clitheroe and Grantham
elections 1802-8, 1818-23 (2 bundles, 1 item);
corresp mainly rel to estate matters 1810-41 (5
bundles); accounts 1794-1850 (11 vols); journals,
accounts and papers rel to travel on the continent
1800-2 (15 vols); school books 1792-9 (7 vols).
Lord Brownlow. Lincolnshire Archives Committee,
Archivists' Report 12, 1960-1, pp63-6.

[154] **DALRYMPLE** (formerly **FERGUSSON**),
Sir Charles (1839-1916), 1st Bt

MP Bute 1868-80, 1880-5, Ipswich 1886-1906; a
lord of the Treasury 1885-6

Political corresp 1866-1915 (3 bundles), incl letters
from AJ Balfour (19 items), Lord Randolph
Churchill (11 items) and Sir Stafford Northcote (14
items); papers rel to Bute and Ipswich elections
1868-86 (12 vols and items); ecclesiastical corresp
and papers 1859-1910 (1 vol, 3 bundles); personal
and family corresp; diaries, journals, account
books, etc (65 vols); masonic and misc papers
*c*1860-1911.
National Library of Scotland (Acc 7228). Accepted
for the nation in lieu of tax and allocated to the
Library 1977-8. NRA 17690.

[155] **DALRYMPLE, John Hamilton** (1771-1853),
8th Earl of Stair 1840

MP Edinburghshire 1832-5; keeper of the Great
Seal of Scotland 1840-1, 1846-52

Political, military and general corresp *c*1810-51 (3
vols, several bundles), incl letters from Lord
Brougham, the Duke of Gloucester and the Duke
of Hamilton; election papers 1832-5, mainly
printed; corresp and papers rel to local affairs (1
box); personal accounts 1819-23.
Scottish Record Office (GD 135). Deposited by the
13th Earl of Stair 1965. NRA 10017.

[156] **DALRYMPLE-HAMILTON, Sir Hew
Hamilton** (1774-1834), 4th Bt

MP Haddingtonshire 1795-1800, Ayrshire 1803-7,
1811-18, Haddington burghs 1820-6

Corresp and papers rel to Ayrshire politics 1801-27
(4 bundles); corresp rel to local, business and
family affairs 1809-34 (6 bundles); commissions,
burgess tickets, etc (1 bundle).
In private possession. Enquiries to NRA (Scotland)
(NRA(S) 2404). NRA 25160.

Political, social and family corresp 1803-32 (*c*100
items), incl letters rel to Ayrshire politics 1803-11;
letter books *c*1804-30 (microfilms only); corresp
and papers rel to taxation and legal matters 1801-25

(2 bundles, 7 items); personal and household accounts 1804-25 (3 vols, 13 items).
Scottish Record Office (GD 109, RH 4/57).
Deposited by Admiral Sir Frederick Dalrymple-Hamilton 1961.

[157] **DANIEL, David Robert** (1859-1931)

Welsh local politician and trade union official

Political and general corresp with Sir Arthur Acland, William Jones MP, Sir Herbert Lewis, David Lloyd George and others c1880-c1930 (c1,900 items); corresp and papers of and rel to TE Ellis (508 items), incl letters from Ellis to Daniel 1873-98 (350 items); corresp and papers rel to the North Wales Quarrymen's Union 1878-1914 (280 items); misc corresp (c8 bundles); diaries 1871-1930 (44 vols); literary and misc notebooks and papers (c70 vols and bundles).
National Library of Wales (DR Daniel Papers). NRA 30323.

[158] **DASHWOOD, Sir George Henry** (1790-1862), 5th Bt

MP Buckinghamshire 1832-5, Chipping Wycombe 1837-62

Corresp and papers rel to Buckinghamshire and Chipping Wycombe elections 1832-52 (108 items); personal, family, financial and estate corresp and papers c1808-63 (1,170 items), incl his letters to his wife on political and other topics.
Bodleian Library, Oxford (MS D.D. Dashwood). Deposited by Sir John Dashwood, Bt, from 1950. NRA 892.

[159] **DAVENPORT, Edward Davies** (1778-1847)

MP Shaftesbury 1826-30

Political corresp c1822-47 (68 items), incl letters from Thomas Attwood, Lord Holland and Lord Westminster; papers rel to the 1847 election, with other political and misc papers 1814-46 (61 items); corresp c1815-46 (141 items), incl letters from JN Fazakerley, Bishop Reginald Heber and Sir Charles Napier; estate and financial corresp and papers.
John Rylands University Library of Manchester (Bromley Davenport Muniments). Deposited by Sir Walter Bromley-Davenport 1948-70. NRA 592.

DAVENPORT, WB, see Bromley-Davenport.

[160] **DAVITT, Michael** (1846-1906)

MP co Meath 1882, co Meath (N division) 1892, co Cork (NE division) 1893, co Mayo (S division) 1895-9

Political and general corresp 1870-1906, incl corresp with Joseph Chamberlain, James Collins, John Dillon, John Morley, William O'Brien, CS Parnell, AM and Margaret Sullivan, Archbishop

Walsh and Alfred Webb; letters and papers rel to the Land League 1879, etc, *The Times*, the Parnell commission,etc 1883-93, the Waterford by-election 1891-2, the Irish parliamentary party and United Irish League c1895-1905, his withdrawal from parliament 1899, the general elections of 1900 and 1906, the education question 1901-6, etc; family corresp and papers; notes for speeches 1878-1906; diaries and notebooks 1877-1906, incl travel diaries 1884-1905; autobiographical writings 1881-1904; accounts 1882-95; bankruptcy papers 1892-4; scrapbooks, press cuttings, pamphlets, addresses and misc papers.
Trinity College Library, Dublin (MSS 9320-9681). Presented 1982.

[161] **DAWSON, George Robert** (1790-1856)

MP co Londonderry 1815-30, Harwich 1830-2; under-secretary for home affairs 1822-7; joint secretary to the Treasury 1828-30

Londonderry election accounts and registers 1832 (4 vols); election diary 1837.
In private possession. Copies are in the Public Record Office of Northern Ireland (T 874, 1048/4).

[162] **DAY, Robert** (d 1841)

MP Tuam 1783-90, Ardfert 1790-7

Diaries 1794, 1801, 1827-39 (4 vols), incl comments on Irish politics, public affairs, etc; papers c1780-c1839 (7 vols).
Royal Irish Academy, Dublin (MSS 12 W 1-13).
Manuscript sources for the history of Irish civilisation, ed RJ Hayes, 1965, i, 811.

Irish circuit diary and English travel journal 1807-13 (1 vol).
Beinecke Library, Yale University, New Haven, Connecticut (Osborn Collection: MS d 147). NRA 18661.

[163] **DE GREY, Thomas** (1748-1818), 2nd Baron Walsingham 1781

MP Wareham 1774, Tamworth 1774-80, Lostwithiel 1780-1; under-secretary for the colonies 1778-80; a commissioner of the Board of Control 1784-90; joint postmaster-general 1787-94; chairman of the committee for privileges of the House of Lords 1794-1814

General corresp and papers c1770-1818 (c100 bundles), incl corresp rel to the Post Office and the House of Lords; notes and papers, mainly copies, rel to trade, the colonies, India, Spain and the House of Lords c1760-86 (1 box, 41 vols and bundles); letters and draft speech on retirement as chairman of the committee for privileges 1814 (2 bundles); Wareham and Tamworth election papers 1774-80 (1 bundle); travel journals 1769-70 (2 vols); accounts c1772-1818 (4 vols), with other financial and misc papers.
Norfolk Record Office (MS 21554). Deposited by the 9th Baron Walsingham 1967-77. NRA 21634.

Copies made for him of official papers rel to Post
Office business 1787-92.
Post Office Archives (POST 97). *Guide to Post Office
Archives*, 1985, p78.

[164] **DE GREY, Thomas** (1843-1919), 6th Baron
Walsingham 1870

MP W Norfolk 1865-70

Political corresp and papers 1865-90 (11 bundles,
7 items), incl corresp as president of the Eastern
Union of Conservative Associations 1885-9; corresp
and papers rel to financial, local and other affairs
1865-1912 (*c*140 bundles and items), incl
agricultural associations and unionism 1873-91 (2
bundles).
Norfolk Record Office (MS 21554). Deposited by
the 9th Baron Walsingham 1967-77. NRA 21634.

[165] **DELANE, John Thadeus** (1817-1879)

Editor of *The Times* 1841-77

Corresp *c*1841-77 (27 vols), incl letters from John
Walter III 1847-77 (2 vols); office diaries 1857-77.
The Times Archives. See *The history of* The Times,
ii, 1939, p538. Enquiries to the Archivist, *The
Times* Archives, 214 Gray's Inn Road, London
WC1X 8EZ.

Corresp with WH Russell (1 box).
The Times Archives. Enquiries to the Archivist.

Letters to him and William Stebbing, assistant
editor, 1870-7 (13 vols).
*Humanities Research Center, University of Texas,
Austin*. Bequeathed to the London Library by
WPD Stebbing in 1961 and sold at Sotheby's 18
July 1967, lot 525.

[166] **DELAVAL, John Hussey** (1728-1808),
Baron Delaval 1783

MP Berwick-upon-Tweed 1754-61, 1765-74,
1780-6

Corresp and papers rel to politics and elections in
Berwick 1754-1807 (48 vols and bundles),
Northumberland and Durham 1760-1807 (6
bundles), Lincoln 1768-1807 (3 bundles) and
Andover and Lancaster 1761-1807 (1 bundle);
parliamentary corresp and papers 1757-*c*1804 (11
vols, 5 bundles), incl draft speeches and notes on
debates; corresp and papers rel to estate,
household, business, legal and local affairs (*c*110
bundles); corresp with relatives and rel to family
affairs *c*1753-1808 (*c*32 bundles); personal accounts
and financial papers 1754-1807 (20 vols and
bundles); memoranda *c*1760-77 (5 vols), incl
parliamentary notes; literary and misc papers (4
vols, 9 bundles).
Northumberland Record Office (2 DE). Presented to
the Northumberland County History Committee
by his descendant the 6th Marquess of Waterford
*c*1907, given to Newcastle Central Public Library
1919, and transferred to Northumberland Record
Office 1963. NRA 10635.

Estate, business and personal corresp 1751-99 (4
bundles); papers rel to the Seaton Delaval
volunteers 1798-1800 (1 bundle).
Northumberland Record Office (NRO 650).
Deposited on behalf of the 22nd Baron Hastings,
a descendant of his sister, 1971. NRA 10635.

[167] **DENISON, John Evelyn** (1800-1873),
Viscount Ossington 1872

MP Newcastle-under-Lyme 1823-6, Hastings
1826-30, Nottinghamshire 1831-2, S
Nottinghamshire 1832-7, Malton 1841-57, N
Nottinghamshire 1857-72; Speaker of the House of
Commons 1857-72

Corresp and papers 1818-73, nd (1,460 items), incl
letters from politicians, churchmen and
agriculturalists; diaries as Speaker 1857-71 (6 vols);
personal diaries, notebooks, etc 1824-72 (12 vols);
corresp and papers rel to the *Speaker's Commentary
on the Bible* *c*1862-71 (1 vol, 486 items).
Nottingham University Library (Os, Os2). Deposited
by Colonel WME Denison 1964 and by his widow
Mrs Pamela Goedhuis 1979. NRA 205.

[168] **DENMAN, Thomas** (1779-1854), 1st Baron
Denman 1834

MP Wareham 1818-20, Nottingham 1820-6,
1830-2; solicitor-general to Queen Caroline 1820-1;
attorney-general 1830-2; Speaker of the House of
Lords 1835

Letters from Lord Brougham 1828-54, nd (176
items).
University College London (Brougham Papers).
NRA 31344.

Political and family corresp *c*1828-52 (*c*65 items),
incl letters from Brougham.
In private possession.

Judicial notebooks 1832-49 (75 vols), with related
unbound papers 1832-44; commonplace book with
copies of legal opinions.
Lincoln's Inn Library, London (Misc MSS 609-703,
714). Presented by Arthur Denman 1920.

Letters and papers rel to Queen Caroline and to
his legal career 1821-40 (25 items).
West Sussex Record Office (Add MS 733). Deposited
by Mrs W Burrell and CS Denman 1955. NRA
6777.

[169] **DE VERE, Sir Stephen Edward** (1812-1904),
4th Bt

MP co Limerick 1854-9

Letter books 1846-54 (2 vols); manuscript articles
on political subjects, press cuttings and privately
printed pamphlets, with copies of letters *c*1874-86
(7 vols); journals 1847-77 (12 vols), incl references
to Limerick elections and parliamentary debates;
notebooks 1840-57, with accounts and a few copies
of letters (3 vols); accounts 1866-85 (5 vols).
Trinity College Library, Dublin (MSS 5056-83).

[170] **DICK** (formerly **HUME**), **William Wentworth Fitzwilliam** (1805-1892)

MP co Wicklow 1852-80

Corresp and papers rel to co Wicklow politics 1848-80 (c100 items), incl papers rel to the elections of 1848, 1857 and 1880 and to a protectionist meeting 1850; personal, family and legal corresp and papers c1830-86 (several hundred items), incl letters from Sir Fitzroy Kelly.
Public Record Office of Ireland. Deposited by Williams & James, solicitors, through the British Records Association 1987.

Misc corresp and papers 1866-81 (c35 items), mainly rel to the Parnell estates in Ireland.
British Library (Add MS 62443). Purchased among papers of his grandson Lord Long at Sotheby's 20 July 1981, lot 141.

Election accounts, co Wicklow 1857 (1 bundle); misc corresp 1863-72 (4 items); will 1883; photograph albums.
Wiltshire Record Office (WRO 2016). Deposited by Williams & James, solicitors, 1983, 1985.

[171] **DICKINSON, Francis Henry** (1812-1890)

MP Somerset 1841-7

Political, local, religious and family corresp and papers 1833-85 (95 bundles), incl corresp rel to Somerset politics mainly 1837-47, letters from Archdeacon Denison and Samuel Wilberforce, and papers rel to Wells Theological College.
Somerset Record Office (DD/DN 293-387). Deposited by Captain WF Dickinson 1951. NRA 16967.

[172] **DICKINSON, William** (1745-1806)

MP Great Marlow 1768-74, Rye 1777-90, Somerset 1796-1806

Political, constituency and other corresp 1763-1806 (42 bundles); accounts (incl Somerset election expenses) 1762-1806 (8 vols); letter book and papers rel to Jamaican estates c1792-1805 (1 vol, c10 bundles).
Somerset Record Office (DD/DN 232-73, 417-21, 467-76). Deposited by Captain WF Dickinson 1951. NRA 16967.

[173] **DICKINSON, William** (1771-1837)

MP Ilchester 1796-1802, Lostwithiel 1802-6, Somerset 1806-31; a lord of the Admiralty 1804-6

Political and parliamentary corresp and papers 1797-1828 (3 bundles), incl papers rel to Ireland and to select committees on sewers and county rates; electoral, local, estate, financial and family corresp and papers 1795-1837 (1 vol, 15 bundles).
Somerset Record Office (DD/DN 274-92). Deposited by Captain WF Dickinson 1951. NRA 16967.

[174] **DIGBY, William** (1849-1904)

Secretary of the National Liberal Club 1882-7; journalist and supporter of Indian self-government

Corresp and papers rel to Dadabhai Naoroji's candidature at Central Finsbury 1889-92 (6 bundles); letters from Charles Bradlaugh, Mortilal Ghose and Sir Dinshaw Wacha 1889-1904 (1 box).
India Office Library and Records (MSS Eur D 767). Purchased 1971, 1980. NRA 25885 (partial list).

[175] **DILKE, Ashton Wentworth** (1850-1883)

MP Newcastle-upon-Tyne 1880-3; proprietor and editor of the *Weekly Dispatch* 1875-83

Letters from politicians 1868-83 (78 items), incl Joseph Chamberlain (8 items) and John Morley (19 items); misc papers rel to his election and resignation as an MP, etc c1875-83 (1 bundle); letters from Russians 1873-83 (58 items); MS of an unpublished work on 'Russian Power' with related papers c1870-5 (4 bundles); family and misc corresp and papers c1860-83 (c300pp), incl corresp with his brother Sir Charles Dilke.

Churchill College, Cambridge (Dilke-Roskill-Enthoven Collection). Deposited by Sir Ashton Roskill 1973-4. NRA 21872.

[176] **DILLON, John** (1851-1927)

MP co Tipperary 1880-3, co Mayo (E division) 1885-1918

Corresp with GW Balfour, Augustine Birrell, James Bryce, Michael Davitt, TC Harrington, John Morley, William O'Brien, TP O'Connor, JE Redmond and others c1877-1927 (106 vols); shorthand letter books 1887-97 (9 vols); minutes, accounts, corresp and papers rel to the Irish Parliamentary Party, Evicted Tenants' Committee, Home Rule Fund, etc 1878-1924 (60 vols, etc); speech notes and misc political and other papers (10 vols); journals, diaries, notes and memoranda 1876-1922 (79 vols, etc); accounts and financial papers 1885-1922 (8 vols, etc); addresses, scrapbooks, etc (18 vols and items); misc family corresp and papers.
Trinity College Library, Dublin (MSS 6500-6666, 6727-6867). Purchased 1971. NRA 23146.

Letters from Michael Davitt 1880-1902, nd (12 vols).
Trinity College Library, Dublin (MSS 9403-14). Presented with the Davitt papers 1982.

Lists of members of the Irish National Federation c1893-6 (1 vol); notes on Irish and general politics 1919-21 (2 vols).
Department of Special Collections, Kenneth Spencer Research Library, University of Kansas, Lawrence (O'Hegarty MSS C216-17, G19).

Diary 1916.
Trinity College Library, Dublin (MS 9820). Presented 1984.

[177] **DILLON, Luke Gerald** (1834-1917), 4th
Baron Clonbrock 1893

Private secretary to the lord lieutenant of Ireland
1866-8, 1874-6; Irish representative peer 1895-1917

Corresp and papers, incl papers rel to the land and
Home Rule questions.
National Library of Ireland. See *Manuscript sources
for the history of Irish civilisation, Supplement,* 1979,
i, 131.

[178] **DOMVILE, Sir Charles Compton William**
(1822-1884), 2nd Bt

Stood for co Dubin 1857

Corresp and papers rel to co Dublin elections
1857-65, with earlier election papers from 1746 (3
vols); general and family corresp 1848-60, 1871-2
(2 vols).
National Library of Ireland (MSS 9361, 9363, 9365,
11854-5). Acquired from JR Stewart and Son,
Dublin, agents to the Domvile estate.

DOUGLAS, EG, see Douglas-Pennant.

[179] **DOUGLAS, Hon Frederick Sylvester
North** (1791-1819)

MP Banbury 1812-19

Corresp *c*1806-19 (*c*1,300 items), mainly rel to
Banbury affairs but incl letters from Stratford
Canning (13 items) and Lord Wellesley (15 items);
family corresp *c*1809-19, incl letters from his father
(*c*140 items) and mother (*c*125 items); travel diaries
1804, 1814-15 (4 vols, etc).
Bodleian Library, Oxford. Purchased from a dealer
1981 (formerly sold at Phillips's 2 July 1981, lot
309).

[180] **DOUGLAS, Sylvester** (1743-1823), Baron
Glenbervie 1800

MP Irishtown 1794-6, Fowey 1795-6, Midhurst
1796-1800, Plympton Erle 1801-2, Hastings
1802-6; chief secretary for Ireland 1794-5; a
commissioner of the Board of Control 1795-1806;
joint paymaster-general 1801-3; vice-president of
the Board of Trade 1801-4; surveyor-general of
woods and forests 1803-6, 1807-10; first
commissioner of woods and forests 1810-14

His papers were bequeathed to his executors, who
included the 5th Earl of Guilford. On Guilford's
death in 1827 those of the papers in his possession
passed to the 2nd Earl of Sheffield. Some were
sold after the death of the 3rd Earl of Sheffield in
1909, and others at Phillips's on 2 July 1981.

Political, social and family corresp 1800-23 (*c*400
items), incl letters from correspondents with
surnames beginning A and B and copies of out-
letters; letters to his wife 1810-16, nd (*c*100 items).
National Library of Scotland (Acc 8059). Purchased

from DP White (formerly sold at Phillips's 2 July
1981, part of lot 308). NRA 24836.

Corresp of him and his wife and of Lady Sheffield
*c*1808-20 (213 items).
Untraced. Sold at Phillips's 2 July 1981, part of lot
308.

Letters to him and his wife from the 5th Earl of
Guilford *c*1808-23 (over 18 items); letters from
Lady Charlotte Lindsay *c*1814-23 (55 items).
British Library (Add MSS 61981-3, 61986).
Purchased at Phillips's 2 July 1981, lots 298, 303.

Corresp and papers rel to a projected biography of
Lord North *c*1796-1800, with later endorsements
by Glenbervie.
British Library (Add MS 61876). Purchased in 1980
with Lord North's papers.

Corresp, accounts and papers 1795-1814 as attorney
for Frederick North while governor of Ceylon (6
bundles, *c*520 items), incl corresp with Lord Minto.
Kent Archives Office (U 471/C 39-62, 127).
Deposited by the 9th Earl of Guilford 1954. NRA
5392.

Letters from various correspondents 1819-20 (32
items).
National Library of Scotland (Crawford Muniments
35/4). Transferred from the John Rylands
University Library of Manchester 1988. *Hand-list
of personal papers from the muniments of the Earl of
Crawford and Balcarres,* 1976, p66.

Letters of recommendation and passports during
his European tour 1767-8.
National Library of Scotland (Acc 7079). Purchased
1977. NRA 29292.

Journals 1793-1811, 1815-19 (11 vols).
In private possession. See *The diaries of Sylvester
Douglas, Lord Glenbervie,* ed FL Bickley, 1928.

Journals 1793, 1811-15 (2 vols).
Untraced. Purchased by WS Sichel after the
Sheffield Park sale 1910. See *The Glenbervie
journals,* ed Walter Sichel, 1910.

Memorandum and sketch of French society written
*c*1770-1 (copied *c*1794 and annotated *c*1819) (1 vol).
British Library (Add MS 62139). Purchased at
Lawrence's of Crewkerne 11 March 1982, lot 263
(formerly Phillips's, 2 July 1981, part of lot 308).

Accounts and financial papers, Bushy Park
household and estate 1810-16 (*c*180 items).
Untraced. Sold at Phillips's 10 Dec 1987, lot 421.

[181] **DOUGLAS-PENNANT** (formerly
DOUGLAS), **Edward Gordon** (1800-1886), 1st
Baron Penrhyn 1866

MP Carnarvonshire 1841-6

Political papers of him and his son the 2nd Baron
*c*1850-*c*1907 (several hundred items), mainly rel to
Carnarvonshire elections.
University College of North Wales, Bangor (Penrhyn
MSS). Deposited by the 6th Baron Penrhyn 1983.

[182] **DOUGLAS-PENNANT, George Sholto Gordon** (1836-1907), 2nd Baron Penrhyn 1886

MP Carnarvonshire 1866-8, 1874-80

Political papers of him and his father *c*1850-*c*1907 (several hundred items) rel to Carnarvonshire elections, industrial relations, the Property Defence League, etc.
University College of North Wales, Bangor (Penrhyn MSS). Deposited by the 6th Baron Penrhyn 1983.

[183] **DOUGLAS-SCOTT-MONTAGU** (formerly **MONTAGU-DOUGLAS-SCOTT**), **Henry John** (1832-1905), 1st Baron Montagu of Beaulieu 1885

MP Selkirkshire 1861-8, S Hampshire 1868-84

Political corresp and papers 1837-1906 (*c*45 bundles), incl papers rel to elections in Selkirkshire 1837-69 and S Hampshire 1868-92; corresp and papers rel to ecclesiastical matters *c*1866-94 (13 bundles); corresp and papers as verderer of the New Forest 1867-99 (54 bundles), incl papers rel to the New Forest Bill 1875-7; family corresp 1841-93 (*c*80 bundles), incl corresp with his father the 5th Duke of Buccleuch on political matters 1851-83; personal and social letters *c*1849-99 (17 bundles), mainly from WCD Esdaile; commissions, passports and corresp rel to his peerage 1851-1904 (10 bundles and items); legal and misc corresp and papers 1842-1905 (35 bundles), incl patronage corresp *c*1870-90; diaries 1869-96 (17 vols).
Lord Montagu of Beaulieu. Enquiries to the Heritage Education Officer and Archivist, Beaulieu Abbey, Brockenhurst, Hampshire SO4 7ZN. NRA 4880.

[184] **DRENNAN, William** (1754-1820)

United Irishman

Political, literary and general corresp 1776-1819, incl letters to the Revd William Bruce *c*1782-92 (76 items) and corresp with Samuel and Martha McTier (*c*1,400 items); political and literary papers, commonplace books, notes, etc 1737-1820, incl papers rel to parliamentary reform and the Belfast Academical Institution.
Public Record Office of Northern Ireland (D 456, 531, 553, 591, 729; T 965, 2884).

[185] **DRUMMOND** (formerly **WALKER**), **Sir Francis Walker** (1781-1844), 2nd Bt

Scottish politician

Letters from Lord Brougham, the Duke of Buccleuch, JC Douglas, Lord Tweeddale and others mainly rel to Scottish elections 1827-37 (*c*4 bundles); papers rel to his dispute with the Bank of Scotland 1830-1 (*c*2 bundles); passport 1821.
Scottish Record Offiice (GD 230). Deposited by Brodies, WS 1977. NRA 10137.

[186] **DRUMMOND, Henry** (1786-1860)

MP Plympton Erle 1810-12, W Surrey 1847-60

Political and general corresp and papers 1809-60 (*c*730 items), incl letters from Benjamin Disraeli, Lord Palmerston, Sir Robert Peel and Sir Charles Wood; religious corresp and papers 1814-60 (*c*350 items), incl letters from JB Cardale (27 items) and Edward Irving (45 items); corresp and papers rel to architectural work at Albury Park *c*1807-85 (*c*160 items), incl letters from AWN Pugin (65 items); genealogical and heraldic papers rel to *Histories of noble British families* 1840-8 (215 items); letters to CK Sharpe 1810-41 (18 items); misc letters and papers 1802-60 (58 items).
The Duke of Northumberland. Enquiries to the Archivist, Alnwick Castle, Alnwick, Northumberland NE66 1NQ. NRA 836.

[187] **DUFF** (formerly **ABERCROMBY**), **Sir Robert William** (1835-1895)

MP Banffshire 1861-93; a lord of the Treasury 1882-5, of the Admiralty 1886

Political corresp 1873-92 (15 items); corresp with the 5th and 6th Earls Fife on political and financial matters 1862-89 (20 items); notebook containing political comments, speeches and quotations *c*1861 (1 vol); naval logbooks and papers 1847-60 (2 vols, 15 items); misc corresp and papers 1863-90 (44 items).
Scottish Record Office (GD 105). Deposited 1946. NRA 29898.

[188] **DUFFY, Sir Charles Gavan** (1816-1903)

MP New Ross 1852-5; prime minister of Victoria 1871-2

Political, literary and general corresp 1840-1914 (6 vols, 53 folders), incl letters from Thomas Carlyle, Archbishop Croke, John Dillon, WEH Lecky, WS O'Brien, the 1st Baron O'Hagan, JE Pigot and GO Trevelyan; historical notes, literary papers and drafts *c*1870-1900 (9 vols, 7 folders); commonplace book *c*1864.
National Library of Ireland (MSS 1627, 2642, 3738-9, 4193-8, 4559, 4722, 5756-8, 7404, 8005-6, 8098).

Corresp and papers *c*1842-8 (5 boxes, 1 vol), incl papers rel to *The Nation* and diaries and papers rel to his trial.
Royal Irish Academy, Dublin (MSS 23 O 47, 12 P 15-20). *Manuscript sources for the history of Irish civilisation*, ed RJ Hayes, 1965, i, 962-3.

Corresp rel to Australian federation 1856-77 (32 items).
La Trobe Library, Melbourne. See *Guide to collections of manuscripts relating to Australia*, 1965, A 80.

[189] **DUNDAS, Sir David** (1799-1877)

MP Sutherland 1840-52, 1861-7; solicitor-general
1846-8; judge advocate-general 1849-52

Political and general corresp and papers 1818-75
(c100 items); family and social corresp 1816-45
(c250 items); personal accounts 1842-67 (9 vols);
estate corresp 1850-65 (c50 items).
,Scottish Record Office (GD 35). Deposited by Lt-
Colonel JC Dundas 1956 and Dundas and Wilson,
CS 1975. NRA 8399.

[190] **DUNDAS, George** (1819-1880)

MP Linlithgowshire 1847-59

Letter book mainly rel to Linlithgowshire politics
1846-8, 1855-9 (1 vol); corresp 1847-78 (1 vol);
misc commissions, etc 1859-78 (5 items).
National Library of Scotland (Adv MS 80.1.11, 15;
Ch B 1335-6, 1338-9, 1349).

[191] **DUNDAS, Lawrence** (1844-1929), 3rd Earl
of Zetland 1873, 1st Marquess of Zetland 1892

MP Richmond 1872-3; lord lieutenant of Ireland
1889-92

Corresp as lord lieutenant, mainly rel to patronage,
1889-92 (400 items), with other corresp and papers.
North Yorkshire County Record Office (ZNK).
Deposited by the 3rd Marquess of Zetland 1965,
1979. *Annual report 1971*, p48; *Accessions to
repositories . . . 1979*, 1980, p44.

[192] **DUNDAS, Robert** (1758-1819), Lord
Arniston

MP Edinburghshire 1790-1801; solicitor-general
(Scotland) 1784-9; lord advocate 1789-1801

Political, official and general corresp 1781-1814 (6
boxes), incl letters from the 1st Viscount Melville;
letters mainly rel to taxation 1795-1801 (1 vol).
Edinburgh University Library (La.II.500-1; add 3).
Bequeathed by David Laing 1878. HMC *Report on
the Laing Manuscripts*, ii, 1925, pp503-692 *passim*.

General corresp c1780-1819 (2 vols), incl letters
from Lord Melville and the 3rd Duke of Portland;
letters to John Spottiswood 1800-14 (1 vol);
transcripts of letters from Lord Melville 1782-1811
(1 vol); copies of letters to Alexander Dirom rel to
the malt tax 1803 (1 bundle); journals 1772-5,
1804-19 (4 vols); Arniston diary 1790-9 (1 vol); fee
book 1778-92 (1 vol); account books 1800-18 (5
vols); misc papers 1819 (1 bundle).
In private possession. Enquiries to NRA (Scotland)
(NRA(S) 0077). NRA 8398. A microfilm of some
of the papers is in the Scottish Record Office.

Misc corresp and papers 1792-1810 (30 items),
mainly rel to his legal career.
Scottish Record Office (GD 214). Presented by Lt-
Commander RSE Hannay 1940.

DUNDAS, RA, see Nisbet-Hamilton.

[193] **DUNDAS, Thomas** (1741-1820), 1st Baron
Dundas 1794

MP Richmond 1763-8, Stirlingshire 1768-94

Business and political corresp and papers 1773-1820
(2,112 items); parliamentary and patronage papers
c1789-91 (14 vols and items); corresp and papers
rel to elections in Scotland and Yorkshire 1779-1819
(50 items); diaries, memoranda and accounts
1770-1816 (17 vols); corresp rel to Yorkshire affairs
1779-1814 (c370 items); financial, estate and misc
corresp and papers (c900 items).
North Yorkshire County Record Office (ZNK X2).
Deposited by the 3rd Marquess of Zetland 1965.
NRA 16269.

[194] **DUNLOP, John** (1789-1868)

Secretary of the Society for the Abolition of Slavery;
temperance reformer

Political, business and family corresp c1800-67 (27
bundles), rel to slavery, suffrage, temperance and
other topics, and incl letters from Joseph Sturge;
notebook, draft speeches, lectures and other papers
rel to slavery, reform, etc c1820-65 (8 vols and
bundles); papers rel to North American travels
1831-4 (2 bundles); diary 1844; commonplace
book; personal and household accounts 1819-66
(15 vols, 3 bundles); estate and misc corresp and
papers c1831-58 (3 bundles).
National Library of Scotland (Dep 360). Deposited
by Dr JCH Dunlop 1983. NRA 19325.

Diaries, mainly rel to the temperance movement,
and autobiography 1833-60 (3 vols); genealogical
and misc corresp and papers c1817-68 (3 vols);
literary MSS 1842-56 (2 vols).
National Library of Scotland (MSS 9254, 9261-3,
9272-3, 9297, 9300). Presented by Mrs LCC Bell
1962.

[195] **DYKE, Sir William Hart** (1837-1931), 7th
Bt

MP W Kent 1865-8, Mid Kent 1868-85, Kent
(Dartford division) 1885-1906; patronage secretary
to the Treasury and chief whip 1874-80; chief
secretary for Ireland 1885-6; vice-president of the
Committee of Council for Education 1887-92

Letters from Lord Beaconsfield 1868-80, nd (26
items).
*Douglas Library, Queen's University, Kingston,
Ontario* (Disraeli Project Collection). Acquired
1976. NRA 23298.

[196] **DYOTT, Richard** (1808-1891)

MP Lichfield 1865-80

Political corresp and papers 1826-87 (7 bundles), incl letters from Sir Robert Peel, 2nd Bt (24 items); corresp and papers mainly rel to Lichfield elections 1841-80 (11 bundles); Lichfield and Staffordshire poll books, printed papers, etc 1745-1880 (14 vols, c50 items); estate, local, financial and family corresp and papers 1842-90 (c22 bundles, 7 items); travel diaries 1835-40 (2 vols, 1 bundle); personal and household accounts 1826-47 (4 vols).
Staffordshire Record Office (D 661). Deposited by Major RA Dyott 1962. NRA 9000.

[197] **EASTHOPE, Sir John** (1784-1865), Bt

MP St Albans 1826-30, Banbury 1831-2, Leicester 1837-47; proprietor of the *Morning Chronicle* 1834-47

Political corresp and papers 1809-61 (498 items), incl letters from Lord Brougham, the 1st Earl of Durham, Lord Palmerston and Lord John Russell rel to domestic and foreign affairs.
William R Perkins Library, Duke University, Durham, North Carolina. Acquired 1958. *Guide to the cataloged collections,* 1980, pp159-60.

Letters from Lord Palmerston 1838-55, nd, mostly originals (33 items).
Southampton University Library (Broadlands Papers GC/EA/26-58). Deposited by the Broadlands Archives Trust 1985. NRA 12889.

[198] **EDEN, William** (1744-1814), 1st Baron Auckland 1789

MP New Woodstock 1774-84, Heytesbury 1784-93; under-secretary for the northern department 1772-8; a commissioner for conciliation with America 1778-9; chief secretary for Ireland 1780-2; joint vice-treasurer (Ireland) 1783-4; joint postmaster-general 1798-1804; president of the Board of Trade 1806-7

Political, diplomatic and general corresp and papers mainly 1776-1813 (50 vols), incl letters from John Beresford, Edward Cooke, Henry Dundas, Lord Grenville, John Hatsell, Lord Henley and William Pitt; corresp and papers rel to the East India Company 1776-1802 (4 vols); misc diplomatic papers 1785-95 (4 vols).
British Library (Add MSS 33412-69). Purchased 1893.

Political, diplomatic and general corresp and papers mainly 1764-1814 (6 vols), incl letters to Lord Sheffield 1781-c1814 and papers rel to North America 1775-9.
British Library (Add MSS 45728-30, 46490-1, 46519). Presented by OE and Miss VM Dickinson, grandchildren of the 3rd Baron Auckland, 1941, 1948.

Letters to him, mainly from politicians 1768-1811 (c30 items).
British Library (Add MS 29475). Purchased from Charles Law 1873.

Letters to him, mainly from politicians and diplomats c1777-1812 (c20 items).
British Library (Add MS 54328). Purchased 1968 (formerly sold at Hodgson's 30 March 1967, lot 542).

Letters from Lord Clare 1784-1801 (40 items); letters rel to Irish affairs 1784-1802 (72 items).
Keele University Library (S 21). Purchased 1957 from Raymond Richards, who had acquired them from the Sneyd family 1949. NRA 1248.

[199] **EGERTON** (formerly **LEVESON-GOWER**), **Francis** (1800-1857), 1st Earl of Ellesmere 1846

MP Bletchingley 1822-6, Sutherland 1826-31, S Lancashire 1835-46; under-secretary for the colonies 1828; chief secretary for Ireland 1828-30; secretary at war 1830

Letter books as chief secretary 1829-30.
Public Record Office of Ireland (M 736-8).

Estate, business and canal corresp 1837-46 (c525 items), incl letters from James Loch; charitable and patronage corresp 1835-56 (1,788 items).
Northamptonshire Record Office (EB 1496-1500). Deposited 1954. NRA 4357.

Bank account 1834-42 (1 vol).
Staffordshire Record Office (D 593/N/1/2/1/3). NRA 10699.

Estate, business and canal corresp c1833-7, 1846-57.
The Duke of Sutherland. See FC Mather, *After the Canal Duke,* 1970, p367.

[200] **ELIOT, Edward Granville** (1798-1877), 3rd Earl of St Germans 1845

MP Liskeard 1824-32, E Cornwall 1837-45; a lord of the Treasury 1827-30; chief secretary for Ireland 1841-5; postmaster-general 1846; lord lieutenant of Ireland 1853-5; lord steward 1857-8, 1859-66

Political and official corresp 1829-66 (1 box), incl letters from Lord Aberdeen (15 items), Sir James Graham (14 items) and Sir Robert Peel (22 items); corresp rel to his mission to Spain 1835 (1 vol); letter books as lord lieutenant of Ireland 1853-5 (2 vols); general corresp 1822-72 (1 box); family corresp (5 boxes); election speeches 1835 (1 bundle); commonplace book nd (1 vol); accounts 1851-2 (1 bundle).
The Earl of St Germans. NRA 28659.

[201] **ELIOT, Hon Edward James** (1758-1797)

MP St Germans 1780-4, Liskeard 1784-97; a lord of the Treasury 1782-3, 1783-93; a commissioner of the Board of Control 1793-7

Letters from William Pitt 1782-92 (39 items). *Suffolk Record Office, Ipswich* (Acc 435). Deposited by GMT Pretyman 1953. NRA 174.

Letters from Hester, Lady Chatham 1786-93 (37 items). *Cambridge University Library* (Add 6958-9). Purchased from GMT Pretyman at Sotheby's 15 Nov 1937, lot 232.

[202] **ELLICE, Edward** (1810-1880)

MP Huddersfield 1837, St Andrews burghs 1837-80

Corresp of him and his father rel to political and public affairs 1820-80 (61 vols), incl corresp rel to St Andrews and Inverness politics 1847-80 (1 vol); family corresp 1819-80 (6 vols); journals and logbooks of tours and cruises 1829-80 (6 vols); family, business and estate corresp and papers c1765-1917 (122 vols, 163 items). *National Library of Scotland* (MSS 15001-15195 *passim*; Ch 12601-12763 *passim*). Deposited by Russell Ellice 1949-50; purchased 1973. NRA 883.

Ellice family corresp and papers 1764-1873 (3 vols), incl papers of Edward Ellice junior. *University of Toronto Library*. See *Union list of manuscripts in Canadian repositories*, 1975, p375.

[203] **ELLIOT, Hon Arthur Ralph Douglas** (1846-1923)

MP Roxburghshire 1880-92, Durham 1898-1906; financial secretary to the Treasury 1903

Political and general corresp c1857-1923 (17 vols); political papers 1879-1912 (28 vols), incl Roxburghshire political papers and annotated registers 1879-92 and notes for speeches c1881-1912; family corresp c1850-1918 (6 vols); literary papers c1873-1921 (7 vols), incl notes for his *Life* of Lord Goschen; diaries 1861-1923 (34 vols); legal fee-book 1871-81. *National Library of Scotland* (MSS 19479-19571). Presented by Mr and Mrs HWA Elliot 1967, 1977.

Letters from his brother the 4th Earl of Minto 1862, 1880, 1901-4 (88ff). *National Library of Scotland* (MS 12372, ff1-88). Purchased from the 5th Earl of Minto 1958, 1960. NRA 10476.

[204] **ELLIOT, William** (1766-1818)

MP Portarlington 1801-2, Peterborough 1802-18; chief secretary for Ireland 1806-7

Corresp and papers as chief secretary 1806-7 (20 vols), incl corresp with the Duke of Bedford, Lord Grenville, Sir John Newport, Lord Spencer and others; political, general and family corresp

1775-1818 (4 vols), incl letters from the 1st and 2nd Earls of Minto and corresp with Lord Fitzwilliam rel to Peterborough; political notebooks, papers and drafts of speeches 1813-17, nd (5 vols); estate and legal corresp and papers 1805-18 (1 vol). *National Library of Scotland* (MSS 12899-12927, 12931). Purchased from the 5th Earl of Minto 1958, 1960. NRA 10476.

[205] **ELLIOT MURRAY-KYNYNMOUND** (formerly **ELLIOT**), **Gilbert** (1751-1814), 1st Baron Minto 1797, 1st Earl of Minto 1813

MP Morpeth 1776-7, Roxburghshire 1777-84, Berwick-upon-Tweed 1786-90, Helston 1790-5; president of the Board of Control 1806

Corresp and papers as president of the Board of Control 1806 (11 vols); as governor-general of India 1806-14 (457 vols); election corresp and papers, Morpeth, Helston and Roxburghshire, mainly 1776-1814 (20 vols); political corresp and papers c1778-1811 (17 vols), incl notebooks of parliamentary proceedings 1778, 1797-8 (2 vols), corresp and papers rel to the impeachment of Sir Elijah Impey c1787-8 (4 vols), and notes and drafts of speeches; diplomatic corresp and papers 1793-1822 (63 vols); general and family corresp 1773-1814 (113 vols), incl corresp with Lord and Lady Auckland, William Elliot, Lord Glenbervie, Lord and Lady Malmesbury and Lord and Lady Palmerston; travel journals 1781-1807 (7 vols); financial and legal corresp and papers 1777-1816 (29 vols); literary papers 1783-1810 (7 vols). *National Library of Scotland* (MSS 11042-11739, 12824-30, 13330-9, 13356-64). Purchased from the 5th Earl of Minto 1958, 1960. NRA 10476.

See also *Diplomats*.

[206] **ELLIOT MURRAY-KYNYNMOUND, William Hugh** (1814-1891), 3rd Earl of Minto 1859

MP Hythe 1837-41, Greenock 1847-52, Clackmannan and Kinross-shire 1857-9

Election and constituency corresp 1838-59 (5 vols); political corresp and papers 1835-90 (20 vols), incl papers rel to Scottish education and the Lunacy Commission, and a political notebook 1837-c1860; general corresp 1822-91 (10 vols); financial and legal corresp and papers 1844-91 (8 vols); family corresp and papers 1822-91 (22 vols); diaries, notebooks and memoranda books 1853-91 (57 vols). *National Library of Scotland* (MSS 12238-12362). Purchased from the 5th Earl of Minto 1958, 1960. NRA 10476.

[207] **ELLIS, Thomas Edward** (1859-1899)

MP Merionethshire 1886-99; patronage secretary to the Treasury 1894-5; Liberal chief whip 1894-9

Political and general corresp c1878-99 (1 vol, c3,650 items), incl letters from DR Daniel, David Lloyd George, John Morley and Lord Rosebery;

patronage corresp 1894-5 (273 items); notebooks, drafts of speeches and other papers rel to elections, education and Welsh affairs 1886-98 (1 bundle, *c*230 items); corresp as a charity commissioner (164 items); family corresp and papers (*c*200 items): diaries 1889-97 (5 vols); misc corresp and papers (2 boxes, 4 vols, *c*350 items), incl notebooks and press cuttings.
National Library of Wales (TE Ellis Papers). Deposited by his son TI Ellis *c*1958-68. NRA 26129.

Political corresp 1877-98 (65 items), mainly letters from DR Daniel; diaries 1875-8 (3 vols).
National Library of Wales (DR Daniel Papers). NRA 30323.

[208] **ELLIS-GRIFFITH** (formerly **GRIFFITH**), **Sir Ellis Jones** (1860-1926), 1st Bt

MP Anglesey 1895-1918, Carmarthenshire (Carmarthen division) 1923-4; under-secretary for home affairs 1912-15

Corresp and papers *c*1890-*c*1926, incl letters from TE Ellis (80 items) and other politicians, addresses, notes, etc rel to Welsh politics, disestablishment, education, etc.
National Library of Wales. Presented by Mrs Gwilym Davies 1956. *Annual report 1955-6*, p26.

Notes of sermons heard 1878 (1 vol).
National Library of Wales (CM Archives, MS 771a). Deposited by the Presbyterian Church of Wales 1934. NRA 28416.

[209] **ELPHINSTONE, William Buller Fullerton** (1828-1893), 5th Lord Elphinstone 1861

Scottish representative peer 1867-85; a lord in waiting 1874-80, 1885-6, 1886-92

Corresp and papers rel to the representative peerage *c*1868-75 (*c*12 bundles); letters rel to the Balmerino peerage 1862-6 (18 items); royal corresp 1866-81 (12 items); misc financial corresp *c*1850-60 (1 bundle); naval logbooks 1841-55 (4 vols).
Scottish Record Office (GD 156). Deposited by the 17th Lord Elphinstone 1961.

[210] **ERNEST AUGUSTUS** (1771-1851), Duke of Cumberland 1799, King of Hanover 1837-51

Grand master of the Orange Order

Corresp and papers, mainly as Duke of Cumberland and King of Hanover, 1779-1850 (5 boxes, vols and bundles), incl letters from Lord Eldon 1827-36, Lord Londonderry 1816-38, the Duke of Wellington 1822-48 and Orange lodges 1829-36, nd, corresp with the British and Prussian royal families 1814-50 and papers rel to Catholic emancipation, parliamentary affairs, etc 1817-43, nd.
Niedersächsisches Hauptstaatsarchiv, Hanover (Dep 103). Access restricted. NRA 28404.

ESTCOURT, GTJ, see Sotheron-Estcourt.

[211] **ESTCOURT, Thomas** (1748-1818)

MP Cricklade 1790-1806

Cricklade election corresp and papers 1790-1807 (83 items); political and general corresp 1774-1818 (215 items); corresp and papers rel to the yeomanry and local affairs 1770-1805 (145 items); financial papers 1772-1817 (5 vols, 5 items); diaries 1790-1814 (7 vols).
Gloucestershire Record Office (D 1571). Deposited by TDG Sotheron-Estcourt 1958-73. NRA 2630.

[212] **ESTCOURT, Thomas Grimston Bucknall** (1775-1853)

MP Devizes 1805-26, Oxford University 1826-47

Corresp and papers rel to Wiltshire elections 1805-19 (35 items) and as MP 1826-47 (1 vol, 67 items); political, general and family corresp 1790-1850 (*c*1,350 items), incl letters from Sir Robert Peel and Lord Sidmouth; corresp and papers rel to national affairs 1821-51 (1 vol, 530 items); corresp and papers rel to local affairs 1791-1848 (1 vol, 2 files, 338 items) and to a memorial to General Lord Edward Somerset 1843-50 (3 vols, 37 items); diaries 1796-1853 (56 vols); corresp and papers rel to European tours (3 vols, 2 bundles, 39 items); misc financial papers.
Gloucestershire Record Office (D 1571). Deposited by TDG Sotheron-Estcourt 1958-73. NRA 2630.

[213] **EVANS, Sir Edward** (1846-1917)

President of Liverpool Liberal Federal Council 1887-1917; chairman of the National Liberal Federation 1894-1917

Political corresp and papers 1880-1917 (208 items), incl letters from HH Asquith (12 items) and Lord Rosebery (23 items).
Liverpool Record Office (Acc 2662). Purchased from Mrs A Gornall 1974. NRA 18343.

[214] **FARQUHARSON, Robert** (1836-1918)

MP Aberdeenshire (W division) 1880-1906

Diaries 1888-92, 1895, 1903, 1910-13 (7 vols), incl references to parliamentary and political events and constituency business; medical case books *c*1864, *c*1873 (2 vols).
In private possession. Enquiries to NRA (Scotland) (NRA(S) 1391). NRA 20361.

[215] **FAWCETT, Henry** (1833-1884)

MP Brighton 1865-74, Hackney 1874-84; postmaster-general 1880-4

Letters from JS Mill 1860-70 (41 items) and WT Thornton 1862 (1 item).
British Library of Political and Economic Science,

London (Mill-Taylor LVII). Presented by his daughter Philippa Fawcett 1943. NRA 7531.

[216] FAWCETT, Dame Millicent (1847-1929)

President of the National Union of Women's Suffrage Societies 1897-1918

Corresp rel to women's suffrage 1871-1915 (361 items); indexes of corresp 1886-97, 1910 (2 vols); analyses of parliamentary divisions 1867-83 (2 vols); notes for speeches, etc 1890-2, nd (27 items); corresp and papers of the NUWSS, the International Woman Suffrage Alliance and other bodies *c*1867-1920 (*c*730 vols and items), with notes by her; corresp and papers rel to women's education, employment and welfare 1880-1920 (457 items); misc papers 1873-1920 (78 items).
Manchester Central Library (M 50/2-8). Presented 1922. NRA 20885.

General and political corresp and papers 1870-1925 (*c*230 items), mainly rel to suffrage issues; corresp and papers rel to the Henry Cust case 1894-5 (*c*120 items); papers rel to the Ladies' Commission of Inquiry into Boer War concentration camps 1901-2 (3 vols); addresses and misc papers 1912-25 (6 vols and items).
Fawcett Library, London (FL 28). NRA 20625.

[217] FAZAKERLEY, John Nicholas (1787-1852)

MP Lincoln 1812-18, 1826-30, Great Grimsby 1818-20, Tavistock 1820, Peterborough 1830-41

Corresp and papers, mainly political, 1809-51 (70 items).
William R Perkins Library, Duke University, Durham, North Carolina. Presented 1964. *Guide to the cataloged collections*, 1980, p171.

Family and political corresp 1809-53 (1 vol), incl letters from the 4th Baron Holland to Mrs Fazakerley 1825-32 (*c*40 items).
British Library (Add MS 61937). Purchased at Sotheby's 15 Dec 1980, lot 300.

FECTOR, see Laurie.

FERGUSSON, see Dalrymple, Charles.

[218] FERRAND (formerly **BUSFEILD**), **William Busfeild** (1809-1889)

MP Knaresborough 1841-7, Devonport 1863-6

Poll books 1837-47 (7 vols); printed political papers 1835-92 (*c*600 items), incl polling cards, posters and press cuttings, rel to the Bradford election 1837 and other contests.
West Yorkshire Archive Service, Bradford (51D79). Acquired 1979. NRA 1108.

Diaries 1843, 1847-89 (45 vols).
Yorkshire Archaeological Society, Leeds (MD 290). Deposited by Lt-Colonel GW Ferrand 1955. NRA 12919.

[219] FFOLKES, Sir William John Henry Browne (1786-1860), 2nd Bt

MP Norfolk 1830-2, W Norfolk 1832-7

Letters and papers rel to Norfolk elections and politics 1830-47 (7 bundles); misc family corresp 1827-44 (1 bundle); misc estate and business corresp and papers 1822-47 (1 bundle, 1 item); cash book 1810-12; passport 1814.
Norfolk Record Office (NRS 7949, 7958, 8721, 8738, 8740-2, 8753, 11781; MC 50/72-4). Deposited by Norfolk Record Society. NRA 4635.

[220] FIELDEN, John (1784-1849)

MP Oldham 1832-47

Political, business and family corresp and papers, mainly 1811-49 (3 boxes), incl letters from the Cobbett family 1834-44 and accounts 1836-40 rel to the *Champion and Weekly Herald*, etc (*c*60 items), letters from and papers rel to Richard Oastler 1836-43, nd (10 items), corresp and papers rel to the New Poor Law, the Ten Hours Bill and the Anti-Corn Law League, and an address to the electors of Oldham 1832.
John Rylands University Library of Manchester. Purchased 1974-5, 1981.

Letters from Lord Ashley 1833-43 (9 items).
Untraced. Francis Edwards Ltd catalogue 1034, 1981, item 366.

[221] FINCH-HATTON, George William (1791-1858), 10th Earl of Winchilsea 1826

Ultra-Tory

Political corresp rel to the opposition to Catholic emancipation mainly 1828-9 (*c*130 items); misc legal and other corresp and papers 1809-57 (*c*85 items).
Northamptonshire Record Office (F-H). Deposited 1956. NRA 4485.

[222] FITZALAN-HOWARD, Henry (1847-1917), 15th Duke of Norfolk 1860

Postmaster-general 1895-1900

Political corresp 1870-1915 (13 bundles), incl letters from Lord Beaconsfield, RW Hanbury, the 3rd Marquess of Salisbury and others; papers as postmaster-general (3 bundles); papers rel to Ireland 1887 (2 files); to the royal commission on education 1887-8 (2 bundles); religious and educational corresp and papers (*c*40 bundles and items); general and charitable corresp 1860-1917 (over 500 bundles), incl corresp of his private secretaries; estate, legal, local and family corresp;

registers of corresp 1875-7 (3 vols); papers as Earl Marshal; addresses, press cuttings, passports, engagement diary, etc.
The Duke of Norfolk. Enquiries to the Librarian and Archivist, Arundel Castle, West Sussex BN18 9AB. *Arundel Castle archives: a catalogue*, ed FW Steer, i-iv, 1968-80, *passim*. Papers less than one hundred years old are closed to research.

Corresp and papers rel to the Sheffield estate and civic affairs c1860-1915.
Sheffield Record Office (Arundel Castle MSS). Deposited by the 16th Duke of Norfolk 1960. *Catalogue of the Arundel Castle manuscripts*, 1965, *passim*.

[223] **FITZGERALD, Augustus Frederick** (1791-1874), 3rd Duke of Leinster 1804

Lord lieutenant of co Kildare 1831-74

Corresp and papers mainly rel to politics and patronage 1809-74 (44 bundles), incl corresp with the 6th and 7th Dukes of Bedford, the 4th Earl of Clarendon and Lord John Russell; commissions and appointments, etc 1808-41 (15 items); grand tour journal 1811-12 (1 vol).
Public Record Office of Northern Ireland (D 3078). Purchased 1975. NRA 27429.

[224] **FITZGERALD, Maurice** (1774-1849), 18th Knight of Kerry

MP co Kerry 1795-1831; a lord of the Treasury 1827-8, of the Admiralty 1834-5

Corresp and reminiscences, mainly political, 1783-1849 (13 vols), incl letters from Lord Castlereagh, the 1st Earl of Kenmare, the 3rd Marquess of Lansdowne, Daniel O'Connell and Sir Robert Peel rel to the Catholic question, Kerry elections, etc.
In private possession. Enquiries to the Public Record Office of Northern Ireland. NRA 29433.

Letters to him and his son from the Duke of Wellington and others 1796-1884 (1 vol).
National Library of Ireland (MS 2077).

[225] **FITZHERBERT, Alleyne** (1753-1839), Baron St Helens 1791

Chief secretary for Ireland 1787-9

General, political, business and family corresp and papers 1785-1839 (2,840 items), incl papers rel to elections for Rutland 1805, York 1808 and Stafford 1832; papers as a privy councillor 1801-19 and a lord of the Bedchamber 1802-30 (169 items); diplomatic corresp and papers 1777-1817 (458 items).
Derbyshire Record Office (D 239M). Presented by Sir John Fitzherbert, Bt 1963.

[226] **FITZPATRICK, General the Hon Richard** (1747-1813)

MP Okehampton 1770-4, Tavistock 1774-1807, 1812-13, Bedfordshire 1807-12; chief secretary for Ireland 1782; secretary at war 1783, 1806-7

Political and general corresp 1767-1813 (4 vols), incl letters from CJ Fox and the Marquis de Lafayette.
British Library (Add MSS 47580-3). Presented by Professor GM Trevelyan 1951.

Corresp and misc papers 1774-1807 (1 vol); journal 1803 (1 vol); catalogue of his library 1813 (1 vol).
British Library (Add MSS 51454-6). Purchased from the trustees of the 5th Earl of Ilchester 1960.

[227] **FITZROY, George Henry** (1760-1844), 4th Duke of Grafton 1811

MP Thetford 1782-4, Cambridge University 1784-1811

Political and general corresp 1795-1837 (63 items), incl letters from his father; corresp and papers rel to family affairs 1813-39 (172 items); letter books as lord lieutenant of Suffolk 1801-14 (2 vols); financial and misc corresp 1791-1829 (1 vol, 18 items).
Suffolk Record Office, Bury St Edmunds (HA 513). Deposited by the 10th Duke of Grafton 1952 and by the 11th Duke 1972. NRA 2567.

[228] **FLOOD, Henry** (1732-1791)

MP co Kilkenny 1759-60, Callan 1761-76, Enniskillen 1777-83, Kilbeggan 1783-90, Winchester 1783-4, Seaford 1786-90; joint vice-treasurer (Ireland) 1775-81

Letters mainly rel to Irish politics 1765-83 (16 items); corresp with Archbishop Markham 1767-80 (43 items) and the 2nd Earl of Rosse 1784-91 (85 items, mainly letters to Rosse); drafts and reports of speeches, political pamphlets, notes and extracts c1765-90 (10 vols and bundles).
The Earl of Rosse. NRA 25548.

Political and general corresp 1765-88 (1 vol), incl letters from Lord Charlemont.
British Library (Add MS 22930). Purchased at the sale of the Dawson Turner collection 1859.

[229] **FOLJAMBE** (formerly **MOORE**), **Francis Ferrand** (1750-1814)

MP Yorkshire 1784, Higham Ferrers 1801-7

Political and misc corresp and papers 1780-1804 (c95 items), incl letters from Lord Fitzwilliam, Sir George Savile and the Revd Christopher Wyvill 1780-4 and papers rel to the Yorkshire Association 1780-3; letters from the Revd William Mason 1771-4 (1 vol).
Nottinghamshire Archives Office (Foljambe XI, vols I, V, VI, XIII). Deposited 1977. NRA 20442.

Letters to him 1790-1814 (2 bundles); personal and household accounts of him and his wife c1790-1815 (5 bundles).
Nottinghamshire Archives Office (DD/SR 215/5-6, 25-7; 221/49-50). Deposited 1957. NRA 6119.

[230] **FORBES, John** (1750-1797)

MP Ratoath 1776-83, Drogheda 1783-96

Political corresp 1775-96 (34 items), incl letters from George Ponsonby.
National Library of Ireland (MS 978). Presented by TJ Kiernan, to whom they had been given by Dr JG Forbes. Three further letters were presented by Dr Forbes to the Corporation of Drogheda.
Analecta Hibernica, viii, 1938, pp315-71; NRA 23756.

Corresp 1783-95 (mainly 1785) (c57 items), incl letters from Lord Charlemont, Henry Grattan and the Duke of Portland.
National Library of Ireland (MS 10713). Acquired as part of the FS Bourke collection. NRA 23756.

[231] **FORBES, William** (1806-1855)

MP Stirlingshire 1835-7, 1841-55

Corresp mainly rel to political, family and local affairs 1831-54 (over 2,000 items), incl some rel to Stirlingshire elections from 1832.
Scottish Record Office (GD 171). Deposited by Lt-Colonel William Forbes 1953.

[232] **FORTESCUE, Hugh** (1783-1861), 2nd Earl Fortescue 1841

MP Barnstaple 1804-7, St Mawes 1807-9, Buckingham 1812-17, Devon 1818-20, 1830-2, Tavistock 1820-30, N Devon 1832-9; lord lieutenant of Ireland 1839-41; lord steward 1846-50

Corresp and papers as lord lieutenant 1839-41 (3 portfolios); Dublin household accounts (2 boxes, 5 vols); election corresp and papers, Barnstaple 1804-7, 1820, Devon 1816-37 (3 vols, 12 bundles); political corresp and papers 1814-61 (3 portfolios, 4 bundles), incl corresp with the 2nd Earl Grey and the 3rd Baron Holland; family and misc corresp and papers (2 vols, 17 bundles); diaries 1808-61 (c17 vols), mainly of European travels; accounts 1800-61 (9 vols).
Devon Record Office (1262 M). Deposited by the 6th Earl Fortescue 1963-4. NRA 6304.

Corresp rel to the celibacy of fellows of Trinity College 1840 (25 items).
Trinity College Library, Dublin (MS 2091). Presented by the 4th Earl Fortescue 1931.

[233] **FORWOOD, Sir Arthur Bower** (1836-1898), 1st Bt

MP SW Lancashire (Ormskirk division) 1885-98; secretary of the Admiralty 1886-92

Corresp and papers rel to naval affairs 1885-90 (several bundles and files), incl letters from Lord George Hamilton; corresp and papers rel to local politics and elections 1880-92 (3 bundles); letters from politicians 1860-90 (7 bundles), incl Lord Randolph Churchill (c50 items), the 3rd Earl of Harrowby (95 items) and Lord Salisbury (36 items); corresp and papers (mainly printed) rel to parliamentary and economic matters 1883-97 (several bundles and files); corresp and reports rel to the creation of the see of Liverpool 1878-9 (2 bundles); business and family corresp and papers 1854-98 (24 bundles); misc personal corresp and papers 1854-98 (9 bundles), incl diary 1854.
Hampshire Record Office (19M62). Acquired 1962. NRA 25330.

[234] **FOSTER, John** (1740-1828), 1st Baron Oriel 1821

MP Dunleer 1761-8, co Louth 1768-1800, 1801-21; chancellor of the Exchequer (Ireland) 1784-5, 1804-6, 1807-11; Speaker of the Irish House of Commons 1785-1800

Corresp and papers rel to Irish trade and revenues 1745-1800, mainly 1777-1800 (c2,000 items), incl corresp with Sackville Hamilton and Sir Robert Heron; Irish Exchequer corresp and papers 1804-11 (c6,000 items), incl corresp with William Huskisson (30 items), Spencer Perceval (over 200 items), Sir Arthur Wellesley (100 items), William Wellesley-Pole (100 items) and various officials; papers as Speaker (200 items); corresp and papers rel to politics, patronage, etc in co Louth (c3,000 items), incl letters from Robert Peel; corresp rel to politics, trade and patronage 1812-28 (c1,300 items), incl letters from Denis Browne, Lord Camden, JL Foster (260 items) and Lord Norbury; corresp and papers rel to the Irish linen industry c1760-1827 (c3,000 items); family, financial, estate, agricultural and other corresp and papers.
Public Record Office of Northern Ireland (D 207, 562, 1739, 2681). Deposited 1927-69. NRA 6701.

Corresp and papers 1770-1827 (c1,420 items), incl further corresp as chancellor of the Irish Exchequer c1805-11 (c1,000 items), and corresp rel to patronage, co Louth affairs, the Linen Board and his private finances 1812-17 (291 items).
Viscount Massereene and Ferrard (his great-great-great-grandson). Copies are in the Public Record Office of Northern Ireland (T 2519/4). NRA 6701.

Copies of letters from him 1819 (25 items).
National Library of Ireland (MS 4128). Copies are in the Public Record Office of Northern Ireland (T 2519/3).

[235] **FOSTER, John Leslie** (c1781-1842)

MP Dublin University 1807-12, Yarmouth 1816-18, Armagh 1818-20, co Louth 1824-30

Letters from Sir Robert Peel 1813-39 (81 items) and from other politicians 1807-38 (48 items); misc papers rel to patronage, financial and estate matters 1814-41 (1 bundle).
Royal Irish Academy, Dublin (MS 23 G 39). *Manuscript sources for the history of Irish civilisation*, ed RJ Hayes, 1965, ii, 188.

[236] **FOWNES LUTTRELL, John** (1752-1816)

MP Minehead 1776-1806, 1807-16

Minehead election papers c1780-1812 (2 boxes); printed parliamentary papers 1782-1816 (1 box); corresp and accounts; journals 1782-1816.
Somerset Record Office (DD L). Deposited by the Luttrell family 1958. NRA 6670.

[237] **FOX-STRANGWAYS, Henry Stephen** (1787-1858), 3rd Earl of Ilchester 1802

Captain of the Yeomen of the Guard 1835-41

Corresp and papers rel to Dorset, Devon and Somerset politics 1829-57, mainly 1830s (c130 items); papers rel to the Yeomen of the Guard 1835-41, incl his resignation 1841; to the Dorset militia and yeomanry 1803-56; family and local corresp and papers 1794-1858.
Dorset Record Office (D 124). Deposited by the 7th and 8th Earls of Ilchester 1959-68.

Letters from the 3rd Marquess of Lansdowne and Lady Lansdowne nd (2 vols); family and general corresp 1812-55 (1 vol).
British Library (Add MSS 51363-5). Purchased from the trustees of the 5th Earl of Ilchester 1960.

[238] **FREDERICK, Sir John** (1750-1825), 5th Bt

MP Newport 1774-80, Christchurch 1781-90, Surrey 1794-1807

Surrey election accounts 1794-6 (1 vol); proceedings of parliamentary committees on election petitions, Bedfordshire 1785 (4 vols, 1 item), Southwark 1796 (6 vols) and Weymouth 1804 (1 vol); Surrey militia accounts 1794 (1 vol); misc personal and financial papers 1782-1824.
Surrey Record Office, Kingston-upon-Thames (183). Deposited 1954-70. NRA 10698.

[239] **FREEMAN-MITFORD** (formerly **MITFORD**), **John** (1748-1830), 1st Baron Redesdale 1802

MP Bere Alston 1788-99, East Looe 1799-1802; solicitor-general 1793-9; attorney-general 1799-1801; Speaker of the House of Commons 1801-2; lord chancellor (Ireland) 1802-6

Semi-official corresp as lord chancellor (Ireland) 1802-6 (130 items), incl letters from Lord

Hardwicke (48 items), Lord Sidmouth (28 items) and William Wickham (10 items); corresp rel to English and Irish politics 1786-1826 (302 items), incl letters from Spencer Perceval (32 items) and from Lords Arden, Eldon, Farnborough and Stowell; misc appointments, patents and corresp 1771-1804 (13 items); personal and family corresp 1773-1827 (90 items); travel journals 1776-91 (11 vols); sketch books (3 vols); catalogue of his library c1800 (1 vol).
Gloucestershire Record Office (D 2002). Deposited by the 5th Baron Redesdale 1964. NRA 23794.

Opinions as a law officer 1793-1800 (4 vols); notebooks as lord chancellor 1802-6 (11 vols); fee books 1786-1800 (4 vols); other legal notes and papers mainly 18th cent (60 vols).
Inner Temple Library, London. Presented by the 2nd Baron Dulverton 1957. *Catalogue of manuscripts in the Library . . . of the Inner Temple*, ed J Conway Davies, 1972, iii, 1084-1150.

General and antiquarian corresp 1792-1829 (1 vol), incl letters from him to John Caley 1816-24; legal, literary and theological writings (1 vol).
British Library (Add MSS 36650-1). Presented by AB Freeman-Mitford 1901.

[240] **FREEMAN-MITFORD, John Thomas** (1805-1886), 2nd Baron Redesdale 1830, Earl of Redesdale 1877

Chairman of committees and deputy Speaker of the House of Lords 1851-86

Personal and political corresp 1805-86 (135 items), incl letters from Sir Robert Peel, 3rd Bt (17 items) and corresp with the 1st Duke of Wellington (48 items); accounts 1829-38 (1 vol).
Gloucestershire Record Office (D 2002). Deposited by the 5th Baron Redesdale 1964. NRA 23794.

[241] **FREMANTLE, Thomas Francis** (1798-1890), 1st Baron Cottesloe 1874

MP Buckingham 1827-46; joint secretary to the Treasury 1834-5, 1841-4; secretary at war 1844-5; chief secretary for Ireland 1845-6

Treasury corresp and papers 1834-5, 1841-4 (15 boxes, 1 bundle); Irish corresp and accounts 1845-6 (3 bundles), incl letters from Sir Robert Peel; Buckingham election corresp and papers 1831-80 (1 vol, 13 bundles); corresp and papers as a Conservative whip 1837-44 (4 vols, 7 bundles, 13 items); general parliamentary corresp and papers 1830-83 (1 box, 10 bundles), with minutes of Stafford and Horsham election committees 1833, 1835 (2 vols); corresp and papers as chairman of the Board of Customs 1841-73 (24 boxes); misc official corresp and papers 1834-89 (20 bundles); political and general corresp 1820-44 (36 bundles); corresp and papers rel to local affairs 1808-90 (2 boxes, 36 bundles) and as acting lord lieutenant of Buckinghamshire 1875-81 (12 bundles); personal corresp, accounts and papers 1813-90 (1 box, 19 vols, 140 bundles); family corresp and papers

1814-90 (26 boxes); estate and household corresp and papers (36 vols, 127 bundles); diaries 1814-36 (17 vols); travel journals 1820-2 (4 vols); school and university exercise books 1814-18 (38 vols, 2 bundles).
Buckinghamshire Record Office (D/FR). Deposited by Commander the Hon JT Fremantle 1967. NRA 15283.

Corresp with WE Gladstone 1853-81 (*c*60 items) and other letters (19 items), mainly rel to duties on wine, tea, and tobacco.
Untraced. Offered for sale at Bloomsbury Book Auctions 28 June 1985, lot 202 and 20 June 1986, lot 216.

Letters and reports sent to him as chief secretary rel to the Irish potato crop 1845 (52 items).
Nottingham University Library (Ne C 9151-9202). Deposited among the papers of his successor Lord Lincoln 1955; accepted for the nation in lieu of tax and allocated to the Library 1981. NRA 7411.

[242] **FREMANTLE, Sir William Henry** (1766-1850)

MP Enniskillen 1806, Harwich 1806-7, Saltash 1807, Tain burghs 1808-12, Buckingham 1812-27; resident secretary for Ireland 1789-1800; joint secretary to the Treasury 1806-7; a commissioner of the Board of Control 1822-6

Political, personal and family corresp and papers 1787-1850 (13 boxes), incl letters from the 1st Duke of Buckingham and Lord Grenville, corresp and papers rel to Ireland 1788-1824 (3 packets, 2 bundles) and to the Tain burghs 1808 (1 bundle), notes for drafts of parliamentary speeches *c*1806-13 (3 bundles), and personal and household accounts 1835-50 (8 vols).
Buckinghamshire Record Office (D/FR). Deposited by Commander the Hon JT Fremantle 1967. NRA 15283.

[243] **FREWEN, Moreton** (1853-1924)

MP co Cork (NE division) 1910-11; Irish nationalist and monetary reformer

Corresp and papers *c*1871-1924 (47 boxes), incl letters from AJ Balfour, the 4th Earl Grey, Lord Lansdowne and Andrew Bonar Law, papers rel to currency and trade, speeches and misc papers.
Library of Congress, Washington. NRA 22522.

[244] **GIFFARD, Stanley Lees** (1788-1858)

Editor of the *Standard* 1827-58

General and political corresp 1823-56 (2 vols), incl letters from Lord George Bentinck, Sir Robert Inglis, the 4th Duke of Newcastle and the 7th Earl of Shaftesbury.
British Library (Add MSS 56368-9). Presented by his great-grandson the 3rd Earl of Halsbury 1970. NRA 6238.

General and political corresp 1825-54, nd (1 vol), incl letters from Lord Brougham, Bishop Phillpotts and RB Seeley.
Bodleian Library, Oxford (MS Eng. lett. c. 56). Presented by Lady Evelyn Giffard 1938.

General corresp 1812-54 (*c*40 items); family corresp *c*1808-27 (*c*25 items); misc papers (1 bundle).
The Earl of Halsbury. NRA 6238.

[245] **GILL, Thomas Patrick** (1858-1931)

MP co Louth (S division) 1885-92

Political corresp and papers 1881-99 (*c*1,000 items), incl corresp rel to the Plan of Campaign and the Parnell crisis; corresp with Sir Horace Plunkett 1891-1927 (*c*550 items); corresp and papers rel to Irish agriculture and politics 1900-20 (3 folders, *c*220 items); general corresp 1877-1921 (*c*2,000 items), incl letters rel to journalism and Irish agricultural administration; diaries 1900, 1907-8, 1915-16 (5 vols); notebooks, drafts and copies of articles, etc *c*1882-1922.
National Library of Ireland (MSS 13478-13525). *Manuscript sources for the history of Irish civilisation, Supplement*, 1979, i, 283-5.

Misc corresp (autographs) and papers 1890-1921, nd (97 items), incl letters from Lord Dudley (13 items).
In private possession. Photocopies are in Trinity College Library, Dublin (MS 4733). NRA 22036.

[246] **GILPIN, Charles** (1815-1874)

MP Northampton 1857-74; secretary of the Poor Law Board 1859-65

Corresp 1832-75 (239 items), mainly with reformers.
William R Perkins Library, Duke University, Durham, North Carolina. Purchased 1968. *Guide to the cataloged collections*, 1980, p200.

[247] **GLADSTONE, Herbert John** (1854-1930), Viscount Gladstone 1910

MP Leeds 1880-5, Leeds (W division) 1885-1910; financial secretary to the War Office 1886; under-secretary for home affairs 1892-4; first commissioner of Works 1894-5; Liberal chief whip 1899-1905; home secretary 1905-10

Papers rel to the Home Office 1892-5, 1906-10 (7 vols); to the Board of Works 1884-96 (3 vols); diaries and papers as chief whip 1899-1906 (8 vols); as governor-general of South Africa 1910-14 (6 vols); royal, political and official corresp 1880-1929 (61 vols), incl corresp with prime ministers, Liberal politicians, civil servants and South African politicians; general and family corresp 1873-1930 (46 vols); speech notes and parliamentary notebooks 1905-29 (4 vols); diary, literary papers, etc *c*1875-1929 (12 vols).
British Library (Add MSS 45985-46118, 46474-86). Presented by his widow 1935.

Family and misc corresp 1863-1930 (c2,980 items); political diary 1880-5 (1 vol); election speeches 1900 (1 vol); papers rel to honours and peerage 1894-1930 (1 bundle); misc personal papers 1890-1902 (4 bundles, 4 items).
St Deiniol's Library, Hawarden (Glynne-Gladstone MSS). Deposited by Sir William Gladstone, Bt 1968, and Ogilvy, Gillanders and Co 1974. Access through Clwyd Record Office. NRA 14174.

Family corresp and papers rel to WE Gladstone 1913-36 (6 vols).
Lambeth Palace Library, London (MSS 2758-9, 2771-4). Presented by Viscount Gladstone and HN Gladstone 1928 and by the Octagon Trustees 1938. Access partially restricted. *Catalogue of manuscripts in Lambeth Palace Library (MSS 2341-3119)*, 1983, pp 74-5.

[248] **GLADSTONE, Sir John** (1764-1851), 1st Bt

MP Lancaster 1818-20, New Woodstock 1820-6, Berwick-upon-Tweed 1826-7

Political, business, family and general corresp 1790-1851 (270 bundles), incl letters from John Backhouse 1812-37 (5 bundles), George Canning 1812-27 (6 bundles), Kirkman Finlay 1812-41 (14 bundles), Thomas Gladstone 1817-51 (29 bundles), WE Gladstone 1821-51 (8 bundles) and William Huskisson 1814-30 (5 bundles); corresp arranged by subject 1791-3, 1817-49 (26 bundles), incl elections 1825-41 (3 bundles), slavery, the corn laws and Liverpool commerce; letter books 1820-51 (15 vols); papers rel to elections 1818-42 (20 bundles and items); to George Canning 1814-29 (8 bundles and items); to Liverpool affairs 1818-35 (8 bundles and items); to railways 1825-48 (27 vols and bundles); to Leith Asylum 1829-47 (3 bundles); to business matters 1760-1829 (17 vols, bundles and items); to executorships 1828-50 (3 vols, 11 bundles); to the division of his estate 1838-56 (5 bundles); memoranda 1816-47 (9 bundles and items); accounts 1803-51 (6 vols, 9 bundles); misc papers 1786-1851 (c40 bundles and items).
St Deiniol's Library, Hawarden (Glynne-Gladstone MSS). Deposited by Sir William Gladstone, Bt 1968-82, SG Checkland 1973 and Ogilvy, Gillanders & Co 1973. Access through Clwyd Record Office. NRA 14174.

Family, business and estate corresp and papers 1829-51 (24 bundles); pamphlets, etc 1813-46 (1 bundle).
Sir William Gladstone, Bt. Enquiries to NRA (Scotland) (NRA(S) 2607). NRA 10151.

[249] **GLADSTONE, Sir Thomas** (1804-1889), 2nd Bt

MP Queenborough 1830-1, Portarlington 1832-5, Leicester 1835-7, Ipswich 1842

Political, family and general corresp 1817-88 (119 bundles), incl letters from Sir John Gladstone 1817-51 (10 bundles) and from WE Gladstone

1822-88 (5 bundles); election corresp 1830-41 (9 bundles); other corresp arranged by subject 1839-55 (9 bundles); poll books, addresses, vouchers, etc rel to elections 1830-65 (42 vols and bundles); pocket diaries 1828, 1843 (2 vols); notebooks and memoranda 1828-59 (16 vols, bundles and items); estate, executorship and misc papers 1819-87 (19 vols and bundles), incl MS of *Thoughts on practical reverence* (1863).
St Deiniol's Library, Hawarden (Glynne-Gladstone MSS). Deposited by Sir William Gladstone, Bt 1968 and SG Checkland 1973. Access through Clwyd Record Office. NRA 14174.

Personal, financial and estate corresp and papers 1826-88 (14 vols, 10 bundles).
Sir William Gladstone, Bt. Enquiries to NRA (Scotland) (NRA(S) 2607). NRA 10151.

[250] **GLADSTONE, William Henry** (1840-1891)

MP Chester 1865-8, Whitby 1868-80, E Worcestershire 1880-5; a lord of the Treasury 1869-74

Chester election accounts 1865 (3 items); letters, petitions, etc addressed to him as MP for Whitby 1868-74 (5 bundles); family and political corresp 1844-89 (442 items), incl letters from WE Gladstone 1844-89 (102 items); general papers 1851-91 (1 vol, 5 bundles, 9 items), incl press cuttings rel to his career 1865-90 (1 vol).
St Deiniol's Library, Hawarden (Glynne-Gladstone MSS). Deposited by Sir William Gladstone, Bt 1968. Access through Clwyd Record Office. NRA 14174.

[251] **GLASIER, John Bruce** (1859-1920)

Chairman of the Independent Labour Party 1900-3

Political corresp of him and his wife Katharine 1879-1950 (2,085 items), incl letters from JK Hardie, JR MacDonald and Philip Snowden; diaries 1892-1919; notebooks, commonplace book, sketch book, album and misc papers c1876-1919 (15 vols, 1 bundle); family corresp mainly of Katharine Glasier, with her diaries and notebooks, c1888-1976.
Liverpool University Library. Presented by Malcolm Bruce Glasier 1976. NRA 25263.

Letters from William Morris and others 1886-1900 (64 items).
William Morris Gallery, Walthamstow (J 78-141). Presented by Katharine Bruce Glasier. *Catalogue of the Morris collection*, 1969, p45.

[252] **GLYNNE, Sir Stephen Richard** (1780-1815), 8th Bt

Stood for Flint boroughs 1806, 1807

Corresp 1796-1814 (c36 items), incl some rel to the 1806 and 1807 elections; election addresses, canvass

books, voters' lists, etc 1806-7 (c165 items); misc papers 1801-15 (c15 items).
National Library of Wales (Hawarden Papers). Deposited by his grandson Lord Gladstone of Hawarden 1935. NRA 11469.

Misc letters from his wife, the 2nd Baron Braybrooke and others 1799-1815 (70 items).
St Deiniol's Library, Hawarden (Glynne-Gladstone MSS). Deposited by Sir William Gladstone, Bt 1968. Access through Clwyd Record Office. NRA 14174.

[253] **GODLEY, John Arthur** (1847-1932), 1st Baron Kilbracken 1909

Private secretary to WE Gladstone 1872-4, 1880-2

Corresp with WE Gladstone 1874-98 (2 vols); political and literary corresp 1881-1927 (1 vol), incl letters from Lord Rosebery and corresp with Lord Morley of Blackburn.
British Library (Add MSS 44900-2). Presented by the 2nd Baron Kilbracken 1936.

Corresp and papers as permanent under-secretary for India 1883-1909 (62 vols and bundles).
India Office Library and Records (MSS Eur F 102). Left by him at the India Office 1909 and transferred to the Library 1961. NRA 27523.

[254] **GORDON** (formerly **HAMILTON-GORDON**), **John Campbell** (1847-1934), 7th Earl of Aberdeen 1870, 1st Marquess of Aberdeen and Temair 1916

Lord lieutenant of Ireland 1886, 1905-15

Corresp and papers rel to Ireland 1877-1934 (5 bundles), incl letters from John Morley 1886 and Augustine Birrell 1907-15; expenses as lord lieutenant 1906-14 (8 vols); corresp and papers as governor-general of Canada 1893-8 (20 bundles); as lord high commissioner to the General Assembly 1881-5 (3 bundles); as lord lieutenant of Aberdeenshire 1861-93 (5 bundles); general and political corresp 1870-1934 (3 vols, 5 bundles), incl letters from Henry Drummond, WE Gladstone and Lord Stanmore; personal, family, business and misc corresp and papers 1879-1934 (1 box, 17 bundles); press cuttings and commemorative volumes (c50 vols); estate corresp 1886-98 (14 bundles).
The Haddo Trustees. Enquiries to NRA (Scotland) (NRA(S) 0055). NRA 9758.

See also *Colonial Governors.*

GOULD, see Morgan, Charles.

[255] **GRAHAM** (formerly **GRAEME**), **Robert** (d 1859)

A lord of the Treasury 1834; stood for Perthshire 1834

Corresp and papers rel to Perthshire politics 1811-41 (21 vols); canvass and poll books, election

papers and ephemera 1812, 1832-42 (31 vols); corresp rel to patronage matters 1833-4 (2 vols); general and political corresp 1797-1858, nd (14 vols); family corresp 1795-1854 (3 vols); misc corresp 1809-39 (3 vols); travel journals, corresp and notes 1816-49 (12 vols); account book 1829-39; engagement books 1838, 1843 (2 vols); historical notes c1805 (1 vol); inventory of library, etc 1848 (1 vol).
National Library of Scotland (MSS 16020-39, 16047-57, 16125-78). Presented by Anthony Maxtone Graham 1955.

[256] **GRAHAM, General Thomas** (1748-1843), Baron Lynedoch 1814

MP Perthshire 1794-1807

Corresp and papers rel to elections 1773-1815 (15 vols), incl lists of freeholders and canvass books; general, military, political and family corresp 1775-1843 (61 vols); military notebooks, memoirs and papers (24 vols); journals 1776-1839 (48 vols); engagement books 1838, 1843 (2 vols); personal and bank account books 1770-1842 (12 vols); estate corresp and papers 1769-1843 (7 vols).
National Library of Scotland (MSS 3590-3645, 3863, 16001-16420; Ch 2525-35, 12841 *et seq*). Presented or deposited by Anthony Maxtone Graham and his sister, Mrs Patrick Smythe 1941-66; purchased 1965-80.

Letters from Perthshire freeholders 1794 (49 items); general corresp 1789-1826 (10 items).
Major JJ Graham. Enquiries to NRA (Scotland) (NRA(S) 2148). NRA 23600 (12/6-7).

Letter book, Italy 1830 (1 vol).
Edinburgh University Library (Gen 721 D).

[257] **GRANT, General James** (1720-1806)

MP Tain burghs 1773-80, Sutherland 1787-1802

Corresp and papers c1758-1806 (c500 vols and bundles), mainly rel to military affairs and as governor of East Florida, but incl corresp rel to Banffshire, Sutherland and Tain burghs 1773-96 and political corresp with the 4th Duke of Atholl, Henry Dundas, the Countess of Sutherland and others.
In private possession. Enquiries to NRA (Scotland) (NRA(S) 0771). NRA 17173.

[258] **GRANT, Sir William** (1752-1832)

MP Shaftesbury 1790-3, New Windsor 1794-6, Banffshire 1796-1812; solicitor-general 1799-1801; master of the rolls 1801-17

Political, official and literary corresp 1788-1836 (51 items).
William R Perkins Library, Duke University, Durham, North Carolina. Presented 1970. *Guide to the cataloged collections*, 1980, p208.

[259] **GRANT DUFF, Sir Mountstuart Elphinstone** (1829-1906)

MP Elgin burghs 1857-81; under-secretary for India 1868-74, for the colonies 1880-1

Political, official, literary and general corresp 1855-1905 (32 vols), incl letters from Lords De Tabley, Dufferin, Kimberley and Lytton and John Morley; corresp and papers as governor of Madras 1881-6; engagement diaries.
Mrs Shiela Sokolov Grant (his granddaughter). NRA 24627 (partial list).

[260] **GRATTAN, Henry** (1746-1820)

MP Charlemont 1775-90, Dublin 1790-7, 1806-20, Wicklow 1800, Malton 1805-6

Political and other corresp 1782-1808 (c15 items).
Brynmor Jones Library, Hull University (DDLA). Deposited by the Countess Fitzwilliam. NRA 6488. Briefly described in *Public Record Office of Northern Ireland: deputy keeper's report 1960-5*, p84.

Personal account books 1786-91, 1816-18 (3 vols); historical notes; family and other corresp c1794-1820, mainly letters from him to his son Henry and others.
National Library of Ireland (MSS 2111, 3715-17, 14164, 27805, 27814). Acquired from various sources.

Drafts or notes for speeches nd (2 items), and notes on Irish imports and exports 1784.
Trinity College Library, Dublin (MS 4232). Presented 1967. NRA 22022.

[261] **GRATTAN, James** (1783-1854)

MP co Wicklow 1821-41

Journals of parliamentary proceedings 1818-41 (15 vols); political and general notebooks c1809-37 (19 vols); travel diaries 1837-44 (5 vols).
National Library of Ireland (MSS 3847-53, 5775-9, 14136-63).

Misc political, financial and other papers mainly 1823-54 (38 items).
Trinity College Library, Dublin (MS 4232). Presented 1967. NRA 22022.

[262] **GREENE, Thomas** (1794-1872)

MP Lancaster 1824-52, 1853-7; chairman of the Committee of Ways and Means 1841-7

Political corresp and papers 1822-56 (160 items), incl letters from the 14th Earl of Derby and rel to the Lancaster election 1847; corresp, memoranda and printed papers as a commissioner for building the new palace of Westminster mainly 1848-51 (1 vol, 110 items).
House of Lords Record Office (Historical Collection 298). Purchased from his great-granddaughter the Dowager Countess of Lichfield 1982. Formerly deposited in Lancashire Record Office. *House of Lords Record Office memorandum no 69*, 1984.

Papers as an MP 1831-56 (1 parcel); notebooks on parliamentary procedure (4 vols); papers rel to parliamentary committees 1840s (1 bundle); general corresp c1796-1869 (6 boxes); notebooks as chairman of Lancaster quarter sessions 1861-5 (3 vols); misc official papers c1816-67 (1 box); accounts 1809-72 (9 vols, 2 bundles); travel journals, notes, etc.
Lancashire Record Office (DDGr). Deposited by the Dowager Countess of Lichfield 1962. NRA 14794.

[263] **GREGORY, William** (1766-1840)

MP Portarlington 1798-1800; under-secretary for Ireland 1812-31

Personal and political corresp with Lord Talbot of Hensol 1819-35, nd (18 bundles).
Staffordshire Record Office (D 240/J/5). Returned to Talbot's great-grandson, Lord Shrewsbury, by Augusta, Lady Gregory 1903. NRA 8481.

[264] **GREGORY, Sir William Henry** (1817-1892)

MP Dublin 1842-7, co Galway 1857-71

Corresp and papers rel to political, colonial and artistic affairs c1835-90 (several thousand items), incl letters from the 4th Earl of Carnarvon, WE Forster, Lord Houghton, Lord Kimberley, Sir Robert Peel, 2nd Bt, the 5th Earl of Rosebery and the 1st Earl Russell.
In private possession.

[265] **GREVILLE, Charles Cavendish Fulke** (1794-1865)

Clerk to the Privy Council 1821-59

Political journal 1814-60 (29 vols).
British Library (Add MSS 41095-41123). Bequeathed by him to Henry Reeve, and presented by Reeve's widow 1895.

Corresp with Henry Reeve 1839-65 (2 vols).
British Library (Add MSS 41184-5). Purchased 1925.

[266] **GREY, Albert Henry George** (1851-1917), 4th Earl Grey 1894

MP S Northumberland 1880-5, Northumberland (Tyneside division) 1885-6

Corresp and papers c1880-1917 (162 boxes), incl letters, memoranda and printed papers rel to constituency and parliamentary politics c1880-6 (c3 boxes), proportional representation c1880-c1917 (3 boxes), church reform c1880-c1900 (2 boxes), co-operation c1880-c1915 (5 boxes) and public house trusts c1900-4 (3 boxes); letters to and from the 3rd Earl Grey 1870-94 (884 items).
Durham University Department of Palaeography and Diplomatic (Grey of Howick Collection). Deposited by the 5th Earl Grey 1955.

Letters to him from Major H Craufurd and others rel to public house trusts 1900-2 (1 file), among the papers of the 2nd Earl of Lytton.
Lady Cobbold. NRA 25520.

See also *Colonial Governors.*

[267] **GREY, General the Hon Charles**
(1804-1870)

MP Chipping Wycombe 1832-7; private secretary to the 2nd Earl Grey 1832-4, Prince Albert 1849-61, Queen Victoria 1861-70

General, political, military and family corresp and papers c1821-70 (1 vol, c4,000 items), incl letters from WE Gladstone, Lord Halifax, Sir Charles Phipps, Viscount Ponsonby, Lord John Russell and Queen Victoria; transcripts of corresp with his wife 1848-69 (2 vols); transcripts of the 2nd Earl Grey's corresp 1802-40 (5 vols) and an account of his life c1861 (1 vol); journals 1831-65 (18 vols); diaries 1840-68 (19 vols); memoranda books 1868-70 (3 vols); commonplace book nd; account books 1835-68 (7 vols); game books 1818-42 (2 vols); misc accounts and papers 1826-70 (2 boxes, 18 vols and bundles).
Durham University Department of Palaeography and Diplomatic (Grey of Howick Collection). Deposited by the 5th Earl Grey 1955-63, and by the 6th Earl Grey 1967-79. NRA 6228.

Diaries 1839, 1841 (2 vols).
National Archives of Canada, Ottawa (MG24 A10). Presented by the 4th Earl Grey while governor-general of Canada.

[268] **GREY, Mary Elizabeth** (1776-1861),
Countess Grey

Political hostess

Letters to her 1796-1850 (c1,300 items), incl letters from Lord Brougham 1843-5 (124 items), Edward Ellice 1836-45 (26 items) and Lord Grey 1796-1843 (836 items).
Durham University Department of Palaeography and Diplomatic (Grey of Howick Collection). Deposited by the 5th Earl Grey 1955. NRA 6228.

Letters from Thomas Creevey, the 3rd and 4th Barons Holland, Viscount Ponsonby, the Revd Sydney Smith, the 2nd Duke and Duchess of Sutherland and others 1792-1851 (4 boxes); diaries 1822-43 (2 vols).
Borthwick Institute, York University (Halifax Papers A1/4, A7/1A). Deposited 1980 by the 3rd Earl of Halifax, a descendant of her youngest daughter. NRA 8128.

Letters to her and her husband from Sydney Smith 1808-44 (185 items).
New College, Oxford (MSS 4433-4). FW Steer, *The archives of New College, Oxford,* 1974, p111.

GRIFFITH, see Ellis-Griffith.

[269] **GRIMSTON, James Bucknall** (1747-1808),
3rd Viscount Grimston 1773

MP St Albans 1783-4, Hertfordshire 1784-90

Corresp rel to political, patronage, family and estate affairs, etc 1775-1808 (c1,800 items), incl St Albans and Hertfordshire election corresp; misc election papers; letter books 1778-1808 (6 vols); travel journals, accounts and sketch books 1768-70, nd (12 vols); latin verses (1 vol).
Hertfordshire Record Office (D/EV) Deposited by the 6th Earl of Verulam 1962-3. NRA 7246; HMC *Report on the manuscripts of the Earl of Verulam,* 1906.

[270] **GROSVENOR, Hugh Lupus** (1825-1899),
3rd Marquess of Westminster 1869, 1st Duke of Westminster 1874

MP Chester 1847-69; master of the Horse 1880-5

Chester election accounts and papers 1847-59 (19 items); royal, political, ecclesiastical and general corresp 1866-99 (187 items), incl letters from WE Gladstone, Queen Victoria and the Prince of Wales; papers rel to public affairs 1895-9 (2 files, 11 items); family corresp 1853-99 (24 items); misc papers 1842-99 (1 vol, 4 files, 37 items).
The Duke of Westminster. Enquiries to Cheshire Record Office. NRA 13470.

[271] **GROSVENOR, Richard** (1795-1869), 2nd Marquess of Westminster 1845

MP Chester 1818-30, Cheshire 1830-2, S Cheshire 1832-5; lord steward 1850-2

Parliamentary and election papers (1 box); Flintshire election accounts 1861 (1 vol); general corresp and papers (1 box).
The Duke of Westminster. Enquiries to Cheshire Record Office. NRA 13470.

[272] **GROSVENOR, Robert** (1767-1845), 2nd Earl Grosvenor 1802, 1st Marquess of Westminster 1831

MP East Looe 1788-90, Chester 1790-1802; a lord of the Admiralty 1789-91; a commissioner of the Board of Control 1793-1801

Parliamentary and election papers (4 boxes); registers, poll books and accounts, Chester elections 1767-1826 (21 vols); general corresp and papers (2 boxes); Flintshire yeomanry papers 1831-40 (5 boxes).
The Duke of Westminster. Enquiries to Cheshire Record Office. NRA 13470.

[273] **GROSVENOR, Robert** (1801-1893), 1st Baron Ebury 1857

MP Shaftesbury 1822-6, Chester 1826-47, Middlesex 1847-57

Letters and papers rel to elections, etc (1 box).
The Duke of Westminster. Enquiries to Cheshire Record Office. NRA 13470.

Corresp 1820-91 (3 vols); journal of a Mediterranean tour 1829 (2 vols).
Bodleian Library, Oxford (MSS Eng. lett. c.439-41, Eng. misc. c.667-8). Deposited by Mrs Margaret Dorling 1975; purchased 1977.

Journal 1826 (1 vol).
Beinecke Library, Yale University, New Haven, Connecticut (Osborn Collection fd 30). NRA 18661.

[274] **GUEST, Sir Josiah John** (1785-1852), 1st Bt

MP Honiton 1826-31, Merthyr Tydfil 1832-52

Corresp 1807-52 (20 vols *passim*), mainly rel to the Dowlais Iron Co, but incl corresp rel to elections, Chartism and other political affairs; notebook 1820-9.
Glamorgan Archive Service (Dowlais Iron Co Records). Acquired 1955. NRA 7863; *Bulletin of the National Register of Archives*, viii, 1956, p18.

[275] **GUEST, Montagu John** (1839-1909)

MP Youghal 1869-74, Wareham 1880-5

Election and other political corresp 1868-99 (3 vols); general, family and misc corresp and papers 1827-1905 (5 vols), incl letters rel to Dorset affairs 1867-92.
British Library (Add MSS 57934-41). Transferred from the British Museum Department of Prints and Drawings 1973.

[276] **GURDON, Sir William Brampton** (1840-1910)

Private secretary to WE Gladstone 1865-6, 1868-74; stood for Norfolk (SW division) 1885, Southwark (Rotherhithe division) 1886, Colchester 1888; MP Norfolk (N division) 1899-1910

Corresp rel to his private secretaryship, Treasury affairs, South Africa, national and local politics, etc 1865-1908 (*c*390 items), incl letters from WE Gladstone 1865-92 (*c*35 items), Lord Kimberley, Lord Northbrook, Sir Henry Ponsonby, Sir Reginald Welby and Sir Evelyn Wood; corresp and papers rel to Norfolk and Rotherhithe constituencies and elections 1884-6 (*c*120 items); letters rel to candidates for Norwich and E Essex 1885 (2 bundles); press reports, N Norfolk elections 1899-1900 (3 bundles); papers rel to Treasury and revenue business 1851-85 (24 items), the Post Office 1868-84 (*c*110 items) and the finances of the Transvaal 1877-84 (*c*150 items); personal and genealogical corresp and papers 1847-1908 (*c*240

items); account books 1889-94 (2 vols); Eton diaries nd (3 vols); appointments diaries 1856, 1858, 1874-85, 1887-94, 1897-8, 1905-6 (26 vols); travel journals 1878-96, nd (8 vols); sketch books 1879-96, nd (12 vols).
Suffolk Record Office, Ipswich (HA 54/1, 2, 8, 9). Deposited 1964.

[277] **HALDANE, Richard Burdon** (1856-1928), Viscount Haldane 1911

MP Haddingtonshire 1885-1911; secretary for war 1905-12; lord chancellor 1912-15, 1924

Political and general corresp 1872-1928 (17 vols), incl letters from HH Asquith 1885-1926, Lord Balfour 1892-1928, Lord Morley of Blackburn 1886-1922 and Lord Rosebery 1887-1927; letters describing his career to his mother 1866-1925 (81 vols) and his sister 1874-1928 (4 vols); letters to him from his mother 1877-1924 (2 vols); cabinet papers and other confidential memoranda 1897-1928 (1 vol); notes mainly for lectures and essays 1875-1928 (12 vols), incl notes for speeches in the House of Commons 1881 and while campaigning in his constituency 1888-92 (1 vol); drafts of his autobiography, autobiographical memoranda, notes on contemporaries and misc papers 1872-1928 (28 vols, 1 item); press cuttings 1877-1937 (16 vols).
National Library of Scotland (MSS 5901-6013, 6105-6, 6108A, 6109, 20035-6, 20049-78, 20205, 20213-23; Ch 15508). Presented by Sir William Haldane and Mrs Campbell Fraser 1945, and by TGN Haldane 1971-3.

[278] **HALIDAY, Alexander Henry** (*c*1728-1802)

Belfast politician and physician

Letters to him 1774-1802 (3 vols), mainly from Lord Charlemont.
Royal Irish Academy, Dublin (MSS 12 R 23-5).
HMC *Twelfth Report App X* and *Thirteenth Report App VIII, Manuscripts and correspondence of James, first Earl of Charlemont*, 2 vols 1891, 1894; *Manuscript sources for the history of Irish civilisation*, ed RJ Hayes, 1965, i, 539.

[279] **HAMILTON, Alexander** (1767-1852), 10th Duke of Hamilton 1819

MP Lancaster 1802-6

Lanarkshire electoral roll 1832, poll books 1832, 1835; minutes of Mid-Lanarkshire Liberal registration committee 1838; political and personal corresp and misc papers 1788-1851 (*c*140 bundles), incl letters from Lords Grey, Holland, Lansdowne, Melbourne and Palmerston, the 4th and 5th Dukes of Newcastle and the Duke of Wellington mainly 1825-40, letters and papers rel to Lanarkshire militia and yeomanry 1794-1855, lieutenancy business and local patronage 1815-51, and elections 1827-51, and corresp rel to his artistic, literary and antiquarian interests; legal and estate corresp and

papers 1802-51, incl letters between him, his
agents, architects and others (*c*40 bundles); further
corresp 1802-51, incl letters to his father rel to the
Lancaster election 1802 and corresp with Robert
Peel, Lord Sidmouth and others rel to volunteer
corps and industrial unrest in Lanarkshire 1819-25
(*c*730 items); papers rel to local defence in Glasgow
and Lanarkshire 1794-1811 (*c*200 items); passports
1826, 1830.
The Duke of Hamilton. Enquiries to NRA
(Scotland) (NRA(S) 0332). NRA 10979.

Letters from his wife 1809-*c*1844 (*c*69 items);
corresp with William Beckford 1783, 1806-44 (1
vol); corresp mainly rel to Beckford's business
affairs 1813-48 (1 vol).
Bodleian Library, Oxford (MSS Beckford c.21,
38-9). Presented 1984 by BH Blackwell Ltd, after
purchase from the 15th Duke of Hamilton at
Sotheby's 19 July 1977, lot 272. NRA 22980.

Misc papers 1813-58, incl reports on Scottish
railways and a petition from the Greenock
magistrates in favour of the reform bill 1832 (*c*40
items).
Scottish Record Office (GD 406). Purchased from
the 15th Duke of Hamilton 1983. NRA 10979 (M9/
295-306).

[280] **HAMILTON, Sir Edward Walter**
(1847-1908)

Private secretary to Robert Lowe 1872-3, to WE
Gladstone 1873-4, 1880-5

Corresp with members of the royal family and royal
household 1880-1908 (9 vols); with WE Gladstone,
his private secretaries and members of the
Gladstone family 1874-1908 (8 vols); with Lord
Goschen, Sir William Harcourt, Lord Rosebery
and other politicians and journalists 1870-1908 (10
vols); letters from members of the Hamilton and
Herbert families 1870-1908 (2 vols); general corresp
1870-1908 (8 vols); political and social diaries 1867,
1880-1906 (55 vols); engagement diaries 1890-5,
1897-1906 (16 vols).
British Library (Add MSS 48599-48699). Presented
by JA Godley 1915.

Semi-official corresp, memoranda, notes and other
papers rel to Treasury business mainly 1872-1907
(102 vols).
Public Record Office (T 168/5-99). NRA 28800.

Letters to him from various correspondents 1880-7
(12 items).
St Deiniol's Library, Hawarden (Glynne-Gladstone
MSS). Deposited by Sir William Gladstone, Bt
1968. Access through Clwyd Record Office. NRA
14174.

[281] **HAMILTON, James** (1811-1885), 2nd
Marquess of Abercorn 1818, 1st Duke of Abercorn
1868

Lord lieutenant of Ireland 1866-8, 1874-6

Corresp and papers, mainly as lord lieutenant,
1866-8, 1874-6 (22 bundles), incl letters from Lord

Mayo 1866-8 (91 items) and Sir Michael Hicks
Beach 1874-6 (51 items); political, royal and
personal corresp 1825-66, with that of his wife
1818-1904 (14 bundles); estate and financial corresp
1834-78 (19 bundles); corresp and papers rel to his
claim to the dukedom of Chatelherault, mainly
1818-65 (17 bundles); misc corresp 1870-85 (5
bundles).
Public Record Office of Northern Ireland (D 623).
Deposited by the 4th and 5th Dukes of Abercorn.
NRA 15790.

[282] **HAMILTON, John James** (1756-1818), 9th
Earl of Abercorn 1789, 1st Marquess of Abercorn
1790

MP East Looe 1783-4, St Germans 1784-9

Letters to him rel to Irish political, patronage and
estate affairs 1790-1819 (98 bundles), incl letters
from George Knox and Lord Ranfurly 1790-1809
(7 bundles) and from John Stewart 1793-1817 (6
bundles), and letters to him as colonel of the
Tyrone militia 1793-8 (5 bundles); corresp rel to
his Scottish estates, local affairs etc 1790-1817 (36
bundles); corresp and papers rel to English affairs
1767-1817 (24 bundles and items), incl speech notes
1784-1810 (1 bundle), engagement diaries
1798-1802 (5 vols) and financial papers 1788-1817,
etc; letter books 1789-1817 (11 vols), incl copies of
letters to Lord Castlereagh, Lord Clare, Henry
Dundas, Lord Hardwicke, William Pitt and others.
Public Record Office of Northern Ireland (D 623).
Deposited by the 4th and 5th Dukes of Abercorn.
NRA 15790.

HAMILTON-GORDON, see Gordon.

[283] **HAMILTON-TEMPLE-BLACKWOOD**
(formerly **BLACKWOOD**), **Frederick Temple**
(1826-1902), 5th Baron Dufferin 1841, 1st Earl of
Dufferin 1871, 1st Marquess of Dufferin and Ava
1888

Under-secretary for India 1864-6, for war 1866;
chancellor of the Duchy of Lancaster and
paymaster-general 1868-72

Papers and pamphlets, India 1854-65 (1 bundle,
12 items); War Office corresp 1866 (26 items);
administrative and patronage corresp as chancellor
of the Duchy of Lancaster 1868-72 (6 vols); papers
as a member of the committees on military
education 1869-70 (2 vols, 1 item) and design of
warships 1870-1 (*c*155 items); corresp and papers
mainly as lord lieutenant of co Down *c*1855-80 (2
vols, 17 bundles), and rel to Irish politics, land
tenure, education, etc (mainly printed) 1832-1902
(63 boxes, vols and bundles); papers as warden of
the Cinque Ports 1892-5 (1 vol, 1 bundle); extensive
corresp and papers as special commissioner to Syria
1860-1, governor-general of Canada 1872-8,
ambassador to Russia 1879-81, Turkey 1881-4,
Italy 1888-91 and France 1891-6, and viceroy of
India 1884-8; political and general letters received

1846-1902 (156 bundles); copies of letters from him to Queen Victoria, AJ Balfour, WE Gladstone, politicians, diplomats and others, incl references to British and Irish politics, 1889-97 (1 vol, 101 items); corresp and papers mainly rel to honours and appointments 1846-91, publications and speeches c1850-1901, yachting 1850-1900 and business interests 1895-1902; diaries and journals 1839, 1842, 1847-63, 1865, 1879-82, 1885-1902 (32 vols).
Public Record Office of Northern Ireland (D 1071H). Deposited by the Marchioness of Dufferin and Ava 1957. NRA 5700.

Letters from politicians, diplomats, artists, authors and others 1857-64 (10 vols); corresp and papers, partly printed, rel to India 1879-88 (c108 vols).
The Dowager Marchioness of Dufferin and Ava. A microfilm is in the Public Record Office of Northern Ireland (MIC 22). NRA 5700.

See also *Diplomats* and *Colonial Governors*.

[284] HARCOURT, Lewis (1863-1922), 1st Viscount Harcourt 1917

Private secretary to his father Sir William Harcourt 1880-1904; MP NE Lancashire (Rossendale division) 1904-16; first commissioner of Works 1905-10, 1915-16; secretary for the colonies 1910-15

Letters from his father 1875-1904 (10 vols); special corresp 1882-1922 (9 vols), incl letters from Lord James of Hereford 1884-1909, Lord Morley of Blackburn 1887-1922, Lord Ripon 1890-1908 and Lord Spencer 1888-1905; corresp and papers as first commissioner of Works 1905-10, 1915-16 (9 vols); corresp with governors and others, memoranda, reports, etc as colonial secretary 1910-15 (48 vols); political, administrative and personal corresp and papers arranged by subject, mainly 1906-21, but incl desk diaries 1886, 1899 and appointments diaries 1899-1908, 1913 (28 boxes and vols); general corresp 1882-1922 (23 vols); family corresp 1880-1919 (17 vols); corresp rel to a biography of his father 1905-22 (1 vol); printed Foreign Office telegrams and cabinet memoranda 1907-16 (63 vols); journals 1880-7, 1892-5 (74 vols); loose items removed from journals for 1880-3 (3 vols).
Bodleian Library, Oxford (MS Harcourt dep.347-600, 649-58, 671-88, 749-51). Deposited by the 2nd Viscount Harcourt 1972. NRA 3679.

[285] HARDIE, James Keir (1856-1915)

MP West Ham (S division) 1892-5, Merthyr Tydfil 1900-15; chairman of the Independent Labour Party 1893-1900, 1913-15

Letter book 1879-89; corresp with his family, his secretary Margaret Symons and others 1884-1915 (4 files); parliamentary desk diary 1915; corresp and papers mainly of Margaret Symons rel to women's suffrage 1905-12 (2 files); drafts of speeches or articles 1902-8 (1 file); papers rel to his world tour 1907-8 (7 vols, files and items); legal

and financial papers 1892-1914 (1 file); membership register, Scottish Labour Party 1892; press cuttings and misc papers, mainly printed, 1888-1915 (13 vols and files).
National Library of Scotland (Dep 176). Deposited with the papers of his son-in-law Emrys Hughes MP by Mrs Martha Hughes 1971-81.

Minutes in his hand of a committee for the publication of the *Daily Herald* 1911.
National Library of Scotland (Acc 5121). Purchased at Lawrence of Crewkerne sale 15 Oct 1970, lot 186.

Diary 1884 (1 vol); misc letters and papers 1888-1909 (7 items).
Labour Party Archives, London (JKH). NRA 14863.

[286] HARDY, Thomas (1752-1832)

Secretary of the London Corresponding Society 1792-4

Drafts of letters to editors of periodicals and others 1796-c1829 (1 vol); sketch of the history of the London Corresponding Society nd (1 vol).
British Library (Add MSS 27814, 27818). Acquired with the papers of Francis Place 1868.

[287] HARE, Thomas (1806-1891)

Radical reformer

Letters mainly from politicians and political economists 1828-71.
St John's College, Oxford (MS 356). Presented by DL Roberts 1981. NRA 7453.

Letters from JS Mill and others rel to proportional representation 1859-63, 1867 (1 vol).
British Library (Add MS 43773). Presented by Hare's grandson Harold Clayton 1934.

[288] HARNEY, George Julian (1817-1897)

Chartist; stood for Tiverton 1847

Corresp and papers 1841-96 (c240 items), incl letters from Louis Blanc 1848-54 (c20 items), Guiseppe Mazzini 1844-58 (16 items) and Feargus O'Connor 1845-50 (5 items).
In private possession. FG and RM Black, *The Harney papers*, 1969.

[289] HARRINGTON, Timothy Charles (1851-1910)

MP co Westmeath 1883-5, Dublin (Harbour division) 1885-1910

Political corresp with Michael Davitt, John Dillon, CS Parnell, JE Redmond and others 1881-1910 (4 boxes and vols); corresp and papers mainly rel to the activities and finances of the Irish National League 1880-1903 (3 boxes, 4 items); warrant for his arrest 1881, corresp, notes and press cuttings on the Maamtrasna murders case 1882-4, papers

rel to the Parnell commission 1888, and other material rel to his legal career 1887-1910 (6 boxes, 1 item); letters to him and Parnell rel to the establishment of a Parnellite newspaper 1891-2 (1 box); parliamentary pledges by candidates standing for election as members of the Irish Parliamentary Party 1885-6, and misc telegrams from members to headquarters 1886-96 (2 boxes); corresp on the formation of the Dublin Dockyard Co 1901-3 (1 box); letters from Lord Dunraven and other papers rel to the land conference 1902 (1 box); diary of his American tour 1890 (1 vol); corresp and papers of and rel to Richard Pigott 1870-89 (1 box); misc political and personal papers c1841-1904 (8 boxes, vols and items).
National Library of Ireland (MSS 2195, 5384-5, 5388, 8314, 8576-95, 8930-4). *Manuscript sources for the history of Irish civilisation*, ed RJ Hayes, 1965, ii, 419-20, and *Supplement*, 1979, i, 316. Further papers are reported to be in private possession.

HART DYKE, see Dyke.

[290] **HARTLEY, David** (1732-1813)

MP Hull 1774-80, 1782-4

Letters from constituents 1774-89, and papers rel to Hull and to his candidatures at Callington 1768 and 1772, Beverley 1780 and Bath 1790 (6 bundles); letters, speeches, notes, etc mainly rel to domestic politics c1753-1794, incl commercial and financial questions, the abolition of slavery, Catholic emancipation and parliamentary reform (3 vols, 8 bundles, 66 items); corresp, memoranda, printed papers, etc rel to the American war and peace negotiations 1766-88 (7 bundles); general political and personal corresp 1760-95, with politicians, churchmen and others incl Charles Grey, George and William Hammond, Samuel and WH Hartley, Newton Ogle and Sir George Savile (22 bundles); corresp and papers rel to his invention of fire-plates 1772-95 (9 bundles); personal and household bills and vouchers 1761-89 (2 bundles); misc papers c1750-1789 (5 bundles, c40 items).
Berkshire Record Office (D/EHy/O6-8, 15-43; F83-111; A10; B1-5; L4; Z7). Deposited by members of the Hartley Russell family 1957-60. NRA 844.

Corresp with Lord Carmarthen, CJ Fox and others 1783-5 (5 vols).
William L Clements Library, University of Michigan, Ann Arbor. Purchased 1933. *Guide to the manuscript collections*, 1942, p136.

[291] **HAVELOCK-ALLAN** (formerly **HAVELOCK**), **Lieutenant-General Sir Henry Marshman** (1830-1897), 1st Bt

MP Sunderland 1874-81, co Durham (SE division) 1885-92, 1895-7

Corresp and papers, incl diary of the Sunderland election 1874, election and other addresses to

constituents 1874-92, corresp and papers rel to election expenses 1880, and papers rel to military affairs, Ireland, Afghanistan, the Eastern Question, etc 1874-97.
North Yorkshire County Record Office (ZDG (H) III 7).

[292] **HAWKINS, Sir Christopher** (1758-1829), Bt

MP Mitchell 1784-99, Grampound 1800-7, Penryn 1818-20, St Ives 1821-8

Corresp and papers rel to constituency business, elections and patronage in Tregony 1789-1820 (1 bundle, 264 items), Helston 1792, 1801-28 (348 items), Grampound 1807-16 (c20 items) and St Ives 1820-9 (66 items); political and general corresp and misc papers 1791-1829 (5 bundles, c300 items); letters from agents rel to estate, mining and political matters 1780-1829 (c54 bundles); letters from the Trelawney-Brereton family 1793-1829 (164 items).
Cornwall Record Office (DD.J). Deposited mainly in 1960 by Miss Elizabeth Johnstone, a descendant of his brother John, and in 1985 by M Galsworthy. NRA 29664.

Personal and family corresp 1799-1829 (308 items).
In private possession. NRA 29664 (pp155-6).

Letters to and from his brother John, Sir John Hobhouse and others 1802-27 (1 vol).
West Sussex Record Office (Hawkins Papers 7). Deposited in 1960 by Mrs GH Johnstone and Miss Elizabeth Johnstone. *The Hawkins papers: a catalogue*, 1962, p15.

[293] **HAY, Field Marshal George** (1787-1876), 8th Marquess of Tweeddale 1804

Scottish representative peer 1818-76

Military, political and general corresp 1806-76 (5 vols), incl corresp rel to parliamentary elections 1816-18, 1841 and the representative peerage 1831-7 (1 vol); family corresp of him and his wife 1803-76 (8 vols), incl letters from Lord John Hay rel to politics, elections, etc 1808-47; legal, financial and estate corresp 1807-76 (7 vols); papers as quartermaster-general in Spain 1811-13 (2 vols, 1 item), and as governor of Madras mainly 1842-8 (6 vols); military memoirs nd (1 vol); accounts 1842-50 (1 vol); misc papers 1807-73 (3 vols); appointments, commissions, etc 1821-75 (24 items).
National Library of Scotland (MSS 14441-53, 14457-63, 14532-4, 14555-63, 14601, 14808; Ch 10971-94). Bequeathed by the 11th Marquess of Tweeddale 1969.

Corresp, minutes and reports as governor of Madras 1842-8 (24 vols).
India Office Library and Records (MSS Eur F 96). Deposited by the 11th Marquess of Tweeddale 1959. NRA 27520.

[294] **HAY, George** (1822-1862), styled Earl of Gifford

Private secretary to the Duke of Newcastle 1854-5; MP Totnes 1855-62

Corresp, notes, speeches, etc 1832-62 (*c*60 vols, folders and bundles), incl misc official corresp 1843-60 (1 folder), notes on electoral and parliamentary reform (1 folder), and notes on banking and currency questions (9 folders and bundles).
Public Record Office of Northern Ireland (D 1071G). Deposited by the Marchioness of Dufferin and Ava 1957. NRA 5700.

Corresp 1852-63 (1 vol), incl letters from constituents1855-62, and corresp of RB Sheridan rel to Gifford's debts 1862-3; notes of requests for assistance from constituents 1859-62 (1 vol); accounts 1856-63 and bank books 1859-62 (2 vols).
British Library (Add MSS 42768-71). Presented 1932 by the Dorset Natural History and Archaeological Society, which had acquired them from the 11th Duke of Bedford.

Personal, family and legal corresp 1840-62 (3 vols).
National Library of Scotland (MSS 14442, 14455-6). Bequeathed 1969 by his nephew the 11th Marquess of Tweeddale.

[295] **HEATHCOTE, Sir Gilbert** (1773-1851), 4th Bt

MP Lincolnshire 1796-1807, Rutland 1812-41

Political, election and general corresp and misc papers 1794-1842 (220 items); sporting corresp and papers 1794-1842 (138 items); political and election expenses 1809-20 (1 vol); personal accounts and bank books 1793-6, 1814-45 (4 vols).
Lincolnshire Archives Office (ANC 12A/11, 12C/7; 2 ANC 12/6; 3 ANC 6/29-31, 9/3-9; 5 ANC 6E/2-3). Deposited by his great-great-grandson the 3rd Earl of Ancaster 1951-8. NRA 5789.

[296] **HEATHCOTE, Gilbert John** (1795-1867), 1st Baron Aveland 1856

MP Boston 1820-30, 1831-2, S Lincolnshire 1832-41, Rutland 1841-56

Corresp with landowners, constituents, agents and others, addresses, notes, canvassing memoranda, poll books, press cuttings and other election papers, Boston 1818-35 (331 items), Lincolnshire 1818-41 (407 items), Rutland 1841-52 (36 items) and miscellaneous mainly 1830-1 (41 items); speech notes, memoranda, press cuttings, etc rel to the ballot, corn laws, militia, railways, tenant-right and other political issues 1833-66 (179 items); corresp and papers rel to the Rutland yeomanry 1819-25 (4 items) and South Lincolnshire militia 1857-63 (128 items); misc political and social corresp 1820-65 (229 items); misc papers rel to local and personal affairs 1827-67 (53 items); travel journals and misc papers *c*1812-14 (3 vols, 8 items); bank books 1860, 1862-3 (3 vols); newspapers containing copies of his speeches 1834-46 (37 items).

Lincolnshire Archives Office (ANC 12A/12-13, 12C/7-9, 13A, 13B/4-11, 15A, 15B/1-3; 3 ANC 9/10-16; 5 ANC 9/1-2; 9 ANC 3A/4). Deposited by his great-grandson the 3rd Earl of Ancaster 1951-8. NRA 5789.

[297] **HELY-HUTCHINSON, Hon Francis** (1759-1827)

MP Dublin University 1790-7, Naas 1798-1800

Letters mainly rel to politics and family affairs from his brothers Richard 1792-1825 (332 items), John 1804-27 (172 items), Abraham 1796-1824 (1 bundle) and Christopher 1799-1819 (45 items); misc political, patronage and business corresp and papers 1792-1827 (1 bundle), incl speeches on Catholic relief; Wexford political and estate corresp 1790-1822 (2 bundles); corresp and papers rel to West Iffa and Offa yeomanry 1797-9 (1 bundle), and as collector of Dublin port 1799-1825 (1 bundle); letters from his wife, his sons and other members of his family 1786-1827 (1 vol, 6 bundles).
Trinity College Library, Dublin (Donoughmore F). Deposited by the 7th Earl of Donoughmore 1980. NRA 22331.

[298] **HELY-HUTCHINSON** (formerly **HELY**), **John** (1724-1794)

MP Lanesborough 1759-61, Cork 1761-90, Taghmon 1790-4; provost of Trinity College, Dublin 1774-94

Corresp 1758-94 with successive lords lieutenant, chief secretaries and under-secretaries for Ireland, peers, politicians, bishops, lawyers, estate agents and others, with misc papers, rel to British and Irish politics, constituency business, Trinity College, and legal, estate and family affairs (462 items); papers rel to Trinity College *c*1775-91 (10 vols and bundles), incl the disputed parliamentary election 1790; notebooks mainly on legal and constitutional history *c*1748-94 (8 vols); legal case book and fee book 1760-72 (2 vols).
Trinity College Library, Dublin (Donoughmore C). Deposited by the 7th Earl of Donoughmore 1980. NRA 22331; HMC *Twelfth Report App IX*, 1891, pp227-333.

[299] **HELY-HUTCHINSON, Richard Hely** (1756-1825), 2nd Baron Donoughmore 1788, 1st Viscount Donoughmore 1797, 1st Earl of Donoughmore 1800

MP Dublin University 1776-8, Sligo 1778-83, Taghmon 1783-8; Irish representative peer 1801-25; joint postmaster-general (Ireland) 1806-7

Corresp and papers rel to politics, patronage and elections in Clonmel 1802-24 (44 items), Cork 1801-24 (1 bundle, 68 items), co Cork 1817-23 (17 items), Tipperary 1797-1824 (1 vol, 121 items) and Waterford 1803-24 (38 items); corresp and papers rel to the Union 1798-1801 (52 items); to Catholic emancipation 1807-25 (199 items), incl letters from

Edward Hay, Daniel O'Connell and Archbishops Murray and Troy; corresp with Sir Benjamin Bloomfield, JW Croker, Lord Liverpool, Sir John Newport, Lord Wellesley and other politicians rel to Irish politics, Catholic emancipation, the Prince of Wales, etc 1800-24 (180 items); misc political corresp, speeches and papers 1778-1821 (138 items); memoranda of conversations, corresp, expenses, etc 1807-25 (90 items); family and personal corresp 1793-1825, incl letters from his brothers rel to British and Irish politics (25 vols and bundles); estate and business corresp and papers 1789-1825 (21 bundles).
Trinity College Library, Dublin (Donoughmore D). Deposited by the 7th Earl of Donoughmore 1980. NRA 22331.

[300] **HENEAGE, Edward** (1840-1922), 1st Baron Heneage 1896

MP Lincoln 1865-8, Great Grimsby 1880-92, 1893-5; chancellor of the Duchy of Lancaster 1886

Corresp and printed papers rel to proportional representation, the Education Act of 1906 and Grimsby hospitals and charities, and press cutting books rel to agricultural and political subjects 1881 and the Great Grimsby election 1887 (1 box); letters from him to his Grimsby agents Grange and Wintringham on local and national politics and estate matters 1864-1920, with other agency papers incl Grimsby election accounts 1886 (1 vol, *c*50 bundles).
Lincolnshire Archives Office (HEN, 2 HEN). Deposited by the Heneage trustees 1958-9. NRA 5437.

[301] **HENLEY, Robert** (1747-1786), 2nd Earl of Northington 1772

MP Hampshire 1768-72; lord lieutenant of Ireland 1783-4

Copies of letters to and from him as lord lieutenant May 1783-Feb 1784 (1 vol).
British Library (Add MS 38716). Purchased at Sotheby's 19 May 1913, lot 988 (Phillipps MS 24152).

Letter book June 1783-Feb 1784 (1 vol).
Beinecke Library, Yale University, New Haven, Connecticut (Osborn Collection c44). NRA 18661.

Letters from Lord North and others 1770-83 (7 items).
Northamptonshire Record Office (Northington Papers, envelope F). Deposited by the 6th Baron Henley before 1954. NRA 14944.

[302] **HEPBURNE-SCOTT, Henry Francis** (1800-1867), 7th Lord Polwarth 1841

MP Roxburghshire 1826-32; Scottish representative peer 1843-67; a lord in waiting 1852, 1858-9, 1866-7

Corresp and papers rel to elections in Roxburghshire 1826-32 and Berwick 1832 (*c*300 items); corresp and papers mainly rel to political,

antiquarian and family matters 1810-67 (*c*300 items), incl letters fom Sir Robert Peel (13 items); letter book 1844.
Scottish Record Office (GD 157). Deposited by the 9th Lord Polwarth 1930.

[303] **HERBERT, Edward James** (1818-1891), 3rd Earl of Powis 1848

MP N Shropshire 1843-8

Letters from politicians and others rel to ecclesiastical and social legislation, the Irish representative peerage, Welsh church affairs, etc 1852-73 (12 bundles); corresp and papers rel to the Roxburghe Club, Powis Scholarships and trusteeships 1843-91 (17 bundles).
National Library of Wales (Powis MSS). Deposited by the 6th Earl of Powis 1979.

Letters from politicians, clergymen and others rel to the proposed union of the dioceses of Bangor and St Asaph 1843-8 (*c*140 items).
National Library of Wales (Powis MSS). Deposited by the 4th Earl of Powis 1939. NRA 20150.

Corresp rel to the foundation of the University College of North Wales 1883-9 (200 items).
University College of North Wales, Bangor (Bangor MSS 4248-4545).

[304] **HERBERT, General George Augustus** (1759-1827), 11th Earl of Pembroke 1794

MP Wilton 1780-4, 1788-94

Political, military, personal and family corresp and papers 1775-1827 (*c*19 bundles), incl letters from George III, the 1st Baron Amherst, the 3rd Earl Bathurst, Sir John Hippisley, the 1st Earl of Malmesbury, the 3rd Viscount Palmerston, Spencer Perceval, William Pitt, the 3rd Duke of Richmond, Sir George Yonge and the Duke of York; papers rel to his military career 1773-1816 (17 bundles); official, military and estate letter books 1798-1827 (14 vols); précis of despatches from various diplomats to Lord Howick 1806-7 (5 vols) and Lord Castlereagh 1814-15 (1 vol); memorandum books 1805-23 (5 vols).
Wiltshire Record Office (WRO 2057/F4/3-8, 11-24, 28-46; F6/60-80). Deposited by the 17th Earl of Pembroke 1984. NRA 22080.

European travel journals 1779-83 (4 vols); engagement diaries 1789-92 (3 vols); personal accounts 1779-1827 (22 vols).
The Earl of Pembroke. Enquiries to Wiltshire Record Office. NRA 22080 (A6/22-43, F5/5-11).

[305] **HERBERT, Sidney** (1853-1913), 14th Earl of Pembroke 1895

MP Wilton 1877-85, Croydon 1886-95; a lord of the Treasury and Conservative whip 1885-6, 1886-92; lord steward 1895-1905

Royal corresp 1870-1913 (1 bundle); letters mainly from politicians 1890-1912 (1 bundle); corresp and papers (many printed) rel to the royal household

1887-1912 (*c*9 bundles); family corresp *c*1860-1908 (6 bundles).
The Earl of Pembroke. Enquiries to Wiltshire Record Office. Records less than one hundred years old are closed to research. NRA 22080 (F3/1-9, F4/71-2, 79-84).

Grants of foreign orders *c*1900-10.
Wiltshire Record Office (WRO 2057/F2/40-1). Deposited by the 17th Earl of Pembroke 1984. NRA 22080.

[306] **HERVEY, Frederick William** (1769-1859), 5th Earl of Bristol 1803, 1st Marquess of Bristol 1826

MP Bury St Edmunds 1796-1803; under-secretary for foreign affairs 1801-3

Letters mainly from politicians and diplomats 1801-12 (120 items), incl letters from Charles Arbuthnot, the Duke of Gloucester, Lord Liverpool and Sir John Warren; letters to him in support of Lord Hervey's parliamentary candidature for Cambridge University 1822 (47 items); personal and family corresp 1793-1853 (1 vol, 10 bundles, *c*685 items), incl many letters from Lord William Hervey, Lady Jersey, TA Knight and Lord Liverpool; misc papers *c*1795-1832 (16 vols and items), incl brief journal rel to foreign affairs 1803 and printed papers about reform bills 1831-2.
Suffolk Record Office, Bury St Edmunds (Ac 941/1, 11A, 56). Deposited by the National Trust 1958-9. NRA 6892.

[307] **HERVEY, Frederick William** (1800-1864), 2nd Marquess of Bristol 1859

MP Bury St Edmunds 1826-59; treasurer of the Household 1841-6

Letters in reply to his requests for support for the Suffolk address against the reform bill 1831 (25 items); corresp, speech notes, accounts, etc (59 items), mainly rel to the Bury election 1832 and subsequent petition against his return 1833, and to his election expenses 1857; printed poll books, Bury St Edmunds 1832-57 (7 items); misc personal and family corresp and papers 1819-61 (1 vol, 1 bundle, 45 items).
Suffolk Record Office, Bury St Edmunds (Ac 941/2-11, 11C-D, 59). Deposited by the National Trust 1958-9. NRA 6892.

[308] **HILL, Arthur** (1753-1801), 2nd Marquess of Downshire 1793

MP Lostwithiel 1774-80, Malmesbury 1780-4, co Down 1776-93

Corresp and misc papers 1786-1801 rel to Irish politics, local defence, the rebellion of 1798 and the dispute over the Union 1799-1800, and to Irish and English election and estate business (*c*2,265 items), incl many letters from Richard Annesley,

Lord Camden, Robert Hobart, John Reilly and Colonel Robert Ross.
Public Record Office of Northern Ireland (D 607). Deposited by the 7th Marquess of Downshire 1954-6. NRA 21035.

[309] **HILL, Arthur Blundell Sandys Trumbull** (1788-1845), 3rd Marquess of Downshire 1801

Lord lieutenant of co Down 1831-45

Letters to him about national politics, Catholic emancipation, elections, patronage, the co Down lieutenancy, etc 1809-45 (936 items), incl letters from the 2nd Earl Annesley, Sir Thomas Fremantle, the 3rd Marquess of Londonderry, the 3rd Earl of Roden, Sir Herbert Taylor and Lord Wellesley; corresp with agents and others mainly rel to his estates in Ireland and England 1809-45 (*c*16,300 items), incl letters rel to co Down politics and administration from the Reilly family (1,032 items) and the Revd Charles Hamilton (106 items), and corresp rel to tithes and the Church of Ireland (862 items); family and personal corresp 1810-44 (722 items), incl a few letters on politics and elections; general letter book 1823-45.
Public Record Office of Northern Ireland (D 671/C). Deposited by the 7th Marquess of Downshire 1958. NRA 21035.

Family corresp and papers 1790-1845 (1 bundle); autograph collection of letters to him and others 1810-48 (1 bundle); congratulatory letters on his marriage 1811 (1 bundle).
Berkshire Record Office (D/ED/F133A, C70, C73). Deposited by the 7th Marquess of Downshire and his solicitors 1954-5. NRA 7580.

[310] **HILL, Sir George Fitzgerald** (1763-1839), 2nd Bt

MP Coleraine 1791-5, Londonderry 1795-8, 1802-30, co Londonderry 1801-2; a commissioner of the Treasury (Ireland) 1807-17; vice-treasurer (Ireland) 1817-30

Corresp and papers mainly rel to Irish politics, patronage and financial administration *c*1785-1830 (*c*640 items), incl corresp with JC Beresford 1805-*c*1825 (*c*38 items), Lord Castlereagh 1797-1812 (29 items), Edward Cooke 1795-1812 (43 items), GR Dawson *c*1812-1829 (*c*20 items) and Robert Peel 1812-29 (*c*40 items).
Public Record Office of Northern Ireland (D 642, 642A). Some of the papers were presented by his great-great-niece Mrs CE Oldfield in 1953; the remainder were deposited by Sir Cyril Hill, Bt, and purchased in 1986. NRA 19000.

HILL, William, see Noel-Hill.

[311] **HIPPISLEY, Sir John Coxe** (1748-1825),
1st Bt

MP Sudbury 1790-6, 1802-18

Letters from agents, candidates, lawyers and others
rel to Sudbury elections and constituency business
1789-1814 (54 items); patronage applications from
freemen of the borough 1796-1814 (92 items);
Sudbury poll book 1790; notebook rel to
constituency business 1802-8; accounts with agents
and suppliers, papers rel to law suits, etc 1788-1813
(38 bundles and items); addresses, election squibs,
press cuttings, etc 1789-1808 (27 items).
Suffolk Record Office, Bury St Edmunds (HD 744).
Transferred 1977 from the Museum of the History
of Science, Oxford. NRA 21530.

Corresp with and concerning Cardinal York, and
rel to catholic emancipation, 1795-1811 (84ff).
National Library of Scotland (MS 3112 ff54-137).
Purchased *c*1942.

See also *Diplomats*.

[312] **HOARE, Sir Samuel** (1841-1915), 1st Bt

MP Norwich 1886-1906

Corresp 1879-1913 (*c*250 items), incl letters from
AJ Balfour 1897-1911, Sir Thomas Buxton
1885-1909, Joseph Chamberlain 1898-1901, Sir
Michael Hicks Beach 1899-1905, WH Long
1899-1910 and the 4th Marquess of Salisbury
1896-1907; printed and misc papers (1 file).
Cambridge University Library (Templewood Papers,
P3).

[313] **HODGSKIN, Thomas** (1787-1869)

Journalist and radical reformer

Corresp, literary MSS and other papers 1802-1903
(1 box), incl letters to him from John Bright, Lord
Brougham, Richard Cobden, Francis Place and
other radical politicians, letters from him during
his European travels, two lectures by him and
papers rel to his naval career.
*Sterling Memorial Library, Yale University, New
Haven, Connecticut.* See *National union catalog*, MS
71-2020.

[314] **HOLDEN, Sir Isaac** (1807-1897), 1st Bt

MP Knaresborough 1865-8, W Riding of Yorkshire
(N division) 1882-5, (Keighley division) 1885-95

Papers rel to elections in Knaresborough 1865 and
W Riding (N division) 1872 (1 bundle); political
speech notes nd and printed economic statistics
*c*1840-72 (1 bundle); family, social and business
corresp and misc papers 1827-93, incl a few political
letters and notes *c*1866-72 (59 bundles); papers rel
to religious affairs, etc *c*1850-80 (3 bundles);
personal and family papers 1830-1918, incl
reminiscences of his early career, speech notes and
misc corresp and papers of his son-in-law Alfred
Illingworth MP (5 boxes); journals and notebooks

1844-88, incl diary 1865-9 and notebook 1865-8
(12 vols); papers rel to patents and other business
affairs *c*1830-60 (1 box); press cuttings,
parliamentary bills, addresses and political and
religious pamphlets 1863-97 (9 bundles).
Brotherton Library, Leeds University. See P Hudson,
The West Riding wool textile industry, 1975,
pp238-68.

Corresp 1845-96 (31 bundles), mainly rel to
business and family matters, but incl references to
W Riding politics and parliamentary elections
1865-86, and letters from John Bright, Joseph
Chamberlain and WE Gladstone; political and
general memoranda and speeches *c*1860-70, election
address 1865, notes on banking and business and
misc papers 1824-90 (5 bundles); corresp with his
partner SC Lister 1847-60 and papers rel to a
dispute between them 1886-7 (14 bundles); letter
book 1869-85 (1 vol); technical and business notes,
memoranda, etc *c*1833-1894 (13 bundles); press
cuttings and other printed papers 1845-1905 (6
bundles).
Bradford University Library. Presented by Sir
Edward Holden, Bt 1971. NRA 16299.

[315] **HOLMES, Hugh** (1840-1916)

MP Dublin University 1885-7; solicitor-general
(Ireland) 1878-80, attorney-general (Ireland)
1885-6, 1886-7

Memoirs written in 1901 (2 vols), incl three
chapters on the politics and legislation of the period
1885-7.
In private possession. A microfilm is in the Public
Record Office of Northern Ireland (MIC 197).

[316] **HOLMES, William** (1779-1851)

MP Grampound 1808-12, Tregony 1812-18, Totnes
1818-20, Bishop's Castle 1820-30, Haslemere
1830-2, Berwick-upon-Tweed 1837-41; treasurer of
the Ordnance 1818-30; Tory whip

Political and misc corresp 1820-47, nd (*c*33 items),
incl letters from JW Croker, Sir Robert Peel, Lord
Fitzroy Somerset and the Duke of Wellington.
Untraced. NRA 2592.

HOLROYD, see Baker-Holroyd.

[317] **HOLYOAKE, George Jacob** (1817-1906)

Chartist and radical reformer

Corresp, notes, speeches and printed papers rel to
politics, social reform, secularism, the co-operative
movement, journalism, etc 1835-1906 (*c*4,340
items), incl letters to and from William Coningham,
Sir Joseph Cowen, Sir Charles Dilke, WE
Gladstone, TL Hunt, JS Mill and EFS Pigott.
Co-operative Union Library, Manchester. Presented
by his daughter, Mrs Emilie Holyoake Marsh.
NRA 16403.

General corresp 1837-1904 (5 bundles);
autobiographical notes 1831-40, 1845 (2 vols);
diaries 1845-1905 (54 vols); essay on Lord
Brougham and Lord Denman and account of a
visit to Brougham Castle *c*1830 (1 vol); lecture
notes 1838-9 (1 vol); London Atheistical Society
rules 1842-3, and index to letters written by him
1845-8 (1 vol); trust deed of the *Leader* Newspaper
Co 1856; business cash book 1858-61; Central
Garibaldi Committee minute book, with corresp
rel to and muster roll of Garibaldi's British Legion,
1860-1 (1 box); Travelling Tax Abolition
Committee minutes 1877-98 (1 bundle); misc
papers 1839-1905, nd (4 vols, 25 bundles).
Bishopsgate Institute, London. NRA 10203 (partial
list).

Letters to him from or rel to Harriet Martineau
1851-77 (1 vol).
British Library (Add MS 42726). Presented by Mrs
Holyoake Marsh 1932

Letters from WH White 1865-1903 (16 items).
Bedford Central Library (Mark Rutherford Papers
6). Presented to Sir William Hale-White by Mrs
Holyoake Marsh 1919. NRA 19222.

[318] **HOME, Patrick** (1728-1808)

MP Berwickshire 1784-96

Letters to him 1784-90 (1 bundle), mainly rel to
Berwickshire elections; misc parliamentary papers
1789-*c*1792 (1 bundle); family and misc corresp
1785-1808 (*c*38 bundles), incl many letters from
his cousin and factor George Home rel to
Berwickshire local affairs, the elections of 1784 and
1790, political patronage in Scotland, national
political events, and estate and legal business; letter
books 1744-5, 1791-2 (2 vols); notebooks 1754-9,
1791-1804 (5 vols); travel journal 1791-8 (1 vol).
Scottish Record Office (GD 267). Deposited by Mrs
JW Home-Robertson 1971. NRA 11620.

[319] **HOME DRUMMOND, Henry** (1783-1867)

MP Stirlingshire 1821-31, Perthshire 1840-52

Political, patronage, business and family corresp
and misc papers 1797-1865 (*c*24 bundles, *c*20
items), incl letters from Sir Thomas Fremantle,
the 11th Earl of Kinnoull and Sir William Rae;
notes on education and on books read 1808-58 (8
vols).
Scottish Record Office (GD 24). Deposited by Major
JW Stirling Home Drummond Moray 1948, 1969.
NRA 29367.

[320] **HOPE, General Sir Alexander** (1769-1837)

MP Dumfries burghs 1796-1800, Linlithgowshire
1800-34

Political, military and diplomatic corresp and
papers 1791-1837, incl political corresp with the
4th Earl of Hopetoun 1805-20, the 1st Viscount
Melville 1801-9, William Pitt 1803-4, Sir Herbert

Taylor 1818-25, and others 1801-32 (*c*22 bundles),
corresp and papers rel to the Linlithgowshire
election 1812 (1 bundle), letters to him in support
of JT Hope's candidature for Haddingtonshire
1834 (1 bundle), political and private letter books
1806-9 (3 vols), political journal 1804 (1 bundle),
and notes for a parliamentary speech [1799?] (1
bundle).
Scottish Record Office (GD 364). Deposited by
Colonel AJG Hope 1979. NRA 10172.

Letters from Linlithgowshire freeholders 1805-8 (2
bundles), election corresp 1806-7, 1812 (3 bundles),
political and personal corresp 1805-18 (2 bundles),
lists of freeholders 1804-26 and minutes of elections
1806-7, among papers of his election agent James
Hope.
The Marquess of Linlithgow. Enquiries to NRA
(Scotland) (NRA(S) 0888). NRA 17684 (pp451-8).

See also *Diplomats*.

[321] **HOPE, George William** (1808-1863)

MP Weymouth and Melcombe Regis 1837-41,
Southampton 1842-7, New Windsor 1859-63;
under-secretary for war and the colonies 1841-6

Political, colonial and family corresp and papers
1825-63, incl corresp, speech notes, voters' lists,
accounts and printed papers rel to elections,
constituency business and patronage in Weymouth
1837-44 (17 vols and bundles), Southampton
1842-8 (34 vols and bundles), Portsmouth 1850 (1
bundle), Abingdon *c*1852 (1 bundle), Bridgnorth
1853 (2 bundles), Dover 1857-8 (3 bundles), New
Windsor 1859-63 (7 vols and bundles), and
Scotland 1835-61 (5 bundles), papers rel to the
Grammar Schools bill 1840 (5 bundles), corresp
and papers as under-secretary 1841-6 (*c*80 bundles),
and general political corresp and papers 1838-63
(16 bundles).
Scottish Record Office (GD 364). Deposited by
Colonel AJG Hope 1979. NRA 10172.

See also *Colonial Governors*.

[322] **HOPE, Henry Walter** (1839-1913)

Scottish politician

Political, local, estate and family corresp and papers
1844-1912, incl letters, memoranda, addresses,
draft speeches, etc rel to his proposed nomination
as Conservative candidate for Fife 1868 and to Fife
and Lothian elections *c*1863-1895 (*c*14 vols and
bundles), to his proposed candidature for Windsor
1874 (1 bundle), and to the National Union of
Conservative Associations for Scotland and the East
of Scotland Liberal-Unionist Association 1884-1901
(*c*5 bundles), and general political corresp
1864-1910 (*c*6 bundles).
Scottish Record Office (GD 364). Deposited by
Colonel AJG Hope 1979. NRA 10172.

[323] **HOPE, James** (1764-1847)

United Irishman

Memoranda, reminiscences and political reflections
*c*1840-6 (3 vols); misc corresp and papers (2
portfolios).
Trinity College Library, Dublin (MSS 7253/2-3,
7254-6). Presented by Professor TW Moody 1976.

[324] **HOPE, John Thomas** (1807-1835)

MP Gatton 1830-1, Okehampton 1831-2

Corresp, draft speeches, annotated lists of electors,
accounts, etc mainly rel to the Haddingtonshire
election 1834-5 (2 vols, 9 bundles); printed papers
rel to the Manchester election 1832 (3 bundles);
misc memoranda, notes, essays, etc nd, and
continental travel journal 1827-8 (2 bundles).
Scottish Record Office (GD 364, bundles 157-62,
164, 166, 262-3, 350-2, 741, printed vol 90).
Deposited by Colonel AJG Hope 1979. NRA
10172.

[325] **HOPE-JOHNSTONE** (formerly **HOPE**),
James (1741-1816), 3rd Earl of Hopetoun 1781

Scottish representative peer 1784-90, 1794-6

Political corresp and papers (*c*5 bundles), incl
papers rel to Linlithgowshire elections 1784,
1787-8, list of his supporters in the representative
peerage election 1784, letters from Lord Melville
1805-6. and letters from Linlithgowshire
freeholders 1807-24; personal corresp 1760-84,
1806 (*c*12 bundles); private vouchers 1765-6 (1
bundle).
The Marquess of Linlithgow. Enquiries to NRA
(Scotland) (NRA(S) 0888). NRA 17684.

Corresp and papers mainly rel to politics in
Dumfriesshire and representative peerage elections
1785-90 (3 bundles), incl a petition for reform of
the law governing the latter 1785; personal corresp
1782-90 (*c*7 bundles).
The Earl of Annandale. Enquiries to NRA
(Scotland) (NRA(S) 0393). NRA 12630.

[326] **HORNER, Francis** (1778-1817)

MP St Ives 1806-7, Wendover 1807-12, St Mawes
1813-17

On his death his papers passed to his brother
Leonard who returned some letters received by
Francis Horner to their authors, and obtained
letters written by him from their recipients
(*Memoirs and correspondence of Francis Horner MP
edited by his brother*, 2 vols, 1843, p vii).

Political, family and general corresp (incl many
original letters from him) with John Allen, HP
Brougham, Lord Grenville, Lord and Lady
Holland, Francis Jeffrey, James Loch, JA Murray,
Professor and Mrs Dugald Stewart and others
1795-1817 (7 vols); misc political anecdotes,
memoranda, etc 1804-11 (1 vol).

*British Library of Political and Economic Science,
London* (R(SR)1054). NRA 7527.

Corresp with TR Malthus, David Ricardo and
others, speeches, diary Oct-Nov 1816, notes rel to
political economy, etc 1794-1804 (10 vols) and
other papers.
Lord Lyell (Leonard Horner's eldest daughter
married Sir Charles Lyell, Bt). RP Sturges,
Economists' papers 1750-1950, 1975, p45.

Letters from Lady Holland 1810-17, mainly during
his residence abroad 1816-17 (49 items).
British Library (Add MS 51644 ff2-8, 12-16,
19-129). Probably returned by Leonard Horner in
1817. He returned to Sydney Smith the latter's
letters to Francis Horner, and Smith destroyed
them (Smith to Lady Holland 31 July 1817).

[327] **HORSMAN, Edward** (1807-1876)

MP Cockermouth 1836-52, Stroud 1853-68,
Liskeard 1869-76; chief secretary for Ireland 1855-7

Diary 1842-6 (1 vol).
West Yorkshire Archive Service, Leeds (Ramsden
Archives, box 72). Transferred from the
Cumberland and Carlisle Record Office 1965. NRA
7344.

Diary kept intermittently 1850-66 (1 vol); notes on
political and social questions nd (2 vols).
Buckinghamshire Record Office (D/RA
uncatalogued). Deposited 1962 by his great-nephew
Sir William Pennington-Ramsden, Bt. NRA 11704.

Political corresp 1840-62 (14 items).
In private possession. NRA 24077.

[328] **HOTHAM, General Beaumont** (1794-1870),
3rd Baron Hotham 1814

MP Leominster 1820-31, 1831-41, E Riding of
Yorkshire 1841-68

Corresp and press cuttings rel to E Riding elections
1839-68 (*c*120 items); general and estate corresp
1814-67 (8 bundles), incl some rel to Catholic
emancipation and elections; military papers
1853-68 (29 bundles), incl papers rel to the
reorganisation of the Indian army, mainly 1860 (12
bundles); misc corresp and papers 1829-70 (23
bundles).
Brynmor Jones Library, Hull University (DDHO 8).
Transferred in 1974 from the East Riding Record
Office, where they had been deposited by the 7th
Baron Hotham in 1954. NRA 5408.

[329] **HOWARD, Charles** (1746-1815), 11th Duke
of Norfolk 1786

MP Carlisle 1780-6; a lord of the Treasury 1783

Papers rel to Horsham elections and petitions
1790-1812, with deeds for burgage properties, case
papers, etc; corresp and papers rel to Leominster
elections 1784-96 (25 items); papers rel to the
Shoreham election 1807 (1 bundle); to Carlisle,
Horsham and Steyning elections 1789-1808 (2 vols,

*c*40 items); general and political corresp 1766-1815 (*c*300 items); corresp and papers rel to his dismissal as lord lieutenant of the West Riding 1798 (*c*30 items).
The Duke of Norfolk. Enquiries to the Librarian and Archivist, Arundel Castle, West Sussex BN18 9AB. *Arundel Castle archives: a catalogue*, ed FW Steer, i-iv, 1968-80, *passim*.

[330] **HOWARD, George James** (1843-1911), 9th Earl of Carlisle 1889

MP E Cumberland 1879-80, 1881-5

General corresp and related papers 1863-1911 (*c*5,625 items), incl letters from Sir Wilfrid Lawson (*c*32 items), and Sir William Lee-Warner (*c*26 items), and corresp rel to Cumberland constituencies 1881-1900 (*c*47 items), Yorkshire North Riding Liberal Association 1881-6 (*c*220 items), the Eastern Question Association 1876-7 (*c*187 items), temperance movement (*c*17 items), National Gallery (*c*196 items) and Tate Gallery (*c*76 items); family corresp 1879-1908, nd, incl letters from CWG Howard MP and CH Roberts MP (25 boxes); misc corresp nd (1 box); diaries 1860, 1901 (2 vols); notebooks 1861-82 (6 vols); bills and receipts for pictures purchased 1880-1911 (1 box); papers rel to executorships of Lord Taunton and Lady Wensleydale 1869-95 (1 box); sketch books and miscellanea nd.
In private possession. Enquiries to the Keeper of Archives, Castle Howard, York YO6 7DA. NRA 24681.

[331] **HOWARD, Philip Henry** (1801-1883)

MP Carlisle 1830-47, 1848-52

Personal and family corresp and papers, incl corresp rel to Carlisle elections, etc 1831-72 (2 bundles), parliamentary papers 1830-52 (17 items), and other misc political corresp and papers.
In private possession. NRA 7034.

[332] **HOWARD, Rosalind Frances** (1845-1921), Countess of Carlisle

Advocate of women's suffrage and temperance reform; president of the Women's Liberal Federation 1891-1901, 1906-14

Corresp, reports, notes, speeches, circulars, etc rel to the Women's Liberal Federation 1887-1920 (155 vols, bundles, etc); to Liberal politics in Cumberland, Northumberland and Yorkshire 1895-1910 (5 boxes); to the British Women's Temperance Association and other temperance organisations and campaigns 1882-1921 (164 bundles, files, etc); to trade unionism and unemployment 1890-1908 (5 boxes); to peace movements 1895-1916 (6 boxes) and to women's education 1895-1920 (5 boxes); personal corresp 1862-1918 (*c*2,115 items), incl letters from WS Blunt (*c*77 items); letters of congratulation and condolence, and related papers, 1860-1917 (17

boxes); family corresp (41 boxes); misc corresp (6 boxes); private letter books 1899-1921 (6 vols); diaries 1856-1902 and address book nd (31 vols); account books 1862-1915 (51 vols); misc personal, charitable and household corresp, papers, press cuttings and photographs 1864-1919 (*c*50 boxes, vols, bundles, etc).
In private possession. Enquiries to the Keeper of Archives, Castle Howard, York YO6 7DA. NRA 24681.

[333] **HOWELL, George** (1833-1910)

Secretary to the Reform League 1865-9 and to the parliamentary committee of the Trades Union Congress 1871-5; MP Bethnal Green (NE division) 1885-95

Letters from Edmond Beales, Henry Crompton, EC Jones, Arnold Morley, Samuel Morley, Walter Morrison, AJ Mundella, Samuel Plimsoll, George Smith and other politicians, trade unionists, social reformers, etc 1864-1910 (*c*1,600 items); letter books, incl drafts of speeches, reports and election addresses, 1865-79, 1883-4 (13 vols); diaries 1864-1908 (34 vols); printed election papers 1865-95 (1 vol, 2 files); corresp, minute books, financial papers, etc of the Reform League 1865-9 (16 vols, 6 files, 2 bundles), the International Working Men's Association 1866-9 (1 vol, 1 file) and the Beales National Testimonial Fund 1867-70 (1 vol); papers rel to the TUC and its parliamentary committee 1868-76 (1 vol, *c*8 bundles); minutes, reports, corresp, etc rel to the Plimsoll Seamen's Fund 1873-5 (1 vol, 44 items), the Crystal Palace Mansion House committee 1877 (1 vol) and the London School Board election committee 1879 (1 vol); printed papers rel to political agitation and parliamentary legislation concerning trade unions, the payment of MPs, eight hours' legislation, the land question, etc 1867-1909, nd (*c*130 bundles); autobiographical fragments 1896-1907 (6 vols); papers rel to his biography of Ernest Jones and other literary MSS.
Bishopsgate Institute, London. NRA 10204 (partial list).

[334] **HUGHES, William Bulkeley** (1797-1882)

MP Carnarvon boroughs 1837-59, 1865-82

Corresp rel to elections 1838-46, 1868-74 (1 bundle, 10 items); corresp and papers rel to the Carnarvonshire Liberal Registration Society 1869-73 (1 bundle); annotated electoral registers, Carnarvon boroughs 1838-41 (5 vols); canvass books, Carnarvon town 1841, 1859 (2 vols); misc bills and papers 1841-74 (5 bundles and items); papers rel to railway development *c*1840-50; family, personal and estate corresp 1789-1917.
University College of North Wales, Bangor (Plas Coch MSS). Deposited by Sir William Hughes-Hunter 1937 and CW Grove White 1952. NRA 8487.

[335] **HUME, Joseph** (1777-1855)

MP Weymouth and Melcombe Regis 1812,
Aberdeen burghs 1818-30, Middlesex 1830-7,
Kilkenny 1837-41, Montrose burghs 1842-55

His papers are reported to have been destroyed by
fire in 1860.

Letters to and from him on behalf of Jeremy
Bentham 1816, 1830 (7 items).
University College London (Bentham Papers).
Catalogue of the manuscripts of Jeremy Bentham, 2nd
edn 1962.

Letter from Richard Brash 1826 and letters from
Thomas Joplin 1824-32 (6 items).
London University Library (AL 12,64,66,67).
*Catalogue of the manuscripts and autograph letters in
the University Library*, 1921.

Letters to him from various correspondents
1814-31 (5 items); letters from him 1823-54 (30
items).
*Beinecke Library, Yale University, New Haven,
Connecticut* (Osborn Collection).

HUME, WWF, see Dick.

[336] **HUMPHREYS-OWEN** (formerly
HUMPHREYS), **Arthur Charles** (1836-1905)

MP Montgomeryshire 1894-1905

Letters from Lord Rendel rel to Liberal politics in
Wales, party organisation, electioneering,
agricultural questions, education and the
foundation of the University College of Wales, etc
1877-1905 (c850 items); general corresp 1863-1905
(c825 items), incl letters from AH Bright, CH
Tawney, HY Thompson, Sir George Trevelyan and
Sir George Young, rel to national and local politics,
parliamentary and local elections,
Montgomeryshire County Council business, family,
estate and business affairs; letters from him to his
wife rel to political, educational and family matters
1878-1905 (over 1,200 items); papers rel to
Montgomeryshire elections and County Council
c1888-1904.
National Library of Wales (Glansevern Collection).
Deposited by SPF Humphreys-Owen 1936, 1939,
and by Elizabeth Humphreys-Owen 1971. NRA
16469; *Annual report 1935-36* p52, *1939-40* pp34-5,
1970-71 p68.

Letters to him from politicians and others
1868-1905 (c150 items), incl AHD Acland
1891-1904, HM Butler 1898-1904 and Sir John
Gorst 1898-1904.
National Library of Wales. Deposited by the
Borough of Llanidloes 1962. *Annual report 1962-63*,
p58.

[337] **HUNT, Henry** (1773-1835)

MP Preston 1830-2

Corresp and papers 1760-1838 (102 items), incl
letters to him from Joseph Hume, the 11th Earl of
Pembroke, Sir Robert Wilson, Sir Charles Wolseley
and others 1801-31, letters from him to RA
Davenport 1804-34, and misc papers.
*Department of Special Collections, University of
Chicago Library, Illinois* (MS 563). Purchased from
a dealer 1928, formerly Phillipps MSS 23487,
23490. NRA 29425.

Papers rel to his business interests in France
1828-31 (3 vols), with other corresp and papers
c1816-1833 (1 vol).
James Stevens-Cox Esq. JC Belchem, '*Orator' Hunt*,
1985.

Letters from William Cobbett mainly rel to
agricultural matters c1812-29 (35 items).
Adelphi University Library, Garden City, New York.

Diary 1820-1.
Manchester Central Library. Formerly Phillipps MS
23461. NRA 13262.

[338] **HUNTER BLAIR** (formerly **HUNTER**),
Sir James (1741-1787), 1st Bt

MP Edinburgh 1781-4

Letters to him from various correspondents
1761-86 (c26 bundles), many rel to politics and incl
some from Henry Dundas; family and misc corresp
1761-86 (4 bundles, c30 items).
Sir Edward Hunter-Blair,Bt. Enquiries to NRA
(Scotland). NRA 7868.

[339] **HYETT** (formerly **ADAMS**), **William
Henry** (1795-1877)

MP Stroud 1832-5

Political corresp 1831-8 (94 items), mainly with
Gloucestershire politicians, agents and supporters;
committee minutes, addresses, bills and other
election papers, Stroud 1831-2 (5 vols, 85 items);
misc political papers 1823-35 (14 items); corresp
and papers mainly rel to local affairs 1813-77 (1
vol, 120 items); corresp, notes and journals while
travelling in Europe 1815-20, 1825-6 (5 vols, 122
items); literary, scientific and horticultural corresp
and papers c1820-76 (20 vols, 8 bundles, 32 items);
corresp with his sons and rel to their education
1837-68 (189 items); family corresp c1814-76 (1
bundle, loose items); copies of estate corresp from
1836 (1 vol).
Gloucestershire Record Office (D 6). Presented by
Sir Francis Hyett and Misses ME and LC Hyett
1936-59; additional papers acquired 1985. NRA
4506.

[340] **INGLIS, Sir Robert Harry** (1786-1855), 2nd Bt

MP Dundalk 1824-6, Ripon 1828-9, Oxford University 1829-54

Corresp, journals and papers (some transcripts) 1798-1852, nd (3 boxes), incl parliamentary notebooks 1838-52 (9 vols), letters from Bishop Jebb 1817-27 and the Revd C Forster 1817-26, continental travel journals 1814-38, 1845 (20 vols), memoranda rel to Scottish and continental tours 1805, 1836, nd, account books 1838 (3 vols), and historical and literary notebooks nd (3 vols).
Canterbury Cathedral Library (Howley-Harrison Library, MSS 1805-44). Deposited 1887 by Mrs Benjamin Harrison, formerly Inglis's ward.

[341] **JAMES, Walter Charles** (1816-1893), 1st Baron Northbourne 1884

MP Hull 1837-47

Letters to him and his family from WE Gladstone 1846-93 (1 vol); letters to him and his wife from his stepfather Lord Hardinge 1844-7 (162 items); corresp with John Ruskin 1851 (1 vol); corresp rel to his peerage 1884 (1 vol); misc family corresp and papers 1786-1921, incl letters to him from politicians, churchmen and artists (5 vols, 8 items); recollections of Gladstone and Sir Robert Peel, and other political notes 1883-7 (4 items); sketch books, scrapbooks, photographs, etc.
In private possession. NRA 23887.

Diary 1851.
Lambeth Palace Library (MS 1771). Presented 1960.

[342] **JEFFREY, Francis** (1773-1850), Lord Jeffrey

MP Forfarshire burghs 1831, Malton 1831-2, Edinburgh 1832-5; lord advocate 1830-4

Letter books 1830-4 (3 vols); legal notebook nd (1 vol); diary 1827 (1 vol); travel journals 1800, 1823 (3 vols); verses c1800 (1 vol).
National Library of Scotland (Acc 3445). Purchased from Mrs EM Anstey 1963.

Letters from Francis Horner 1798-1816 (67 items).
British Library of Political and Economic Science, London (R(SR)1054). Returned after Horner's death in 1817. NRA 7527.

Letters from Lord Cockburn 1827-46 (42 items).
National Library of Scotland (Dep 235). Deposited amoung Cockburn's papers by Mrs FB Cockburn 1975. NRA 25498.

Case notes 1821 (1 vol).
National Library of Scotland (Adv MS 24.3.18).

[343] **JENKINSON, Charles Cecil Cope** (1784-1851), 3rd Earl of Liverpool 1828

MP Sandwich 1807-12, Bridgnorth 1812-18, East Grinstead 1818-28; under-secretary for home affairs 1807-9, for the colonies 1809-10; lord steward 1841-6

Official and personal corresp with the 5th Duke of Dorset, the Duchess of Kent, Sir Robert Peel, the 6th Earl of Plymouth, Baron Stockmar, Lord Wellesley, the Duke of Wellington and others mainly 1825-51 (c365ff); official and other papers 1833-51 (158ff); memorandum book 1824-5; naval logbook 1795.
British Library (Add MSS 38190, 38195-6, 38303, 38372, 38381, 38475, 38477, 38479, 38576). Presented by his great-grandson HB Portman 1911-12.

Letters to him from members of the royal family, politicians and others c1800-51, among corresp and papers of the Jenkinsons and related families c1760-1878.
British Library (MS Loan 72). Deposited 1977. NRA 21672.

Corresp and papers as secretary of legation, Austria 1806-7 (1 file); letter books 1808-10 (4 vols); diary 1809 (1 vol); misc papers rel to the volunteer movement c1803-6 (2 files, 4 items).
National Library of Wales (Pitchford Hall MSS). Deposited by his great-grandson Sir Charles Grant.

Letters to him 1808-26 (18 items); Bridgnorth election accounts 1812; financial papers 1808-24 (48 items); memorandum of his dispute with Lord Verulam 1827-8.
Mrs Oliver Colthurst (step-granddaughter of Sir Charles Grant). NRA 9005 (nos 286,289,329,331, 446).

[344] **JOCELYN, Robert** (1788-1870), 3rd Earl of Roden 1820

MP co Louth 1806-7, 1810-20; treasurer of the Household 1812, vice-chamberlain 1812-21; a lord of the Bedchamber 1827-31

Political, religious and misc corresp with the 2nd Earl of Bandon, Lord Londonderry, Bishop Phillpotts, the Duke of Wellington and others 1820-47 (4 vols); letter book 1811-70 (1 vol); misc letters to him in an autograph collection (2 vols).
The Earl of Roden. Enquiries to the Public Record Office of Northern Ireland, which holds copies of the papers (MIC 147, T 2647). NRA 16147.

[345] **JOHNSTON, William** (1829-1902)

MP Belfast 1868-78, Belfast (S division) 1885-1902

Diaries 1847-8, 1850-71, 1873-1902 (54 vols), incl entries rel to national politics, local affairs, Orange lodge meetings, etc.
Public Record Office of Northern Ireland (D 880/2). Deposited by William Johnston 1957.

JOHNSTONE, see Pulteney, William.

[346] **JOLLIFFE, Hylton** (1773-1843)

MP Petersfield 1796-7, 1802-30, 1831-2, 1833-5

Petersfield election papers 1802-34 (3 vols, c10 bundles), incl corresp 1802, 1831-4, letter book 1830, reports of election proceedings 1820, 1830, 1831, poll books and voters lists 1832-3, election petition papers 1825, 1830-3 and bills 1812-18.
Somerset Record Office (DD/HY, boxes 17, 37). Deposited by the 5th Baron Hylton 1970. NRA 3945.

[347] **JOLLIFFE, William George Hylton** (1800-1876), 1st Baron Hylton 1866

MP Petersfield 1830-2, 1837-8, 1841-66; under-secretary for home affairs 1852; Conservative chief whip 1853-9; patronage secretary to the Treasury 1858-9

Letters from the 14th Earl of Derby 1846-66 (c110 items), and from Benjamin Disraeli 1848-68 (c90 items); political and general corresp, reports and misc papers 1840-76 (c2,650 items), mainly as chief whip, incl many letters from GA Hamilton, Sir John Pakington, Sir Philip Rose, Markham Spofforth, TE Taylor, SH Walpole and other politicians, whips and party managers, rel to constituency matters, elections, patronage, registration, etc; papers rel to bills, resolutions and speeches 1846-8 (26 items); corresp as under-secretary 1852 (59 items); papers rel to parliamentary reform 1859 (25 items); list of English boroughs with names of candidates and notes by him 1859 (1 vol); notes on English boroughs nd (1 vol); printed lists of MPs 1852, 1857 (4 vols); printed and lithographed whips (165 items); election addresses 1832-40; personal accounts 1821-48.
Somerset Record Office (DD/HY, boxes 12,18,24,37,45). Deposited by the 5th Baron Hylton 1970-1. NRA 3945.

[348] **JONES, Ernest Charles** (1819-1869)

Chartist

Corresp, family papers and business papers 1819-69 (1,708 items).
Rare Book and Manuscript Library, Columbia University, New York (ERA Seligman Collection).

Letters to him (8 items) and from him (23 items) 1840-69.
International Institute of Social History, Amsterdam.

Diaries 1839-47 (2 vols).
Manchester Central Library (MS 923.2.J18). NRA 13262.

Album of poems and drawings 1834-53.
British Library (Add MS 61971A-C). Purchased at Phillips's sale 1 Oct 1981, lot 268.

[349] **JONES, Leslie Grove** (1779-1839)

Stood for Marylebone 1832

Letter book 1830-2 and misc corresp and papers 1831-2 (35 items) rel to the Marylebone election of 1832 and other political matters.
Westminster City Libraries, Marylebone Local History Library (D/Jon). NRA 714.

[350] **KAY-SHUTTLEWORTH, Ughtred James** (1844-1939), 1st Baron Shuttleworth 1902

MP Hastings 1869-80, NE Lancashire (Clitheroe division) 1885-1902; under-secretary for India 1886; chancellor of the Duchy of Lancaster 1886; chairman of the public accounts committee 1888-92; secretary of the Admiralty 1892-5

Political, local and estate corresp and papers c1869-1939 (c8 boxes), incl corresp rel to India 1885-6 and with Lord Spencer rel to Ireland 1886, and papers rel to the Hastings election 1869, the Municipal Reform League 1886, the public accounts committee 1891, etc; family and misc papers (c4 boxes).
In private possession. NRA 19369.

[351] **KEITH-FALCONER, Algernon Hawkins Thomond** (1852-1930), 9th Earl of Kintore 1880

A lord in waiting 1885-6, 1895-1905

Corresp and papers rel to his election campaign at Chelsea 1879-80 (1 bundle); as a Conservative whip 1885-8 (4 bundles); as governor of South Australia 1889-95 (9 vols, 1 bundle); letters from the royal family 1897-1918 and from the King's private secretary 1903-10 (2 bundles); misc legal, estate and genealogical corresp and papers 1888-c1922.
Aberdeen University Library (MSS 3064, 3161). Deposited by the 13th Earl of Kintore 1980, 1984. NRA 10210.

[352] **KENNEDY, Thomas Francis** (1788-1879)

MP Ayr burghs 1818-34; clerk of the Ordnance 1832-3

Corresp with Lord Dunfermline 1812-50.
In private possession. Enquiries to NRA (Scotland) (NRA(S) 0136). NRA 10208.

[353] **KENYON, Lloyd** (1732-1802), 1st Baron Kenyon 1788

MP Hindon 1780-4, Tregony 1784-8; attorney-general 1782-3, 1783-4; chief justice of the King's Bench 1788-1802

Political, legal and family corresp 1754-1802 (c1,700 items), incl letters from Sir Richard Arden, CJ Fox, Thomas Pennant, William Pitt, the Duke of Richmond, Lord Rockingham, Lord Thurlow and William Wilberforce; diaries 1767-1802 (36 vols); bench notes 1780-1801 (26 vols); case papers (22 boxes); precedent books (7 vols); account books 1750-9, 1772-1802 (9 vols).

Lord Kenyon. A small part of the correspondence is calendared in HMC *Fourteenth Report App IV, Manuscripts of Lord Kenyon,* 1894.

Misc corresp, legal notes, etc 1749-1800 (*c*22 items). *Colonel JF Kenyon.* NRA 29405 (Scrapbook 1).

[354] **KING, George** (1771-1839), 3rd Earl of Kingston 1799

MP co Roscommon 1797-9; Irish representative peer 1807-39

Political and patronage corresp 1808-30 (2 bundles, 98 items), incl letters from Henry Goulburn, the 2nd Viscount Melville and Lord Redesdale. *Doncaster Archives Department* (DD DC/P2). Deposited by Captain PP Davies-Cooke, a descendant of his elder daughter, 1980.

Letters mainly from politicians rel to patronage 1819-39 (13 items). *Clwyd Record Office, Hawarden* (D/GW/B/1134-44, 1146, 1148). Deposited by Captain PP Davies-Cooke 1981. NRA 17586.

[355] **KINLOCH, George** (1775-1833)

MP Dundee 1832-3

Personal and family corresp and papers 1775-1833 (15 folders), incl corresp with John Cartwright, William Cobbett and Henry Hunt rel to the Hampden Clubs and Peterloo 1815-19 (1 folder), letters rel to his pardon for sedition 1821-3 (2 folders), and corresp and papers as MP 1833 (1 folder). *Sir John Kinloch, Bt.* Enquiries to NRA (Scotland) (NRA(S) 0551). NRA 14800.

[356] **KNATCHBULL-HUGESSEN** (formerly **KNATCHBULL**), **Edward Hugessen** (1829-1893), 1st Baron Brabourne 1880

MP Sandwich 1857-80; a lord of the Treasury 1859-66; under-secretary for home affairs 1866, 1868-71, for the colonies 1871-4

Corresp with WE Gladstone 1860-82 (14 items); letters from Lord Salisbury 1874-90 (14 items); from politicians, churchmen and others 1832-88 (1 vol); misc corresp and copies of corresp 1849-74 (14 items); scrapbooks 1843-92 (6 vols), incl election corresp and political papers; political journal 1857-90 (12 vols); political anecdotes 1858-81 (1 vol); diaries 1849-93 (45 vols); travel journals 1851, 1887-8 (2 vols); misc papers 1854, 1893 (6 items). *Kent Archives Office* (U 951, U 1963). Deposited by the 7th Baron Brabourne 1962, 1982. NRA 1301.

[357] **LAMB** (formerly **BURGES**), **Sir James Bland** (1752-1824), 1st Bt

MP Helston 1787-90; under-secretary for foreign affairs 1789-95

Corresp as under-secretary 1789-95 (20 vols), mainly with British diplomats and agents; general corresp 1773-1824 (11 vols), incl letters from JW Croker, Sir William Dolben, Sir William Scott and Lord Thurlow; family corresp 1772-1824 (16 vols); list of letters received 1788-94 (1 vol); originals and copies of official papers rel to foreign affairs mainly 1789-95 (23 vols); personal and literary papers 18th-19th cent (10 vols), incl an account of political events in December 1783, and drafts of memoirs. *Bodleian Library, Oxford* (MS Dep. Bland Burges 2-80). Deposited 1958 by Mrs M Morris Davies, a descendant of his sister Frances. NRA 19920.

Letters from Sir William Hamilton 1774-98 (14 items). *Fitzwilliam Museum, Cambridge.* Bequeathed by SG Perceval 1922.

[358] **LANGHAM, Sir William** (1771-1812), 8th Bt

Stood for Northamptonshire 1806

Corresp rel to his canvass 1806 (*c*80 items); poll book, election papers and pamphlets, mainly printed, 1806 (10 vols, folders and bundles); papers rel to the Cottesbrooke Volunteers 1797-1814 (1 roll, 7 items); accounts 1788-1812 (3 vols, 2 items). *Northamptonshire Record Office* (L(C)105-30). Deposited 1972. NRA 5973.

[359] **LASCELLES, Henry** (1767-1841), 2nd Earl of Harewood 1820

MP Yorkshire 1796-1806, 1812-18, Westbury 1807-12, Northallerton 1818-20

Corresp and papers mainly rel to elections for Yorkshire 1796-1818, Pontefract 1811-13 and Northallerton 1812 (6 boxes); corresp and papers as lord lieutenant of the West Riding 1819-56 (2 boxes); accounts 1804-41 (*c*3 bundles). *West Yorkshire Archive Service, Leeds* (Harewood Archives). Deposited by the 7th Earl of Harewood 1963. NRA 24610.

[360] **LAURIE** (formerly **FECTOR**), **John Minet** (1812-1868)

MP Dover 1835-7, Maidstone 1838-41

Political corresp 1834-40 (3 bundles), some rel to the Carlist war in Spain; misc political papers 1818-57 (1 bundle); misc corresp 1812-40 (*c*6 items), mainly letters from his father; journal of Scottish tour 1827; misc papers 1828, 1852 (2 items). *Sir Bayley Laurie, Bt.* NRA 5405.

[361] **LAYARD, Sir Austen Henry** (1817-1894)

MP Aylesbury 1852-7, Southwark 1860-9; under-secretary for foreign affairs 1852, 1861-6; first commissioner of Works 1868-9

Political corresp rel to Spain and Turkey 1857-85 (6 vols); corresp as under-secretary 1861-6 (20 vols); papers as an MP and as first commissioner of Works 1849-69 (1 vol); memoirs 1817-47, 1869-80 (8 vols); other diplomatic, archaeological and literary papers 1829-94 (99 vols).
British Library (Add MSS 38931-39164). Bequeathed by his widow 1912.

Corresp and papers 1828-1911 (38 vols), incl diary 1854 (1 vol) and accounts 1833-9, 1877-83 (5 vols).
British Library (Add MSS 58149-53, 58159-72, 58174-96). Presented by his great-nephew Gordon Waterfield 1970.

See also *Diplomats*.

[362] **LEADER, John Temple** (1810-1903)

MP Bridgwater 1835-7, Westminster 1837-47

Personal and family corresp and papers 1764-1896 (175 items), incl letters and a memorandum from Lord Brougham rel to radical politics, the Canadian rebellion, etc 1838-44, nd (30 items).
House of Lords Record Office. Presented 1980 by his great-great-great-nephew, the 5th Baron Westbury.

[363] **LEE, John** (1733-1793)

MP Clitheroe 1782-90, Higham Ferrers 1790-3; solicitor-general 1782, 1783; attorney-general 1783

Political and general corresp 1769-93, nd (164 items), incl letters from Lord and Lady Rockingham 1772-91 (25 items); appointments, misc legal papers, etc 1769-85, nd (24 items).
Durham County Record Office (D/Bo/C 1-176, 253-64). Transferred from the Bowes Museum 1963. NRA 23425.

Political, social and family corresp of Lee and his wife 1763-1817 (203 items).
William L Clements Library, University of Michigan, Ann Arbor. Purchased 1932. *Guide to the manuscript collections*, 1978, p74.

[364] **LEE ANTONIE** (formerly **LEE**), **William** (1764-1815)

MP Great Marlow 1790-6, Bedford 1802-12

Letters to him rel to politics, local and personal affairs, etc 1792-1815, nd (170 items), incl letters from Samuel Whitbread 1796-1815 (86 items); letters from him to his lawyer Edward Arrowsmith, Whitbread and others 1786-1814 (102 items); personal and estate accounts and related papers 1771-1813 (c250 items); typescript copies of untraced original letters to him 1793-1815 (107 items).

Bedfordshire Record Office (BS 2093-2138; UN 193-285, 310-535, 558-70). Presented by AC Benedict Eyre 1959, and deposited by Unilever Research Laboratories 1962. NRA 7125.

[365] **LEGGE, George** (1755-1810), 3rd Earl of Dartmouth 1801

MP Plymouth 1778-80, Staffordshire 1780-4; president of the Board of Control 1801-2; lord steward 1802-4; lord chamberlain 1804-10

Corresp and papers rel to India mainly 1801-2 (c380 vols, bundles and items), incl letters from Henry Addington, Lord Clive, Henry Dundas, CF Greville, David Scott and Lord Wellesley; corresp and papers as lord steward and lord chamberlain 1802-10 (c165 bundles and items), incl corresp with the royal family, papers rel to theatres, and accounts 1804-8; corresp and papers as lord warden of the Stannaries 1783-98 (22 bundles and items); general corresp 1771-1810 (c160 items); diary 1801-10 (1 vol), incl detailed entries rel to Board of Control business; sketches and drawings 1763-73 (1 vol); receipt book 1782-6 (1 vol); misc papers 1783-1809 (c70 bundles and items), mainly rel to philanthropy and Staffordshire affairs.
Staffordshire Record Office (D 742, 859, 1501, 1778). Deposited mainly by the 7th and 8th Earls of Dartmouth. NRA 5197; HMC *Eleventh Report App V* and *Fifteenth Report App I, Manuscripts of the Earl of Dartmouth*, i, 1887, pp425-48, iii, 1896, pp223-93; HMC *Thirteenth Report App IV*, 1892, pp497-506.

Journal 1795-8, probably of the 3rd Earl of Dartmouth (1 vol).
Staffordshire Record Office (1548). Purchased c1981. NRA 3515.

[366] **LEGH, George Cornwall** (1804-1877)

MP N Cheshire 1841-7, 1848-68, Mid Cheshire 1868-73

Journals and diaries (38 vols); personal account books (25 vols); sketch books and notebooks (20 vols); estate and business corresp and papers (4 bundles).
John Rylands University Library of Manchester (Cornwall-Legh Muniments). Deposited by CLS Cornwall-Legh 1951. NRA 604.

[367] **LEITH HAY, Sir Andrew** (1785-1862)

MP Elgin burghs 1832-8, 1841-7; clerk of the Ordnance 1834, 1835-8

Political, military, financial and other corresp and papers 1808-62 (c16 vols and bundles), incl political corresp c1831-57, diaries containing notes of parliamentary business 1833, 1835, misc Ordnance Board papers 1831, 1836-7, and papers rel to his *Narrative of the Peninsular War* (1831).
Scottish Record Office (GD 225). Deposited by the National Trust for Scotland 1967. NRA 10212.

[368] **LE MARCHANT, Sir Denis** (1795-1874), 1st Bt

Private secretary to Lord Brougham 1830-4; permanent secretary to the Board of Trade 1836-41, 1848-50; joint secretary to the Treasury 1841; MP Worcester 1846-7; under-secretary for home affairs 1847-8

Corresp and papers, incl letters from Thomas Barnes, Lord Brougham and the 3rd Earl Spencer, and journal 1830-4.
In private possession. Access through the Historical Manuscripts Commission.

Corresp with members of the Baring family 1820-30 (1 parcel).
Baring Brothers and Co Ltd (DEP 193.51). Presented by Sir Edward Le Marchant, Bt. Enquiries to the Archivist, Baring Brothers & Co Ltd, 8 Bishopsgate, London EC2N 4AE. NRA 30566.

[369] **LENNOX, General Charles** (1764-1819), 4th Duke of Richmond 1806

MP Chichester 1790-1806; lord lieutenant of Ireland 1807-13

Corresp and papers as lord lieutenant (14 vols, 6 bundles), comprising letter books and index 1807-8 (3 vols), copies of letters sent, with a few received, 1807-13 (3 vols), audience books and indexes 1808-13 (11 vols), addresses, memorials and petitions to him 1807-13 (2 bundles), and misc papers 1807-10 (1 bundle); corresp and papers as colonel of the 35th Regiment 1805-6 (1 bundle).
Kent Archives Office (U 269/O 213-16). Deposited among the papers of Lord Whitworth by the 4th Baron Sackville 1950. NRA 8575.

Corresp with politicians and others mainly rel to British politics and Irish administration 1794-1818 (1,930 items).
National Library of Ireland (MSS 58-75A). Purchased 1930. *Manuscript sources for the history of Irish civilisation*, ed RJ Hayes, 1965, iv, 231.

See also *Colonial Governors.*

LEVESON-GOWER, Francis, see Egerton.

[370] **LEVESON-GOWER, George Granville** (1758-1833), 2nd Marquess of Stafford 1803, 1st Duke of Sutherland 1833

MP Newcastle-under-Lyme 1779-84, Staffordshire 1787-99; joint postmaster-general 1799-1801

Corresp with Lord Grenville, Thomas Grenville, William Pitt and other politicians and public figures 1785-1826 (c80 items); patronage corresp 1814-29 (1 bundle); letters from James Loch rel to estates in Sutherland 1816-32 (1 bundle); bank books 1792-1834 (8 vols).

Staffordshire Record Office (D 593/P/18, 34; D 868/11). Deposited by the trustees of the will of the 4th Duke of Sutherland 1959, 1966. NRA 10699.

Letters from his wife 1805-20 (1 box) and from James Loch 1813-33 (2 boxes); corresp and papers rel to the Sutherland militia and volunteers 1794-1813 (3 boxes, 1 vol); misc corresp, accounts and papers 1787-1833 (1 box).
National Library of Scotland (Dep 313). Deposited by the Countess of Sutherland 1980. NRA 11006.

[371] **LEVY, Joseph Moses** (1811-1888)

Proprietor of the *Daily Telegraph* 1855-88

Corresp 1855-88 (1 box), mainly rel to political and theatrical matters, incl letters from the 15th Earl of Derby, WE Gladstone and Lord Granville; misc corresp and photographs c1860-70 (1 vol); press cuttings 1877-9, 1888 (2 vols).
Lord Burnham (his great-great-grandson). Access through the Historical Manuscripts Commission. NRA 29865.

[372] **LEWIS, Sir John Herbert** (1858-1933)

MP Flint boroughs 1892-1906, Flintshire 1906-18, University of Wales 1918-22; secretary to the Local Government Board 1909-15, to the Board of Education 1915-22

Political, personal and family corresp and papers 1884-1933 (13 boxes, 10 vols, 2 files), incl letters from David Lloyd George 1891-1907 (101 items) and Lord Rendel 1889-1912 (c50 items), corresp and papers rel to Welsh home rule 1885-1922 (3 bundles), the National Council of Wales and the North and South Wales Liberal Federations 1887-97 (2 bundles, c45 items) and the Welsh Parliamentary Party mainly 1890-6 (3 files, c35 items), draft and printed election addresses with related corresp 1891-1910 (1 file), circulars from Liberal whips and party leaders 1893-1917 (1 bundle), parliamentary reminiscences 1892-5 (1 file), and diaries, travel journals and notebooks 1884-1907 (c35 vols).
National Library of Wales (J Herbert Lewis Papers; NLW MSS 9494-5). Partly presented and partly deposited by his widow 1935-44 and his daughter Mrs K Idwal Jones 1960-78. NRA 16471 (partial list); NLW *Handlist of MSS,* III, p150, *Annual report 1960-1* p57, *1961-2* p29, *1974-5* pp70-1, *1975-6* p79, *1976-7* p42, *1978-9* p48.

Political, personal and family papers 1864-1933 (9 boxes), incl election corresp and accounts, Flint boroughs 1892-1900 and Flintshire 1906 (30 items).
Clwyd Record Office, Hawarden (D/L, D/DM/53). Deposited by Mrs K Idwal Jones. *Guide to the Flintshire Record Office,* 1974, p89; Clwyd Record Office *Annual report 1976* p28, *1978* p31.

[373] **LEWIS, Sir Thomas Frankland**
(1780-1855), 1st Bt

MP Beaumaris 1812-26, Ennis 1826-8, Radnorshire
1828-34, New Radnor boroughs 1847-55; joint
secretary to the Treasury 1827-8; vice-president of
the Board of Trade 1828; treasurer of the Navy
1830

Corresp rel to Welsh elections, parliamentary
affairs, the poor law commission, family affairs,
etc 1801-55 (c225 items); election papers 1813-52
(c22 items); papers as treasurer of the Navy and
privy councillor 1830-2 (7 items); anecdotes of the
Duke of Wellington c1852 (1 item); notes on his
parliamentary career 1854 (1 bundle); papers rel to
Radnorshire affairs 1803-55 (c10 items); diaries
1827, 1841 (2 vols); travel journals and notes 1801,
1841 (3 vols); misc accounts and papers c1803-46
(c16 items).
National Library of Wales (Harpton Court MSS).
Deposited by Sir Douglas Duff Gordon, Bt 1952-3.
NRA 22798.

[374] **LIEVEN, Princess Dorothea
Christoforovna** (1784-1857)

Political hostess

Corresp with members of the British, Russian and
other royal families 1799-1856 (16 vols); with
politicians and diplomats, incl Lords Aberdeen,
Brougham, Grey and Palmerston, c1817-56 (18
vols); with Lady Palmerston c1826-54 (2 vols);
general corresp 1799-1857 (5 vols); family corresp,
incl letters from her husband (c27 vols);
memoranda, diaries, notes and commonplace books
(16 vols).
British Library (Add MSS 47341-408, 47412-19,
58121-3). Purchased 1938, and at Sotheby's 12
March 1974, lot 223.

Corresp with Lord Grey 1823-41 (10 vols).
Staffordshire Record Office (D 593/P/22/5).
Entrusted by her to the 2nd Duke of Sutherland
and deposited in 1959 by the trustees of the will
of the 4th Duke of Sutherland. NRA 10699.

[375] **LINDSAY, Lieutenant-General James**
(1793-1855)

MP Wigan 1825-31, Fife 1831-2

Corresp and papers rel to Fife elections 1831-5 (765
items); to local affairs in Fife 1831-55 (375 items);
to Wigan affairs 1829-36 (35 items); family and
personal corresp and papers 1808-55 (2,700 items);
letter book 1821-31; military papers, travel journals
and notebooks 1808-55 (12 vols); business, legal
and estate corresp and papers 1821-55.
National Library of Scotland (Crawford Muniments
40). Transferred from the John Rylands University
Library of Manchester 1988. *Hand-list of personal
papers from the muniments of the Earl of Crawford
and Balcarres*, 1976, pp67-76.

LINDSAY, RJ, see Loyd-Lindsay.

[376] **LINDSAY, William Schaw** (1816-1877)

MP Tynemouth and North Shields 1854-9,
Sunderland 1859-65

Political, business, maritime, literary and other
corresp mainly c1855-77 (c2,000 items), incl letters
from John Bright, Benjamin Disraeli (12 items),
WE Gladstone and Joseph Hume; corresp and
papers rel to the United States c1860-7 (2 vols);
memoirs (11 vols), with related letters and press
cuttings (2 vols); MS of *History of merchant shipping
and ancient commerce* (1874-6) and related papers
(1 box); MS autobiography, other literary MSS,
account books, legal papers, etc.
Untraced. Sold at Sotheby's 21 July 1988, lot 391.

Letters from Richard Cobden 1854-62 (3 vols).
West Sussex Record Office (Cobden Papers 121-3).
Deposited by the governors of Dunford College
1961-4. *The Cobden papers: a catalogue*, 1964,
pp19-20.

[377] **LINTON, William James** (1812-1898)

Political reformer

Letters to him from about 140 correspondents;
letters from him 1849-96; notebooks, journals and
literary MSS.
*Beinecke Library, Yale University, New Haven,
Connecticut* (General Collection: MS Vault Shelves,
Linton).

Personal and political corresp (c400 items), incl
corresp with WB Adams, Alexander Herzen,
Guiseppe Mazzini and other European nationalists;
minutes of the provisional committee 1847 and
council 1847-8 of the People's International
League.
Feltrinelli Foundation, Milan. NRA 20471.

[378] **LISTER, Thomas** (1752-1826), 1st Baron
Ribblesdale 1797

MP Clitheroe 1773-90

Political corresp and papers mainly rel to Clitheroe
1729-1807 (1 box), incl corresp rel to the Clitheroe
election 1784 and to the Yorkshire election 1806;
misc political and other corresp and papers
1776-1826 (c10 boxes).
Yorkshire Archaeological Society, Leeds (MD 335).

[379] **LITTLETON** (formerly **WALHOUSE**),
Edward John (1791-1863), 1st Baron Hatherton
1835

MP Staffordshire 1812-32, S Staffordshire 1832-5;
chief secretary for Ireland 1833-4

Letters received as chief secretary 1833-4 (10 vols);
letter books 1833-4 (4 vols); Irish papers arranged
by subject mainly 1833-5 (c2,870 items), incl tithes,
church revenues and education; papers given to

him by Lord Anglesey on his appointment 1833 (1 vol); notes about Ireland 1834-7 (1 vol); chief secretary's audience book 1830-4 and engagement book 1834 (2 vols); corresp rel to Staffordshire elections 1812-54 (3 vols, 1 bundle); political scrapbook 1817-20 (1 vol) and notebooks *c*1817-19, 1850 (2 vols); papers as lord lieutenant of Staffordshire 1854-61 (*c*51 bundles); general and family corresp 1812-62 (57 vols, *c*5 bundles); journals, with indexes and extracts, 1817-62 (97 vols); draft memoirs written *c*1850; trusteeship and other financial papers.
Staffordshire Record Office (D 260, 1121, 1178, 4028). Deposited by the 5th Baron Hatherton and his executors 1953-83. NRA 4022.

[380] LLOYD, Thomas Edward (1820-1909)

MP Cardiganshire 1874-80

Papers rel to Cardiganshire election expenses 1874 (1 vol, 5 bundles, 48 items); misc political and patronage corresp and papers 1874-80 (*c*65 items); personal account books 1865-1906 (6 vols); misc legal, financial, estate and personal corresp and papers *c*1824-1909 (*c*1,500 items).
Carmarthenshire Area Record Office (Coedmor Collection). Deposited by EH Lloyd and EDM Lloyd. NRA 25681.

[381] LLOYD GEORGE, David (1863-1945), 1st Earl Lloyd George 1945

MP Carnarvon boroughs 1890-1945; president of the Board of Trade 1905-8; chancellor of the Exchequer 1908-15; minister of munitions 1915-16; secretary for war 1916; prime minister 1916-22

Political and misc personal corresp and papers 1882-1945 (1,054 boxes, 88 vols), incl papers rel to his early political career to 1905, mainly speeches and papers about social, economic and political questions (13 boxes).
House of Lords Record Office (Historical Collection 192). Deposited by the Beaverbrook Foundation 1975, 1978. NRA 15700; *Guide to historical collections*, 1978, p7.

Corresp and papers, with those of his family, *c*1885-1965 (1 box, 90 vols), incl letters and telegrams to him from politicans and other public figures 1890-1940 (2 vols), letters to his first wife 1886-1936 (40 vols), diaries 1887, 1889 (2 vols), and speech notes 1885-1931 (9 vols); corresp and papers mainly rel to Welsh affairs 1898-1919 (*c*200 items); additional corresp, speech notes, etc mainly 1908-20 (over 1,050 items).
National Library of Wales (MSS 20403-93, 21787-92, and uncatalogued). Purchased 1969, 1982, 1986. NRA 28941 (partial list); *Annual report 1981-2* p63, *1986-7* p64.

Political and business letter book 1891-8 (1 vol).
National Library of Wales. Presented by Mrs Mari Ellis 1980. *Annual report 1979-80* p47.

Papers 1914-32 (1 foot).
Public Record Office (MUN 9). Acquired 1975.

Early corresp and diaries.
In private possession. Not available for research in 1987.

Letters and notes from Winston Churchill 1907-32 (19 items).
Untraced. Sold at Sotheby's 10 July 1986, lots 319-37.

[382] LLOYD MOSTYN (formerly LLOYD), Edward Mostyn (1795-1884), 2nd Baron Mostyn 1854

MP Flintshire 1831-7, 1841-2, 1847-54, Lichfield 1846-7

Political and election corresp and papers 1831-61 (over 500 items), mainly rel to Flintshire.
University College of North Wales, Bangor (Mostyn Collection 7845-8448 *passim*). Deposited by the 4th Baron Mostyn 1962. NRA 22953.

[383] LOCH, James (1780-1855)

MP St Germans 1827-30, Tain burghs 1830-52

Corresp and papers (*c*163 bundles), mainly rel to estate management but incl letters from Lord Brougham and a copy of his diary 1808-23 (1 vol).
Scottish Record Office (GD 268). Deposited by the Hon SD Loch 1971-9.

Letters to him and his family from politicians and others 1807-53 (1 bundle).
Scottish Record Office (GD 2/117). Deposited by the British Records Association. NRA 21901.

Personal and family corresp 1803-65 (212 items), mainly rel to University College London and the Society for the Diffusion of Useful Knowledge.
University College London (MS Add 131). Presented by the Hon SD Loch 1971. NRA 18113.

Letters from Francis Horner 1800-10 (31 items).
British Library of Political and Economic Science, London (R(SR)1054). Returned after Horner's death in 1817. NRA 7527.

Letters from HP Brougham 1809, 1825-9 (17 items).
University College London (Brougham Papers). NRA 31344.

[384] LOCKHART ROSS, Lieutenant-General Sir Charles (1763-1814), 7th Bt

MP Tain burghs 1786-96, Ross-shire 1796-1806, Linlithgow burghs 1806-7

Personal, family and estate corresp and papers, incl corresp and papers rel to Lanarkshire and Ross-shire politics 1789-1813 (*c*8 bundles) and to military affairs 1804-13 (1 vol, 5 bundles).
Scottish Record Office (GD 129). Deposited 1970, 1982. NRA 10533.

[385] **LONG, Richard Penruddocke** (1825-1875)

MP Chippenham 1859-65, N Wiltshire 1865-8

Election addresses and accounts, Chippenham 1859
(1 bundle); letters rel to the N Wiltshire election
1865 (c100 items); family corresp 1851-70 (3
bundles), incl corresp with his father rel to N
Wiltshire politics c1859-66; personal and household
vouchers 1853-6, 1866-73.
Wiltshire Record Office (WRO 2016). Deposited by
Williams & James, solicitors, 1983, 1985.

Misc corresp 1852-75 (12 items), incl four letters
from Lord Derby 1855, 1862.
British Library (Add MS 62443). Purchased among
papers of the 1st Viscount Long at Sotheby's 20
July 1981, lot 141.

[386] **LONG, Walter** (1793-1867)

MP N Wiltshire 1835-65

Corresp and papers rel to N Wiltshire elections
1834-41, 1851-66 (2 bundles); family corresp
1840-66 (4 bundles), incl corresp with JC
Colquhoun and RP Long rel to Wiltshire politics
c1859-66; personal and household vouchers 1821-3,
1842-4, 1856-67 (several hundred items).
Wiltshire Record Office (WRO 2016). Deposited by
Williams & James, solicitors, 1985.

Misc letters, speech notes, etc 1821-66 (c36 items),
incl a few letters rel to the 1852 election.
British Library (Add MS 62443). Purchased among
papers of the 1st Viscount Long at Sotheby's 20
July 1981, lot 141.

[387] **LOVEDEN** (formerly **TOWNSEND**),
Edward Loveden (c1751-1822)

MP Abingdon 1783-96, Shaftesbury 1802-12

Abingdon election accounts 1784-5, corresp 1789
(1 bundle) and list of voters 1802; Shaftesbury poll
books 1802, 1806, 1807 (2 vols); misc corresp and
papers 1777-1822 (2 bundles, 1 item).
Berkshire Record Office (Acc 633). Deposited by
Sir Pryse Saunders-Pryse, Bt 1954.

Political corresp with Lord Rawdon and others
mainly 1788-96 (c24 items); misc corresp
c1795-c1820 (c5 bundles); Breconshire freeholders'
book 1799 (1 vol); papers rel to his divorce 1809
(2 bundles).
National Library of Wales (Gogerddan MSS).
Deposited by Sir Pryse Saunders-Pryse, Bt 1949.

LOVEDEN, Pryse (1774-1849), see Pryse.

[388] **LOVEDEN** (formerly **PRYSE**), **Pryse**
(1815-1855)

MP Cardigan boroughs 1849-55

Corresp, bills, accounts, etc, Cardigan boroughs
elections 1849-53 (c5 vols and bundles).
National Library of Wales (Gogerddan MSS).
Deposited by Sir Pryse Saunders-Pryse, Bt 1949.

[389] **LOVETT, William** (1800-1877)

Chartist

Corresp and papers, mainly printed, rel to the
Working Men's Association, the Complete Suffrage
Union and the People's League c1836-50 (2 boxes),
incl misc original corresp (c20 items).
Birmingham Central Libraries Archives Department
(Lovett Collection).

Corresp and papers as secretary of the 'General
Convention of the Industrial Classes' 1839 (2 vols).
British Library (Add MS 34245A,B). Presented by
EA Parry 1892.

Minutes of the Working Men's Association, mainly
compiled by him as secretary, 1836-49 (4 vols).
British Library (Add MSS 37773-6). Presented 1909
by MH Truelove, whose father had acquired them
from Lovett.

[390] **LOWRY-CORRY, Montagu William**
(1838-1903), Baron Rowton 1880

Private secretary to Benjamin Disraeli 1866-81

Letters from Disraeli 1866-81 (415 items); personal
and official corresp and papers 1866-72 (309 items);
misc corresp and papers intermingled with those
of Disraeli.
Bodleian Library, Oxford (MS Disraeli dep).
Deposited by the National Trust 1978. NRA 842.

Corresp with Disraeli, Queen Victoria and others
(several bundles).
Prince Rupert Loewenstein (son-in-law of Rowton's
great-nephew MW Lowry-Corry).

Family corresp and papers c1877-1916, incl letters
to him from his sister Alice (c50 items).
Bodleian Library, Oxford. Presented 1987 by his
great-great-nephew RA Salisbury-Jones. NRA
20352.

[391] **LOWRY-CORRY, Somerset** (1774-1841),
2nd Earl Belmore 1802

MP co Tyrone 1797-1800, 1801-2; Irish
representative peer 1819-41

Political corresp and papers 1800-38 (6 bundles),
incl corresp rel to co Fermanagh and co Tyrone
elections, and corresp of the 2nd Earl of Enniskillen
as his representative rel to local politics and his
election to the representative peerage 1819-37 (76
items); corresp and papers as governor of Jamaica
1828-32 (52 bundles), incl papers rel to the
vindication of his conduct in the House of Lords,
etc 1832-3 (3 bundles); estate, financial and misc
corresp 1799-c1841 (8 bundles).
Public Record Office of Northern Ireland (D 3007/
G-H). Deposited by the 8th Earl Belmore 1974.
NRA 18797.

See also *Colonial Governors*.

[392] **LOWRY-CORRY, Somerset Richard**
(1835-1913), 4th Earl Belmore 1845

Irish representative peer 1857-1913; under-secretary for home affairs 1866-7

Corresp, journal and day book as under-secretary 1866-7 (2 vols, 93 items); corresp and papers rel to representative peerage elections 1856-c1904 (140 items); to co Tyrone elections and local government 1856-1905 (3 vols, 1,608 items); to general political and patronage matters 1855-1911 (613 items); to the Irish land question 1860-1903 (426 items); to education, mainly in Ireland, 1872-1904 (191 items); to the Church of Ireland 1872-1909 (549 items); corresp and papers as governor of New South Wales and related papers 1867-1904 (8 vols, 623 items); personal, family, estate, antiquarian, and other corresp and papers 1850-1913 (c15 vols, c6,300 items).
Public Record Office of Northern Ireland (D 3007/ J-X). Deposited by the 8th Earl Belmore 1974. NRA 18797.

See also *Colonial Governors*.

[393] **LOWTHER, James** (1736-1802), Earl of Lonsdale 1784

MP Cumberland 1757-61, 1762-8, 1774-84, Westmorland 1761-2, Cockermouth 1769-74; lord lieutenant of Westmorland 1758-1802, Cumberland 1759-1802

Political and general corresp 1751-c1802 (c13 bundles, 1 file), incl letters from CJ Fox, Lord North, William Pitt and the 3rd Duke of Portland; election papers for Appleby 1754 (7 boxes), Carlisle 1768-80, Cumberland 1768-80, Lancaster 1784-6 and Westmorland 1768-74; Cumberland and Westmorland land tax and freeholders' lists 1761-1825; files of 'stray letters', incl corresp rel to Lancaster elections 1784-90 (203 items); notes on public finance c1765 (1 vol) and misc parliamentary papers; Cumberland and Westmorland militia papers 1760-1808.
Cumbria Record Office, Carlisle (D/LONS/L). Deposited by the 7th Earl of Lonsdale 1963-75. NRA 17777; HMC *Thirteenth Report App VII, Manuscripts of the Earl of Lonsdale*, 1893, pp127-48.

[394] **LOWTHER, Sir John** (1759-1844), 1st Bt

MP Cockermouth 1780-6, Carlisle 1786, Haslemere 1786-90, Cumberland 1796-1831

Papers of him and his son JH Lowther rel to Cumberland, Lancashire, Westmorland and Yorkshire elections 1784-1835 (2 bundles, c240 items); general and family corresp 1779-1844 (31 bundles), incl letters from JH Lowther rel to parliamentary affairs 1834-7 (c40 items); account book 1792-4; corresp, journal and papers rel to the Grand Tour 1784-5 (1 vol, c40 items); misc corresp and papers (1 vol, c166 items).
Clwyd Record Office, Ruthin (DD/L). Deposited by Sir William Lowther, Bt 1976. NRA 19944.

[395] **LOWTHER, William** (1757-1844), 2nd Viscount Lowther 1802, 1st Earl of Lonsdale 1807

MP Carlisle 1780-4, Cumberland 1784-90, Rutland 1796-1802; lord lieutenant of Cumberland and Westmorland 1802-44

Political and general corresp 1770-1841 (c66 bundles), incl letters from Lords Bathurst and Camden, George Canning, JW Croker, Lords Eldon, Essex and Farnborough, the 2nd Earl of Liverpool, Lords Melville and Mulgrave, William Pitt, Lord Spencer and RP Ward; letters from his son Lord Lowther 1805-41 (31 bundles); corresp arranged by subject 1802-55 (17 bundles), incl civil disturbances 1819-20, 1830-1 (2 bundles) and the Westmorland election 1820 (3 bundles); files of 'stray letters', incl election corresp 1818-35; election papers for Appleby 1807 (3 boxes), Carlisle 1816, 1827, Cumberland 1826-41, and Westmorland 1818-41 (c13 boxes); Cumberland and Westmorland land tax and freeholders' lists 1761-1825; letters from his Whitehaven agents 1801-41 (29 bundles); bank books 1774-84, 1803-41 (11 vols).
Cumbria Record Office, Carlisle (D/LONS/L). Deposited by the 7th Earl of Lonsdale 1963-75. NRA 17777; HMC *Thirteenth Report App VII, Manuscripts of the Earl of Lonsdale*, 1893, pp146-244.

[396] **LOYD, Samuel Jones** (1796-1883), Baron Overstone 1850

MP Hythe 1819-26

Political, financial and personal corresp and papers 1804-83 (c2,300 items), incl corresp with GW Norman (over 350 items, mainly letters from Overstone), Robert Torrens 1847-63 (c80 items) and other economists and politicians.
London University Library (MS 804). Presented by CL Loyd 1972. NRA 17743 (partial list); DP O'Brien, *The correspondence of Lord Overstone*, 3 vols, 1971.

[397] **LOYD-LINDSAY** (formerly **LINDSAY**), **Robert James** (1832-1901), Baron Wantage 1885

MP Berkshire 1865-85; financial secretary to the War Office 1877-80

Corresp and papers.
National Library of Scotland (Crawford Muniments).

Corresp and papers of him and his wife rel to the British National Society for Aid to the Sick and Wounded in War 1870-1905 (c1,270 items).
British Red Cross Archives, Guildford (D/Wan). Presented by CL Loyd 1985. NRA 30569.

Letters from various correspondents 1871, 1878, 1882 (5 items).
London University Library (MS 804/1448, 1528, 1589-90). Presented by CL Loyd 1972 with the papers of Wantage's father-in-law Lord Overstone. NRA 17743.

[398] **LUBBOCK, John** (1834-1913), 1st Baron
Avebury 1900

MP Maidstone 1870-80, London University
1880-1900

General corresp 1855-1911 (39 vols); family and
political corresp 1870-1913 (3 vols), incl corresp
rel to his election 1870; corresp rel to his published
works (10 vols); diaries 1853-1913 (6 vols);
commonplace book 1850-84 (1 vol); notebooks
1875-99 (2 vols); illuminated addresses (3 items).
British Library (Add MSS 49638-81, 62679-89, Add
Ch 76145-7). Presented by Mrs Adelaide Lubbock
1958 and by the 4th Baron Avebury 1983.

Papers rel to shop hours and the early closing
movement 1886-1900 (3 vols, c70 items).
Warwick University Modern Records Centre (MSS
246). Deposited by the 4th Baron Avebury 1982.
NRA 25596.

Notebooks (25 vols).
Royal Society, London.

[399] **LUSHINGTON, Stephen** (1782-1873)

MP Great Yarmouth 1806-8, Ilchester 1820-6,
1831-2, Tregony 1826-30, Winchelsea 1831, Tower
Hamlets 1832-41

Political and family corresp c1830-73 (c260 items),
incl letters from Lord Brougham, Sir Francis
Burdett, the 3rd Baron Holland, Joseph Hume and
the 3rd Viscount Melbourne.
Untraced. Offered for sale at Sotheby's 10 July
1986, lot 80.

LUTTRELL, see Fownes Luttrell.

[400] **LYGON, Frederick** (1830-1891), 6th Earl
Beauchamp 1866

MP Tewkesbury 1857-63, W Worcestershire
1863-6; lord steward 1874-80; paymaster-general
1885-6, 1886-7

Corresp and papers.
In private possession. Not available for research.

Letters from Lord Beaconsfield to Beauchamp and
his brother the 5th Earl, with several letters from
Beauchamp to Beaconsfield, 1859-80 (1 vol).
British Library (Add MS 61892). Purchased at
Sotheby's 15 Dec 1980, lot 127.

LYON-BOWES, see Bowes-Lyon.

[401] **LYTTELTON, George William**
(1817-1876), 4th Baron Lyttelton 1837

Under-secretary for war and the colonies 1846

Letters to him rel to parliamentary legislation,
ecclesiastical reform and education from politicians,
churchmen and others 1839-75 (250 items), incl
letters from Lord Clarendon 1863-8 (14 items).

John Rylands University Library of Manchester.
Purchased at Sotheby's 12 Dec 1978, lot 166.
Formerly in Hereford and Worcester Record
Office, Worcester.

Corresp, diaries, political papers, etc 1848-68
(5 boxes).
*Canterbury Museum Archives, Christchurch, New
Zealand.* See *National register of archives and
manuscripts in New Zealand,* A 354.

Letters from his son Alfred 1859-76 (48 items) and
from masters at Eton 1872-5 (8 items); copy of a
letter from him to Alfred 1859; Alfred's school
reports 1865-6.
Churchill College, Cambridge (CHAN 2/18).
Deposited by his grandson the 1st Viscount
Chandos 1970-1. NRA 19700.

Letters from William Whewell 1839-63 (13 items).
Trinity College, Cambridge (Add MS a 80). NRA
8804.

[402] **MACAULAY, Zachary** (1768-1838)

Abolitionist

Corresp and papers, with papers of his son-in-law
and daughter Sir Charles and Lady Trevelyan, rel
to the anti-slavery movement, his governorship of
Sierra Leone, family, business and religious affairs,
etc 1793-1888 (1,014 items), incl corresp with Lord
Brougham, Thomas Clarkson, James Stephen and
William Wilberforce.
Huntingdon Library, San Marino, California.
Purchased from Maggs Bros Ltd 1952. *Guide to
British historical manuscripts in the Huntington
Library,* 1982, pp330-2.

[403] **McCARTAN, Michael** (1851-1902)

MP co Down (S division) 1886-1902

Letter book incl copies of c300 letters to John
Dillon, TC Harrington, TM Healy, John Morley,
CS Parnell and other politicians 1882-1900.
University College Library, Dublin (P 11/B). *Guide
to the Archives Department,* 1985, p20.

[404] **MACFIE, Robert Andrew** (1811-1893)

MP Leith 1868-74

Political, business and family corresp and papers
1824-94 (c2,500 items), incl letters from Sir George
Baden-Powell, the 15th Earl of Derby, WE
Gladstone and the 5th Earl of Rosebery, and papers
rel to elections c1859-81, patent law reform, free
trade and colonial and emigration questions.
Glasgow University Archives (DC 120). Deposited
by his great-grandson RL Paton 1984. NRA 30783.

Letters to him 1828-57 mainly rel to the sugar
trade, the Free Church and family matters.
National Library of Scotland (Acc 8605). Purchased
from Donald McCormack 1984.

[405] **McILQUHAM, Harriet** (fl 1881-1910)

Suffragette

Letters to her from Elizabeth Wolstenholme Elmy, secretary of the Women's Franchise League, 1881-1910, with related corresp and papers (7 vols). *British Library* (Add MSS 47449-55). Presented by her daughter Miss Mary McIlquham 1950.

[406] **MACKAY, Donald James** (1839-1921), 11th Lord Reay 1876

Under-secretary for India 1894-5

Papers rel to his public service in the Netherlands, Great Britain and India 1861-1913 (1 vol, 13 envelopes, 1 item); papers rel to political and social affairs 1862-1905 (1 file, 13 envelopes, 2 items); personal and family corresp 1855-1929 (24 envelopes); financial corresp and papers 1841-1918 (6 envelopes); misc papers 1839-1915, nd (1 file, 12 envelopes, 1 item).
Netherlands State Archives, The Hague. Deposited by the 14th Lord Reay c1963. GJW de Jongh, *Mackay van Ophemert en van leden van aanverwante geslachten*, 1967.

Papers as governor of Bombay 1885-90 (5 boxes). *School of Oriental and African Studies, London* (MS 254560). *Guide to archives and manuscripts in the University of London*, i, 1984, p95.

His speeches and declarations at the Second International Peace Conference 1907. *Scottish Record Office* (GD 84/238). Presented 1929.

[407] **MACKINTOSH, Sir James** (1765-1832)

MP Nairnshire 1813-18, Knaresborough 1818-32; a commissioner of the Board of Control 1830-2

Corresp rel to politics, patronage, etc 1780-1832 (3 vols); journals 1804-28 (13 vols); misc notes 1820-6 (1 vol); collections for his projected history of Great Britain from 1688 to 1789 (40 vols). *British Library* (Add MSS 34487-34526, 52436-53). Presented by Miss Eva Mackintosh 1893 and by the Dowager Lady Farrer 1964.

Misc letters to him, etc 1804-8, nd (7 items). *National Library of Scotland* (MS 5319). Purchased 1950-8.

[408] **MACLAREN, John** (1831-1910), Lord Maclaren

MP Wigtown burghs 1880, Edinburgh 1881; lord advocate 1880-1

General corresp 1850-1909 (9 folders); family corresp 1841-1902 (17 folders), incl letters from his father Duncan Maclaren 1841-84 and his uncle John Bright 1862-81.
National Library of Scotland (Acc 7726, 7841). Acquired 1980-1 among papers of his son-in-law FS Oliver. NRA 29194.

[409] **MACLEOD, John Norman** (1788-1835)

MP Sudbury 1828-30

Addresses to the electors of Sudbury 1828 (1 vol); election papers 1834, etc (1 box); corresp 1806-35 (1 box), incl political corresp 1822-35 (c1 bundle). *Scottish Record Office* (GD 187). Enquiries to NRA (Scotland) (NRA(S) 0361). NRA 11847.

[410] **MACLEOD, Lieutenant-General Norman** (1754-1801)

MP Inverness-shire 1790-6

Election papers late 18th cent (2 boxes), incl freeholders' rolls 1782-8; Indian, military and misc corresp and papers 1781-1801 (2 boxes, c8 vols and bundles), incl letters to David Scott and others (1 bundle) and a fragment of autobiography (23pp). *Scottish Record Office* (GD 187). Enquiries to NRA (Scotland) (NRA(S) 0361). NRA 11847.

[411] **MACPHERSON GRANT, Sir George** (1839-1907), 3rd Bt

MP Elginshire and Nairnshire 1879-86

Corresp and papers c1865-87 (c38 bundles), incl letters rel to political and local affairs. *In private possession.* Enquiries to NRA (Scotland) (NRA(S) 0771). NRA 17173.

[412] **MAHON, Charles James Patrick** (1800-1891), The O'Gorman Mahon

MP co Clare 1830-1, 1879-85, Ennis 1847-52, co Carlow 1887-91

Corresp 1824-91 (mainly 1869 onwards) (6 boxes, 3 folders), incl letters from Mitchell Henry, Justin M'Carthy, Daniel O'Connell, WH O'Shea, Lord Palmerston, CS Parnell and JE Redmond; letter books 1871-8 (1 folder); diary 1870-4; speeches, scrapbooks and memoranda; business, legal and misc papers.
Department of Special Collections, University of Chicago Library, Illinois (Mahon Papers). Presented 1930. NRA 29426.

[413] **MAITLAND, James** (1759-1839), 8th Earl of Lauderdale 1789

MP Newport 1780-4, Malmesbury 1784-9; Scottish representative peer 1790-6; keeper of the Great Seal of Scotland 1806-7

Diplomatic corresp 1806 (3 vols); corresp and papers rel to the abolition of local token currency 1812-14 (1 vol), and to the corn laws 1814-28 (2 vols); parliamentary diary 1827-8 with misc letters 1775-1808 (1 vol); essay on the public wealth c1804 (1 vol); list of office holders in Scotland 1806 (1 vol); letters to him and his family 1756-1863 (3 bundles).
In private possession. Enquiries to NRA (Scotland) (NRA(S) 0131). NRA 10211.

Letters from CJ Fox 1796-1806 (1 vol).
British Library (Add MS 47564). Presented among
Fox's papers by Professor GM Trevelyan 1951.

[414] **MANNERS, Charles Cecil John**
(1815-1888), 6th Duke of Rutland 1857

MP Stamford 1837-52, N Leicestershire 1852-7

Corresp and papers.
In private possession. Not available for research.

[415] **MANNERS, John Henry** (1778-1857), 5th
Duke of Rutland 1787

Lord lieutenant of Leicestershire 1799-1857

Corresp.
In private possession. Not available for research.

[416] **MANNERS SUTTON, Charles**
(1780-1845), 1st Viscount Canterbury 1835

MP Scarborough 1806-32, Cambridge University
1832-5; judge advocate-general 1809-17; Speaker
of the House of Commons 1817-34

Political corresp c1810-45 (80 items), mainly as
Speaker, incl letters from Lords Brougham,
Liverpool and Melbourne, and from Sir Robert
Peel (12 items), and draft letters by Manners Sutton
(16 items).
Untraced. Sold at Phillips's 7 June 1984, lot 764.
Formerly in the possession of Robert Bright, a
descendant of the 3rd Viscount Canterbury.
Miscellaneous personal papers also in Mr Bright's
possession were not included in the sale. NRA
7640.

[417] **MARLING, Sir Samuel Stephens**
(1810-1883), 1st Bt

MP W Gloucestershire 1868-74, Stroud 1875-80

Election and other political corresp and papers
1860-80 (2 vols, 94 items); personal, family and
financial corresp 1835-82 (645 items); financial and
misc papers 1821-83 (8 vols, 26 items).
Gloucestershire Record Office (D 873). Deposited by
Sir John Marling, Bt 1952-9. NRA 10646.

[418] **MARTIN, John** (1812-1875)

MP co Meath 1871-5; secretary of the Home Rule
League

Corresp 1840-64, nd (107 items), incl letters from
JE Pigot and PJ Smyth 1860-4 rel to his
transportation 1849 and to Irish nationalism; misc
memoranda, speeches and drafts of articles
c1840-72 (c100 items).
Public Record Office of Northern Ireland (D 2137).

Diary 1848-58 covering his transportation and
subsequent exile.

Public Record Office of Northern Ireland (D 560).
Presented 1948 by Mrs FV Ryan, widow of his
great-nephew.

[419] **MARTIN, Sir Richard Biddulph**
(1838-1916), Bt

MP Tewkesbury 1880-5, Worcestershire
(Droitwich division) 1892-1906

Political and constituency corresp and papers
1879-82 (3 bundles); personal, legal and financial
corresp and papers c1877-1913 (c12 bundles).
Barclays Bank PLC (Martins Bank Archives). NRA
14254.

Tewkesbury election papers 1880-6, diaries and
travel journals, with other personal and family
papers.
In private possession.

[420] **MAXSE, Admiral Frederick Augustus**
(1833-1900)

Stood for Southampton 1868, Tower Hamlets 1874

Political corresp and papers 1872-98 (10 bundles),
incl corresp and papers rel to women's suffrage,
etc 1872-3 (1 bundle) and Tower Hamlets election
papers 1873-4 (4 bundles); personal corresp and
papers 1845-99 (22 vols and bundles), incl letters
from Joseph Chamberlain 1872-99 (1 vol) and John
Morley 1875, 1894-9 (1 vol); family and misc
corresp and papers 1855-1900 (29 bundles); naval
and Crimean War papers 1846-75 (20 vols and
bundles); notebooks (11 vols); business and
financial papers 1887-98 (3 vols, 3 bundles).
West Sussex Record Office (Maxse Papers). *The
Maxse papers: a catalogue*, 1964, pp6-11.

Personal corresp 1894-5 (30 items); printed copies
of speeches, notebook, etc (1 bundle, 3 items).
Kent Archives Office (U 1599). Deposited by Helen,
Lady Hardinge of Penshurst and the Hon JA
Hardinge 1971. NRA 20659.

Letters from Georges Clemenceau 1884-99 (81
items).
Untraced. Sold at Sotheby's 22 July 1985, lot 409.
NRA 20659.

[421] **MAXWELL, Henry** (1799-1868), 7th Baron
Farnham 1838

MP co Cavan 1824-38; Irish representative peer
1839-68

Corresp rel to co Cavan politics and elections
1823-37 (c700 items); papers rel to the Irish
representative peerage 1838-9 (c100 items); letters
from his cousin Charles Fox, MP for co Longford,
1824-43 (c340 items); estate, etc, corresp 1838-63
(37 items); registers of corresp 1836-62 (2 vols);
political and other notebooks c1817-50 (10 vols);
diaries 1820-63 (26 vols); journals of continental
tours 1836-42 (6 vols); passports 1839-50 (3 items);
cash books 1833-49 (7 vols).

National Library of Ireland (MSS 3504-8, 4103-4, 11494, 18602, 18613-14, 19091-19147 *passim*). *Manuscript sources for the history of Irish civilisation*, ed RJ Hayes, 1965, ii, 91, and *Supplement*, 1979, i, 241-4.

[422] **MAXWELL, Sir Herbert Eustace** (1845-1937), 7th Bt

MP Wigtownshire 1880-1906; a lord of the Treasury and Conservative whip 1886-92

General corresp 1863-1937 (27 boxes); letters from friends (3 boxes); diaries and notebooks 1868-1926, nd (13 vols), incl notebook as a whip; papers mainly rel to his membership of boards, commissions and committees 1890-1934 (1 box); literary and misc papers (23 boxes and vols); financial papers 1901-36 (4 bundles).
National Library of Scotland (Accs 7043, 7111, 8816). NRA 29224.

[423] **MAXWELL, Sir John** (1791-1865), 8th Bt

MP Renfrewshire 1818-30, Lanarkshire 1832-7

Election, parliamentary and other political papers 1806-55 (379 items); general and political corresp 1811-65 (772 items); lieutenancy, militia and local government papers 1811-44, nd (23 items); account books 1841-55 (6 vols); travel journals, Europe and Egypt 1813-16 (2 vols); misc papers 1813-63 (94 items).
Strathclyde Regional Archives (T-PM 117, 129). Deposited by Mrs Anne Maxwell Macdonald 1969. NRA 10559.

[424] **MAXWELL, John Waring** (1788-1869)

MP Downpatrick 1820-30, 1832-5

Corresp and papers rel to Downpatrick and co Down politics 1805-57 (254 items); freeholders' certificates for tenants 1832, 1839 (17 items); papers rel to local administration *c*1811-67 (4 bundles); business and family papers 1818-69.
Public Record Office of Northern Ireland (D 3244).

[425] **MAXWELL-BARRY, John** (1767-1838), 5th Baron Farnham 1823

MP co Cavan 1787-8, 1806-23, Doneraile 1792-7, Newtown Limavady 1798-1800; Irish representative peer 1825-38

Corresp rel to co Cavan elections 1811-18 (120 items); to Irish representative peerage elections 1823-35 (*c*550 items); political corresp 1823-37 (*c*530 items), incl corresp rel to Catholic emancipation and the Orange interest, and letters from Charles Arbuthnot, TL Lefroy and others; corresp and papers rel to a Dublin disturbance and grand jury controversy 1822-3; letters from his wife 1806-26.

National Library of Ireland (MSS 5011, 18600-12). *Manuscript sources for the history of Irish civilisation*, ed RJ Hayes, 1965, ii, 90, and *Supplement*, 1979, i, 242-3.

[426] **MELLY, George** (1830-1894)

MP Stoke-on-Trent 1868-75

Political, personal and misc corresp 1844-94 (36 vols), incl letters to him rel to Lancashire, Preston and Stoke elections, local politics and constituency business; travel journal, Egypt 1850-1 (1 vol); press cuttings and pamphlets 1856-62 (1 vol).
Liverpool Record Office (920 MEL). Presented to Liverpool Central Library by WH Rawdon Smith 1944. NRA 16027.

[427] **MIDDLETON, Richard William Evelyn** (1846-1905)

Chief agent of the Conservative party 1885-1903

Letter book as chief agent 1885-92.
Kent Archives Office (U 564/CLp 1). Deposited by the 3rd Viscount Chilston 1956. NRA 9550.

[428] **MILL, John Stuart** (1806-1873)

MP Westminster 1865-8

His papers passed successively to his step-daughter Helen Taylor and to her niece Mary, and were sold by the latter's executors at Sotheby's 27 March 1922, lots 712-32, and 25 July 1927, lots 659-72. The present whereabouts of several lots has not been traced.

Corresp with politicians, economists and others 1817-73 (14 vols), incl letters from JE Cairnes, Henry Fawcett, Albany Fonblanque, GJ Holyoake, William Longman and Helen Taylor; botanical and other notebooks nd (10 vols); honorary degrees, etc 1858-70 (1 vol); accounts 1866-70 (1 vol); speeches, press cuttings and other printed material 1864-74 (1 box, 1 vol).
British Library of Political and Economic Science, London (Mill-Taylor Collection). Mainly purchased from a dealer 1926 (formerly Sotheby's 27 March 1922, lot 731). Further material was acquired by gift and purchase at later dates. NRA 7531.

Corresp and misc papers 1812-73 (*c*500 items), incl letters to him from politicians, economists and others (*c*200 items), letters from him to his wife and others (237 items), and journal of a tour in Berkshire, Buckinghamshire and Surrey 1828.
Beinecke Library, Yale University, New Haven, Connecticut. Purchased 1930. *National union catalog*, MS 66-1537.

Letters from politicians, reformers, authors and others 1828-73 (317 items); drafts of replies 1819-73 (257 items); letters to Auguste Comte 1841-7 (44 items).
Special Collections, Milton S Eisenhower Library, Johns Hopkins University, Baltimore, Maryland

(John Stuart Mill Letters). Formerly Sotheby's 27 March 1922, lots 724-5.

Letters from Thomas Carlyle 1831-69 (87 items); letters to Carlyle 1832-45 (29 items).
National Library of Scotland (MS 618). Purchased at Sotheby's 10 Nov 1930, lots 379-80 (lot 379 formerly Sotheby's 27 March 1922, lot 729).

Letters from Herbert Spencer 1863-9, with draft replies (c50 items).
Special Collections, Northwestern University Library, Evanston, Illinois. Formerly Sotheby's 27 March 1922, lot 728. *Guide to archives and manuscripts in the United States*, ed PM Hamer, 1961, p162.

Draft letters to various correspondents 1847-64 (66 items), and original letters to John Sterling 1840-4 (9 items).
Brotherton Library, Leeds University (Brotherton Collection). NRA 30440.

Journal-letters to his father while touring France 1820 (1 vol); revised MS of *A system of logic* (1843) (4 vols).
British Library (Add MSS 31909, 41624-7). Presented by his sister Mrs CE Digwood 1882, and by Margaret Lady Magnay 1928.

Journal of tour in Yorkshire and the Lake District 1831 (1 vol).
Bodleian Library, Oxford (MS Don.d.26). Presented by the Friends of the Bodleian Library 1932; formerly Sotheby's 27 March 1922, lot 714.

Press-copy of his *Autobiography* (1873) (1 vol).
John Rylands University Library of Manchester (Eng MS 1243). Purchased 1959; formerly Sotheby's 27 March 1922, lot 720. Other MSS of the *Autobiography* are in Columbia University Library, New York and the University of Illinois Library, Urbana.

MS of *Principles of political economy* (1848).
Pierpont Morgan Library, New York.

[429] **MILNE, Admiral Sir David** (1763-1845)

MP Berwick-upon-Tweed 1820

Berwickshire election corresp 1824-35 (3 bundles); letters from his wife 1820, some rel to the Berwick election (1 bundle); misc corresp 1816-41.
Scottish Record Office (GD 267). Deposited by Mrs JW Home-Robertson 1971. NRA 11620.

General corresp 1796-1845, nd (19 bundles), incl letters from Sir George Cockburn, JW Croker, the 9th Earl of Dalhousie and the 2nd Viscount Melville; letter books, logs and other naval papers 1779-1845 (31 vols, 8 bundles).
National Maritime Museum (MLN). Deposited by AJF Milne-Home 1949, 1965. NRA 30121.

[430] **MILNER, Alfred** (1854-1925), Baron Milner 1901, Viscount Milner 1902

Private secretary to GJ Goschen 1884-9; minister without portfolio 1916-18; secretary for war 1918-19, for the colonies 1919-21

Political, colonial and personal corresp and papers 1868-1925 (c690 vols, etc), incl corresp with Sir Clinton and Lady Dawkins 1887-1912 (2 vols), PL Gell 1873-1923 (2 vols), and Lord Goschen 1884-1907 (3 vols), general corresp 1872-1925 (31 vols), papers rel to the Board of Inland Revenue and the Royal Commission on Agriculture 1892-7 (2 vols), and diaries and notebooks 1875-1925 (73 vols).
Bodleian Library, Oxford (MSS Milner Dep. 1-663, MSS Eng.hist.c.686-707, d.362, e.307). Deposited 1964 by New College to which they had been presented by Lady Milner in 1933, with further papers presented by JG Milner in 1972. NRA 14300.

See also *Colonial Governors*.

[431] **MILNES, Richard Monckton** (1809-1885), 1st Baron Houghton 1863

MP Pontefract 1837-63

Corresp and papers, with political papers of his father RP Milnes MP, 1806-85 (over 100 boxes), incl letters to him from HCE Childers 1856-82 (20 items), Lord Clarendon 1852-70 (20 items), the 15th Earl of Derby 1852-81 (26 items), WE Gladstone 1835-84 (60 items), Lord Granville 1853-83 (36 items), Lord Halifax 1855-76 (21 items), Lord Lansdowne 1872-8 (27 items), Lord Lytton c1840-73 (40 items), Lord Macaulay 1845-58 (25 items), John Morley 1871-84 (40 items), Lord Palmerston 1839-62 (40 items), Lord Ripon 1861-82 (20 items) and the 3rd Marquess of Salisbury 1862-79 (25 items), political and election papers rel to Pontefract 1806-47, commonplace books 1840-65, and literary MSS.
Trinity College, Cambridge.

Letters from politicians, his family and others 1866-83, nd (c50 items).
Nottingham University Library (Ga 2D). Deposited by his great-great-nephew the 9th Viscount Galway 1953. NRA 6741.

Literary, personal and misc corresp and papers c1830-c1885 (1 box, 4 bundles, 2 items).
In private possession. Formerly among the estate papers of the Marquess of Crewe.

MILNES, ROA, see Crewe-Milnes.

MITFORD, see Freeman-Mitford, John.

[432] **MONCK, Sir Charles Miles Lambert** (1779-1867), 6th Bt

MP Northumberland 1812-20

Election corresp 1812-53, with misc political papers 1719-1858 (1 box); letters from Lord Wallace 1826-43 (19 bundles), mainly rel to political affairs; European travel journals 1804-6, 1830-1 (4 vols); diary rel to horticulture, etc 1815-36; commonplace

books (2 vols); household accounts 1826-34 (1 vol), with other financial papers; local, estate, family and other corresp and papers c1801-67 (c4 boxes), incl papers rel to his pamphlet on the reform of the House of Lords 1856-8.
Northumberland Record Office (Belsay MSS). NRA 811.

[433] **MONCK, Charles Stanley** (1819-1894), 4th Viscount Monck 1849

MP Portsmouth 1852-7; a lord of the Treasury 1855-8

Letters mainly to him and his wife from British, Irish and Canadian politicians and others 1805-89 (2 vols); letters from him to his elder son 1855-69 (2 vols); draft replies to addresses 1861-8, with misc addresses and petitions received 1862, 1867 (2 vols).
National Archives of Canada, Ottawa (MG27 IB1). Presented by the 6th Viscount Monck 1950 and purchased at Sotheby's 23 March 1981, lot 353. NRA 28104.

Personal, family, Canadian and estate corresp 1847-1918, incl corresp with JR Godley 1850-2, nd (3 items) and the 5th Earl Spencer 1882-6 (15 items).
The Hon Mrs Batt (his great-granddaughter). NRA 26697. A microfilm of the Godley and Spencer letters is in the National Library of Ireland (P 6071).

See also *Colonial Governors*.

[434] **MONCKTON-ARUNDELL, George Edmund Milnes** (1844-1931), 7th Viscount Galway 1876

MP N Nottinghamshire 1872-85

Political, personal, family, business and estate corresp and papers 1849-1931 (c7,800 items), incl letters from Lord Beaconsfield, the Earl of Crewe, the 5th and 6th Dukes of Portland and the 5th Earl of Rosebery, and papers rel to N Nottinghamshire elections 1872-85, Bassetlaw Conservative Association, and parliamentary business c1875-c1913; diaries 1859-78 (8 vols); additional papers rel to family and local affairs mainly 20th cent (2 boxes).
Nottingham University Library (Galway MSS). Deposited 1953-84. NRA 6741.

[435] **MONCREIFF, James** (1811-1895), 1st Baron Moncreiff 1874

MP Leith burghs 1851-9, Edinburgh 1859-68, Glasgow and Aberdeen Universities 1868-9; solicitor-general (Scotland) 1850-1; lord advocate 1851-2, 1852-8, 1859-66, 1868-9

Political, personal and family corresp and misc papers c1851-95 (4 bundles); political journal and notebook 1850-3 (1 vol).
Lord Moncreiff. Enquiries to NRA (Scotland) (NRA(S) 0333). NRA 10980.

[436] **MONK, Charles James** (1824-1900)

MP Gloucester 1859, 1865-85, 1895-1900

Political corresp and papers 1848-98 (6 bundles, 3 items), incl letters from the 2nd Earl Granville and the 3rd Marquess of Salisbury, and Gloucester election and constituency papers; legal papers, commissions and appointments (1 bundle, 9 items); personal and family corresp and papers 1849-1900.
Dr HA Sanford (his great-great-nephew). NRA 26344.

[437] **MONSELL, William** (1812-1894), 1st Baron Emly 1874

MP co Limerick 1847-74; president of the Board of Health 1857; vice-president of the Board of Trade 1866; under-secretary for the colonies 1868-71; postmaster-general 1871-3

Political, religious, general and family corresp c1831-94 (1 vol, 40 folders, c300 items), incl letters from Cardinal Cullen, Sir Stephen De Vere, the 3rd Earl of Dunraven, WE Gladstone, JR Godley, Cardinal Manning and others.
National Library of Ireland (MSS 8317-18, 8629, 19337, 20676-91, 20697). Partly acquired in the 1930s and partly purchased 1975. *Manuscript sources for the history of Irish civilisation*, ed RJ Hayes, 1965, ii, 45-6 and *Supplement*, 1979, i, 236.

Letters from churchmen, politicians and others c1842-94, with some misc papers (29 bundles).
Public Record Office of Ireland (Acc 1075). Acquired 1976 from Monaghan County Museum. NRA 28043.

[438] **MONSON, William John** (1829-1898), 7th Baron Monson 1862, Viscount Oxenbridge 1886

MP Reigate 1858-62; captain of the Yeomen of the Guard 1880-5, 1886; master of the Horse 1892-4

Corresp and papers rel to the Liberal party in North Lincolnshire 1852-7 (c1 box, 50 bundles and items), incl 1852 election accounts; corresp rel to Lincolnshire and general political matters 1858-97; corresp and papers rel to Reigate and East Surrey politics 1857-85 (c7 bundles); corresp as a Lords whip 1881-97 (1 bundle); letters from his father 1835-62 (c19 bundles), his brother Sir Edmund Monson and other members of his family; corresp and papers rel to Lindsey quarter sessions c1866-88 (2 bundles); militia papers 1854-90 (1 vol, 7 bundles); estate corresp, business papers, accounts, vouchers and misc personal papers c1843-90.
Lincolnshire Archives Office (MON). Deposited by the 10th Baron Monson 1951. NRA 7153 (partial list); *Archivists' Report 3, 1951-2*, pp14-19.

Corresp rel to college life 1847-8 (2 vols).
Lord Monson. Enquiries to Lincolnshire Archives Office. NRA 7153.

Letters mainly from Sir Edmund Monson rel to
Hungarian and Balkan affairs, British politics, etc
1872-6 (204 items).
*William R Perkins Library, Duke University,
Durham, North Carolina.* See *Guide to the cataloged
collections,* 1980, p382.

Letters from Sir Edmund Monson rel to the
Turkish-Serbian war 1875-7 (83 items).
Bodleian Library, Oxford (MS Eng.hist.c.590).
Purchased from George Greer 1972. NRA 23418.

[439] **MONTAGU, John** (1744-1814), 5th Earl of
Sandwich 1792

MP Brackley 1765-8, Huntingdonshire 1768-92;
master of the Buckhounds 1783-1806; joint
postmaster-general 1807-14

Corresp and papers rel to Huntingdon and
Huntingdonshire elections, incl some of his son
Viscount Hinchingbrooke, 1767-1812 (*c*20 vols and
bundles).
Cambridgeshire Record Office, Huntingdon.
Deposited by Viscount Hinchingbrooke 1956.
NRA 5472.

Political and patronage corresp 1794-1813
(3 bundles); corresp rel to the borough of
Huntingdon 1795-1806 (1 bundle); personal, estate
and misc corresp and papers 1763-1811
(12 bundles).
In private possession. NRA 5472.

[440] **MONTAGU, John William** (1811-1884), 7th
Earl of Sandwich 1818

Master of the Buckhounds 1858-9

Corresp and papers *c*1829-84 (11 vols, 7 box files,
21 bundles and folders), incl papers as captain of
the Gentlemen-at-Arms 1852 and master of the
Buckhounds 1858-9 (2 bundles), political corresp
(Huntingdonshire, etc) 1831-59 (8 bundles),
corresp rel to Huntingdon and Huntingdonshire
politics and other local affairs *c*1844-64 (8 bundles),
family, business and general corresp *c*1816-84,
accounts 1838-58 (3 vols), and diaries 1827,
1832-65.
In private possession. NRA 5472.

Papers (mainly printed) rel to Huntingdon and
Huntingdonshire politics, etc 1826-59 (1 folder,
4 items); militia corresp and papers 1841-83
(8 bundles).
Cambridgeshire Record Office, Huntingdon.
Deposited by Viscount Hinchingbrooke 1956.
NRA 5472.

[441] **MONTAGU, Mary Ann Julia Louisa
Harriet** (1781-1862), Countess of Sandwich

Widow of the 6th Earl of Sandwich

Corresp and papers *c*1802-61 (8 vols, 10 box files,
19 bundles, etc), incl political and patronage
corresp 1814-37 (9 bundles), corresp and papers

rel to the borough of Huntingdon mainly 1824-9
(3 bundles), misc corresp with relatives, politicians
and others, accounts 1824-61 (7 vols), and travel
journals and memoranda 1815-30 (3 vols).
In private possession. NRA 5472.

Corresp and papers rel to Huntingdon elections
1807-31 (2 packets); to the Cambridge election
1826 (1 bundle).
Cambridgeshire Record Office, Huntingdon.
Deposited by Viscount Hinchingbrooke 1956.
NRA 5472.

[442] **MONTAGU, William** (1771-1843), 5th
Duke of Manchester 1788

Postmaster-general 1827-30

Letters from the 2nd Earl of Liverpool and the
Duke of Wellington, with other political and
general corresp 1793-*c*1830 (7 bundles and items);
papers rel to his governorship of Jamaica 1807-26
(2 bundles); to his sinecure collectorship of customs
*c*1790 (1 bundle); to the Huntingdonshire
lieutenancy and militia 1743-1800, 1842 (33 items).
Cambridgeshire Record Office, Huntingdon (ddM
10.6,12-13; 21b. 7-8; 26.12; 49.9,11-12,16-18;
85.11-12). Deposited by the 10th Duke of
Manchester 1948, 1954. NRA 902.

MONTAGU-DOUGLAS-SCOTT, see Douglas-
Scott-Montagu.

[443] **MONTAGU SCOTT, Charles William
Henry** (1772-1819), 4th Duke of Buccleuch 1812

MP Marlborough 1793-6, 1806-7, Ludgershall
1796-1804, Mitchell 1805-6

Scottish peerage and parliamentary election papers,
incl some of the 3rd Duke, 1787-1818 (7 bundles);
corresp with Lord Elibank rel to patronage 1812-16
(1 bundle); letters from Sir Walter Scott *c*1811-19
(*c*57 items) and copies of his letters to Scott
(1 bundle); letters from Alexander Maconochie-
Welwood rel to seditious movements in Scotland
(1 bundle); family, militia and misc papers.
Scottish Record Office (GD 224). Deposited by the
8th Duke of Buccleuch 1967. NRA 6184.

Memorandum rel to the representation of
Dumfriesshire 1818; family and business corresp
1794-1817 (1 bundle).
The Duke of Buccleuch. Enquiries to NRA
(Scotland) (NRA(S) 1275). NRA 6184.

[444] **MONTGOMERIE, Archibald William**
(1812-1861), 13th Earl of Eglinton 1819

Lord lieutenant of Ireland 1852-3, 1858-9

Corresp rel to Ireland 1852-3, 1858-9 (*c*500 items),
incl corresp with Lord Derby (127 items),
Lord Naas (141 items) and SH Walpole (99 items);
personal, family and estate corresp 1821-61
(*c*30 bundles).
Scottish Record Office (GD 3). Deposited by the
17th Earl of Eglinton 1952.

[445] **MONTGOMERY, Hugh de Fellenberg** (1844-1924)

Liberal Unionist; Northern Ireland senator

Political, estate and general corresp and papers 1866-1923 (c1,600 items), incl letters from the 2nd Earl of Selborne, AC Sellar and others rel to Liberal Unionist and Irish agrarian politics, etc 1873-1900 (c300 items), letters and papers rel to Home Rule and the Irish Unionist Alliance mainly 1916-20, and letters concerning his relations with the Roman Catholic clergy.
Public Record Office of Northern Ireland (D 627). Presented by Captain P Montgomery. NRA 16154.

[446] **MOORE, George Henry** (1811-1870)

MP co Mayo 1847-57, 1868-70

General corresp 1826-70 (11 vols), incl corresp rel to politics and elections; speeches c1840-70; draft speeches, copies of corresp, etc, mainly rel to politics, 1855-61 (1 vol); travel journals 1836-7 (2 vols).
National Library of Ireland (MSS 889-99, 1391, 3509-10, 8597). *Manuscript sources for the history of Irish civilisation*, ed RJ Hayes, 1965, iii, 421.

[447] **MOORE, John Bramley** (1800-1886)

MP Maldon 1854-9, Lincoln 1862-5

Corresp and papers rel to elections, constituency affairs, etc 1848-61 (7 bundles); printed election papers 1854-9 (5 vols, 5 items); misc printed papers.
Liverpool University Library (D 40). Deposited 1972-3 by Mrs Janet Veitch, to whose husband they had passed from Miss Eva Bramley-Moore. NRA 18347.

[448] **MORE, Robert Jasper** (1836-1903)

MP S Shropshire 1865-8, Shropshire (Ludlow division) 1885-1903

Corresp, mainly social, 1876-1901, incl letters from Joseph Chamberlain, the 8th Duke of Devonshire and WE Gladstone; account written c1890 of his election campaign 1865 (11pp).
In private possession. C Cook, *Sources in British political history 1900-1951*, iv, 1977, p66. A photocopy of the account of his election campaign is in Shropshire Record Office.

Memoirs late 19th cent.
Shropshire Record Office. See *Accessions to repositories 1982*, 1983, p38.

[449] **MORGAN** (formerly **GOULD**), **Sir Charles** (1760-1846), 2nd Bt

MP Brecon 1787-96, Monmouthshire 1796-1831

Letters, memoranda, bills, etc rel to elections in Monmouthshire 1796, 1802, 1812, Brecon 1812 and Breconshire 1816-19 (c200 items); business,

estate and local corresp and papers c1800-46 (over 800 items).
National Library of Wales (Tredegar MSS). Deposited by the Hon FCJ Morgan 1949-50. NRA 28351.

[450] **MORGAN, Charles Octavius Swinnerton** (1803-1888)

MP Monmouthshire 1841-74

Corresp and papers rel to Monmouthshire elections and politics 1840-1, 1846-7, 1851-2, 1857-9, 1865, 1868-9 (c900 items); corresp and papers rel to Chartism 1837-48 (85 items); antiquarian and personal corresp, notes, transcripts, etc 1827-86 (over 400 items).
National Library of Wales (Tredegar MSS). Deposited by the Hon FCJ Morgan 1949-50. NRA 28351.

Journals of tours in England and Wales 1820-1 and Europe 1827-8 (2 vols); Monmouthshire historical collections (8 vols).
Society of Antiquaries of London (MSS 341-2, 680-1). NRA 27819.

[451] **MORRIS, William** (1834-1896)

Socialist

Family and general corresp and papers 1860-1938 (16 vols); literary MSS c1853-1896 (43 vols), incl lectures, addresses and misc papers mainly rel to his political activities 1877-92 (5 vols), and a political diary 1887 (1 vol); journals 1881-96 (5 vols); account of a journey up the Thames 1880 (1 vol); Kelmscott Manor visitors' book 1889-1904 (1 vol).
British Library (Add MSS 45298-45353, 45407-12). Partly bequeathed by Miss May Morris, and partly presented by her literary executor, 1939.

Corresp, literary MSS and misc papers 1860-96 (c110 items).
Huntington Library, San Marino, California. See *Guide to literary manuscripts in the Huntington Library*, 1979, pp331-3.

Letters to various correspondents 1848-96 (c170 items); literary MSS c1865-1896 (18 items).
William Morris Gallery, Walthamstow. See *Catalogue of the Morris collection*, 1969, pp44-6.

Corresp with Philip Webb and related papers 1884-96 (1 vol); notes rel to tapestry, etc c1879 (1 vol).
Victoria and Albert Museum Library. See *Catalogue of English non-illuminated manuscripts*, 1975, pp69,95.

Complete draft of *The Earthly Paradise* (1868-70); journal of travels in Iceland 1871; misc letters, poems and fragments.
Fitzwilliam Museum, Cambridge. WE Fredeman, *Pre-Raphaelitism: a bibliocritical study*, 1965, p45.

Literary MSS *c*1870-6 (10 vols).
Bodleian Library, Oxford (MSS Eng.misc.c.265,
d.265-8, e.233, g.59; Lat.class.e.38). Bequeathed
by Miss May Morris 1939.

MSS of three lectures nd.
International Institute of Social History, Amsterdam.

[452] **MORRISON, James** (1790-1857)

MP St Ives 1830-1, Ipswich 1831-5, 1835-7,
Inverness burghs 1840-7

Corresp and papers.
In private possession. Not available for research.

[453] **MOSTYN, Sir Roger** (1734-1796), 5th Bt

MP Flintshire 1758-96

Corresp rel to the Flintshire election 1784 (2 vols);
estate and misc corresp 1765-95 (*c*20 items).
University College of North Wales, Bangor (Mostyn
Collection). Deposited by the 4th Baron Mostyn
1962 and the 5th Baron 1969. NRA 22953.

[454] **MUNRO-FERGUSON, Ronald Crawford**
(1860-1934), Viscount Novar 1920

MP Ross and Cromarty 1884-5, Leith burghs
1886-1914; private secretary to Lord Rosebery
1886, 1892-4; secretary of state for Scotland 1922-4

Letters to his wife rel to political affairs 1891-1912,
incl comments on Liberal leaders and other public
figures (325 items).
ABL Munro-Ferguson Esq. Enquiries to NRA
(Scotland) (NRA(S) 0505). NRA 14552.

Corresp, despatches, memoranda, speeches, etc
mainly as governor-general of Australia 1914-20
(10,650 items).
National Library of Australia, Canberra (MS 696).
Deposited 1961 by ABL Munro-Ferguson and the
Novar trustees. NRA 22805.

Corresp 1914-20 (3 bundles).
Australian War Memorial, Canberra (DRL 2574,
3rd Series). Presented by Lady Novar 1935.
C Hazlehurst and C Woodland, *Guide to the papers
of British cabinet ministers 1900-1951*, Royal
Historical Society 1974, p53.

Letters from Alfred Deakin *c*1914-19 (33 items).
National Library of Australia, Canberra (MS 1540/
18). Presented by Deakin's eldest daughter 1965.
NRA 25702.

[455] **MURRAY, David William** (1777-1840), 3rd
Earl of Mansfield 1796

Ultra-Tory

Political corresp, memoranda, speeches, notes of
conversations, printed papers, etc 1812-39
(*c*50 bundles), rel to political disturbances 1819,
his opposition to Catholic emancipation 1829 and
parliamentary reform 1830-2, the poor laws

*c*1829-39, the East India Co 1832-8, Ireland 1832-9,
a proposal to nominate him as chancellor of Oxford
University 1833, etc; corresp and papers as colonel
of the East Middlesex militia 1798-1803
(9 bundles); estate, local and personal corresp and
papers 1804-40.
The Earl of Mansfield. Enquiries to NRA (Scotland)
(NRA(S) 0776). NRA 10988.

[456] **MURRAY, Sir George Herbert** (1849-1936)

Private secretary to WE Gladstone 1892-4, to Lord
Rosebery 1894-5

Corresp and papers 1885-1934 (17 bundles), incl
letters to him from Gladstone 1892-5 (1 bundle)
and Rosebery 1894-1921 (1 bundle), letters from
Gladstone to other correspondents 1853-67
(1 bundle), and memoranda by Gladstone 1892,
copies of reports to the Prince of Wales on Cabinet
proceedings 1894-5 and other papers 1892-5
(3 bundles).
The Duke of Atholl (a great-grandson). Enquiries
to NRA (Scotland) (NRA(S) 0234). NRA 11000.

Corresp (1 box).
In private possession. C Cook, *Sources in British
political history 1900-1951*, ii, 1975, p177.

[457] **MURRAY, John** (1755-1830), 4th Duke of
Atholl 1774

Scottish representative peer 1780-6

Corresp and papers *c*1773-1830 (several thousand
items), incl lists of voters and other papers rel to
Perthshire politics 1773-*c*1830 (5 bundles), and
corresp and papers rel to Perthshire lieutenancy
business and local defence 1794-1825 (*c*5 vols,
*c*70 bundles, incl letters from the 2nd Earl of
Liverpool, Lord Palmerston, Robert Peel and Lord
Sidmouth).
The Duke of Atholl. Enquiries to NRA (Scotland)
(NRA(S) 0234). NRA 11000.

[458] **MURRAY, John Archibald** (1779-1859),
Lord Murray

MP Leith burghs 1832-9; lord advocate 1834,
1835-9

Corresp rel to politics, patronage and legal affairs
1807-58, nd (2 vols), incl letters from Lord Minto
1837 (18 items); European travel journal 1814
(1 vol); misc papers 1826, 1855 (2 items).
National Library of Scotland (MSS 19735-9).
Purchased 1965-6.

Letters to him, mainly as lord advocate, rel to
Scottish politics and patronage 1813-57 (140 items).
National Library of Scotland (Acc 6553). Purchased
1976. *Annual report 1975-6*, p61.

Letters from Francis Horner 1795-1816
(222 items).
*British Library of Political and Economic Science,
London* (R(SR)1054). Returned after Horner's
death in 1817. NRA 7527.

Letters from the 1st and 2nd Barons Brougham, mainly rel to politics, 1823-58, nd (1 vol).
British Library (Add MS 40687). Purchased 1922.

Letters from the 1st Baron Brougham 1844-59 (c100 items).
William L Clements Library, University of Michigan, Ann Arbor. Purchased 1925-7. *Guide to the manuscript collections,* 1978, p16.

[459] **MURRAY, William David** (1806-1898), 4th Earl of Mansfield 1840

MP Aldborough 1830-1, Woodstock 1831-2, Norwich 1832-7, Perthshire 1837-40; a lord of the Treasury 1834-5

Political and personal corresp 1823-79, nd (2 bundles); parliamentary speeches and papers c1830-74 (2 bundles); corresp and papers as lord high commissioner to the General Assembly 1858 (2 bundles); estate, local, financial and other corresp and papers.
The Earl of Mansfield. Enquiries to NRA (Scotland) (NRA(S) 0776). NRA 10988.

[460] **MURRAY PULTENEY** (formerly **MURRAY**), **General Sir James** (c1755-1811), 7th Bt

MP Weymouth and Melcombe Regis 1790-1811; secretary at war 1807-9

Military, political and personal corresp, mainly of Murray Pulteney, c1764-c1840 (30 vols), incl letters from Lord Grenville (22 items), the 1st Viscount Melville (100 items), the 2nd Earl of Moira (10 items), the 1st Earl of Mulgrave (12 items) and the 3rd Duke of Richmond (23 items); military papers 1795-1805, nd (3 vols).
Pierpont Morgan Library, New York (MA 297, 487, 1260-90). Purchased by J Pierpont Morgan 1899. NRA 30863.

[461] **MYDDELTON-BIDDULPH, Robert** (1805-1872)

MP Denbigh boroughs 1830-2, Denbighshire 1832-5, 1852-68

Election corresp and papers 1832-52 (39 vols, 2 bundles, 6 items), incl canvass books, etc for Denbighshire 1847.
National Library of Wales (Chirk Castle MSS C 87-98). Deposited by Colonel RE Myddelton 1932; purchased by the Library 1974. NRA 10568.

[462] **NAOROJI, Dadabhai** (1825-1917)

MP Finsbury (Central division) 1892-5; president of the Indian National Congress 1886, 1893, 1906

Corresp and papers 1870-1917 (several thousand pages), incl letters from WS Caine, William Digby and AJ Webb, and papers rel to his election campaigns in London.
National Archives of India, New Delhi. NRA 20504.

[463] **NAPIER, Francis** (1758-1823), 8th Lord Napier 1775

Scottish representative peer 1796-1806, 1807-23

Corresp and misc papers c1742-early 19th cent (c250 items), incl many letters from Scottish peers rel to representative peerage elections c1783-c1802, and copies of his speeches as lord high commissioner to the General Assembly c1802-16.
Edinburgh University Library (La.II.461). Bequeathed by David Laing 1878.

[464] **NEPEAN, Sir Evan** (1751-1822), 1st Bt

MP Queenborough 1796-1802, Bridport 1802-12; permanent under-secretary for home affairs 1782-94, for war 1794-5; secretary of the Admiralty 1795-1804; chief secretary for Ireland 1804; a lord of the Admiralty 1804-6

Private letters from Lord St Vincent rel to naval and political affairs 1793-1802 (2 vols); letters from William May, Sir Sidney Smith and others 1796-1801 (2 vols); secret Admiralty account book 1795-1804 (1 vol).
National Maritime Museum (NEP). Purchased at Sotheby's 1931-72. NRA 30121.

Copies of official letters and reports to him 1797-8, mainly rel to the Irish rebellion (1 vol).
British Library (Add MS 21142). Purchased 1855.

Misc corresp and papers 1780-1822 (4 vols), incl letters to him 1793-1819 and papers rel to the West Indies 1792-6.
Mitchell Library, Sydney (ML MSS 66/2-5). Presented by Mrs Eric Crewdson 1948. NRA 28290.

See also *Colonial Governors.*

[465] **NEWDEGATE, Charles Newdigate** (1816-1887)

MP N Warwickshire 1843-85

Political and general corresp c1841-87 (c80 bundles and items), incl letters from Benjamin Disraeli 1846-68 (11 items) and Lord Stanley 1846 (21 items) and corresp with George Dixon 1885 (1 bundle); printed parliamentary and election papers, pamphlets and press cuttings 1841-85 (1 vol, 7 bundles); papers rel to the Colwich nunnery case 1857, his quarrel with HE Manning 1869-73, and a draft bill for an enquiry into monastic and conventual institutions 1872 (1 vol, 7 bundles and items); personal, family and estate corresp and papers c1840-86.
Warwick County Record Office (Newdegate Papers).

[466] **NEWDIGATE-NEWDEGATE** (formerly **NEWDIGATE**), **Sir Francis Alexander** (1862-1936)

MP Warwickshire (Nuneaton division) 1892-1906, (Tamworth division) 1909-17

Corresp and papers from 1873, incl corresp with Aretas Akers-Douglas, AJ Balfour, Sir Henry

Campbell-Bannerman, Joseph Chamberlain, Lord
Curzon, the Duke of Norfolk and other politicians
and public figures 1881-1906 (*c*160 bundles and
items), corresp and papers rel to the 1909 and 1910
elections, and corresp, papers and journal as
governor of Tasmania and Western Australia
1917-24.
Warwick County Record Office (Newdegate Papers).
NRA 26325 (partial list).

[467] **NEWPORT, Sir Simon John** (1756-1843),
1st Bt

MP Waterford 1803-32; chancellor of the
Exchequer (Ireland) 1806-7

Corresp with British and Irish politicians,
churchmen and others 1798-1842 (244 items), incl
letters from Lords Duncannon, Ebrington, Grey,
Monteagle and Plunket and Bishop Thomas
Elrington; papers mainly rel to his financial affairs
*c*1826-41, but incl reminiscences of Lord Wellesley
and draft resolutions on the Church of Ireland 1831
(40 items).
Queen's University Library, Belfast (MS 7).
Purchased from Colbeck Radford & Co, cat 58,
1937, items 118, 118*. NRA 29769.

Letters mainly from Lord Grenville and Sir Robert
Peel rel to British and Irish political and economic
affairs 1792-1834 (68 items).
*William R Perkins Library, Duke University,
Durham, North Carolina*. Acquired 1956. NRA
29598.

Letters from Lord Duncannon, William Elliot,
Henry Grattan, Lords Grey, Lansdowne, Plunkett
and others rel to Irish politics and administration
1806-41 (*c*90 items).
National Library of Ireland (MS 796). *Manuscript
sources for the history of Irish civilisation*. ed RJ
Hayes, 1965, iii, 495.

Letters from constituents and other papers
1825-40.
Public Record Office of Ireland (M 482). *Manuscript
sources for the history of Irish civilisation*, ed RJ
Hayes, 1965, iii, 495.

[468] **NICHOLL, Sir John** (1759-1838)

MP Penryn 1802-6, Hastings 1806-7, Great
Bedwyn 1807-21, 1822-32

Letters to him from statesmen, churchmen and
others rel to trade, the war with France, Catholic
emancipation, etc 1798-1835 (4 boxes, 2 bundles);
corresp rel to his parliamentary candidature for
Oxford University 1814-21 (2 bundles); to county
and borough politics in Glamorgan 1814-*c*1832 (*c*6
bundles); misc political papers 1812-30 (3 bundles);
admiralty and ecclesiastical court papers 1780-1852,
incl some of his son John Nicholl, with misc legal
accounts and papers 1786-1835 (*c*150 bundles);
corresp and papers rel to Merthyr Mawr church,
estate and local affairs *c*1790-1838 (*c*8 bundles);
personal and family corresp and papers 1787-1894

(180 bundles), incl his diaries 1816-38 (21 vols),
travel journals and notebooks *c*1788-1816 (8 vols),
and memoranda and account books 1787-1838 (*c*44
vols, 9 bundles).
Glamorgan Archive Service (Merthyr Mawr Estate).
NRA 9673.

Papers rel to maritime and international law
1787-1832 (39 bundles), mainly as King's advocate
1798-1809.
Public Record Office (PRO 30/42). Presented by
Farrer and Co, solicitors, 1941, through the British
Records Association. NRA 8660.

[469] **NICHOLL, John** (1797-1853)

MP Cardiff boroughs 1832-52; judge advocate-
general 1841-6

Corresp and papers rel to elections and politics in
Glamorgan, incl some of his father, 1814-52 (18
bundles), with other papers rel to county affairs
1787-1884 (162 bundles); papers as judge advocate-
general *c*1830-46 (1 vol, *c*6 bundles); parliamentary
papers rel to enquiries and arbitration 1814-45 (29
bundles); misc political and legal corresp and
papers 1835-52, nd (1 vol, 2 bundles); corresp and
papers, with those of his father, rel to ecclesiastical
legislation 1812-47 and ecclesiastical court cases
1781-1852 (143 bundles); letters from his family
and others 1801-52 (*c*12 bundles); journals,
notebooks and accounts while at Christ Church,
Oxford, with household accounts, passports, etc
1814-57 (5 vols, 16 bundles, 3 items); corresp rel
to Merthyr Mawr church and estate 1838-52 (*c*18
bundles).
Glamorgan Archive Service (Merthyr Mawr Estate).
NRA 9673.

[470] **NIGHTINGALE** (formerly **SHORE**),
William Edward (1794-1874)

Stood for Andover 1835

Political, family and general corresp of him and
his wife *c*1801-1874, incl letters to him from Lord
Palmerston 1835-63 (*c*30 items), John Parker MP
1830-67 (2 bundles), and his son-in-law Sir Harry
Verney *c*1858-73; election papers 1835, mainly
printed (1 packet); travel journals of him and his
wife 1809-47 (1 vol, 3 bundles).
Sir Ralph Verney, Bt. NRA 21969.

[471] **NISBET-HAMILTON** (formerly
CHRISTOPHER, formerly **DUNDAS**), **Robert
Adam** (1804-1877)

MP Ipswich 1826-31, 1835-7, Edinburgh 1831-2,
N Lincolnshire 1837-57; chancellor of the Duchy
of Lancaster 1852

Political corresp *c*1830-68 (1 file), incl letters from
the 14th Earl of Derby, Benjamin Disraeli and Sir
Robert Peel, 2nd Bt; misc political and business
corresp *c*1830-77 (1 file); letters from his wife (1
file).
Scottish Record Office (GD 205). Deposited by Sir
David Ogilvy, Bt 1963.

[472] **NOEL-HILL** (formerly **HILL**), **William**
(1773-1842), 3rd Baron Berwick 1832

MP Shrewsbury 1796-1812, Marlborough 1814-18

Accounts and vouchers rel to the Shrewsbury
election 1796 (4 boxes); printed election papers
1796; political corresp *c*1796 (*c*8 items); diplomatic
and personal corresp and papers 1800-42.
Shropshire Record Office (SRO 112). Deposited by
the Dowager Lady Berwick 1947 and by the
National Trust 1973. NRA 26124.

See also *Diplomats*.

NUGENT-TEMPLE-GRENVILLE, see
Temple-Nugent-Brydges-Chandos-Grenville.

O'BRIEN, AS, see Stafford.

[473] **O'BRIEN, James Francis Xavier**
(1828-1905)

MP co Mayo (S division) 1885-95, Cork 1895-1905;
treasurer of the Irish Parliamentary Party

Political corresp 1883-1904 (*c*800 items), incl letters
from Edward Blake, John Dillon, Justin M'Carthy,
William O'Brien and JE Redmond; corresp and
papers *c*1869-1905 (*c*750 items), mainly rel to party
organisation and finances but incl some
constituency and other papers; account books
1885-99 and financial papers *c*1886-1904 (*c*600
items), mainly rel to the Irish Parliamentary Party
and the Evicted Tenants Fund; minutes 1890-5
and letter books 1896-1905 (Irish Parliamentary
Party, etc); drafts for articles, speeches, etc
*c*1890-1905 (*c*150 items); draft autobiography
*c*1900.
National Library of Ireland (MSS 5834-7, 9222-36,
9698, 13376, 13418-74, 16695-6). *Manuscript sources
for the history of Irish civilisation*, ed RJ Hayes,
1965, iii, 544, and *Supplement*, 1979, i, 521-2.

[474] **O'BRIEN, William** (1852-1928)

MP Mallow 1883-5, co Tyrone (S division) 1885-6,
co Cork (NE division) 1887-92, Cork 1892-5,
1900-3, 1904-9, 1910-18

Political corresp 1890-1928, incl letters from
Michael Davitt 1893-1904, nd (1,192 items), John
Dillon 1890-1902 (103 items) and JE Redmond
1891-1902 (173 items); literary papers 1902-25.
National Library of Ireland (MSS 913-14, 7998,
8554-9, 10496). *Manuscript sources for the history of
Irish civilisation*, ed RJ Hayes, 1965, iii, 549-50,
and *Supplement*, 1979, i, 524.

Corresp with politicians and others 1889-1927 (84
items).
National Library of Ireland (MSS 11439-40).
Acquired among the MacDonagh Papers.
Manuscript sources for the history of Irish civilisation,
ed RJ Hayes, 1965, iii, 207.

Political and general corresp 1872-1928 (26 boxes),
incl many letters rel to the United Irish League
and Irish Parliamentary Party 1898-1900; corresp
with his wife 1889-1927 (10 boxes), mainly letters
to her; misc notebooks, addresses, literary MSS,
press cuttings, etc (16 boxes).
University College Library, Cork. Philip Bull, 'The
William O'Brien Manuscripts in the Library of
University College, Cork', *Journal of the Cork
Historical and Archaeological Society*, lxxv, 1970,
pp129-41.

[475] **O'BRIEN, William Smith** (1803-1864)

MP Ennis 1828-31, co Limerick 1835-49

Political and general corresp 1819-64 (23 vols), incl
corresp rel to the Repeal movement and Young
Ireland 1843-8 and to his trial and transportation
1848-54; family and misc corresp 1819-64, incl
letters from him to his wife; journals and diaries
1830-52 (5 vols); commonplace books 1836-47, nd
(4 vols); addresses and other misc papers.
National Library of Ireland (MSS 426-66, 3923,
8653-66, 9049-50; MS G309, 313). *Manuscript
sources for the history of Irish civilisation*, ed RJ
Hayes, 1965, iii, 550-2.

Collected papers rel to Irish history and literature
(25 items).
Trinity College Library, Dublin (MS 4298).
Presented by Dr Brendan O'Brien 1968. NRA
19217.

[476] **O'CONNELL, Daniel** (1775-1847)

MP co Clare 1829-30, co Waterford 1830-1, co
Kerry 1831-2, Dublin 1832-6, 1837-41, Kilkenny
1836-7, co Cork 1842-7

Political and general corresp 1800-46 (83 folders);
family corresp 1798-1846, incl letters from his wife
1801-30; personal and business corresp *c*1809-47;
political papers, rel to the co Clare election 1828,
etc; addresses and petitions; journal 1795-7;
financial and misc papers.
National Library of Ireland (MSS 13629-51).
Acquired 1952. *Manuscript sources for the history of
Irish civilisation, Supplement*, 1979, i, 535-6.

Political corresp 1810-47 (219 items); misc political
papers (*c*75 items), incl a political notebook nd and
misc accounts 1834-45; personal and family corresp
1801-46 (156 items); misc papers rel to his legal
practice, incl fee book 1803-14.
University College Library, Dublin (P 12). Acquired
1939-40. NRA 30001.

Misc personal and political corresp 1801-46, nd
(*c*120 items), incl letters from him; family corresp
*c*1758-1904, incl corresp of Daniel O'Connell with
his uncles Daniel and Maurice.
In private possession. A microfilm is in the National
Library of Ireland (P 1620-4).

Political and family corresp and papers 1808-1947
(4 vols), incl letters to Edward Dwyer, Edward
Hay and James Sugrue 1808-*c*1844 (1 vol), and

notes on Sir Robert Peel and the Irish education question c1843-4.
British Library (Add MSS 62712-15). Purchased from Mrs NM Evans 1982.

Journal incl political observations 1795-1802.
Royal Irish Academy, Dublin (MSS 12 P 13).

Fee book 1798-1805.
National Library of Ireland (MS 130). Purchased from Miss Ellen O'Connell 1900.

[477] **O'CONOR, Charles Owen** (1838-1906), The O'Conor Don

MP co Roscommon 1860-80

Political corresp and papers 1858-1903 (c830 items), incl letters from Isaac Butt, WE Gladstone and CS Parnell, and letters and papers rel to elections, prison reform, the Catholic university, proportional representation, Home Rule, the Land League and the Land Purchase Act 1903; patronage corresp 1860-83 (c165 items); canvass book 1879 (1 vol); diaries 1861-1906 (46 vols); journal of American tour 1865-6 (1 vol); draft essays and speeches nd (1 vol); general, family, antiquarian and estate corresp 1849-1906 (c1,700 items); MS of and notes for *The O'Conors of Connaught* (1891); 'Recollections of my life' to 1897.
In private possession. GW and JE Dunleavy, *The O'Conor papers: a descriptive catalog and surname register of the materials at Clonalis House*, 1977.

[478] **O'CONOR, Denis** (1794-1847), The O'Conor Don

MP co Roscommon 1831-47; a lord of the Treasury 1846-7

Political corresp and papers 1830-47 (c370 items), incl letters from his brother Edward as his election agent 1831-6, corresp rel to constituency affairs, parliamentary reform, Irish Catholic education and the Famine, notes about his duties as an MP, minutes of a meeting of Irish MPs on proposed alterations in the Irish reform bill 1831, and a Roscommon voters' list 1839; letters to him mainly rel to family and estate matters 1809-47 (c230 items).
In private possession. GW and JE Dunleavy, *The O'Conor papers: a descriptive catalog and surname register of the materials at Clonalis House*, 1977.

[479] **O'CONOR, Owen** (1763-1831), The O'Conor Don

MP co Roscommon 1830-1

Letters to him from JP Curran, the 1st Earl of Donoughmore, Henry Grattan, Edward Hay, Daniel O'Connell and others, with drafts of replies, memoranda, committee papers, addresses, etc rel to Catholic emancipation and repeal of the Union c1798-1829 (c490 items); political and election

corresp and papers 1830-1 (c210 items); general, family and estate corresp 1782-1831 (c1,200 items), incl letters from his sons Denis and Edward and his brother Charles; account book 1795-1831.
In private possession. GW and JE Dunleavy, *The O'Conor papers: a descriptive catalog and surname register of the materials at Clonalis House*, 1977.

O'GORMAN MAHON, The, see Mahon.

[480] **O'HAGAN, Thomas** (1812-1885), 1st Baron O'Hagan 1870

MP Tralee 1863-5; solicitor-general (Ireland) 1860-1; attorney-general (Ireland) 1861-5; lord chancellor (Ireland) 1868-74, 1880-1

Corresp with Lord Spencer 1868-84 (235 items); with Lord Hartington, DR Pigot and others c1840-84 (c270 items); rel to constituency politics 1857-69 (53 items); legal and official papers 1836-82 (753 items); corresp and papers rel to Irish education and religious affairs 1845-84 (319 items); misc literary, charitable, personal and family corresp and papers c1825-85 (c770 items); manuscript and printed speeches and addresses 1831-84 (43 items).
Public Record Office of Northern Ireland (D 2777). Deposited by the 4th Baron O'Hagan. NRA 18813.

Corresp rel to Irish politics, administration, education, etc 1850-85 (c800 items), incl letters from Dr Thomas Andrews, DB Dunne, Lord Emly, Sir Patrick Keenan and Lord Spencer.
National Library of Ireland (MSS 17864-74). Acquired with the papers of his great-nephew Sir William Teeling. *Manuscript sources for the history of Irish civilisation, Supplement*, 1979, i, 554-5.

[481] **O'HARA, Charles** (1746-1822)

MP Dungannon 1776-83, co Sligo 1783-1800, 1801-22

Corresp and papers rel to co Sligo politics and Volunteers 1776-1820 (c130 items); political corresp with John Hely-Hutchinson 1772-4 (6 items); with Caesar Colclough 1790-1818 (61 items); parliamentary notebooks 1777-84 (2 vols) and papers c1775-1806 (38 items); memorandum on the 1798 rebellion; personal, estate and family corresp c1765-1875 (c1,950 items), incl letters from the Trench and King families and letters to his son.
National Library of Ireland (MSS 20280-20307, 20393-20402). NRA 18831; *Manuscript sources for the history of Irish civilisation, Supplement*, 1979, i, 556-7.

Misc family papers, incl papers rel to horse-breeding and racing 1762-1806.
In private possession. See *Manuscript sources for the history of Irish civilisation*, ed RJ Hayes, 1965, iii, 658.

[482] ONSLOW, William Hillier (1853-1911), 4th Earl of Onslow 1870

Under-secretary for the colonies 1887-8, 1900-3; secretary to the Board of Trade 1888; under-secretary for India 1895-1900; president of the Board of Agriculture 1903-5; chairman of committees of the House of Lords 1905-11

Political and personal corresp and papers 1884-1911 (*c*18 vols, *c*50 loose items), incl letters from AJ Balfour, Joseph Chamberlain, JA Chamberlain, Lewis Harcourt, Lord Lansdowne and the 3rd Marquess of Salisbury, and corresp and papers rel to allotments and small-holdings; diaries 1869-92 (12 vols); travel journals 1861-97 (7 vols).
Surrey Record Office, Guildford (173). Deposited by the Dowager Countess of Onslow 1972. NRA 1088.

[483] ORD, William (1781-1855)

MP Morpeth 1802-32, Newcastle-upon-Tyne 1835-52

Letters to him and printed papers rel to political and social affairs 1801-54 (167 items); Northumberland and Newcastle election corresp and papers 1826-52 (1 bundle, 64 items); corresp and papers rel to Northumberland and Durham affairs 1779-1851 (2 bundles, 125 items); travel journals, accounts, lecture notes, etc 1812-25, nd (13 vols, 1 bundle, 3 items); family, trusteeship and misc papers *c*1746-1854 (19 bundles and items).
Northumberland Record Office (NRO 324/A). Deposited by JC Blackett-Ord 1968. NRA 24799.

[484] ORDE-POWLETT (formerly **ORDE**), **Thomas** (1740-1807), 1st Baron Bolton 1797

MP Aylesbury 1780-4, Harwich 1784-96, Rathcormick 1784-90; under-secretary for home affairs 1782; secretary to the Treasury 1782-3; chief secretary for Ireland 1784-7

Official and political corresp and papers 1782-7 (*c*18 vols, 400 items), mainly as chief secretary, incl corresp with William Pitt and the Duke of Rutland, letter books 1784-7 (3 vols) and memoranda and other papers rel to the Irish parliament, patronage and pensions, Irish civil and military establishments, trade and commerce, education and the Irish Church; notes of letters received mainly 1793-4, etc (1 vol).
National Library of Ireland (MSS 15800-15978, 16326, 16349-74). Purchased from the 7th Baron Bolton 1969. *Manuscript sources for the history of Irish civilisation, Supplement*, 1979, i, 60-9; NRA 8638.

Corresp and papers as secretary to the Treasury 1780-3 (4 vols, 1 bundle, *c*90 items); corresp and papers rel to India 1762-92, mainly 1782-3 (2 bundles, *c*80 items); to the duchy of Lancaster 1770-1807 (2 bundles, *c*12 items); to political, patronage and misc affairs 1775-1807 (2 vols, 2 bundles, *c*50 items); personal corresp, accounts and papers *c*1760-1808 (10 vols, *c*20 items); European

travel journals 1772, 1774 (5 vols); printed papers, etc.
North Yorkshire County Record Office (ZBO). Purchased from the 7th Baron Bolton 1982. NRA 8638.

Corresp and papers as lord lieutenant of Hampshire 1801-7 (13 vols, *c*160 items); as governor of the Isle of Wight 1791-1807 (5 bundles).
Hampshire Record Office. Deposited by the 6th Baron Bolton 1949 and purchased by the record office 1982. NRA 16. One volume (NRA 8638, item 613) was transferred from North Yorkshire Record Office 1982.

Corresp rel to the government and defence of the Isle of Wight 1797-8.
Isle of Wight County Record Office. See *List of accessions to repositories in 1970,* 1971, p102.

Scheme for a 'system of education in Ireland' 1787 (2 vols).
Bodleian Library, Oxford (MS Top.Irel.d.2-3).

Misc Irish papers 1784-92 (6 items), incl lists of members of the Irish House of Commons 1784-7 (2 items).
House of Lords Record Office (Historical Collection 111). Deposited by the 3rd Baron Ashbourne 1972. AB Cooke and APW Malcomson, *The Ashbourne papers 1869-1913,* 1974, pp204-14.

[485] O'SHEA, Wiliam Henry (1840-1905)

MP co Clare 1880-5, Galway 1886

Political corresp 1881-9, nd (1 vol), incl corresp with Joseph Chamberlain (39 letters from him 1882-9 and 16 copies or drafts of letters to him), WE Gladstone, CS Parnell and others.
National Library of Ireland (MS 5752).

Letters from politicians and others 1884, nd (1 vol).
Untraced. Sold at Sotheby's 9 May 1983, lot 368.

[486] PACKE, Hussey (1846-1908)

Stood for N Leicestershire 1874, 1880, Leicestershire (Loughborough division) 1900

Corresp and papers 1857-1908, mainly personal but incl corresp rel to his parliamentary candidatures 1880, 1900 (52 items), election accounts 1874, 1880 (2 vols, 1 item) and list of voters *c*1874.
Leicestershire Record Office (DE 1346, DE 1749). Deposited by SJ Packe-Drury-Lowe 1973, 1977. NRA 21104.

[487] PAGET, Henry (1797-1869), 2nd Marquess of Anglesey 1854

MP Anglesey 1820-32; a lord in waiting 1837-9; lord chamberlain 1839-41

Corresp with Lord Grey 1832-4 (3 bundles); circular letters to his constituents 1828-*c*1831 (1 bundle); corresp mainly as lord chamberlain 1839-41 (6 bundles, etc).
The Marquess of Anglesey. NRA 10.

[488] **PAGET, Sir Richard Horner** (1832-1908), 1st Bt

MP E Somerset 1865-8, Mid Somerset 1868-85, Somerset (Wells division) 1885-95

Political, local, estate and family corresp and papers 1834-1907, incl papers rel to the 1885 general election (746 items), political and other papers 1872-90 (54 items), and papers rel to Somerset county affairs.
Bristol University Library (DM 106). Deposited by Sir Richard Paget, Bt. NRA 28090.

[489] **PAKENHAM, General William Lygon** (1819-1887), 4th Earl of Longford 1860

Under-secretary for war 1866-8

Corresp and papers, incl War Office corresp and diaries.
In private possession. Enquiries to the Public Record Office of Northern Ireland. NRA 30594.

[490] **PALMER, William Waldegrave** (1859-1942), 2nd Earl of Selborne 1895

MP Hampshire (Petersfield division) 1885-92, Edinburgh (W division) 1892-5; under-secretary for the colonies 1895-1900; first lord of the Admiralty 1900-5; president of the Board of Agriculture 1915-16

Corresp with AJ Balfour 1892-1915, Joseph Chamberlain 1888-1911, Lord Curzon 1882-1924, the 8th Duke of Devonshire 1887-1904, the 1st Earl of Midleton 1883-1941, Lord Milner 1896-1921, and the 3rd and 4th Marquesses of Salisbury 1885-1940 (12 vols); corresp and papers as Liberal Unionist chief whip 1885-95 (2 vols); as under-secretary for the colonies 1895-1900 (2 vols); as first lord of the Admiralty 1900-5 (73 vols); corresp and papers rel to British politics 1900-14, service in the war cabinet 1915-16, ecclesiastical affairs 1894-1940, etc (20 vols); South African corresp, travel journals and papers 1905-41 (43 vols); general corresp 1883-1942 (6 vols); family and personal corresp 1867-1942 (29 vols); financial and legal papers 1883-1945 (22 vols); reminiscences written in 1937 (3 vols); misc personal papers 1880-1942 and typescript copies of letters 1895-1923 (5 vols); printed papers 1854-1939 (42 vols).
Bodleian Library, Oxford (MSS Selborne, MSS Selborne adds). Presented by the 4th Earl of Selborne 1970-9. NRA 17810, 22802.

See also *Colonial Governors*.

[491] **PANKHURST, Richard Marsden** (1836-1898)

Radical reformer and advocate of women's suffrage

Letters from Lydia Becker; press cuttings 1863-96 (8 vols); misc personal and family papers 1860s-90s, incl letters to his wife Emmeline from Mrs Jacob Bright early 1890s.

International Institute of Social History, Amsterdam (E Sylvia Pankhurst Collection). Presented by Dr RKP Pankhurst 1960. NRA 17176.

[492] **PARKER, Albert Edmund** (1843-1905), 3rd Earl of Morley 1864

A lord in waiting 1868-74; secretary of the Local Government Board 1873-4; under-secretary for war 1880-5; first commissioner of Works 1886; chairman of committees and deputy Speaker of the House of Lords 1889-1905

Journals rel to political and personal affairs 1879-1904 (3 vols); family corresp and papers 1854-98 (1 vol); general corresp and papers 1853-1903, nd (2 vols); notebooks 1859-85, nd (23 vols); travel journals, Europe and Egypt, 1861-82 (7 vols).
British Library (Add MSS 48265-48300). Presented by the 5th Earl of Morley 1954.

Letters from and rel to Lord Grey while in Africa 1896-7 (1 bundle); letters from Morley to his wife 1876-90 (2 bundles), incl references to political and official matters.
West Devon Record Office (Acc 69).

[493] **PARKER, John** (1772-1840), 2nd Baron Boringdon 1788, 1st Earl of Morley 1815

Canningite Tory

Corresp with Lord Amherst 1808-27, George Canning 1789-1826, Lord Granville 1784-1826, Lord Holland 1793-1820 and Lord Morpeth 1792-1822 (8 vols); memoirs to 1794, with texts of his speeches in the House of Lords, etc 1795-1823 (2 vols); diaries 1799-1803 (3 vols); travel journals 1790-3 (3 vols); family and general corresp, incl that of his second wife, 1789-1849 (17 vols).
British Library (Add MSS 48219-51). Presented by the 5th Earl of Morley 1954.

[494] **PARKES, Joseph** (1796-1865)

Radical reformer; parliamentary solicitor

Letters from Richard Cobden, JC Hobhouse, Lord Palmerston, the 3rd Earl Spencer, the 2nd Baron Stanley of Alderley and others 1822-65 (over 240 items).
University College London (Parkes Papers). Purchased from his great-granddaughter Lady Iddesleigh 1960. NRA 6318.

Letters from Lord Brougham 1825-38, 1856-65, nd (112 items).
University College London (Brougham Papers). Purchased from Lady Iddesleigh and incorporated into Brougham's papers. NRA 31344.

Corresp and papers rel to his work on the Junius letters 18th-19th cent (*c*9 vols, *c*30 items).
Birmingham University Library (MSS 7/iv/2). Acquired from Lady Iddesleigh 1967. NRA 13201.

Letters from Richard Cobden 1846-65 (128ff).
British Library (Add MS 43664, ff1-128). Presented by Mrs EJC Cobden Unwin 1933.

Letters from Richard Cobden 1846, 1855-6, nd (8 items).
West Sussex Record Office (in Add MSS 2767, 6014). Presented by Richard Cobden-Sanderson 1961-4. *The Cobden papers: a catalogue*, 1964, pp88-9.

Letters to 'Dear P' [?Parkes] from Edward Ellice senior 1851-62 (23 items).
National Library of Scotland (MS 15196). Purchased from Miss Marion Ellice. NRA 883.

Letters from his daughter Bessie Rayner Parkes, William Hazlitt and others 1821-62, nd (26 items).
Girton College, Cambridge (BRP I, IV). Purchased from Lady Iddesleigh and Mrs Lowndes Marques 1982.

[495] **PARNELL, Henry Brooke** (1776-1842), 1st Baron Congleton 1841

MP Maryborough 1797-1800, Queen's County 1802, 1806-32, Portarlington 1802, Dundee 1833-41; secretary at war 1831-2; paymaster-general 1835-41

Corresp and papers 1780-1842 (2 vols, 33 bundles), incl corresp and papers mainly as secretary at war and paymaster-general 1798-1842 (3 bundles), election and Dundee constituency corresp and papers 1826-41 (5 bundles), and corresp and papers rel to political and economic affairs 1807-42 (1 vol, *c*6 bundles) and to roads 1817-40 (1 vol, 2 bundles).
Southampton University Library. Deposited by the 8th Baron Congleton 1989.

[496] **PARSONS, Lawrence** (1758-1841), 2nd Earl of Rosse 1807

MP Dublin University 1782-90, King's County 1791-1800, 1801-7; Irish representative peer 1809-41; joint postmaster-general (Ireland) 1809-31

Corresp rel to political, personal and business affairs 1791-1834 (24 bundles), incl letters from Peter Burrowes 1792-1828 (18 items) and Lord Castlereagh 1793-1817 (14 items); corresp and papers arranged by subject 1791-1841 (53 vols and bundles), incl corresp and papers as joint postmaster-general 1809-30 (99 items) and political corresp, etc 1780-1839 (5 bundles); speeches, notes on parliamentary precedents, political recollections, commonplace books, etc *c*1765-*c*1840 (1 box, 21 bundles); papers rel to Henry Flood's career and death 1791-*c*1820 (1 vol, *c*4 bundles).
The Earl of Rosse. NRA 25548.

[497] **PAXTON, Sir Joseph** (1803-1865)

MP Coventry 1854-65

Corresp, with that of his wife and family, 1826-1907 (*c*2,000 items), incl corresp rel to Coventry elections, constituency affairs and national politics 1854-64 (*c*100 items) and corresp with Lord Panmure and others rel to the Army Works Corps 1855-9 (152 items).
The Trustees of the Chatsworth Settlement. Enquiries to the Librarian and Keeper of the Devonshire Collections, Chatsworth, Bakewell, Derbyshire DE4 1PP. NRA 20594/1.

[498] **PAYNE, Ralph** (1739-1807), Baron Lavington 1795

MP Shaftesbury 1768-71, Camelford 1776-80, Plympton Erle 1780-4, Fowey 1790-1, New Woodstock 1795-9

Letters to him and his wife rel to political and personal affairs, mainly from Lord North, 1769-83 (1 bundle).
In private possession. NRA 26045.

Letters from Lord Northington rel to Irish politics 1773-86 (76 items).
National Library of Ireland (MS 888). Purchased at Hodgson's 13 July 1938, lot 273.

Letters to him and his wife from public figures mainly rel to personal, social and family affairs 1774-1807 (15 items).
Public Record Office of Northern Ireland (D 3196/N/1). Deposited by the 7th Earl of Dunraven 1976. NRA 26717.

Corresp with his brother and others 1762-1805 (53 items); misc papers (1 bundle).
University of British Columbia Library, Vancouver. Purchased from Francis Edwards Ltd 1966. NRA 27225.

[499] **PEARSON, Charles John** (1843-1910), Lord Pearson

MP Edinburgh and St Andrews Universities 1890-6; solicitor-general (Scotland) 1890-1; lord advocate 1891-2, 1895-6

Letters to him from the 8th Duke of Argyll, AJ Balfour, the 2nd Earl of Selborne, Lord Shand and other politicians, lawyers and scholars 1866-1906 (283 items).
Edinburgh University Library (Gen 756). Acquired 1964. *Index to manuscripts: first supplement*, 1981, p441.

[500] **PEASE, Henry Fell** (1838-1896)

MP N Riding of Yorkshire (Cleveland division) 1885-96; president of the National Liberal Federation 1881-2

Political corresp and papers 1853-96 (3 files, *c*190 items); personal, business, family and misc corresp and papers *c*1844-96 (*c*450 items); letter books 1863-86 (3 vols); diaries and travel journals 1850-96 (26 vols).
Durham County Record Office (D/Pe). Deposited by MO Pease 1969-75. NRA 25741.

[501] **PEASE, Joseph Albert** (1860-1943), 1st
Baron Gainford 1917

MP Northumberland (Tyneside division)
1892-1900, Essex (Saffron Walden division)
1901-10, W Riding of Yorkshire (Rotherham
division) 1910-16; patronage secretary to the
Treasury 1908-10; chancellor of the Duchy of
Lancaster 1910-11; president of the Board of
Education 1911-15; postmaster-general 1916

Personal and family corresp and papers (162 boxes),
incl official corresp and papers 1908-16, misc
Cabinet memoranda, corresp 1886-1943 (40 boxes),
political and election papers, political scrapbooks
and diaries from 1892 and press cuttings 1881-1938
(16 vols).
Nuffield College, Oxford (Gainford Papers).
Deposited by the 3rd Baron Gainford.

[502] **PEASE, Sir Joseph Whitwell** (1828-1903),
1st Bt

MP S Durham 1865-85, co Durham (Barnard
Castle division) 1885-1903

Election papers 1857-1902 (2 boxes); general
corresp 1854-1903 (11 boxes); business papers (8
boxes); domestic papers (3 boxes); Bowes Museum
papers (1 box); legal papers (1 box).
Nuffield College, Oxford (Gainford Papers).
Deposited by his great-grandson the 3rd Baron
Gainford.

Diary *c*1872-*c*1902.
J Gurney Pease Esq. See MW Kirby, *Men of business
and politics: the rise and fall of the Quaker Pease
dynasty of north-east England 1700-1943*, 1984.

[502A] **PEEL, Arthur Wellesley** (1829-1912), 1st
Viscount Peel 1895

MP Warwick 1865-85, Warwick and Leamington
1885-95; patronage secretary to the Treasury
1873-4; under-secretary for home affairs 1880;
Speaker of the House of Commons 1884-95

Letters from Lord Randolph Churchill, Sir
Mountstuart Grant Duff, Sir Erskine May, WH
Smith and others 1870s-1880s (1 vol); notes on
House of Commons business, etc 1879-85 (1 vol);
diaries 1860-85 (8 vols); press cuttings 1884-9 (1
vol); game book 1857-68.
In private possession. Not available for research.

[503] **PEGGE BURNELL** (formerly **STEADE**),
Edward Valentine (1805-1878)

Nottinghamshire politician

Corresp and misc papers 1814-*c*1860, incl letters
from his brother-in-law John Parker MP rel to
political and family affairs 1829-55 (3 bundles) and
from Lord Lincoln and others rel to
Nottinghamshire politics mainly 1835-50 (3
bundles), and misc political letters to John Parker

from various correspondents 1819-*c*1850.
Nottinghamshire Archives Office (DD CW).
Deposited 1959, 1985. NRA 6898 (partial list).

[504] **PELHAM-CLINTON, Henry Pelham**
(1785-1851), 4th Duke of Newcastle 1795

Ultra-Tory

Corresp and papers rel to political and public affairs
1806-50 (382 items), incl letters from Sir Robert
Peel 1821-43 (25 items) and the Duke of Wellington
1825-40 (39 items), and corresp rel to WE
Gladstone's candidature at Newark 1832-41 (46
items); corresp and papers rel to elections in
Nottinghamshire and Yorkshire 1822-46 (135 vols,
bundles and items); corresp and papers as lord
lieutenant of Nottinghamshire 1810-39 (430 items),
incl corresp rel to the reform riots 1831 and his
dismissal 1839; personal, family, estate and local
corresp and papers 1792-1850 (over 3,000 items);
genealogical and antiquarian corresp and papers
1814-41 (513 items); diaries 1822-50 (8 vols).
Nottingham University Library (Ne C, O, X, 2F).
Deposited by the trustees of the will of the 7th
Duke of Newcastle 1955, 1966; accepted for the
nation in lieu of tax and allocated to the Library
1981. NRA 7411.

[505] **PENNINGTON, John** (1741-1813), 1st
Baron Muncaster 1783

MP Milborne Port 1781-96, Colchester 1796-1802,
Westmorland 1806-13

Corresp with politicians and others 1770-1813 (241
items), incl the Duke of Grafton 1770-83, Lord
Lonsdale 1803-10 and JBS Morritt 1806-13; family
corresp and papers 1762-1813 (365 items), incl
political papers 1786-*c*1812 (28 items); political
memoranda 18th-19th cent (8 vols); diaries
1779-82, 1796-1813 (14 vols); military journal 1758,
travel journal 1771, letter books and notebooks
1773-*c*1800, nd (13 vols); business and estate
corresp and papers 1775-1813 (869 items).
National Library of Scotland (Crawford Muniments
55). Transferred from the John Rylands University
Library of Manchester 1988. *Hand-list of personal
papers from the muniments of the Earl of Crawford
and Balcarres*, 1976, pp84-7.

Letters from William Wilberforce 1788-1811 (16
items).
Bodleian Library, Oxford (MSS Wilberforce
d.15–16). Purchased from the executors of Dr
Octavia Wilberforce 1965-6. NRA 7132.

[506] **PERCEVAL, Charles George** (1756-1840),
2nd Baron Arden 1784

MP Launceston 1780-90, Warwick 1790-6, Totnes
1796-1802; a lord of the Admiralty 1783-1801;
master of the Mint 1801-2; a commissioner of the
Board of Control 1801-3

Family corresp and papers 1791-1846, nd (6 vols),
incl his memorandum on the position of the Irish

peers before the Union 1799-1800, papers as master
of the Mint 1800-2 and a commonplace book with
diary entries 1784-96, nd.
British Library (Add MSS 47140-3). Presented 1950
by the trustees of Lucy, Countess of Egmont,
widow of his grandson.

Corresp with politicians and others 1812-39 (1 vol);
corresp as lord lieutenant of Surrey 1830-9 (5 vols).
Bodleian Library, Oxford (MS Eng. lett. d.167,
MSS Top. Surrey c.1–5). Presented by PA Landon
1954. NRA 5762.

[507] **PERCY, General Hugh** (1742-1817), 2nd
Duke of Northumberland 1786

MP Westminster 1763-76; lord lieutenant of
Northumberland 1786-99, 1802-17

Political, military and general corresp and papers
*c*1760-1816 (*c*31 vols), incl political corresp with
CJ Fox, John McMahon, the 2nd Earl of Moira,
the 3rd Duke of Portland and others *c*1786-1812,
corresp and papers rel to the American war
1774-87, and diplomatic and military corresp rel
to the Napoleonic war with Sir John Elley, Sir
James Leith, Sir Edward Pellew, Lord Strangford
and others; unbound corresp and papers, incl
papers rel to the Westminster election 1806 and to
the Northumberland lieutenancy, militia and
yeomanry; letter books mainly rel to estate, local
and military affairs 1788-1816 (12 vols).
The Duke of Northumberland. Enquiries to the
Archivist, Alnwick Castle, Alnwick,
Northumberland NE66 1NQ. NRA 836 (partial
list).

[508] **PERCY, Hugh** (1785-1847), 3rd Duke of
Northumberland 1817

MP Buckingham 1806, Westminster 1806,
Launceston 1806-7, Northumberland 1807-12; lord
lieutenant of Ireland 1829-30

Corresp and papers as lord lieutenant mainly
1829-30 (8 vols), incl corresp with the Duke of
Wellington and Robert Peel, returns, memorials,
etc; general corresp 1813-47 (2 vols); corresp with
that of the 2nd Duke 1796-1834 (1 vol); misc
unbound corresp and papers, incl corresp as
chancellor of Cambridge University 1841-6 (53
items); general letter books 1817-47 (4 vols);
Northumberland lieutenancy and vice-admiralty
papers; bank books 1817-47 (5 vols).
The Duke of Northumberland. Enquiries to the
Archivist, Alnwick Castle, Alnwick,
Northumberland NE66 1NQ. NRA 836 (partial
list).

[509] **PERY, Edmond Sexten** (1719-1806),
Viscount Pery 1785

MP Wicklow 1751-60, Limerick 1760-85; Speaker
of the Irish House of Commons 1771-85

Corresp rel to Irish politics and patronage 1759-90
(347 items), incl letters from WG Hamilton (32
items), Lord Hawkesbury (12 items), Lord Lucan

(18 items), Lord Mendip (14 items), Thomas Orde
(13 items) and Lord Townshend (12 items).
Huntington Library, San Marino, California.
Purchased from Sotheran & Co 1926. *Guide to
British historical manuscripts in the Huntington
Library*, 1982, pp341-2; HMC *Eighth Report App
I*, 1881, pp174-208 and *Fourteenth Report App IX*,
1895, pp155-99.

Copies of corresp and papers mainly rel to Irish
politics and patronage *c*1760-*c*1806 (1 vol).
Walter Armytage, Esq. Photocopies are in the Public
Record Office of Northern Ireland (T 3052). NRA
17230.

[510] **PETTY-FITZMAURICE, Edmond George**
(1846-1935), Baron Fitzmaurice 1906

MP Calne 1868-85, Wiltshire (Cricklade division)
1898-1906; under-secretary for foreign affairs
1882-5, 1905-8; chancellor of the Duchy of
Lancaster 1908-9

Corresp with Lord Bryce 1900-21, Sir Henry
Campbell-Bannerman 1900-7, Lord Crewe
1906-33, Sir Charles Dilke 1876-1908, WE
Gladstone 1874-98, Lord Granville 1880-9 and
others (7 box files); general corresp (1 box file);
papers arranged by subject (3 box files), incl drafts
and printed copies of Foreign Office letters and
memoranda.
The Earl of Shelburne (his great-great-nephew). C
Hazlehurst and C Woodland, *Guide to the papers
of British cabinet ministers 1900-1951*, Royal
Historical Society 1974, pp54-5.

Letters from Sir Robert Morier 1883-5 (1 bundle).
Balliol College, Oxford. Returned by Fitzmaurice
to Morier's daughter. NRA 26599.

[511] **PHILIPPS** (formerly **FISHER**), **Sir Charles
Edward Gregg** (1840-1928), 1st Bt

Stood for Pembrokeshire 1880, 1885, 1886, 1892

Corresp and papers rel to elections and
Conservative party organisation in Pembrokeshire
1876-*c*1911 (12 bundles); to Pembrokeshire county
affairs 1876-1921 (13 bundles); political, personal,
family and estate corresp 1855-1922 (*c*100 bundles,
*c*750 items); papers rel to his legal career 1868-75
(5 vols and bundles); diaries 1868-1906 (7 vols);
accounts and memoranda 1859-1918 (64 vols and
bundles).
National Library of Wales (Picton Castle
Collection). Deposited by his granddaughter Mrs
Sheila Plunkett 1949. NRA 28426.

[512] **PHILIPPS, John George** (1761-1816)

MP Carmarthen 1784-96, 1796-1803

Political, family and financial corresp and papers
1780-1816 (*c*600 items), mainly rel to Carmarthen
politics and elections.
Carmarthenshire Area Record Office (Cwmgwili
Papers). Deposited by Sir Grismond Philipps.
NRA 21545.

[513] **PHILLIMORE, Sir Robert Joseph**
(1810-1885), 1st Bt

MP Tavistock 1853-7; judge advocate-general
1871-3

Political and other corresp and papers, incl letters
from WE Gladstone and diaries.
Christ Church, Oxford. Acquired 1976.

[514] **PHILLIPPS, Sir Thomas** (1792-1872), Bt

Stood for Great Grimsby 1826

Grimsby election papers 1826-34 (7 vols); family,
topographical and misc corresp and papers (1,911
vols and bundles).
Bodleian Library, Oxford (MSS Phillipps-
Robinson). Presented by Lionel and Philip
Robinson 1958. NRA 26260.

[515] **PINNEY, William** (1806-1898)

MP Lyme Regis 1832-42, 1852-65, E Somerset
1847-52

Corresp and papers rel to elections and constituency
affairs at Lyme Regis 1831-61 and in Somerset
1847-52 (c18 bundles), with other personal,
business and family corresp and papers.
Bristol University Library (Pinney Papers). Acquired
1947-8. NRA 16668.

[516] **PLACE, Francis** (1771-1854)

Radical reformer

Political, misc and collected papers 1714-1847, nd
(61 vols), incl papers rel to Westminster elections
and politics, etc 1714-1838, mainly 1790-1818 (18
vols), to the combination laws 1734-1826 (8 vols),
to the London Corresponding Society 1791-8, nd
(8 vols) and to working men's associations,
education, etc; papers of the Metropolitan
Parliamentary Reform Association 1842 (1 vol); his
narrative of political events in England 1830-5 (9
vols).
British Library (Add MSS 27789-27859). Acquired
1868.

Political corresp with Richard Cobden, Sir John
Cam Hobhouse, Joseph Hume, Joseph Parkes and
others 1827-50 (4 vols); personal corresp 1810-37
(2 vols); selected political, literary and misc corresp
1813-52 (2 vols); autobiography (6 vols); misc
papers 1819-39 (1 vol).
British Library (Add MSS 35142-54, 37949-50).
Presented by Charles Miers 1897, and by Dr HA
Miers and FR Miers 1909.

Political memoranda and commonplace books
mainly 1816-44 (6 vols).
British Library (Add MSS 36623-8). Presented by
Graham Wallas 1901.

The . . . proceedings against Queen Caroline (1820),
annotated by Place (2 vols).
British Library (Add MSS 57841A-B). Purchased
at Sotheby's sale 6 Dec 1972 (formerly Phillipps
MS 74539).

Press cuttings (180 vols), incl misc original letters.
British Library, Department of Printed Books (Place
Collection).

[517] **PLAYFAIR, Lyon** (1818-1898), 1st Baron
Playfair 1892

MP Edinburgh and St Andrews Universities
1868-85, Leeds (S division) 1885-92; postmaster-
general 1873-4; chairman of the Committee of Ways
and Means 1880-3; vice-president of the Committee
of Council for Education 1886

Personal and family corresp and misc papers
1839-1910 (c1,150 items), incl letters from Joseph
Chamberlain 1894-6 (12 items), Lord Granville
1850-86, nd (40 items), Sir Robert Peel 1842-50
(13 items), Lord Rosebery 1876-96 (17 items) and
Lord Spencer 1865-98 (12 items), and corresp with
WE Gladstone 1859-92 (37 items).
Imperial College London (Playfair Papers).
Presented by his great-nephew Sir Edward Playfair
1962. NRA 11556.

See also *Scientists*.

[518] **PLEYDELL-BOUVERIE** (formerly
BOUVERIE), **Jacob** (1750-1828), 2nd Earl of
Radnor 1776

MP Salisbury 1771-6; lord lieutenant of Berkshire
1791-1819

Corresp and papers rel to Downton borough
elections and election petitions 1774-1831 (62
bundles and items); to the recordership of Salisbury
18th-19th cent (15 bundles and items); political
memoranda c1800 (6 items); charges to grand juries
1786-1813 (c50 items).
Wiltshire Record Office (WRO 490/1315-1416
passim). Deposited by the 8th Earl of Radnor 1972.
NRA 17343.

Misc Cricklade election papers 1794 (16 items);
accounts, etc as executor of Sir Mark Pleydell
1768-77 (1 vol, 1 bundle).
Berkshire Record Office (D/EPb/A2-3, O10).
Deposited by Miss ME Pleydell-Bouverie 1951.
NRA 5476.

Corresp and papers rel to the lieutenancy of
Berkshire 1794-1815 (3 vols, 7 bundles, 75 items).
Berkshire Record Office (D/ERa/O3-28). Deposited
by the 8th Earl of Radnor 1971. NRA 5476.

Parliamentary notebooks containing details of
proceedings and the text of his speeches.
The Earl of Radnor. See *The history of Parliament:
the House of Commons 1754-1790*, 1964, iii, 302.

[519] **PLEYDELL-BOUVERIE, William**
(1779-1869), 3rd Earl of Radnor 1828

MP Downton 1801-2, Salisbury 1802-28

Political and election corresp and papers mainly
1801-19 (9 vols, 5 bundles, 31 items), incl letters,
notes, etc rel to the Mary Anne Clarke scandal
1809-10 (4 vols, 1 bundle), papers rel to cases of
seditious libel 1811 (1 bundle), an account of events
at the Salisbury election 1818 (1 vol) and Cricklade
election papers 1818 (3 vols, 22 items); general
corresp 1802-68 (1 vol, 61 bundles, c1,410 items),
mainly rel to family, estate and local affairs, but
incl corresp rel to Salisbury 1802-18 (1 bundle),
and letters and papers rel to reform associations
1842-58 (1 bundle); papers rel to quarter sessions,
militia, lieutenancy and other local business
1800-59 (3 vols, 18 files, 7 bundles, 140 items);
student notes and exercises c1784-97 (71 vols, 1
file, 1 bundle); sermons composed by him, with
other personal corresp and papers, 1843-64 (1 vol,
c290 items); cash books and bank pass books
1828-59 (9 vols).
Berkshire Record Office (D/EPb/A14, A16, C1-135,
F6-32, F34-6, F38-43, O11-20, O24-54). Deposited
by Miss ME Pleydell-Bouverie and the National
Trust 1951. NRA 5476.

Corresp and papers rel to Downton borough
elections and election petitions 1774-1831 (62
bundles and items); to the Wiltshire county
elections 1831-4 (51 items); to the recordership of
Salisbury 18th-19th cent (15 bundles and items).
Wiltshire Record Office (WRO 490/1315-1416
passim). Deposited by the 8th Earl of Radnor 1972.
NRA 17343.

Corresp rel to his bill for the abolition of
subscription to the Thirty Nine Articles within the
University of Oxford 1834-5 (38 items).
Pusey House, Oxford. Presented by EO Pleydell-
Bouverie 1908. NRA 30608.

Papers rel to quarter sessions business late 18th
cent-1818 (1 bundle).
Berkshire Record Office (D/ERa/O29). Deposited
by the 8th Earl of Radnor 1971. NRA 5476.

[520] **PLUNKET, William Conyngham**
(1764-1854), 1st Baron Plunket 1827

MP Charlemont 1798-1800, Midhurst 1807, Dublin
University 1812-27; solicitor-general (Ireland)
1803-5; attorney-general (Ireland) 1805-7, 1822-7;
lord chancellor (Ireland) 1830-4, 1835-41

Political and semi-official corresp 1799-1844 (c300
items).
In private possession. National Library of Ireland,
report no 495.

Letters from Lord Brougham 1819-38, nd (22
items).
University College London (Brougham Papers).
NRA 31344.

Patent, grant of pension and other formal
documents as lord chancellor.
Public Record Office of Northern Ireland (D 3406/
A/14). Acquired 1979.

[521] **PLUNKETT, Arthur James** (1759-1836),
8th Earl of Fingall 1793

Irish Catholic politician

Corresp with Lord Redesdale on the Catholic
question, with related papers, 1803-4 (3 folders);
political and general corresp c1794-1829, nd (4
folders); militia and yeomanry papers 1793-1810;
misc business and estate papers, incl papers rel to
the guardianship of the 12th Viscount Gormanston
1786-9 (1 folder).
National Library of Ireland (MSS 8021-3, 8029,
11294). Presented by the 12th Earl of Fingall 1951
and R Quinn 1961.

[522] **POLE CAREW** (formerly **POLE**), **Reginald**
(1753-1835)

MP Penryn 1782-4, Reigate 1787-90, Lostwithiel
1790-6, 1812-16, Fowey 1796-9, 1802-12; under-
secretary for home affairs 1803-4

Political, personal and estate corresp 1767-1832 (64
bundles), mainly letters to him, incl political
corresp rel to Sprotborough 1790-1 (1 bundle) and
parliamentary reform 1831-2 (c2 bundles); letter
books 1783-1817, 1832-3 (7 vols), incl private letter
book as under-secretary 1804; parliamentary and
official papers 1774-1834 (2 vols, 24 bundles); misc
political and official corresp and papers 1802-32
(12 bundles); misc corresp and papers rel to Cornish
politics, defence and local affairs mainly 1779-1833;
accounts 1768-1835 (6 vols).
Sir John Carew Pole, Bt. Enquiries to Cornwall
Record Office. NRA 5960.

[523] **POLE-TYLNEY-LONG-WELLESLEY**
(formerly **WELLESLEY-POLE**), **William**
(1788-1857), 4th Earl of Mornington 1845

MP St Ives 1812-18, 1830-1, Wiltshire 1818-20,
Essex 1831-2

Political, personal and family corresp 1807-30, nd
(4 vols), mainly letters from his father, but incl
letters from Sir Charles Bagot, Edward Ellice,
Joseph Hume, Douglas Kinnaird and Lord
Palmerston.
Redbridge Central Reference Library, Ilford
(Wellesley-Pole Papers). Purchased at Sotheby's 29
June 1965, lot 291 (formerly Phillipps MSS
20126-7, 20130, 20135). NRA 24051.

[524] **PONSONBY, George** (1755-1817)

MP Wicklow 1778-83, Inistigoe 1783-97, Galway 1797-1800, co Wicklow 1801-6, 1816-17, Tavistock 1808-12, Peterborough 1812-16; lord chancellor (Ireland) 1806-7

Corresp and vouchers c1810-17 (c100 items).
National Library of Ireland (Dunalley Papers). *Manuscript sources for the history of Irish civilisation, Supplement*, 1979, i, 613. The greater part of his papers was destroyed at Kilboy in 1922 (*Analecta Hibernica 12*, 1943, p131).

[525] **POTTER, Richard** (1778-1842)

MP Wigan 1832-9

Parliamentary journals and diaries 1833-7 (4 vols); diaries 1800-38 (4 vols); letter books 1798-1837 (2 vols); misc corresp and papers 1800-38 (1 vol); memorandum book 1793-9 (1 vol); account book 1798-1812 (1 vol); extracts from the press nd (1 vol).
British Library of Political and Economic Science, London (Coll Misc 146). NRA 7535.

[526] **POTTER, Thomas Bayley** (1817-1898)

MP Rochdale 1865-95

Letters from Richard Cobden 1845, 1857-65 (92 items).
West Sussex Record Office (Add MS 2761). Presented by Richard Cobden-Sanderson 1961-4. *The Cobden papers: a catalogue*, 1964, p90.

Letters mainly from John Bright 1864-5 (1 vol).
Manchester Central Library (MS 923.2 Br 13).

Letters from Cobden and others 1866-78 (12ff).
British Library (Add MS 43678, ff49-60). Presented by Mrs EJC Cobden Unwin 1933.

[527] **POWELL, Sir Francis Sharp** (1827-1911), Bt

MP Wigan 1857-9, 1881, 1885-1910, Cambridge 1863-8, W Riding of Yorkshire (N division) 1872-4

Political, local, estate and family corresp and papers 1844-1910, incl corresp and papers rel to elections and politics in Wigan 1850-9, 1876-1901 (1 box, 1 vol, c8 bundles), Cambridge 1863-9 (2 bundles), the West Riding 1872-4 (2 bundles) and Manchester 1875 (1 bundle), misc political corresp, speech notes, etc 1851-1910 (several bundles), papers rel to the select committee on theatrical licenses 1866 (1 box), printed parliamentary papers 1907 (1 bundle), diaries and pocket books 1875-1906, memorandum book nd and press cuttings books 1863-1911.
West Yorkshire Archive Service, Bradford (16D86). Deposited in Leeds District Archives by the trustees of FSE Bardsley-Powell 1979 and by Mrs Bardsley-Powell 1985, and transferred 1986. NRA 30578.

[528] **PRICE, William Edwin** (1841-1886)

MP Tewkesbury 1868-80

Corresp and papers 1864-91 (2 boxes, 5 drawers), incl Tewkesbury election corresp 1879-80 (3 bundles), speech notes (1 bundle), and letters from him and others to WV Ellis rel to local politics 1876-88 (2 bundles).
Mrs Tania Rose (his granddaughter).

[529] **PRIMROSE, Archibald John** (1783-1868), 4th Earl of Rosebery 1814

MP Helston 1805-6, Cashel 1806-7; Scottish representative peer 1818-28

Political corresp 1811-57 (10 bundles), incl corresp with the 2nd Baron Auckland, the 2nd Earl Grey, Lord Lansdowne and Lord Melbourne; personal corresp 1814-82 (c14 bundles); letter book 1803-30; notes and memoranda nd (12 vols); travel journals 1815-16, 1824, 1840 (2 vols); accounts 1811-68 (63 vols, 1 bundle); family, legal and estate papers.
The Earl of Rosebery. Enquiries to NRA (Scotland) (NRA(S) 2244). NRA 10461.

[530] **PRIMROSE, Sir Henry William** (1846-1923)

Private secretary to Lord Ripon 1880-4, to WE Gladstone 1886

Corresp and papers 1864-1923 (259 items), incl letters to him from WE Gladstone, Sir Henry Ponsonby and Lord Rosebery, letters from him to his wife, and papers rel to the Gladstone administrations of 1886 and 1892, the international conference on sugar bounties 1901 and the committee on Irish finance 1911-12.
William R Perkins Library, Duke University, Durham, North Carolina. Acquired from Professor WB Hamilton 1970. NRA 29599.

[531] **PRYSE** (formerly **LOVEDEN**), **Pryse** (1774-1849)

MP Cardigan boroughs 1818-41, 1842-9

Corresp, bills and other papers, Cardigan boroughs elections 1812-42 (3 vols, 6 bundles); Cardiganshire freeholders' books 1799, 1817-18, 1823 (6 vols); misc corresp c1820-40 (c4 bundles); personal accounts 1811-21 (1 vol).
National Library of Wales (Gogerddan MSS). Deposited by Sir Pryse Saunders-Pryse, Bt 1949.

PRYSE, Pryse (1815-1855), see Loveden, Pryse.

PULTENEY, JM, see Murray Pulteney.

[532] **PULTENEY** (formerly **JOHNSTONE**), **Sir William** (1729-1805), 5th Bt

MP Cromarty 1768-74, Shrewsbury 1775-1805

Political, personal and family corresp 1750-1818 (2,087 items), incl corresp rel to Shropshire and other elections, the American revolution and the East India Company.
Huntington Library, San Marino, California. Purchased from Maggs Bros Ltd 1952. *Guide to British historical manuscripts in the Huntington Library*, 1982, pp345-8.

[533] **PUSEY, Philip** (1799-1855)

MP Chippenham 1830-1, Cashel 1831-2, Berkshire 1835-52

Letters *c*1800-60 mainly to him from politicians and others (4 bundles); letters from Lord Mahon 1828-35 (1 bundle); corresp rel to the Royal Agricultural Society 1849-54 (1 bundle); corresp and papers rel to the Berkshire declaration against the reform bill 1832 (1 packet); election expenses, Berkshire 1832 and election addresses 1832, 1847, 1852; notes and drafts for speeches, pamphlets and addresses rel to politics, agriculture, etc *c*1830-1854, with printed pamphlets and press cuttings 1827-54 (5 vols, 7 bundles, 30 items); family corresp 1835-54 (3 bundles); misc corresp *c*1830-1854 (4 bundles); personal accounts 1824-47 and bank book 1847-53 (1 vol, 15 items).
Berkshire Record Office (D/EBp). Deposited by EB Bouverie-Pusey 1951. NRA 30567.

Letters to him from politicians and others 1835-51 (1 box).
Bodleian Library, Oxford (Dep.e.155). Deposited by the Oxford University Institute of Agricultural Economics 1971. NRA 8117.

[534] **RAMSDEN, Sir John William** (1831-1914), 5th Bt

MP Taunton 1853-7, Hythe 1857-9, W Riding of Yorkshire 1859-65, W Riding of Yorkshire (E division) 1880-5, (Osgoldcross division) 1885-6, Monmouth boroughs 1868-74; under-secretary for war 1857-8

Corresp and papers as MP for Hythe 1857-9 and as under-secretary for war 1857-8 (1 box, 2 bundles); corresp and papers rel to elections and other political, local and patronage affairs in the West Riding 1859-86 (*c*9 boxes, 6 vols, *c*3 bundles); in Monmouthshire 1868-71 (*c*7 bundles); corresp with his secretary, William Powell, some rel to political affairs, 1859-76, nd (22 bundles); diaries 1863-7 (2 vols); bills 1852-91 (5 boxes); indexes to his general corresp 1852-65 (3 vols); family, estate and misc corresp and papers 1855-96.
West Yorkshire Archive Service, Leeds (Ramsden Archives). Transferred from the Cumberland and Carlisle Record Office 1965. NRA 7344.

Political, family and misc corresp 1855-1911 (1 vol, 271 items), incl letters from his brother-in-law Edward Horsman 1867, mainly rel to the passage of the reform bill, and copies of corresp with Horsman 1855-8 (1 vol); press cuttings rel to Monmouth boroughs 1868 (1 vol); accounts and papers rel to tour in Europe and Asia 1855-6.
Buckinghamshire Record Office (D/RA). Deposited by Sir William Pennington-Ramsden, Bt 1962-4. NRA 11704.

Corresp and papers rel to Huddersfield estate and local affairs *c*1851-1914, incl corresp rel to his possible parliamentary candidature for Huddersfield 1852, etc (1 bundle).
West Yorkshire Archive Service, Kirklees (Muncaster Castle Papers). Transferred from Leeds Archives Department 1971. NRA 7344.

Letters from Edward and Charlotte Horsman 1864-9 (*c*12 items); accounts 1857-60 (1 vol); executorship and guardianship papers *c*1885-90 (1 box).
In private possession. NRA 24077.

[535] **RATHBONE, William** (1819-1902)

MP Liverpool 1868-80, Carnarvonshire 1880-5, Carnarvonshire (Arfon division) 1885-95

Corresp and papers arranged by subject 1856-1902 (*c*418 items), incl political corresp mainly with WE Gladstone and DP Williams of the Arfon Liberal Association 1865-95 (55 items) and papers rel to education in Liverpool and Wales 1874-1902 (*c*200 items); political and general corresp 1850-1905 (236 items); personal and family corresp *c*1824-1902 (4 files, 505 items), incl typescript copies; autograph collection of letters to him and his family, etc; letter book 1858-67; misc papers 1838-1902 (*c*6 vols, *c*130 items), incl parliamentary diary 1869.
Liverpool University Library (Rathbone Papers IX, XXI). Deposited by members of the Rathbone family 1954. NRA 7187.

Letters from Florence Nightingale 1864-1900 (44 items), with related letters and papers 1855-1910 (39 items).
Liverpool Record Office (610 RAT). Deposited by his great-granddaughter Mrs Bridget Gledhill 1987. NRA 30142.

Political and misc letters to him *c*1857-87 (*c*10 items).
Leicestershire Record Office (DE 1274). Deposited by RT Paget, a descendant of his sister, 1972. NRA 16847.

[536] **REDMOND, John Edward** (1856-1918)

MP New Ross 1881-5, co Wexford (N division) 1885-91, Waterford 1891-1918

Corresp with politicians, Roman Catholic bishops and others, arranged alphabetically, 1878-1919 (*c*5,000 items), incl letters from HH Asquith, Augustine Birrell, Michael Davitt, John Dillon, TP Gill, David Lloyd George, Lord Morley of Blackburn, William O'Brien and George Wyndham; overseas corresp 1890-1917 (*c*585

items); general corresp and papers 1890-1918
(c3,200 items), incl papers rel to the Irish
Parliamentary Party and the United Irish League;
misc corresp and papers, incl draft speeches 1912
(1 vol), lectures, press cuttings and addresses.
National Library of Ireland (MSS 3667, 9025-33,
15164-15274, 15277-80, 15519-24, 18290-2).
Manuscript sources for the history of Irish civilisation,
ed RJ Hayes, 1965, iv, 196, and *Supplement*, 1979,
i, 638-42.

[537] **REEVE, Henry** (1813-1895)

Foreign editor of *The Times* 1840-55; editor of the
Edinburgh Review 1855-95

His 'voluminous correspondence' and brief diaries
in the possession of his widow were used extensively
in JK Laughton, *Memoirs of the life and
correspondence of Henry Reeve* (2 vols 1898). The
papers were later dispersed, and many remain
untraced, including letters from JT Delane and
other papers owned by H Reeve Wallace and used
in *The history of* The Times, ii, 1939.

Letters from Lord Brougham 1842-64 (1 vol).
*William L Clements Library, University of Michigan,
Ann Arbor*. Purchased 1925-7. *Guide to the
manuscript collections*, 1978, p16.

Letters from Comte Adolphe de Circourt rel to
French and European politics 1849-53 (2 vols).
British Library (Add MSS 37422-3). Purchased
1906.

Letters from Lord Clarendon 1843-69 (4 folders).
Bodleian Library, Oxford (MSS Clar.dep.c.534-5).
Deposited by the 7th Earl of Clarendon 1959. NRA
6302.

Corresp with CCF Greville 1839-65 (2 vols).
British Library (Add MSS 41184-5). Purchased
1925.

Letters from FPG Guizot 1840-74.
Cambridge University Library (Add 7615).

Letters from Lord William Hervey 1846-8 (67
items).
Suffolk Record Office, Bury St Edmunds (Ac 941/
61/1). Deposited by the National Trust 1958-9.
NRA 6892.

Corresp with Comte Alexis de Tocqueville and his
wife 1835-59.
All Souls College, Oxford. Presented by H Reeve
Wallace 1923.

[538] **RENDEL, Stuart** (1834-1913), Baron Rendel
1894

MP Montgomeryshire 1880-94

Political, personal and misc corresp and papers
1866-1913, nd (11 bundles, c3,500 items), incl
letters from TE Ellis, WE Gladstone, AC
Humphreys-Owen, JH Lewis and John Morley;
notes on political conversations with WE Gladstone
and others 1886-1910 (84 items); family corresp

1853-1905 (2 vols, c80 items); diaries 1863-9 (5
vols), mainly rel to business affairs.
National Library of Wales (Rendel Papers).
Deposited by HS Goodhart-Rendel 1955 and Miss
Rosemary Rendel 1959-86, and purchased 1969.
NRA 7517.

Letters from Sir Robert Hart and JD Campbell
and misc papers rel to Chinese affairs 1882-1904
(146 items).
National Library of Wales (Rendel Papers).
Transferred from Tyne and Wear Archives Service
1987.

Corresp and papers rel to Sir WG Armstrong
Whitworth & Co Ltd 1863-1913 (8,943 items), incl
letters from Lord Armstrong 1863-80 (676 items)
and his brother GW Rendel 1863-82 (1,066 items).
Tyne and Wear Archives Service (Accession 31).
NRA 31574.

[539] **RICE-TREVOR** (formerly **RICE**), **George
Rice** (1795-1869), 4th Baron Dynevor 1852

MP Carmarthenshire 1820-31, 1832-52

Election papers 1820-47 (8 vols, 2 envelopes), incl
letters of support 1820-41, electoral registers
1832-8, canvass books 1832 and accounts 1832-3;
accounts and pay book of the Carmarthenshire
Yeomanry 1819-27 (2 vols).
Carmarthenshire Area Record Office (Dynevor
Muniments, boxes 159/10-11, 160/4-7, 161/4-5,
278/17). Deposited by the 9th Baron Dynevor
1964-6. NRA 21613.

[540] **RICHARD, Henry** (1812-1888)

MP Merthyr Tydfil 1868-88; secretary of the Peace
Society

Letters to him rel to politics, the peace movement,
education and Welsh affairs 1856-88 (c180 items);
corresp, mainly rel to Richard Cobden, 1872-87 (1
vol); account of an interview with WE Gladstone
1870 and draft letter to Gladstone rel to education
in Wales 1883 (2 items); diary 1853-4, 1863 (1 vol);
travel journals 1849-86 (9 vols); sermon and misc
notes 1826, nd (1 vol).
National Library of Wales (MSS 5503-5, 5509,
10198-10208, 11340). Mainly presented by his
nieces, the Misses Magdalen and Mary Evans,
1935. *Handlist of manuscripts*, ii, 1951, pp107-8, iii,
1961, pp198-9, 328.

Letters from Richard Cobden rel to political,
economic and foreign affairs, international
arbitration, etc 1849-64, nd (3 vols).
British Library (Add MSS 43657-9). Presented by
Mrs EJC Cobden Unwin 1933.

[541] **RIDLEY, Sir Matthew White** (1745-1813), 2nd Bt

MP Morpeth 1768-74, Newcastle-upon-Tyne 1774-1812

Political and election corresp and papers c1768-1807 (3 vols, 5 bundles, c13 items); diary 1791 and expenses 1774-91 as mayor of Newcastle (1 bundle); letters to him on his resignation as alderman 1807 (1 bundle); family corresp 1766-1802 (2 bundles, 4 items); diary 1810-12 (3 vols); notebook 1795-1805.
Northumberland Record Office (ZRI). Deposited by the 4th Viscount Ridley 1964. NRA 4468.

[542] **RIDLEY, Sir Matthew White** (1778-1836), 3rd Bt

MP Newcastle-upon-Tyne 1812-36

Political and election corresp and papers 1812-36 (67 vols, bundles and items), incl letters from Lords Eldon and Grey, corresp rel to Northumberland politics 1824-6, 1832, and political letter book 1813-17; corresp and papers rel to local affairs, freemasonry, etc 1807-35 (c4 bundles); to hunting, with those of his son, 1818-74 (16 bundles); to his London house, the purchase of Italian paintings, etc 1818-32 (7 bundles and items).
Northumberland Record Office (ZRI). Deposited by the 4th Viscount Ridley 1964. NRA 4468.

[543] **RIDLEY, Sir Matthew White** (1807-1877), 4th Bt

MP N Northumberland 1859-68

Political and election corresp and papers 1850-68 (1 vol, 10 bundles), incl corresp rel to Northumberland politics 1850-2 and parliamentary notebook 1863-8; railway papers 1844-5 (2 bundles); family and misc corresp 1836-60 (4 bundles); hunting corresp and papers, with those of his father, 1818-74 (16 bundles); travel journals 1830 (2 vols).
Northumberland Record Office (ZRI). Deposited by the 4th Viscount Ridley 1964. NRA 4468.

[544] **ROBERTS, John Bryn** (1847-1931)

MP Carnarvonshire (Eifion division) 1885-1906

General corresp 1868-1930 (c520 items), incl letters rel to elections, local politics and the Liberal parliamentary party; letter book 1885-7 (1 vol), mainly rel to the 1885 election campaign; election addresses and leaflets of Roberts and others 1885-1927 (55 items); election accounts 1885-1900 (4 bundles); political speech notes 1885-1905 (2 vols, 13 items); notes on politics c1883-1926 (90 items); on other topics 1860-1930 (3 vols, 36 bundles and items); copies of his letters to the press 1888-1926 (43 items); diaries 1863-76, 1910-30 (22 vols).

National Library of Wales (John Bryn Roberts Collection). Deposited 1931 by his niece's husband, AS Davies. NRA 16470.

[545] **ROBINSON, Hon Frederick** (1746-1792)

MP Ripon 1780-7

Corresp 1776-92, nd (1,000 items), incl letters from the 1st Baron Boringdon 1780-8 (86 items), Lord Grantham 1776-86 (c200 items) and the corporation of Ripon 1780-6 (26 items).
Bedfordshire Record Office (L 30/15). Deposited 1961 by Baroness Lucas, a descendant of his nephew Lord De Grey. NRA 6283.

Letters from the 2nd Baron Boringdon, RD Waddilove and others 1792 (128 items).
Hampshire Record Office (9M73/137). Deposited 1973 by Viscount FitzHarris, a descendant of his brother-in-law, whose permission to consult the letters should be obtained through the record office. NRA 6589.

Letters from his sisters Anne and Theresa 1771-6 (56ff).
British Library (Add MS 48218 *passim*). Presented 1954 by the 5th Earl of Morley, a descendant of Theresa.

Letters from his sister Anne 1780-8 (166 items).
West Devon Record Office (Acc 430). Deposited by the 6th Earl of Morley. NRA 31187.

[546] **ROBINSON, John** (1727-1802)

MP Westmorland 1764-74, Harwich 1774-1802; joint secretary to the Treasury 1770-82; surveyor-general of woods and forests 1787-1802

Political corresp and papers c1754-1799, mainly 1770-99 (712 items), incl letters from Lord Sandwich and corresp with George III, Henry Dundas, Lord Liverpool and Lord North; political and misc corresp and papers 1751-1802 (1 box), incl papers rel to parliamentary management, electoral calculations and election accounts 1751-85 (1 vol, c8 bundles), papers rel to America, India and Ireland 1770-84 (c3 bundles), and corresp with, or rel to, the 1st and 2nd Earls of Abergavenny 1781-96, nd (c127 items); papers rel to the borough of Harwich; corresp and papers rel to the East India Company, incl letters from Richard Barwell, Warren Hastings and Sir Thomas Rumbold.
The Marquess of Abergavenny. HMC *Tenth Report* App VI, 1887, pp3-72; *Parliamentary papers of John Robinson, 1774-1784*, ed WT Laprade, Royal Historical Society, Camden Third Series xxxiii, 1922. Copies of the political papers are in the British Library (MS Facs 340(1)-(5)).

Corresp with George III rel to political affairs, etc 1772-84 (3 vols); financial papers, mainly as agent to George III and Lord North, 1751-82 (1 vol).
British Library (Add MSS 37833-6). Purchased 1909.

[547] **ROEBUCK, John Arthur** (1801-1879)

MP Bath 1832-7, 1841-7, Sheffield 1849-68, 1874-9

Corresp and papers mainly rel to Canada 1831-55 (6 vols), incl letters from the 3rd Earl Grey, Joseph Hume, Henry Labouchere, Lord Monteagle and Joseph Parkes 1834-55, papers as agent in England for the Lower Canada assembly 1834-6 and rel to the Canadian rebellion 1837-8, and literary MSS.
National Archives of Canada, Ottawa (MG24 A19). *General inventory: manuscripts*, iv, 1972, pp142-3.

[548] **ROGERS, James Edwin Thorold** (1823-1890)

MP Southwark 1880-5, Southwark (Bermondsey division) 1885-6

Corresp rel to political, economic and university affairs and misc papers 1854-91 (778 items), incl letters from John Bright 1864-85 (92 items), Richard Cobden 1854-65 (55 items) and WE Gladstone 1854-87, nd (21 items).
Bodleian Library, Oxford (Thorold Rogers Papers). Purchased from Dr MAT Rogers 1982. NRA 12396.

Family corresp 1852-1937 (1 vol); diaries 1854-7 (3 vols); draft of his *Joseph Rogers MD* (1889) (1 vol); verses, epigrams and misc papers (1 vol, 1 bundle, 17ff).
Bodleian Library, Oxford (MSS Eng. misc. c.583, c.585, d.902, f.476-8; Eng. lett. c.334; Eng. poet. e.131). Presented by Mrs TF Higham 1953. NRA 19554.

[549] **ROSE, George** (1744-1818)

MP Launceston 1784-8, Lymington 1788-90, Christchurch 1790-1818; joint secretary to the Treasury 1782-3, 1783-1801; vice-president of the Board of Trade 1804-6, 1807-12; joint paymaster-general 1804-6; treasurer of the Navy 1807-18

Corresp with, and papers rel to, William Pitt 1783-1809 (1 vol); corresp with Lord Bathurst, George Canning and the Bishop of Lincoln 1801-16 (1 vol); papers as secretary to the Treasury 1782 (1 vol); corresp and papers as treasurer of the Navy 1782-1817 (2 vols, 5 rolls); as clerk of the Parliaments 1805-16 (1 vol); rel to his other offices and to misc affairs 1764-1814 (1 vol); general corresp 1777-1817 (1 vol).
British Library (Add MSS 42772-80). Acquired from his great-great-great-grandson ASG Douglas 1932.

Letters from Lord Marchmont 1773-93 (1 vol); general corresp 1776-1817, nd (2 vols).
National Library of Scotland (MSS 3523, 3795-6). Purchased at Sotheby's 17 Dec 1946, lot 391, and 19 May 1947, lot 223.

ROSS, see Lockhart Ross.

[550] **ROUND, Charles Gray** (1797-1867)

MP N Essex 1837-47; stood for Oxford University 1847

Political, personal and family corresp and papers 1813-64, incl corresp and papers rel to the Oxford University election 1847 (2 vols, *c*350 items) and printed papers rel to the Essex election 1830 (11 items).
Essex Record Office, Colchester (D/DRb, D/DRc). Presented by the executors of CJ Round 1946, and by Major JG Round 1946-56. NRA 20947.

[551] **RUGGLES-BRISE, Sir Samuel Brise** (1825-1899)

MP E Essex 1868-83

Political corresp to *c*1879 (1 bundle); general corresp 1852-97 (1 bundle); Essex election papers 1868 and misc appointments, etc 1852-99 (1 bundle); political diary 1878-82; family and misc corresp and papers.
Essex Record Office, Chelmsford (D/DRs).

Commonplace books 1857-69, incl political speeches to Essex societies.
Essex Record Office, Chelmsford (U 328).

[552] **RUSSELL, Edward Richard** (1834-1920), 1st Baron Russell of Liverpool 1919

MP Glasgow (Bridgeton division) 1885-7; editor of the *Liverpool Daily Post* 1869-1919

Letters to him from politicians, journalists and others *c*1866-95 (4 vols).
Liverpool Record Office. Purchased at Bloomsbury Book Auctions 17 Jan 1985, lot 101.

Letters to him from politicians and others 1876-1900 (33 items); press cutting books 1866-93 (4 vols), incl a few letters and other items; letters, telegrams and cuttings rel to his knighthood 1893 (2 vols).
Liverpool Record Office (920 RUS). Presented by Henry Young & Sons Ltd 1921. NRA 16257.

Letters from Joseph Chamberlain, WE Gladstone, Sir Theodore Martin and John Morley 1869-98 (1 vol).
British Library (Add MS 62993). Purchased at Bloomsbury Book Auctions 7 March 1984, lots 146-7, 154-5. The present location of other letters (lots 148-53, 156) is unknown.

Letters from Lord Rosebery 1888-1901 (33 items), with copies of replies (3 items).
Liverpool University Library. Purchased from Edward Hall 1960. *Guide to the manuscript collections in Liverpool University Library*, 1962, p22.

[553] **RUSSELL, Francis** (1788-1861), 7th Duke of Bedford 1839

MP Peterborough 1809-12, Bedfordshire 1812-32

Corresp and papers rel to Bedfordshire politics mainly 1815-47 (2 vols, 5 bundles); corresp and papers rel to public and political affairs c1813-52 (8 bundles), incl the affair of Lady Flora Hastings 1839; political and general corresp 1805-61 (c1,200 items, incl typescript copies), incl letters from Charles Arbuthnot, CCF Greville, JC Hobhouse, Lord Lansdowne, Lord Melbourne and the 5th Duke of Rutland, and original letters to Arbuthnot and Lady Westmorland; family corresp c1806-61 (c43 bundles), incl letters from his father and a few from Lord John Russell; estate corresp and papers 1819-61 (1 vol, 17 bundles); misc papers (2 vols, 9 bundles).
The Trustees of the Bedford Estates. Enquiries to the Archivist, Bedford Office, 29A Montague Street, London WC1B 5BL. NRA 26179.

Letters from Lord Clarendon 1846-60 (mainly 1849-51) (3 boxes).
Bodleian Library, Oxford (MSS Clar.dep.Irish, boxes 80-2). Deposited by the 7th Earl of Clarendon 1962. NRA 6302.

Bedfordshire election corresp and papers 1807-57 (2 boxes, 2 bundles), incl corresp of WG Adam 1811-33 (1 bundle) and London out-voters' registers 1812-32 (6 vols), with other local and estate papers.
Bedfordshire Record Office (Bedford Estate (Russell Family) Papers). NRA 17140.

Tavistock election letters and papers 1841-57 (6 bundles).
Devon Record Office (L 1258 add 8M/E11). Deposited by the trustees of the Bedford Settled Estates. NRA 9813.

[554] **RUSSELL, John** (1766-1839), 6th Duke of Bedford 1802

MP Tavistock 1788-90, 1790-1802; lord lieutenant of Ireland 1806-7

Irish papers 1806-7, comprising corresp with William Elliot, Lord Grenville, Lord Holland and others (18 bundles), letter books (4 vols), patronage, application and audience books (3 vols), establishment book (1 vol), and papers on disturbances, hospitals, tithes, etc (1 vol, 13 bundles); political corresp and papers 1807-18 (6 bundles), incl letters to him from CJ Fox (10 items); family, general and misc corresp and papers 1799-1839 (1 vol, 42 bundles); notebook of letters received and sent 1786-7; papers rel to estate management, farming, horticulture, botany and art collections (4 boxes, 8 vols); journal 1802.
The Trustees of the Bedford Estates. Enquiries to the Archivist, Bedford Office, 29A Montague Street, London WC1B 5BL. NRA 26179.

Corresp with solicitors rel to Camelford elections 1795-1813 (5 bundles).
Devon Record Office (L 1258). Deposited by the trustees of the Bedford Settled Estates. NRA 9813.

[555] **RUSSELL, John** (1842-1876), styled Viscount Amberley

MP Nottingham 1866-8

Election and other political corresp and papers, incl some of his wife, 1865-74 (1 bundle, 208 items); corresp with friends 1862-74 (543 items), incl letters to Lady Amberley from Helen Taylor 1865-73 (101 items); American corresp 1864-73 (1 bundle, 87 items); corresp rel to the deaths of his wife and daughter 1874-6 (72 items); family corresp 1850-75, incl letters from his father 1863-73; journals 1854-74 (4 vols), with those of his wife 1856-72 (4 vols); notebooks, press cutting books and misc papers 1849-97.
McMaster University Archives, Hamilton, Ontario. Purchased from the 3rd Earl Russell 1968. *A detailed catalogue of the archives of Bertrand Russell,* ed B Feinberg, 1967, pp23-33.

[556] **RUSSELL, Thomas** (1767-1803)

United Irishman

Corresp and papers 1791-1802, nd (2 vols), incl letters to him (c128 items), letters from him (17 items), a note on the United Irishmen and fragments of a diary 1791-7.
Trinity College Library, Dublin (MSS 868/1-2). Deposited by the Revd JD'A Sirr 1843. NRA 20231.

Notebooks 1793, nd (2 vols); letters to him and misc papers c1793-7 (c20 items).
State Paper Office, Dublin (620/20-53 *passim*).

[557] **RUTHERFURD, Andrew** (1791-1854), Lord Rutherfurd

MP Leith burghs 1839-51; solicitor-general (Scotland) 1837-9; lord advocate 1839-41, 1846-51

Letters mainly to him from Lord Cockburn, Sir William Craig, Lord Dunfermline, Edward Ellice senior and junior, Sir George Grey, Lord Jeffrey, Lord Murray, the 2nd Baron Panmure, Lord John Russell, Henry Tufnell and others rel to politics, parliamentary business, legal affairs, patronage, the Church of Scotland, etc 1813-72 (24 vols); general corresp 1795-1854 (10 vols); misc notebooks, speeches, press cuttings, etc mainly 1822-51 (9 vols).
National Library of Scotland (MSS 9686-9728). Deposited in 1969 by the Faculty of Advocates, to which they had been bequeathed in 1927 by JH Rutherfurd.

[558] **RYDER, Nathaniel** (1735-1803), 1st Baron Harrowby 1776

MP Tiverton 1756-76

Corresp rel to elections and municipal affairs in Tiverton, incl corresp of his son Dudley Ryder, 1756-99 (c13 vols); general, family and estate corresp 1756-1803 (c7 vols, etc); diaries 1753-1800

(2 vols); parliamentary notes 1765 (1 vol); notes on his estates 1756-1802 (1 vol); accounts 1756-97 (1 vol).
The Harrowby Manuscripts Trust. Enquiries to the Archivist, Sandon Hall, Stafford ST18 0DN. NRA 1561; D Jacobs, *Catalogue of the Harrowby-Tiverton Manuscripts*, 1971.

Notes on civil law 1753 (1 vol).
Lincoln's Inn Library, London (Misc 880). Presented by the 5th Earl of Harrowby 1951.

[559] **ST CLAIR-ERSKINE, James Alexander** (1802-1866), 3rd Earl of Rosslyn 1837

MP Kirkcaldy burghs 1830-1, Great Grimsby 1831-2; master of the Buckhounds 1841-6, 1852; under-secretary for war 1859

Corresp as under-secretary for war rel to patronage, pensions, militia and yeomanry matters 1859 (52 items); misc corresp as master of the Buckhounds 1852 (1 bundle, 1 item).
Scottish Record Office (GD 164/1372-80, 1818, 1820).

[560] **SALUSBURY-TRELAWNY, Sir John Salusbury** (1816-1885), 9th Bt

MP Tavistock 1843-52, 1857-65, E Cornwall 1868-74

Parliamentary diaries 1858-65, 1868-73 (10 vols).
Bodleian Library, Oxford (MSS Eng. hist. d.410-19). Presented by Miss CF Harvey 1974.
Annual report of the curators of the Bodleian Library for 1974-5, p18.

[561] **SAMUEL, Herbert Louis** (1870-1963), 1st Viscount Samuel 1937

Stood for Oxfordshire (Henley division) 1895, 1900; MP N Riding of Yorkshire (Cleveland division) 1902-18, Lancashire (Darwen division) 1929-35; chancellor of the Duchy of Lancaster 1909-10; postmaster-general 1910-14, 1915-16; president of the Local Government Board 1914-15; home secretary 1916, 1931-2

Political corresp and papers 1890-1962 (158 files), incl election corresp and papers 1893-1902 (3 files), general political corresp 1888-1900 (116 items), political notebooks 1893-1910 (2 vols), printed papers rel to Liberal meetings, etc 1890-9 (1 file), and papers rel to the conditions of match box makers, etc (1 file); family corresp, mainly rel to political affairs, 1881-1938 (3 files); personal papers 1871-1962 (22 files); literary, philosophical and scientific papers *c*1885-1962 (84 files); commissions, appointments, etc 1906-59 (54 items); press cuttings and photographs *c*1870-1962 (6 boxes, 1 vol, 78 files).
House of Lords Record Office (Historical Collection 128). Deposited by the 2nd Viscount Samuel 1963. NRA 11187.

Corresp, minutes, memoranda and other papers rel to Palestine and Zionism 1914-62.
Israel State Archives, Jerusalem (Record Group 100). P Jones, *Britain and Palestine 1914-1948*, 1979, pp111-12.

Personal papers.
In private possession. C Hazlehurst and C Woodland, *Guide to the papers of British cabinet ministers 1900-1951*, Royal Historical Society 1974, p126.

[562] **SANDARS, John Satterfield** (1853-1934)

Private secretary to Henry Matthews 1886-92, to AJ Balfour 1892-1905

Royal corresp and papers, with some of AJ Balfour, 1886-1905 (10 vols); political corresp and papers, with some of Balfour and Henry Matthews, 1887-1929 (48 vols), incl letters from Aretas Akers-Douglas 1895-1907, Joseph Chamberlain 1891-1906, Sir Michael Hicks Beach 1896-1902 and Lord Salisbury 1894-1903; misc corresp, papers and maps 1895-1917, nd (4 vols, 10 items).
Bodleian Library, Oxford (MSS Eng.hist.a.21, c.713-73; C1 (538), E59 (126)). Presented by his widow 1934. NRA 19043.

[563] **SANFORD, Edward Ayshford** (1794-1871)

MP Somerset 1830-2, W Somerset 1832-41

Election and constituency corresp and papers 1818-57 (*c*9 bundles), mainly Somerset 1830s; corresp as chairman of the committee on pensions 1838 (1 bundle); petitions 1830-*c*1835 (1 bundle); draft speeches and notes *c*1830-5 (1 bundle); misc personal and business corresp *c*1836-70 (*c*17 bundles), incl letters from the 7th Duke of Bedford; notebooks as chairman of quarter sessions *c*1835-40 (3 vols); misc accounts, etc 1816-71 (6 vols and bundles).
Somerset Record Office (DD/SF). NRA 31387.

[564] **SAUNDERSON, Edward James** (1837-1906)

MP co Cavan 1865-74, co Armagh (N division) 1885-1906

Corresp and papers 1864-1914, incl letters from politicians and other public figures 1886-1906 (35 items), general political corresp 1879-1906 (41 items), letter books 1866-1903 (4 vols), fragmentary political journals 1867-72 (3 vols), Orange Order papers 1887-1907 (15 items), scrapbooks mainly containing political press cuttings 1870-1908 (8 vols), and travel journal and speech notes, South Africa 1897 (1 vol).
In private possession. Copies are in the Public Record Office of Northern Ireland (T 2996).

[565] **SCOTT, Charles Prestwich** (1846-1932)

MP SW Lancashire (Leigh division) 1895-1906; editor of the *Manchester Guardian* 1872-1929

Corresp 1870-1930 mainly as editor of the *Manchester Guardian* (*c*5,000 items), incl corresp with Lord Bryce 1886-1921 (51 items), Lord Courtney 1888-1918 (16 items), Lord Gladstone 1897-1928 (17 items), Lord Loreburn 1898-1922 (42 items), Lord Morley of Blackburn 1888-1920 (46 items) and JE Taylor 1871-1905 (594 items); political diaries 1911-28 (2 boxes); press cuttings and other papers rel to elections, etc 1870-1932 (1 box, 1 vol); press cuttings of his leading articles, etc 1898-1931 (6 vols); bank books 1907, 1915-23 (4 vols), with other misc corresp and papers *c*1879-1932.
John Rylands University Library of Manchester (*Guardian* Archives). Deposited 1971. NRA 18162.

Corresp 1911-27 (2 vols); memoranda 1911-28 (7 vols).
British Library (Add MSS 50901-9). Presented by his son JR Scott 1932.

Letters to him and misc corresp kept as autographs (1 vol).
Balliol College, Oxford (MS 420). Presented by his daughter Mrs CE Montague. RAB Mynors, *Catalogue of the manuscripts of Balliol College, Oxford*, 1963, p369.

Misc letters, articles and obituaries 1896-1946 (1 vol).
Manchester Central Library (MS f 920 5.584).

[566] **SCOTT, Henry** (1746-1812), 3rd Duke of Buccleuch 1751

Lord lieutenant of Edinburghshire and Haddingtonshire 1794-1812, of Roxburghshire 1804-12

Political and military corresp 1774-1810 (*c*12 bundles), incl many letters from Lord Melville 1774-1810 and letters from Buccleuch to Lord Hopetoun and others rel to representative peerage elections *c*1790.
Scottish Record Office (GD 224). Deposited by the 8th Duke of Buccleuch 1967. NRA 6184 (Dalkeith Box VI).

Corresp and papers of him and his wife 1770-1812 (*c*20 bundles), incl corresp rel to peerage elections, politics and patronage 1775-*c*1812 (3 bundles).
The Duke of Buccleuch. Enquiries to NRA (Scotland) (NRA(S) 1275). NRA 6184.

[567] **SCULLY, Denys** (1773-1830)

Irish Catholic politician

Corresp on Catholic affairs 1803-18 (383 items), incl letters from Charles Butler, Lord Fingall and Sir Henry Parnell; papers rel to Catholic politics 1795-1830 (*c*56 vols and items), incl commonplace book 1794-1809, papers rel to the Catholic Deputation to London 1805, and the MS of his

Statement of the penal laws (1812); family and general corresp 1793-1830 (*c*145 items); business corresp 1801-2, 1809-14; notes on family history 1806; accounts 1810-30 (3 vols).
National Library of Ireland (MSS 27485-93 *passim*, 27501-42). Presented by Brian Mac Dermott 1983. NRA 29990.

[568] **SEALE, Sir John Henry** (1780-1844), 1st Bt

MP Dartmouth 1832-44

Corresp and papers, incl parliamentary papers *c*1830-*c*1840 (19 bundles).
Devon Record Office (D 3889). Acquired 1986.

[569] **SEYMOUR, General Francis Hugh George** (1812-1884), 5th Marquess of Hertford 1870

Lord chamberlain 1874-9

Corresp and papers rel to co Antrim and S Warwickshire elections 1869-81 (6 bundles); parliamentary and other political papers 1846-83 (6 bundles); corresp and papers as equerry to the Prince Consort and Queen Victoria mainly 1846-70 (10 bundles); as deputy ranger of Windsor Great Park mainly 1850-70 (2 vols, 11 bundles); as lord chamberlain 1863-80 (30 bundles); papers rel to military affairs 1827-83, nd (18 bundles, 6 items); accounts 1832-84 (4 vols, 14 bundles); diary, travel notes, etc 1835-81 (9 items); family and misc corresp and papers 1839-84 (*c*90 bundles); estate and legal corresp and papers 1849-84 (48 bundles); misc corresp and papers 1817-82 (*c*6 bundles), with other antiquarian and family papers.
Warwick County Record Office (CR 114A, 730). Deposited by the 8th Marquess of Hertford 1951, 1961. NRA 8482.

[570] **SEYMOUR, Horace Alfred Damer** (1843-1902)

Private secretary to WE Gladstone 1880-5

Letters from Sir Charles Dilke 1883-4 (15 items), WE Gladstone 1880-90 (118 items), EW Hamilton 1880-98 (123 items), FW Hill 1882-6 (34 items) and others 1873-1901 (120 items).
St Deiniol's Library, Hawarden (Glynne-Gladstone MSS). Deposited by Sir William Gladstone, Bt 1968. Access through Clwyd Record Office. NRA 14174.

[571] **SEYMOUR, Hugh de Grey** (1843-1912), 6th Marquess of Hertford 1884

MP co Antrim 1869-74, S Warwickshire 1874-80; comptroller of the Household 1879-80

Co Antrim election expenses 1869 (1 bundle); corresp and papers rel to Warwickshire elections and local Conservative party affairs 1880-1909 (10 bundles); political notebook 1880-1 (1 vol); commissions, appointments, etc 1862-1906, nd (1 box, 1 vol, 4 bundles, 3 items); accounts and

financial papers 1863-96 (7 vols, 4 bundles); addresses, diplomas, etc 1869-1911 (2 bundles, 9 items); Irish and Warwickshire estate corresp and papers 1879-1909 (5 bundles); legal corresp and papers 1881-93 (11 bundles); family, historical and misc papers 1884-1911 (9 bundles).
Warwick County Record Office (CR 114A, 730). Deposited by the 8th Marquess of Hertford 1951, 1961. NRA 8482.

[572] **SHARMAN CRAWFORD** (formerly **SHARMAN**), **William** (1781-1861)

MP Dundalk 1835-7, Rochdale 1841-52

Political and other corresp and papers 1804, c1830-61 (c140 bundles and items), incl corresp and papers rel to his plans for reform of the Union c1844 and of the Irish land laws; religious and misc corresp and papers 1831-61 (23 bundles and items); estate corresp and papers 1826-60 (c9 bundles, 18 items); autobiographical memorandum c1844.
Public Record Office of Northern Ireland (D 856). Presented by Crawford & Lockhart, solicitors, Belfast. NRA 18999.

[573] **SHARP, Granville** (1735-1813)

Abolitionist

Corresp and papers rel to parliamentary reform, the abolition of slavery, America, religious affairs, etc c1756-1813 (4 boxes), incl corresp with Thomas Clarkson, James Oglethorpe, the 3rd Duke of Richmond, William Wilberforce and Christopher Wyvill; copies of his diary (4 vols) and commonplace books (6 vols); misc literary papers (1 box); family, executorship and other corresp and papers.
Gloucestershire Record Office (Lloyd Baker Papers). NRA 10000.

Letter book 1768-93, mainly rel to the abolition of slavery.
York Minster Library (COLL 1896/1). NRA 12105.

Papers 1768-73 (3 vols).
New York Historical Society. See *Guide to archives and manuscripts in the United States*, ed PM Hamer, 1961, p420.

[574] **SHAW-LEFEVRE, Charles** (1794-1888), Viscount Eversley 1857

MP Downton 1830-1, Hampshire 1831-2, N Hampshire 1832-57; Speaker of the House of Commons 1839-57

Misc personal corresp and papers 1817-87, incl congratulations on his peerage 1857 (35 items).
Hampshire Record Office (38M49/7/111-35 *passim*). Deposited by Lady Bonham Carter, a descendant of his brother Henry, and converted into a gift 1986. NRA 550.

Misc letters to him and his daughter from politicians and others 19th cent (1 envelope).

Hampshire Record Office (15M50/1204/2). Deposited 1950 by Lt Colonel Michael Wallington, a descendant of his second daughter Helena. NRA 5382.

[575] **SHAW-STEWART** (formerly **STEWART-NICOLSON**), **Sir Michael** (1788-1836), 6th Bt

MP Lanarkshire 1827-30, Renfrewshire 1830-6

Renfrewshire election corresp and papers, incl papers of his brother and son, 1827-38 (12 bundles); political survey of Renfrewshire 1825 (1 vol); financial papers 1816-37.
Strathclyde Regional Archives (T-ARD). Acquired 1975. NRA 14672.

Political, family and financial corresp and papers 1811-36 (c5 bundles).
In private possession. Enquiries to NRA (Scotland) (NRA(S) 2623). NRA 14672.

[576] **SHEE, Sir George** (1754-1825), 1st Bt

MP Knocktopher 1798-1800; secretary to the Treasury (Ireland) 1799-1801; under-secretary for home affairs 1801-3, for war and the colonies 1806-7

Letters from the 2nd Earl of Chichester rel to politics, patronage and Irish affairs 1796-1814, and from the Dukes of Gloucester and York, mainly to Shee as under-secretary for war, 1805-10 (1 vol); political, patronage, Indian and family corresp and misc papers 1771-1823 (2 vols).
British Library (Add MSS 60337-9). Purchased from his great-great-great-nephew Richard Neall 1978. NRA 19146.

[577] **SHERIDAN, Richard Brinsley** (1751-1816)

MP Stafford 1780-1806, Westminster 1806-7, Ilchester 1807-12; under-secretary for foreign affairs 1782; joint secretary to the Treasury 1783; treasurer of the Navy 1806-7

Speech notes and papers rel to domestic, colonial and foreign affairs 1781-1814, with some personal and family corresp and other papers c1772-1826 (5 vols); misc letters to him 1770-92, with papers rel to Drury Lane Theatre c1792-1827 (1 vol).
British Library (Add MSS 35118, 58274-7, 63641). Purchased at Sotheby's 17 May 1897, lot 702 and 13 May 1974, lot 222 and at Christie's 16 Oct 1985, lot 117.

Corresp rel to political, personal and theatrical affairs 1771-1806, nd (56 items).
Public Record Office of Northern Ireland (D 1071B/E1). Deposited by the Marchioness of Dufferin and Ava 1957. NRA 5700.

Misc corresp, speech notes and papers mainly rel to parliamentary elections and Drury Lane Theatre 1782-1812, nd (4 bundles).
William Salt Library, Stafford (S.MS 343). NRA 8254.

Corresp and memoranda rel to the Prince of Wales, etc 1781-1812 (42 items).
Beinecke Library, Yale University, New Haven, Connecticut (Osborn Collection: Sheridan Papers). NRA 18661.

Notes and memoranda rel to the impeachment of Warren Hastings *c*1788-95 (173pp).
Untraced. Sold at Sotheby's 29 Nov 1971, lot 200, and exported. Photocopies are in the British Library (RP 730).

Speech notes (1 vol); family corresp (4 boxes).
Houghton Library, Harvard University, Cambridge, Massachusetts (MS Eng 1142, bMS Eng 1276). Acquired 1960, 1967. NRA 20129.

Additional papers rel solely to his literary career and to the management of Drury Lane Theatre are in the British Library (Add MSS 25906-26036, 29709-11), the Bodleian Library, Oxford (MS Eng.lett.c.214), King's College, Cambridge (Le Fanu Papers), the Theatre Museum, London and the Houghton Library Theatre Collection, Harvard.

[578] **SHERIDAN, Richard Brinsley** (*c*1809-1888)

MP Shaftesbury 1845-52, Dorchester 1852-68

Diaries 1849-75 (11 vols), incl accounts of parliamentary business and Dorchester elections 1857, 1865.
Dorset Record Office (D 51/15). Deposited by Mrs JLM Sheridan 1958-9. NRA 7917.

Political and personal letters from the 12th Duke of Somerset 1843-85 (*c*80 items); misc family corresp and papers 1826-43 (6 items).
Buckinghamshire Record Office (D/RA). Deposited by Sir William Pennington-Ramsden, Bt 1962-4. NRA 11704.

Family and legal corresp 1832-63 (1 vol, 194ff).
British Library (Add MSS 42767, 42768 ff187-380). Presented 1932 by the Dorset Natural History and Archaeological Society, which had acquired them from the 11th Duke of Bedford.

Letters to him rel to family, personal and political affairs 1819-83, nd (13 items).
Public Record Office of Northern Ireland (D 1071B, D 1231C). Deposited by the Marchioness of Dufferin and Ava 1957 and by Lady Hermione Blackwood. NRA 5700.

[579] **SHIFFNER, Sir George** (1762-1842), 1st Bt

MP Lewes 1812-26

Sussex election corresp 1807 (25 items); Sussex, Lewes and Brighton election papers, mainly printed, 1768-1832 (18 vols, 7 bundles, 5 items); papers rel to his baronetcy and to local affairs 1789-1835 (2 vols, 64 items); personal and family corresp and papers, incl diaries 1784-1837.
East Sussex Record Office (Shiffner MSS). Deposited 1954-8. NRA 9204.

[580] **SHIRLEY, Evelyn John** (1788-1856)

MP co Monaghan 1826-31, S Warwickshire 1836-49

Corresp rel to Warwickshire politics and society 1799-1840 (6 vols).
In private possession. NRA 7573.

Personal corresp and papers 1810-56 (several boxes); diaries 1823-56 (23 vols), incl notes of his votes in the House of Commons 1840s.
Warwick County Record Office (CR 229, 464, 2131). Deposited by Major JE Shirley 1952-81. NRA 17508.

Papers (mainly printed) rel to politics and elections in co Monaghan and Warwickshire 1826-1901 (1 box), incl misc letters rel to his candidature for S Warwickshire 1832 and analysis of voting among his tenants in co Monaghan 1826; estate corresp and papers 1807-48 (4 bundles).
Public Record Office of Northern Ireland (D 3531/C/3/1-4, E/1). Deposited by Major JE Shirley 1981. NRA 25608.

SHORE, see Nightingale.

[581] **SINCLAIR, Sir George** (1790-1868), 2nd Bt

MP Caithness 1811-12, 1818-20, 1831-41

Political and personal letters from Sir Francis Burdett 1813-44 (1 vol), JW Croker 1833-57 (1 vol), Joseph Hume 1812-53 (1 vol) and William IV 1818-37 (1 vol), incl some to his father Sir John Sinclair; letters mainly from politicians 1808-52 (1 vol); corresp rel to political and ecclesiastical affairs, incl some of his father, 1814-67 (4 vols); letters from Sir Brooke Boothby rel to literary affairs 1809-24 (1 vol); corresp with Lady Findlater rel to personal affairs 1809-13 and misc foreign corresp 1817-22 (1 vol).
Viscount Thurso (his great-grandson). Enquiries to NRA (Scotland) (NRA(S) 0189). NRA 10552.

[582] **SINCLAIR, Sir John** (1754-1835), 1st Bt

MP Caithness 1780-4, 1790-6, 1802-6, 1807-11, Lostwithiel 1784-90, Petersfield 1797-1802; agriculturist

Political, royal, ecclesiastical, agricultural and other corresp and papers of him and Sir George Sinclair, 2nd Bt 1778-1856 (8 vols), incl letters from George Canning 1803-24, George Dempster 1790-1814, Lord Hastings 1797-1811, Joseph Hume 1812-53, Lord Melville 1799-1811 and the Duke of Northumberland 1797-1816.
Viscount Thurso (his great-great-grandson). Enquiries to NRA (Scotland) (NRA(S) 0189). NRA 10552.

Collected letters and papers 1779-1807 (1 vol), mainly as president of the Board of Agriculture.
Reading University Library. NRA 10552.

Letters from George Washington 1792-7 (1 vol).
British Library (Add MS 5757).

Papers rel to West Indian affairs 1815-24
(1 bundle).
Bodleian Library, Oxford (MS Clar.dep.c.376).
Deposited by the 7th Earl of Clarendon 1959. NRA
6302.

Poems *c*1770 (1 vol).
National Library of Scotland (MS 2253). Purchased
1938.

[583] **SKEFFINGTON, Chichester** (*c*1746-1816),
4th Earl of Massereene 1811

MP Antrim 1768-97

Family corresp 1760-1831 (*c*970 items), incl corresp
of him and his wife rel to politics, patronage, and
personal and financial affairs.
Public Record Office of Northern Ireland (D 562).
NRA 6701.

Letters from him to his wife and misc corresp
1779-1831 (180 items).
Viscount Massereene and Ferrard. Copies are in the
Public Record Office of Northern Ireland
(T 2519/4). NRA 6701.

[584] **SLANEY, Robert Aglionby** (1792-1862)

MP Shrewsbury 1826-35, 1837-41, 1847-52,
1857-62

Diaries 1818-49 (9 vols), incl references to politics
and social reform; notes and essays nd (11 vols);
Italian travel journals 1818, 1836 (2 vols); accounts
1824-7 (1 vol); addresses and other printed election
papers 1826-41.
*Shropshire Libraries Local Studies Department,
Shrewsbury* (Morris-Eyton Collection). Deposited
by his great-great-granddaughter Miss VC Morris-
Eyton 1960-2. NRA 19299.

Diaries 1815-17, 1825-6 (3 vols); travel journals
1835, 1850, nd (2 vols).
Birmingham University Library (MS 9/v/2). NRA
15237.

Letters from Sir Robert Peel, Lord John Russell
and others rel to politics and social reform 1839-61
(23 items).
Birmingham University Library (Eyton Letters).
NRA 13199.

Foreign travel journal 1861-2.
Shropshire Record Office. See JS Batts, *British
manuscript diaries of the 19th century*, 1976, p53.

[585] **SMITH, James Parker** (1854-1929)

MP Lanarkshire (Partick division) 1890-1906

Corresp and papers 1864-1932 (*c*40 vols, *c*270
bundles and items), incl corresp with Joseph
Chamberlain and others rel to tariff reform, Liberal
Unionism, elections, etc and misc political papers
1867-1932 (*c*95 bundles), election and other

political press cuttings 1884-1928 (22 vols), diaries
and travel journals 1874-1906, nd (13 vols),
accounts and financial papers 1895-1926 (6 vols,
1 bundle), and personal, family and misc corresp
and papers.
Strathclyde Regional Archives (TD 1). Presented by
Captain AHC Parker Smith 1966-76. NRA 20864.

Letters from him as a pupil at Winchester College
1867-73, and letters to him as warden 1915-20.
Winchester College.

[586] **SMITH, John Abel** (1802-1871)

MP Midhurst 1830-1, Chichester 1831-59, 1863-8

Parliamentary and election papers *c*1828-68 (*c*90
items); corresp and papers rel to Sarawak 1842-67
(163 items), incl corresp with Sir James Brooke;
business, political, personal and family corresp and
papers 1816-71 (*c*400 items); journals, with
enclosures, 1820-69 (21 vols, 9 bundles);
commonplace books *c*1849-66 (3 vols).
West Sussex Record Office (Add MSS 27338-27568).
Deposited by Lt-Colonel and Mrs Anthony Dudley
Smith 1978. NRA 25734.

Letter books rel to Chichester elections and political
affairs 1831-7 (3 vols).
West Sussex Record Office (Add MSS 7169-71).
Presented by Mrs E Fuller 1965. NRA 7796.

[587] **SMITH, John Benjamin** (1794-1879)

MP Stirling 1847-52, Stockport 1852-74; chairman
of the Anti-Corn Law League

Corresp with John Bright, Richard Cobden,
Duncan Maclaren and CP Villiers 1845-79 (3 vols);
papers rel to elections at Manchester, Salford,
Stirling, Stockport, etc 1832-74 (4 vols); to the
Anti-Corn Law League 1836-80 (1 vol); to
Manchester and Stockport affairs 1836-80 (3 vols);
to banking 1832-69 (1 vol); misc papers (3 vols),
incl reminiscences (typescript copy) and
recollections of Peterloo.
Manchester Central Library (MS 923.2 S330-45).
Presented by his daughter Lady Durning-Lawrence
1914. NRA 18683.

[588] **SMITH, Sidney** (b 1805)

Secretary of the Anti-Corn Law League 1839-46

Autobiographical notes and précis of letters mainly
1839-82 (1 vol), incl material rel to the League
1839-46, elections 1845-81, Jewish disabilities
1848-56 and the reform bill 1867, and original
letters from Lord John Russell and others.
Mrs RW Smith. Enquiries to NRA (Scotland)
(NRA(S) 2637). A microfilm is in the Scottish
Record Office (RH 4/156). NRA 28375.

[589] **SMITH, William** (1756-1835)

MP Sudbury 1784-90, 1796-1802, Camelford 1791-6, Norwich 1802-6, 1807-30

Corresp and papers 1785-1860 (328 items), mainly rel to the anti-slavery movement, incl letters from William Wilberforce 1789-1833 (24 items) and corresp rel to elections, parliamentary reform, Catholic emancipation, the legal position of dissenters, etc.
William R Perkins Library, Duke University, Durham, North Carolina. Acquired at various dates since 1954, incl papers formerly in Sotheby's sale 14 Dec 1953, lot 506. *Guide to the cataloged collections*, 1980, pp523-4.

Personal and family corresp and papers (3 boxes), incl letters from his wife rel to the 1784 and 1802 elections, travel journal 1790 with reflections on the French revolution, and engagement diary 1817-18.
Cambridge University Library (Add 7621). Deposited 1962, 1972 by Philip Leigh-Smith, Victor Bonham-Carter and Katherine Duff.

Letters to him from politicians and others, mainly 1811 (*c*40 items).
Sir Ralph Verney, Bt. NRA 21959.

Corresp with his granddaughter Florence Nightingale.
St Thomas's Hospital, London. Presented by the executors of his great-great-granddaughter Mrs RF Nash *c*1953.

Letters to him and his family from politicians and others *c*1820-60 (25 items).
Untraced. Sold at Sotheby's 22 Oct 1980, lot 14.

[590] **SMITH, William Masters** (1802-1861)

MP W Kent 1852-7

Political and other corresp and papers 1830-59 (175 items), incl letters from the 2nd Earl Amherst 1847-52, *c*1856 (10 items) and corresp with Sir Percyvall Hart Dyke 1852-5 (12 items); misc corresp and papers rel to personal, estate and local affairs 1831-*c*1860.
Kent Archives Office (U 1127). Deposited by the executors of Mrs KA Smith-Masters 1965. NRA 11463.

[591] **SMITH-STANLEY, Edward** (1775-1851), 1st Baron Stanley of Bickerstaffe 1832, 13th Earl of Derby 1834

MP Preston 1796-1812, Lancashire 1812-32

General corresp mainly 1830-50 (several hundred items); political letter books 1826-7 (2 vols); copies of letters to and from him (7 bundles and folders); papers rel to natural history *c*1810-50 (9 folders); notebook 1824.
Liverpool Record Office (920 DER 13). Deposited by the 18th Earl of Derby 1968, 1980. NRA 20761.

Corresp and papers *c*1795-*c*1846 (*c*50 packets), mainly rel to natural history, but incl letters to him rel to elections 1795-1832 (1 packet) and from his son EG Stanley *c*1818-40 (1 packet), and corresp and papers rel to legislation 1828 (1 packet).
The Earl of Derby. Access restricted. Enquiries to the Librarian, Knowsley, Prescot, Merseyside L34 4AG.

Preston election accounts 1795-7 (50 items) and corresp 1794-1820 (29 items); misc papers rel to Lancashire elections 1826, 1837 (2 bundles).
Lancashire Record Office (DDK 1683/5-83, 1740/3-4). Deposited by the 18th Earl of Derby. *Guide to the Lancashire Record Office*, 1985, p268.

Letters from collectors and naturalists 1799-1850.
National Museums and Galleries on Merseyside Archives Department (Liverpool Museums Collection). Bequeathed to the city of Liverpool with his zoological collections.

Knowsley game book 1807-18, incl personal notes.
Merseyside Naturalists' Association. GDR Bridson and others, *Natural history manuscript resources in the British Isles*, 1980, p131.

[592] **SOMERSET, Henry Charles** (1766-1835), 6th Duke of Beaufort 1803

MP Monmouth 1788-90, Bristol 1790-6, Gloucestershire 1796-1803

Corresp and papers rel to elections and politics in Gloucester, Gloucestershire, Breconshire and Glamorgan 1796-1830 (6 vols, 12 bundles, 9 items); personal and family corresp and papers 1792-1835 (3 vols, 724 items), incl letters from his brothers and sons on military and political affairs; official and misc corresp and papers 1790-1834 (17 bundles, 61 items), incl militia papers 1799-1819; accounts and financial papers 1786-1835 (7 vols, 32 bundles, 23 items).
The Duke of Beaufort. Enquiries to the Archivist, Estate Office, Badminton, Gloucestershire GL9 1DB. NRA 6282.

[593] **SOMERVILLE, William Meredyth** (1802-1873), 1st Baron Athlumney 1863

MP Drogheda 1837-52, Canterbury 1854-65; under-secretary for home affairs 1846-7; chief secretary for Ireland 1847-52

Letter book as chief secretary 1847-51, incl copies of letters to Lord Clarendon, Lord John Russell, Sir Charles Wood and others rel to the poor law, famine relief, the general election 1847 and Irish legislation 1848-50.
In private possession. A photocopy is in the Public Record Office of Northern Ireland (T 2982).

[594] **SOTHERON-ESTCOURT** (formerly
ESTCOURT), **George Thomas John**
(1839-1915), Baron Estcourt 1903

MP N Wiltshire 1874-85

Corresp and papers rel to N Wiltshire Conservative
Registration Society 1868-71 (63 items), and to the
N Wiltshire elections of 1874 (85 items) and 1880
(5 items); misc personal corresp and papers
1861-1911 (36 items).
Gloucestershire Record Office (D 1571/F587-9,
X185-91). Deposited by TDG Sotheron-Estcourt
1958-73. NRA 2630.

[595] **SPEIRS, Archibald** (1758-1832)

MP Renfrewshire 1810-18

Corresp and papers rel to Renfrewshire elections
and to national and local politics 1782-1832 (c15
bundles), incl letters from the 1st Viscount
Melville, the 3rd Duke of Portland and Sir John
Shaw-Stewart, and papers rel to the creation of
votes; personal, financial, business and estate
corresp and papers 1781-1832 (c3 vols, c39
bundles).
In private possession. Enquiries to NRA (Scotland)
(NRA(S) 2234). NRA 15232.

SPENCE WATSON, see Watson.

[596] **SPENCER, Vice-Admiral Frederick**
(1798-1857), 4th Earl Spencer 1845

MP Worcestershire 1831-2, Midhurst 1832-5,
1837-41; lord chamberlain 1846-8; lord steward
1854-7

Naval, political, family and general corresp 1811-57
(78 boxes), incl corresp as lord chamberlain (1 box);
corresp of his secretary George Appleyard 1836-54
(27 boxes), incl corresp with the 3rd and 4th Earls
Spencer.
British Library (Althorp MSS J). Purchased from
the 8th Earl Spencer 1985. NRA 10410.

[597] **STACY, Enid** (1868-1903)

Socialist and advocate of women's suffrage

Corresp, engagement diaries and papers rel to
political and personal affairs c1882-1903, incl letters
from JR MacDonald rel to the Fabian Society and
Independent Labour Party 1894-5 (31 items) and
from other prominent socialists.
In private possession. C Cook, *Sources in British
political history 1900-1951*, v, 1978, p185.

[598] **STAFFORD** (formerly **O'BRIEN**),
Augustus Stafford O'Brien (1811-1857)

MP N Northamptonshire 1841-57; secretary of the
Admiralty 1852

Corresp as secretary of the Admiralty with Sir
Francis Beaufort, Lord Derby, the Duke of
Northumberland and others (c50 items); other
corresp c1852-7.
Untraced. Offered for sale at Phillips's 10 Dec
1987, lot 478.

Misc family corresp and papers c1760-c1860 (c90
items), incl letters to him from politicians and
others 1852-7 (c15 items) and letters from him to
his father 1844-5, nd.
Untraced. Henry Bristow catalogue 296, 1988, item
181; formerly Phillips's 24 March 1988, lot 5.

[599] **STANHOPE, Arthur Philip** (1838-1905), 6th
Earl Stanhope 1875

MP Leominster 1868, E Suffolk 1870-5; a lord of
the Treasury 1874-5

General corresp and papers 1852-1905, nd (1 box,
45 vols, 71 bundles, 42 items), incl letters from
Lords Beaconsfield, Rosebery and Salisbury
1874-1903 (1 bundle), election papers 1868-74 (c7
bundles), and diaries and travel journals 1853-1905
(41 vols); corresp and papers rel to Kent affairs
and as an ecclesiastical commissioner 1836-1905 (7
vols, 14 bundles, 29 items); accounts and financial
papers 1869-1905 (16 vols, 2 bundles).
Kent Archives Office (U 1590/A124-30, C513-72,
C716, O188-218). Deposited by the administrative
trustees of the Chevening Estate 1971. NRA 25095.

[600] **STANHOPE, Charles** (1753-1816), 3rd Earl
Stanhope 1786

MP Chipping Wycombe 1780-6

Political, scientific and general corresp 1761-1816
(9 bundles, 153 items), incl letters to Lord
Shelburne 1778-94 (1 bundle, 25 items) and letters
from Christopher Wyvill 1780-91 (1 bundle, 15
items) and other politicians 1770-1811 (2 bundles);
political corresp and papers 1775-1816 (5 vols, 31
bundles, 8 items), incl corresp and papers rel to
the coinage 1775-1811 (7 bundles) and Catholic
emancipation, etc 1788-1820 (6 bundles), and
papers rel to electoral reform 1780-8 (7 bundles, 1
item); papers rel to his inventions and to scientific
affairs 1778-1846 (2 vols, 123 bundles, c50 items);
misc political, personal and legal papers c1770-1813
(2 vols, 3 bundles, 7 items); accounts, etc 1786-1816
(2 bundles, 2 items).
Kent Archives Office (U 1590/A108, C46-112, C711,
O162). Deposited by the administrative trustees of
the Chevening Estate 1971. NRA 25095.

[601] **STANHOPE, Philip Henry** (1781-1855), 4th Earl Stanhope 1816

MP Wendover 1806-7, Hull 1807-12, Midhurst 1812-16

Political corresp and papers 1807-55 (57 bundles, 7 items), incl Hull election papers 1807-13 (1 file), corresp and papers rel to Kent county meetings 1822-50 (6 bundles) and papers rel to the corn laws and protection 1826-51, nd (10 bundles); general corresp 1801-55, nd (1 box, 71 bundles, 258 items), incl letters rel to political affairs from JC Herries 1843-53 (14 items) and Lord Londonderry 1829-30 (11 items); papers as surveyor of the Green Wax and keeper of the records at Dublin Castle 1806-54 (3 bundles, 2 items); literary papers 1801-53, nd (1 vol, 14 bundles, 13 items); financial papers, with those of his wife, *c*1803-54 (13 vols, 19 bundles, 5 items); misc corresp and papers 1782-*c*1855 (12 bundles, 61 items).
Kent Archives Office (U 1590/A111-21, C120-227, C713, O163-6). Deposited by the administrative trustees of the Chevening Estate 1971. NRA 25095.

[602] **STANHOPE, Philip Henry** (1805-1875), 5th Earl Stanhope 1855

MP Wootton Bassett 1830-2, Hertford 1832-52; under-secretary for foreign affairs 1834-5; joint secretary of the Board of Control 1845-6

Papers rel to foreign affairs 1834-5 (1 box, 1 item); corresp and papers rel to India 1843-6 (1 box); political corresp and papers 1830-75 (26 bundles, 3 items), incl Hertford election corresp and papers *c*1832-53 (*c*4 bundles, 3 items), papers rel to the reform bills of 1832 (1 bundle) and 1867 (1 bundle, 1 item), and papers rel to the Irish Church bill 1869 (1 bundle); personal, family and general corresp and papers 1810-75, nd (*c*138 boxes and bundles), incl letters from Lord Aberdeen 1830-59 (1 bundle, 43 items), the 14th Earl of Derby 1840-69 (1 box), Benjamin Disraeli 1835-75 (10 bundles), Lord Ellenborough 1832-66 (1 bundle) and WE Gladstone 1835-75 (1 box); corresp and papers rel to royal commissions and the National Portrait Gallery 1844-73 (8 bundles); literary corresp and papers 1830-75, nd (69 bundles); accounts and financial papers 1823-75 (7 vols, 1 bundle); historical collections, autographs, etc.
Kent Archives Office (U 1590/A122-3, C296-477, C714, O167-87,S2/C6-26). Deposited by the administrative trustees of the Chevening Estate 1971. NRA 25095.

Diary of appointments, addresses, etc 1875.
Lincolnshire Archives Office (RA/4/A/3). Deposited 1971 with other family papers by Mrs CWP Lee of Revesby Abbey, formerly the seat of his son Edward Stanhope. NRA 6329.

Letters to him or collected by him from politicians, authors and others.
Untraced. Sold at Sotheby's 23 March 1981, lot 16.

[603] **STANHOPE, Walter Spencer** (1750-1821)

MP Carlisle 1775-80, 1802-12, Haslemere 1780-4, Hull 1784-90, Cockermouth 1800-2

Hull election and patronage corresp and papers 1784-5, 1796-8 (4 bundles, *c*73 items); misc election and general political papers 1779-1808 (4 bundles, 16 items); corresp and papers rel to militia and volunteers 1779-1815 (*c*269 items); general corresp 1772-1821 (*c*1,210 items), incl letters from Edward Collingwood, Lord Lowther and JS Stanhope; personal, family and estate corresp and papers 1768-1821 (3 bundles, *c*789 items); pocket diaries 1775-1820 (36 vols); account books 1783, 1815-17 (2 vols); library catalogues 1795-8, nd.
Sheffield Record Office (Sp St 60564-89, 60635, 60675). NRA 725.

Corresp and papers rel to militia business 1778-1819 (*c*65 items), canal companies 1775-1818 (*c*45 items) and misc matters 1775-1821 (*c*140 items).
West Yorkshire Archive Service, Bradford (Sp St). NRA 6959.

Library catalogues *c*1770, *c*1807 (2 vols).
Brotherton Library, Leeds University (MSS 508, 514). Presented by JM Spencer Stanhope 1942. NRA 25809.

[604] **STANHOPE, Sir Walter Thomas William Spencer** (1827-1911)

MP W Riding of Yorkshire (S division) 1872-80

Letters from politicians 1884-97 (13 items); letters from Lord St Oswald rel to political affairs, etc 1880-5 (15 items); papers as chairman of Holmfirth divisional Conservative association 1885-6 (119 items); press cuttings rel to West Riding elections 1865-80 (1 vol); letters from his son WS Stanhope in Egypt 1883-4 (43 items); corresp rel to railways, canals, local affairs, etc 1876-1902 (316 items); general corresp 1865-96 (368 items); journal 1849; travel log aboard the *Osprey* 1868; notebook as chairman of the West Riding quarter sessions 1881-4 (2 vols); commonplace book nd; accounts 1839-1908 (5 items).
Sheffield Record Office (Sp St 60615-17, 60648, 60685-6, 60719, 60725). NRA 725.

Family and trusteeship corresp 1871-1904, nd (*c*30 items).
West Yorkshire Archive Service, Bradford (Sp St). NRA 6959.

Political corresp 1865-75 (1 vol); journal 1849-53 (1 vol).
Brotherton Library, Leeds University (MSS 430, 507). Presented by JM Spencer Stanhope 1942. NRA 25809.

STANLEY, ES, see Smith-Stanley.

[605] **STANLEY, Mary Catherine** (1824-1900), Countess of Derby

Political hostess

Corresp and papers, incl letters from Lord Dalling, the Queen of the Netherlands and Lord Sherbrooke.
In private possession. Access (restricted) through the Historical Manuscripts Commission.

[606] **STAPLETON, Augustus Granville** (1800-1880)

Private secretary to George Canning 1824-7; stood for Birmingham 1837

Corresp and papers 1793-1896 (*c*60 bundles), mainly as private secretary, incl letters from Canning 1822-7 (33 items), corresp with John Backhouse 1823-31 (61 items), Lord Dunglas 1824-9 (35 items), Lord William Hervey 1825-7 (14 items) and Lord Morley 1818-33 (32 items), corresp and papers 1824-32 rel to *The political life of George Canning* (1831) and other literary works (99 items), and political and patronage corresp and papers of Canning 1822-7.
West Yorkshire Archive Service, Leeds (Stapleton MSS). Purchased by Leeds City Council 1972; formerly sold at Sotheby's 14 July 1952, lot 398, by his grandson EJ Stapleton. NRA 23599.

Corresp and papers mainly rel to personal affairs (1 box), incl corresp with the 11th Earl of Home 1840-80, autograph albums (2 vols), and memorandum and commonplace books; engagement diaries 1822-80 (42 vols).
The Very Revd HEC Stapleton.

Letters from Charles Kingsley rel to ecclesiastical, public and personal affairs 1845-71 (107 items); letters from the Kingsley family, Lord Carlisle, Lord Macaulay and others 1850-74 (*c*35 items).
Untraced. Sold at Sotheby's 14 July 1952, lots 400-1.

[607] **STAUNTON, Sir George Thomas** (1781-1859), 2nd Bt

MP Mitchell 1818-26, Heytesbury 1830-2, S Hampshire 1832-5, Portsmouth 1838-52

Personal and family corresp and papers 1743-1858 (8 vols, 489 items), incl election and other political corresp and papers 1835-52, political journal 1831-7 and travel journals 1826-7, 1830.
William R Perkins Library, Duke University, Durham, North Carolina. Mainly purchased at Sotheby's 25 July 1960, lots 451-6, from Philip Yorke, a descendant of his aunt Lucy. NRA 25905.

[608] **STEAD, William Thomas** (1849-1912)

Editor of the *Northern Echo* 1871-80, of the *Pall Mall Gazette* 1883-90

Corresp 1876-1912 (76 bundles), incl letters from WB Booth, James Bryce, Sir Henry Campbell-Bannerman, the 4th Earl of Carnarvon, the 1st Marquess of Dufferin, RB Haldane and Lords Milner, Morley of Blackburn and Rosebery; literary MSS (14 bundles), incl draft leading articles, etc for the *Northern Echo* (2 bundles) and papers rel to the Jameson raid (6 bundles); misc papers rel to imperial affairs, etc (8 bundles).
Churchill College, Cambridge (STED). Deposited by his grandson WK Stead 1986.

[609] **STEPHENS, James** (1825-1901)

Fenian

Corresp and papers 1848-96, nd (379 items), incl Fenian corresp 1848-96, letter book 1876-9, misc Fenian papers 1859-78, nd, and letters from him to relatives, etc.
Trinity College Library, Dublin (MS 9659d). Presented with the Davitt papers 1983.

American diary 1858-60.
Public Record Office of Northern Ireland. See *Deputy Keeper's report 1938-45*, pp31-4.

Diary of a stay in Paris 1874.
National Library of Ireland (MS 15517). Acquired 1967.

[610] **STEWART, James** (1742-1821)

MP co Tyrone 1768-1800, 1801-12

Letters from or about Lord Charlemont, mainly rel to the Volunteer movement and other political affairs, 1781-99 (77 items); political, family and misc corresp and papers 1761-1820 (*c*265 items), incl co Tyrone election papers.
Public Record Office of Northern Ireland (D 3167). Partly purchased, and partly deposited by HWB Stewart. NRA 20213.

[611] **STEWART-MACKENZIE** (formerly **STEWART**), **James Alexander** (1784-1843)

MP Ross and Cromarty 1831-7; a commissioner of the Board of Control 1832-4; joint secretary of the Board of Control 1834

Corresp and papers rel to the Board of Control *c*1831-6 (113 items); to Ceylon 1836-41; to the Ionian Islands 1840-3; to Parliament and national affairs 1831-6, nd (291 items); to elections in Ross-shire 1817-37 (*c*1,000 items); to family, estate and local affairs *c*1795-1856 (44 vols, *c*1,000 items); personal corresp and papers 1817-43 (*c*15 bundles); diary 1828; commonplace books 1799, 1815 (2 vols); notebook 1802; travel journal 1815; misc vouchers and accounts *c*1817-53 (4 boxes).

Scottish Record Office (GD 46). Presented by Mr and Mrs FA Stewart-Mackenzie 1954. NRA 30101.

See also *Colonial Governors*.

STEWART-NICOLSON, see Shaw-Stewart.

[612] STIRLING-MAXWELL (formerly **STIRLING**), **Sir William** (1818-1878), 9th Bt

MP Perthshire 1852-68, 1874-8

Political corresp, mainly rel to Perthshire 1839-74 and Falkirk burghs 1845-6 (10 bundles); corresp rel to public affairs and patronage 1852-77 (13 bundles); to personal and family matters 1830-77 (10 bundles, 305 items); to literature and art *c*1833-77 (18 bundles); to estate affairs 1844-77 (15 bundles); general corresp 1828-77 (23 boxes, *c*9 bundles), incl political and patronage letters; misc corresp and papers 1816-77 (506 items); diaries, memorandum books, speeches, etc 1833-78 (29 vols).
Strathclyde Regional Archives (T-SK 28-33). Deposited by Mrs Stirling 1975. NRA 24669.

[613] STOPFORD, James George Henry (1823-1914), 5th Earl of Courtown 1858

Irish politician

Corresp rel to co Wexford elections 1866-86 (275 items); religious corresp and papers 1867-1905 (497 items); legal, estate and local corresp and papers 1861-1927 (*c*850 items), incl papers rel to the Property Defence Association; letters mainly from his father and eldest son rel to politics, etc 1845-59, 1884-1914 (247 items); abstract of corresp 1854-92 (1 vol); journal 1842 and diaries 1847-1914 (20 vols); accounts 1860-1915 (56 vols); religious memorandum book; drafts and notes for a family history.
Trinity College Library, Dublin (Courtown Papers). Deposited by Lady Courtown 1977-8. NRA 23150.

[614] STOPFORD, James Thomas (1794-1858), 4th Earl of Courtown 1835

MP co Wexford 1820-30

Corresp and papers rel to co Wexford politics 1820-31, mainly the 1826 election (137 items); legal, estate and local corresp 1822-60 (87 items); family corresp 1821-5, 1841-2 (2 vols, 25 items); accounts 1826-8 (1 vol).
Trinity College Library, Dublin (Courtown Papers). Deposited by Lady Courtown 1977-8. NRA 23150.

[615] STOREY, Samuel (1841-1925)

MP Sunderland 1881-95, 1910

Corresp and papers 1883-1922, incl corresp and papers rel to politics and elections in Sunderland, co Durham and Newcastle-upon-Tyne.
In private possession. C Cook, *Sources in British political history 1900-1951*, iv, 1977, p187.

[616] STRUTT, Edward (1801-1880), 1st Baron Belper 1856

MP Derby 1830-48, Arundel 1851-2, Nottingham 1852-6; chancellor of the Duchy of Lancaster 1852-4

Letters from politicians *c*1832-79 (252 items); literary, scientific and misc corresp *c*1827-1879 (6 bundles); misc appointments, speech notes, etc 1807-74 (*c*20 items); travel journal 1816.
Nottinghamshire Archives Office (DD. BK 7,8). Deposited 1977. NRA 30442.

[617] STUART, Lord Dudley Coutts (1803-1854)

MP Arundel 1830-7, Marylebone 1847-54

Corresp with politicians and others and papers rel to Polish affairs 1833-*c*1854 (4 vols), incl letters from TW Beaumont 1836-46 (11 items), Prince Adam Czartoryski 1834-*c*1854 (29 items), the 4th Earl of Ilchester 1841-7 (18 items) and Count Ladislas Zamoyski 1834-49 (25 items); corresp rel to his marriage, with other family and general corresp and misc papers 1812-58 (*c*9 vols).
The Harrowby Manuscripts Trust. Enquiries to the Archivist, Sandon Hall, Stafford ST18 0DN. NRA 1561.

[618] STUART-WORTLEY, Hon James Archibald (1805-1881)

MP Halifax 1835-7, Bute 1842-59; judge advocate-general 1846; solicitor-general 1856-7

Letters from Lord Palmerston 1856 (1 bundle); misc family and general corresp, legal notes, etc 1824-81 (8 bundles and items).
Sheffield Record Office (WhM 499, 690). Deposited by the 4th Earl of Wharncliffe 1954 and RA Cecil 1979. NRA 1077.

Letters from his wife and others 1845-68 (40 items).
Brynmor Jones Library, Hull University (DDFA(3)/3). Deposited by Nigel Forbes-Adam 1981. NRA 6494.

[619] STUART-WORTLEY-MACKENZIE, John (1801-1855), 2nd Baron Wharncliffe 1845

MP Bossiney 1823-30, 1831-2, Perth burghs 1830, W Riding of Yorkshire 1841-5; secretary of the Board of Control 1830; under-secretary for war and the colonies 1835

Political and general corresp 1834-55 (5 bundles), incl letters from Lord Fitzwilliam 1841, 1850 and Sir Robert Peel 1834-41, letters rel to the chairmanship of the House of Lords 1851, and West Riding election addresses 1837, 1840.
Sheffield Record Office (WhM 526-30). Deposited by the 4th Earl of Wharncliffe 1953. NRA 1077.

Collection of autograph letters and notes to Wharncliffe and others from politicians, scientists, artists, etc mainly 1820-60 (several hundred items). *Lord Montagu of Beaulieu* (his great-grandson). Enquiries to the Heritage Education Officer and Archivist, Beaulieu Abbey, Brockenhurst, Hampshire SO4 7ZN. NRA 4880 (MI H236).

[620] **STURGE, Joseph** (1793-1859)

Abolitionist

Corresp with John Bright 1842-59 (1 vol), Richard Cobden 1839-59 (2 vols), and other politicians and public figures 1833-58 (1 vol). *British Library* (Add MSS 43722-3, 43845, 50131). Acquired 1934-60.

Journal of his West Indian tour [1837] (1 vol). *Rhodes House Library, Oxford* (MSS Brit.Emp.s.22/ G48). Purchased from the British and Foreign Anti-Slavery Society 1951. NRA 1095.

[621] **SUTHERLAND-LEVESON-GOWER, Anne** (1829-1888), Duchess of Sutherland

Mistress of the Robes 1870-4

Corresp and misc papers rel to personal, political and social affairs 1841-88 (4 vols, *c*30 bundles), incl letters and telegrams from Queen Victoria 1868-88 (80 items) and the Prince of Wales 1872-80, nd (3 bundles), and letters from Lord Beaconsfield 1860-80, nd (50 items) and Lord Palmerston 1859-63 (17 items). *Staffordshire Record Office* (D 593/P/24, 28). Deposited by the trustees of the will of the 4th Duke of Sutherland 1959. NRA 10699.

[622] **SUTHERLAND-LEVESON-GOWER** (formerly **LEVESON-GOWER**), **George Granville** (1786-1861), 2nd Duke of Sutherland 1833

MP St Mawes 1808-12, Newcastle-under-Lyme 1812-15, Staffordshire 1815-20

Corresp and papers rel to the Staffordshire election 1820 (21 bundles); political and general corresp and papers 1806-61 (*c*60 vols and bundles), incl letters from Lord Ellesmere 1823-50 (5 bundles) and the 2nd Earl Grey, Lord Lansdowne, Lord Melbourne and other politicians 1832-57, nd (4 bundles), corresp rel to a reform association in North Staffordshire 1837 (1 bundle), and election accounts 1815-18 (1 bundle); Sutherland militia corresp 1831-61 (3 bundles). *Staffordshire Record Office* (D 593/P/20,22,34, R/2/ 42, S/14, 16/2). Deposited by the trustees of the will of the 4th Duke of Sutherland 1959. NRA 10699.

Corresp mainly rel to Scottish affairs 1803-61 (61 bundles), incl letters from William Mackenzie on burgh elections 1840-1 (1 bundle); diaries, mainly copies, 1806, 1835-48 (8 vols); personal and household accounts 1808-61 (22 vols, bundles and

items); misc papers *c*1834-46, nd (1 vol, 1 bundle, 2 items). *National Library of Scotland* (Dep 313). Deposited by the Countess of Sutherland 1980. NRA 11006.

[623] **SUTHERLAND-LEVESON-GOWER, Harriet Elizabeth Georgiana** (1806-1868), Duchess of Sutherland

Mistress of the Robes 1837-41, 1846-52, 1853-8, 1859-61

Letters to her from Lord Melbourne and others *c*1826-61 among her husband's corresp (*c*12 bundles); begging letters received and vouchers for personal expenses 1844-50 (8 vols, 1 bundle). *Staffordshire Record Office* (D 593/P/20,22, R/2/ 41-3; D 868/11). Deposited by the trustees of the will of the 4th Duke of Sutherland 1959, 1966. NRA 10699.

Corresp, mainly letters from her sister Lady Dover, 1826-61 (3 boxes); commonplace book 1829. *National Library of Scotland* (Dep 313). Deposited by the Countess of Sutherland 1980. NRA 11006.

Diary of a journey to Berlin 1864 (1 vol). *British Library* (Add MS 45109). Bequeathed by Frank Hird 1938.

[624] **SWINBURNE, Sir John Edward** (1762-1860), 6th Bt

MP Launceston 1788-90

Launceston election corresp and papers 1786-8 (1 bundle); political papers rel to the sedition acts, parliamentary reform, etc 1789-1849 (9 bundles); militia and lieutenancy papers 1793-1807 (19 bundles); corresp and papers rel to local affairs 1798-*c*1860 (19 bundles); turnpike papers 1820-59 (9 bundles); accounts and financial papers 1786-1847 (36 vols, 3 bundles); personal, family, legal and estate papers 1762-1853 (*c*28 bundles); misc papers. *Northumberland Record Office* (Swinburne (Capheaton) MSS 195-607 *passim*). Deposited by Mrs RG Browne-Swinburne. NRA 8746.

[625] **TALBOT, John Gilbert** (1835-1910)

MP W Kent 1868-78, Oxford University 1878-1910; secretary to the Board of Trade 1878-80

Corresp and papers, incl political, personal and family corresp, some from the Gladstone and Lyttelton families, *c*1855-1910 (7 boxes), letters from him to his wife (1 box) and diaries 1854-1910 (53 vols). *Kent Archives Office*.

[626] **TAYLOR, Helen** (1831-1907)

Advocate of women's rights

Corresp rel to women's suffrage and social position, etc 1865-95 (3 vols); to the London School Board, etc 1867-89 (2 vols); to Irish and other political

and public affairs 1868-95 (1 vol); to the land question and literary work 1867-1900 (1 vol); to the Moral Reform Union (2 vols); to JS Mill and his works 1867-1901 (5 vols); to personal and family affairs 1848-1905 (12 vols); press cuttings and posters 1876-85, nd (165 items); business and misc papers (1 box, 1 vol, 60 items), incl some of JS Mill; notebooks, etc (4 vols); diary 1842-7 (1 vol).
British Library of Political and Economic Science, London (Mill-Taylor Collection). Mainly purchased from a dealer 1926, after sale by her niece's executors at Sotheby's 27 March 1922, lot 731. NRA 7531.

Personal and misc corresp 1874-95 (10 items); misc literary papers 1881-7, nd (6 items).
John Rylands University Library of Manchester. Purchased from Winifred A Myers (Autographs) Ltd 1980.

[627] **TAYLOUR, Thomas** (1787-1870), 2nd Marquess of Headfort 1829

MP co Meath 1812-29; a lord of the Bedchamber 1835-7; a lord in waiting 1837-41

Corresp and papers c1793-1865, incl co Meath election corresp and papers 1807-20 (1 vol, 56 items), co Meath and Cavan election letters and papers 1830 (8 items), militia papers 1793-1828 and misc corresp and papers 1829-65.
National Library of Ireland. NRA 29336 (catalogue of photocopies in the Public Record Office of Northern Ireland).

[628] **TEMPLE, Emily Mary** (1787-1869), Viscountess Palmerston

Political hostess

Letters from Princess Lieven 1822-56 (2 vols); corresp mainly with her mother and her brother Lord Beauvale c1802-51 (4 vols, 25ff).
British Library (Add MSS 45548-56 *passim*, 45911). Presented by her great-granddaughter Mabell, Countess of Airlie 1940, 1944.

Corresp with Princess Lieven 1823-54 (124 items).
Southampton University Library (Broadlands Papers GC/LI/42-165). Deposited by the Broadlands Archives Trust 1985. NRA 12889.

Family corresp c1820-65 (1 box), incl letters from Lord Palmerston 1828-32, 1840-65 (c75 items).
Southampton University Library (Broadlands Papers). Deposited by the Broadlands Archives Trust 1987.

Diaries 1835-69 (33 vols).
In private possession. Enquiries to the Librarian/Archivist, Hatfield House, Hatfield, Hertfordshire.

[629] **TEMPLE, Sir Richard** (1826-1902), 1st Bt

MP Worcestershire (Evesham division) 1885-92, Surrey (Kingston division) 1892-5

Journal-letters written to his wife recording proceedings in the Commons 1886-95 (11 vols); character sketches of prominent members of Parliament 1886-95 (2 vols).
British Library (Add MSS 38916-28). Presented by Sir Richard Temple, Bt 1914.

Corresp and papers 1849-1900 (6 boxes, 240 vols), mainly as an Indian administrator, but incl parliamentary speeches mainly on Indian subjects 1887-93 (34 items) and printed parliamentary and official papers 1882-98 (4 boxes).
India Office Library and Records (MSS Eur F 86). Presented by Sir Richard Temple, Bt 1922. NRA 11216.

[630] **TEMPLE-NUGENT-BRYDGES-CHANDOS-GRENVILLE** (formerly **NUGENT-TEMPLE-GRENVILLE**), **Richard** (1776-1839), 2nd Marquess of Buckingham 1813, 1st Duke of Buckingham and Chandos 1822

MP Buckinghamshire 1797-1813; vice-president of the Board of Trade and joint paymaster-general 1806-7; lord steward 1830

Political, personal, literary and antiquarian corresp and papers 1796-1839, incl Buckinghamshire election papers 1802-13, political and general letter books 1806-9, 1818-32, 1836-8 (6 vols), political journal with copies of letters and speeches 1811-16 (1 vol), draft speeches, notes, etc rel to Ireland 1816 (1 vol), and political and personal diaries 1823, 1827-8 (2 vols).
Huntington Library, San Marino, California. Purchased 1925 after sale in 1921 by his great-granddaughter Baroness Kinloss. *Guide to British historical manuscripts in the Huntington Library, 1982, pp155-97 passim.*

[631] **TENNANT, Sir Charles** (1823-1906), 1st Bt

MP Glasgow 1879-80, Peebles and Selkirk 1880-6

Misc political and personal corresp and papers c1857-c1903 (c14 bundles), incl letters from WE Gladstone and his wife (2 bundles); corresp and papers mainly rel to the purchase of works of art 1872-1903 (9 bundles).
Lord Glenconner (his great-grandson). Enquiries to NRA (Scotland) (NRA(S) 1369). NRA 20770.

[632] **TENNENT, Sir James Emerson** (1804-1869), 1st Bt

MP Belfast 1832-7, 1838-41, 1842-5, Lisburn 1852; joint secretary of the Board of Control 1841-5; permanent secretary to the Board of Trade 1852-67

Political corresp and papers 1830-67 (35 bundles), incl Belfast and Lisburn election papers 1832-52 (c120 items); letters to him rel to India and Ceylon,

political affairs, patronage, etc 1833-69 (41 bundles), incl letters from Lord and Lady Enniskillen 1835-60 (18 items), Lord Fitzgerald 1841-3 (16 items), Lord Stanley 1851-3 (25 items), Lord Torrington 1847-54 (233 items) and James Whiteside 1843-69 (13 items); travel journals, literary papers and misc personal and family papers 1815-63 (c25 vols and bundles); business and estate corresp and papers 1839-69 (c15 vols and bundles).
Public Record Office of Northern Ireland (D 2922). Deposited 1979 by Lady Langham, widow of his great-grandson Sir John Langham, Bt. NRA 23442.

Corresp, drawings, water-colours and photographs for his *Ceylon: an account of the island* (1859) (2 vols).
Untraced. Offered for sale at Sotheby's 15 Dec 1980, lot 159.

[633] **TENNYSON D'EYNCOURT** (formerly **TENNYSON**), **Charles** (1784-1861)

MP Great Grimsby 1818-26, Bletchingley 1826-31, Stamford 1831-2, Lambeth 1832-52; clerk of the Ordnance 1830-2

Political, business, personal, family and antiquarian corresp and papers c1794-1859 (c8,500 items), incl letters and papers rel to his clerkship of the Ordnance 1831-2, corresp with George Canning, Lord Lytton, Lord Melbourne, Sir Charles Monck, Joseph Parkes and others, corresp and papers rel to Grimsby, Stamford, Lambeth and Lincolnshire elections, and some political and other corresp of his father George Tennyson; diaries 1815, 1818 (2 vols); misc notes, printed items, etc (5 bundles).
Lincolnshire Archives Office (TDE, 2TDE, 4TDE). Deposited mainly by Mrs Ruth Tennyson D'Eyncourt and GS Dixon c1941-70. NRA 5698.

Corresp rel to Grimsby politics 1818-20 (c220 items).
South Humberside Area Record Office. Transferred from Grimsby Central Library.

Corresp and papers 1817-52 (185 items), mainly rel to the Lambeth elections of 1835 and 1852.
Lambeth Archives Department (IV/3). NRA 29984.

Letters from Sir Edward Bulwer-Lytton 1842-50 (31 items).
Hertfordshire Record Office (D/EK/C26). Deposited by Lady Hermione Cobbold 1953, 1962. NRA 4598.

[634] **THOMAS, Alfred** (1840-1927), Baron Pontypridd 1912

MP Glamorgan (E division) 1885-1910; chairman of the Welsh Parliamentary Party 1897-1910

Corresp and papers c1880-c1927 (c1,280 items), incl political corresp (123 items), corresp rel to the Royal Commission on the Poor Laws (67 items) and speech notes (c100 items).
Glamorgan Archive Service (CL/Pp). Transferred from Cardiff City Library 1983. NRA 17024.

Letters to him 1886-1913 (60 items), mainly rel to national and local politics and Welsh education.
National Library of Wales (MS 21958). *Annual report 1983-4*, p51.

[635] **THOMAS, David Alfred** (1856-1918), Baron Rhondda 1916, 1st Viscount Rhondda 1918

MP Merthyr Tydfil 1888-1910, Cardiff boroughs 1910; president of the South Wales Liberal Federation 1893-7; president of the Local Government Board 1916-17; minister of food control 1917-18

Letters to him from Liberal politicians, Welsh leaders, constituents and others mainly 1891-5 (350 items), with genealogical papers, pamphlets, press cuttings, etc.
National Library of Wales (DA Thomas Papers). Deposited by his daughter 1940-1.

[636] **THOMPSON, General Thomas Perronet** (1783-1869)

MP Hull 1835-7, Bradford 1847-52, 1857-9

Many of his papers are reported to have been destroyed by fire in 1874 at the Pantechnicon depository, London (LG Johnson, *General T Perronet Thompson*, 1957, p5).

Political and general corresp and papers 1824-68 (8 bundles, c50 items), incl letters from Sir John Bowring, printers' proofs of letters to the secretary of the Bradford Reform Association 1848-51, and corresp rel to Bradford and Halifax politics 1846-68; corresp and papers rel to his service in Sierra Leone, India and the Persian Gulf 1808-21 (6 bundles, c530 items); corresp and papers of his son Charles and granddaughter Edith mainly rel to their unpublished biographies of him, incl many copies of letters from him (some in his own hand) to his family and political associates 1828-69.
Brynmor Jones Library, Hull University (DTH). Presented by his great-niece Mrs Isabel Hughes. NRA 10609.

Corresp mainly with his family 1808-68, but incl a few letters to and from radical politicians (164 items); misc notes and memoranda nd (7 bundles and items).
Brotherton Library, Leeds University (MS 277). Presented 1970 by the widow of his biographer LG Johnson. NRA 15923.

See also *Colonial Governors.*

[637] **THORNTON, Henry** (1760-1815)

MP Southwark 1782-1815

Political and religious diary, with letter book of him and his wife, 1777-1815 (1 vol).
Wigan Record Office (EHC 18/M786). Presented by Edward Hall 1949. NRA 30192.

Family corresp and papers c1766-1938, incl copies of his corresp and that of his wife with Zachary Macaulay, members of the Thornton family and

others 1774-1815 (10 vols), diary 1795-1814 (1 vol) and 'Recollections', etc (1 vol).
Cambridge University Library (Add 7674).
Deposited by his great-grandson EM Forster 1966 and by Forster's executor WH Sprott 1970. NRA 30090.

[638] **TONE, Theobald Wolfe** (1763-1798)

United Irishman

Diaries and notebooks c1787-98 (9 vols); misc letters and papers c1790-7 (2 vols), incl papers rel to the United Irishmen and political notes; autobiography (1 vol).
Trinity College Library, Dublin (MSS 2041-50, 3805-7). Bequeathed by his great-granddaughter Miss KA Maxwell 1923 and by his great-great-granddaughter Mrs LT Dickason 1964.

TRELAWNY, see Salusbury-Trelawny.

[639] **TROLLOPE, John** (1800-1874), 1st Baron Kesteven 1868

MP S Lincolnshire 1841-68; president of the Poor Law Board 1852

Corresp rel to national and local politics 1839-69 (3 bundles); manuscript poll books 1832 (2 vols); S Lincolnshire registration fund accounts 1872, 1873 (2 items); minutes of evidence, Aylesbury petition 1859 (2 vols); papers rel to Lincolnshire yeomanry and militia, quarter sessions, etc 1802-70 (c24 bundles); corresp rel to his peerage 1868 (1 bundle); hunting and other misc papers.
Lincolnshire Archives Office (TB). Bequeathed by the Hon Mrs N Trollope-Bellew 1976. NRA 6115.

[640] **TWISS, Horace** (1787-1849)

MP Wootton Bassett 1820-30, Newport 1830-1, Bridport 1835-7; under-secretary for war and the colonies 1828-30

Corresp with Lord Brougham, JW Croker, Lord Dudley, Lord Lincoln and others rel to politics, elections, patronage, his biography of Lord Eldon, etc 1807-48 (3 vols).
Bodleian Library, Oxford (MSS Don.d.94-5, MS Eng.lett.e.157). Presented by AB Emden 1951, and purchased from Jarndyce 1978.

[641] **URQUHART, David** (1805-1877)

MP Stafford 1847-52

Corresp and papers rel to Chartism 1838-40, 1853-9 (3 bundles); to the Stafford election 1847 (1 bundle); to the Working Men's Foreign Affairs Committees mainly 1855-62 (c28 bundles); corresp, memoranda, literary MSS, etc 1811-77 (over 100 bundles and items), mainly rel to his diplomatic career and foreign affairs.
Balliol College, Oxford. Bequeathed by FF Urquhart 1934. NRA 11691.

See also *Diplomats*.

[642] **VANE** (formerly **STEWART**), **General Charles William** (1778-1854), 1st Baron Stewart 1814, 3rd Marquess of Londonderry 1822

MP Thomastown 1800, co Londonderry 1800, 1801-14; under-secretary for war and the colonies 1807-9

Personal and political corresp 1809-54 (113 bundles), incl letters from Lord Aberdeen, the 2nd Duke of Buckingham, Lord Hardinge, Sir Robert Peel, Lord Strangford, Lord Adolphus Vane and the Duke of Wellington; political, estate and general corresp and papers 1812-54 (81 bundles), incl letters and papers rel to Catholic emancipation 1827-8, Durham city elections 1841-3 and the co Down election 1852; diplomatic corresp and papers 1813-27 (48 boxes); military papers 1796-1813 (1 bundle, 6 items); appointments 1818-30 (3 bundles); accounts and financial papers 1811-56 (1 vol, 3 bundles, 11 items); misc papers (1 vol, 3 bundles, 3 items).
Durham County Record Office (D/Lo). Deposited by the 9th Marquess of Londonderry 1963, 1969. NRA 11528. (Most of the private letters that he received from his half-brother Lord Castlereagh were lost at sea in 1829 while on loan to the Bishop of Calcutta for a projected biography of Castlereagh.)

Corresp and papers rel to co Down politics, with some of the 1st and 2nd Marquesses, 1805-30 (325 items); corresp and papers rel to political, foreign and military affairs 1808-54 (5 vols, 363 items); misc corresp and papers 1822-47 (c50 items); printed account of his career to 1838 (1 vol).
Public Record Office of Northern Ireland (D 3030). Presented by the National Trust 1976. NRA 12865.

[643] **VANE, Frances Anne Emily** (1800-1865), Marchioness of Londonderry

Political hostess

Personal and political corresp c1816-64 (64 bundles), incl copies of letters from Benjamin Disraeli 1837-64 (c240 items) and letters from James Farrer rel to the S Durham election 1857 (7 items); 'Narrative of a visit to the courts of Vienna, Constantinople, Athens, Naples etc . . .', 1844 (1 vol); social and personal papers 1818-61 (1 vol, 2 bundles, 3 items); accounts and other financial papers 1853-65 (4 bundles, 28 items); estate and business corresp 1844-65 (31 bundles); misc papers 1828-62 (6 vols, 11 items).
Durham County Record Office (D/Lo). Deposited by the 9th Marquess of Londonderry 1963, 1969. NRA 11528.

Letters from Benjamin Disraeli and others rel to political and social affairs c1850-60 (27 items); personal, family and misc corresp and papers 1813-c1860 (6 vols, 38 items); continental travel journal c1840 (1 vol).
Public Record Office of Northern Ireland (D 3030). Presented by the National Trust 1976. NRA 12865.

[644] **VANE-TEMPEST-STEWART** (formerly **VANE-TEMPEST**), **Charles Stewart** (1852-1915), 6th Marquess of Londonderry 1884

MP co Down 1878-84; lord lieutenant of Ireland 1886-9; postmaster-general 1900-2; president of the Poor Law Board 1902-5; lord president of the Council 1903-5

Election and other political papers 1874-1912 (2 vols, 3 bundles, 3 items); personal and social papers 1881-7, 1905-13 (1 vol, 3 bundles, 69 items); accounts and other financial papers 1884-1915 (28 vols, 25 bundles), incl accounts as lord lieutenant 1885-9 (19 vols); misc papers 1885-1915 (35 vols, 4 bundles, 9 items), incl press cuttings 1886-1915 (32 vols). *Durham County Record Office* (D/Lo). Deposited by the 9th Marquess of Londonderry 1963, 1969. NRA 11528.

Election telegrams and press cuttings 1878 (2 vols); corresp mainly rel to British and Irish politics 1886-1912 (63 items). *Public Record Office of Northern Ireland* (D 2846/3/7-9). Deposited by his granddaughter Lady Mairi Bury. NRA 25609.

[645] **VASSALL FOX, Elizabeth** (1770-1845), Lady Holland

Political hostess

Political, literary, social and family corresp of Lord and Lady Holland 1785-1845 (254 vols), incl her corresp with the 6th Duke of Bedford, Lord Brougham, the 5th Earl of Carlisle, Edward Ellice senior, the 2nd Earl Grey, the 2nd Viscount Melbourne and the 3rd Viscount Palmerston and his wife; Lady Holland's general corresp 1791-1845 (12 vols), journals 1791-1815 (15 vols), memorandum books (1 vol) and literary papers (7 vols); Holland House dinner books 1799-1845 (8 vols). *British Library* (Add MSS 51520-51957 *passim*). Purchased from the trustees of the 5th Earl of Ilchester 1960.

Corresp of Lord and Lady Holland with CJ Fox and his wife 1791-1806, nd (5 vols). *British Library* (Add MSS 47571-5). Presented by Professor GM Trevelyan 1951.

Letters from Francis Horner 1805-17 (50 items). *British Library of Political and Economic Science, London* (R(SR)1054). Returned after Horner's death in 1817. NRA 7527.

Letters to Lord and Lady Holland and their family from politicians, authors and others mainly early 19th cent (*c*95 items). *Untraced.* Sold at Sotheby's 6 Dec 1984, lots 137, 157.

[646] **VAUGHAN, Benjamin** (1751-1835)

MP Calne 1792-6

Corresp and papers of Vaughan and members of his family 1746-1900 (43 boxes), incl letters from Sir Joseph Banks, Benjamin Franklin, the 1st Marquess of Lansdowne and William Manning, and notes and memoranda rel to politics, taxation, the peace negotiations of 1782-3, etc. *American Philosophical Society, Philadelphia, Pennsylvania.* Presented by Mrs Mary Vaughan Marvin 1950. *Guide to the archives and manuscript collections,* 1966, pp142-3.

[647] **VERNEY, Sir Edward Hope** (1838-1910), 3rd Bt

MP Buckinghamshire (Buckingham division) 1885-6, 1889-91

Corresp arranged by date 1868-1909 (*c*1,500 items), incl letters from Joseph Chamberlain, HJ Gladstone, WE Gladstone, Sir Wilfrid Lawson, Lord Rosebery and Sir Michael Sadler; misc and family corresp and papers 1847-*c*1910 (several boxes), incl letters rel to the Marlow election 1868 and parliamentary, political and election corresp and papers 1885-91; naval papers 1852-74 (15 vols, 1 file); journals 1863-1910 (10 vols). *The Claydon House Manuscripts Trust, Middle Claydon, Buckinghamshire.* NRA 21959.

[648] **VERNEY** (formerly **CALVERT**), **Sir Harry** (1801-1894), 2nd Bt

MP Buckingham 1832-41, 1857-74, 1880-5, Bedford 1847-52

Political and general corresp *c*1817-90 (*c*3 boxes), incl letters from Sir Henry Acland, Lord William Bentinck, the 3rd Earl of Chichester, Sir Bartle Frere, WE Gladstone, Sir George Grey, JP Plumptre and the 7th Earl of Shaftesbury; corresp and papers rel to Buckinghamshire politics 1832-52 (1 bundle); to the Aylesbury & Buckingham Railway Co 1853-79 (1 box); to the Indian mutiny, the Franco-Prussian war, his antiquarian interests, etc (1 box, 6 bundles); family corresp *c*1814-94 (*c*10 boxes), incl many letters from his sister-in-law Florence Nightingale; misc corresp *c*1817-93 (*c*4 boxes); journals and notebooks *c*1830-61 (13 vols); travel journals and related papers 1811-58 (*c*20 vols, 1 parcel); yearly reviews of his life 1829-41, 1850 (1 vol); political and general reminiscences (2 vols); account book 1883-94. *The Claydon House Manuscripts Trust, Middle Claydon, Buckinghamshire.* NRA 21959.

[649] **VERNON, Sir Harry Foley** (1834-1920), 1st Bt

MP E Worcestershire 1861-8

Corresp and papers rel to politics and elections in E Worcestershire *c*1859-80 (*c*665 items); misc appointments, commissions, etc 1860-94 (*c*13 items).
Hereford and Worcester Record Office, Worcester (705:7). Deposited by Mrs RA Horton 1974. NRA 1483.

[650] **VESEY, John** (1771-1855), 2nd Viscount De Vesci 1804

MP Maryborough 1796-7; Irish representative peer 1839-55

Corresp and papers rel to Queen's County elections 1811-22 (1 vol, 1 bundle); to the co Carlow election 1835 (1 bundle); misc patronage corresp 1814-35 (1 bundle); letters and papers rel to Queen's County affairs 1824-38 (1 bundle); to the Abbeyleix yeomanry 1802, 1832 (1 bundle); estate, local, legal, financial and misc corresp and papers 1799-1855 (2 vols, 13 bundles, 4 items).
Viscount De Vesci. Enquiries to the Public Record Office of Northern Ireland. NRA 30023.

[651] **VESEY, John Robert William** (1844-1903), 4th Viscount De Vesci 1875

Lord lieutenant of Queen's County 1883-1900

Political corresp *c*1872-1900 (1 file), mainly 1886-97, incl letters from the 8th Duke of Argyll, Joseph Chamberlain, the 8th Duke of Devonshire and WE Gladstone; letters rel to his UK peerage 1884 (1 envelope); notes for speeches on Ireland, etc (3 bundles); diaries 1879-1901 (23 vols); military and legal papers (2 bundles).
Somerset Record Office (DD/DRU). Deposited by BAA Dru 1981. NRA 28627.

Journal of Egyptian campaign 1882 (typescript copy); misc estate, local and personal corresp and papers 1872-1900 (*c*10 bundles).
Viscount De Vesci. Enquiries to the Public Record Office of Northern Ireland. NRA 30023.

[652] **VESEY, Thomas** (1803-1875), 3rd Viscount De Vesci 1855

MP Queen's County 1835-7, 1841-52; Irish representative peer 1857-75

Corresp and papers rel to Queen's County and co Carlow politics 1832-76 (2 bundles); corresp and papers rel to Fenianism, Disestablishment and the Irish land question 1866-71 (3 bundles); patronage corresp 1859-72 (1 bundle); estate, local and business corresp and papers 1817-76 (89 bundles); personal and family corresp and papers *c*1815-65 (27 bundles).
Viscount De Vesci. Enquiries to the Public Record Office of Northern Ireland. NRA 30023.

[653] **VILLIERS-STUART, Henry** (1803-1874), Baron Stuart de Decies 1839

MP co Waterford 1826-30, Banbury 1830-1

Corresp and papers rel to politics, mainly co Waterford, 1825-66 (*c*13 folders, 3 bundles); misc estate and personal corresp 1822-53, 1872.
National Library of Ireland (MSS 24629, 24682-93). NRA 25261.

Political corresp and papers 1827-73 (2 bundles); personal and family corresp 1850-73, nd (1 bundle).
JHI Villiers-Stuart Esq. Copies are in the Public Record Office of Northern Ireland (T 3131). NRA 25261.

[654] **VILLIERS-STUART, Henry Windsor** (1827-1895)

MP co Waterford 1873-4, 1880-5

Election and other political corresp and papers 1872-93, nd (2 bundles); papers rel to the Stuart de Decies peerage case 1864-95 (1 vol, etc); business corresp and papers 1867-93 (1 bundle); personal and family corresp 1867-1902, nd (1 bundle); papers rel to his visits to Egypt 1877-88, nd (1 bundle); journal 1857.
JHI Villiers-Stuart Esq. Copies are in the Public Record Office of Northern Ireland (T 3131). NRA 25261.

Political, business and personal corresp and papers 1859-93 (*c*6 bundles, 5 items), incl draft political addresses *c*1880-5 (2 items).
National Library of Ireland (MSS 24639, 24694-9). NRA 25261.

[655] **VIVIAN, Sir Arthur Pendarves** (1834-1926)

MP W Cornwall 1868-85

Corresp, notebooks, speeches, etc mainly rel to elections and politics 1868-95 (7 vols, *c*2,200 items); corresp and papers rel to estate, business and local affairs 1871-1920 (5 vols, 303 items); personal diaries 1869-81, 1883-1923 (54 vols), incl summaries of letters from him; travel journals 1851-1903 (10 vols); memoranda and account books 1860-1920 (5 vols).
Cornwall Record Office (PV 12, PV 290). Deposited by HG Vivian 1952, and Helston Borough Museum 1957. NRA 2686.

[656] **VIVIAN, Henry Hussey** (1821-1894), 1st Baron Swansea 1893

MP Truro 1852-7, Glamorgan 1857-85, Swansea boroughs 1885-93

Political corresp with Lord Aberdare, WE Gladstone, Lord Hartington, CRM Talbot and others 1857-94 (*c*210 items); political and election papers 1860-93 (*c*160 items); business, financial and personal corresp and papers 1829-94 (53 vols

and bundles, c1,600 items); letter books and copies
of letters from him 1844-94 (2 vols, c490 items);
diaries and notebooks 1837-94 (15 vols).
National Library of Wales (Vivian Papers C, H3-4,
H13-282). Deposited by the 4th Baron Swansea
1966. NRA 25196.

[657] **VIVIAN, Lieutenant-General Richard
Hussey** (1775-1842), 1st Baron Vivian 1841

MP Truro 1820-6, 1832-4, New Windsor 1826-31,
E Cornwall 1837-41; master-general of the
Ordnance 1835-41

Letter books 1815-18 (2 vols), 1831-41 (6 vols);
military order books 1815-18 (6 vols); diaries 1804,
1820, 1833 (3 vols); visitors' book 1831-5 (1 vol).
National Army Museum (7709-6, 8011-38).
Purchased 1977, 1980. NRA 23378.

Misc political and personal letters to him 1813-42
(37 items).
National Library of Wales (Vivian Papers A37-73).
Deposited by the 4th Baron Swansea 1966. NRA
25196.

[658] **VYVYAN, Sir Richard Rawlinson**
(1800-1879), 8th Bt

MP Cornwall 1825-31, Okehampton 1831-2, Bristol
1832-7, Helston 1841-57

Corresp and papers rel to national politics and
foreign affairs 1825-79 (1 vol, c325 items); to
Cornish county and borough elections 1824-68 (249
items); to Bristol elections and constituency
business 1832-7 (400 items); to the Cornwall
yeomanry and other local matters mainly 1825-74
(543 items); petitions presented to him, Cornwall
and Bristol 1825-73 (c640 items); philosophical
journals 1841-6 and literary MSS (31 vols, 3
bundles).
Cornwall Record Office (22M/BO/34-9, FC/41).
Deposited by John Vyvyan 1952-3. NRA 2653.

Manuscript memoirs written in 1862, incl a
description of his political activities 1830-4.
In private possession. BT Bradfield, 'Sir Richard
Vyvyan and the country gentlemen 1830-1834',
English Historical Review, lxxxiii, 1968, pp729-43.

[659] **WAINEWRIGHT, William** (1777-1857)

Secretary of the Liverpool Parliamentary Office in
London 1823-57

Letters to him as secretary rel to patronage, trade,
legislation, etc 1823-36 (345 items), with other
papers of the Office 1808-37.
Liverpool Record Office (328 PAR). Purchased from
a bookseller by Liverpool Town Clerk's
Department 1908. NRA 17048.

WALKER, see Drummond, FW.

[660] **WALLACE, Thomas** (1768-1844), Baron
Wallace 1828

MP Grampound 1790-6, Penryn 1796-1802,
Hindon 1802-6, Shaftesbury 1807-12, Weymouth
and Melcombe Regis 1812-13, 1818-28,
Cockermouth 1813-18; a commissioner of the
Board of Control 1800-6, 1807-16, 1828-30; vice-
president of the Board of Trade 1818-23; master
of the Mint (Ireland) 1823-7

Political and personal corresp c1810-1830 (55
bundles), incl many letters from Lords Clancarty,
Liverpool, Melville and Shaftesbury, and rel to
Weymouth elections and patronage, Wallace's
candidature for the governorship of Madras 1813,
unrest in Carlisle and Lancashire 1819, commercial
questions, etc; commercial, Irish and misc papers
c1807-30 (7 bundles).
Northumberland Record Office (ZMI/S76).
Deposited 1962 by Sir Stephen Middleton, Bt,
great-great-grandson of Sir Charles Monck, Bt, to
whom Wallace bequeathed his papers. NRA 811.

Letter book and minutes as chairman of the
committee on the Irish revenue 1821 (3 vols); his
recollections of distinguished contemporaries
written c1830-40 (2 vols); misc corresp c1826-1839
(49 items); address from the City on his resignation
from the Board of Trade 1823 (1 roll).
Northumberland Record Office (ZHW/2/5-34, 2/112,
5/24). Deposited 1966 by Mrs Ruth Cairns, great-
granddaughter of James Hope-Wallace to whom
Wallace bequeathed his estates. NRA 24796.

[661] **WALLOP, Newton** (1856-1917), 6th Earl of
Portsmouth 1891

MP Barnstaple 1880-5, Devon (South Molton
division) 1885-91; under-secretary for war 1905-8

General corresp c1890-1910 (2 bundles); letter
books 1884-1905 (4 vols); Barnstaple and Devon
election papers 1878-91 (1 bundle); political papers
c1900-11 rel to Hampshire and national affairs, his
departure from the government, etc (1 box); War
Office corresp 1906-7, with other papers rel to
foreign and military affairs c1904-17 (1 box, 1
bundle); diaries, with those of his wife, from c1870
(c2 boxes).
Hampshire Record Office (15M84). Deposited 1984.
NRA 28451.

[662] **WALSH, John Benn** (1798-1881), 1st Baron
Ormathwaite 1868

MP Sudbury 1830-5, 1838-40, Radnorshire 1840-68

Corresp with his parents, sister and wife rel to
politics, etc 1811-36 (10 box files); journals
1811-16, 1822-3, 1830-77 (43 vols), incl notes of
political events and conversations, and of his
parliamentary and literary activities; chronological
list of main events in his life to 1871 (1 vol);
biography of his mother (1 vol).
National Library of Wales (Pen-y-Bont Hall Papers).
Deposited by the Hon Jane Walsh and the Hon
Mrs Bromley-Martin 1983.

[663] **WALTER, John** (1776-1847)

MP Berkshire 1832-7, Nottingham 1841, 1842-3; proprietor of *The Times*

Political, business, religious and family corresp c1804-47 (c300 items), incl corresp with his wife rel to the Berkshire election 1832 (7 items) and with EW Gray rel to politics c1835-42 (c80 items), and misc corresp rel to the Nottingham elections and petition 1841-2 (c35 items).
The Times Archives. Enquiries to the Archivist, *The Times* Archives, 214 Gray's Inn Road, London WC1X 8EZ.

Legal papers 1847 (1 bundle), rel to the Nottingham elections 1841-2.
Berkshire Record Office (D/EW1). Deposited by Cooke, Cooper & Barry, solicitors, 1954. NRA 5611.

[664] **WATSON, Robert Spence** (1837-1911)

President of the Newcastle-upon-Tyne Liberal Association 1874-97; president of the National Liberal Federation 1890-1902

Letters from James Bryce, Sir Henry Campbell-Bannerman, Joseph Cowen, the 4th Earl Grey, the 1st Marquess of Ripon and other politicians, social reformers, churchmen and authors 1860-1910 (c455 items); list of meetings about the Irish question 1885-90; scrapbook of articles rel to Russia, etc nd.
Newcastle upon Tyne University Library. Presented by his granddaughter Miss Mabel Weiss 1986. BS Beck, *The whereabouts of original material relating to Robert and Elizabeth Spence Watson*, 1986.

Letters from Lord Morley of Blackburn 1873-1910 (393 items); misc corresp with his wife, the 4th Earl Grey and others 1861-1907 (c70 items); journal letters from Tangier, Morocco and Spain 1879 (16 envelopes).
House of Lords Record Office (Historical Collection 136). Deposited by his grandson WB Morrell 1973. NRA 28248.

Diaries 1859-62 (5 vols); lectures delivered to the Newcastle-upon-Tyne Literary and Philosophical Society 1868-72; press cuttings 1834-1914 (7 vols).
Newcastle upon Tyne Central Library. BS Beck, *op cit*.

Misc letters mainly from his family 1865-1904; Norwegian travel journal 1887; visitors' book 1863-1919; typescript reminiscences and other misc papers.
In private possession (various locations). BS Beck, *op cit*.

[665] **WEBB, Martha Beatrice** (1858-1943), Lady Passfield

Fabian and social reformer

Political and personal corresp and papers, with those of her husband, 1870-1947 (86 boxes, 17 unboxed vols), incl her diaries 1873-1943 (58 vols); papers rel to trade unions, local government, professional workers and the relief of distress, with those of her husband, 19th-20th cent; misc papers 1885-1917 (2 vols).
British Library of Political and Economic Science, London (Passfield Papers; Webb Local Government and Trade Union Collections; MISC COLL 43, 238). NRA 7533 (partial list); *Guide to archives and manuscripts in the University of London*, i, 1984, pp26–8.

[666] **WEBB, Sidney James** (1859-1947), Baron Passfield 1929

Member of the London County Council 1892-1910; MP co Durham (Seaham division) 1922-9; president of the Board of Trade 1924; secretary for dominion affairs and the colonies 1929-30, for the colonies 1930-1

Political and personal corresp and papers, with those of his wife, 1870-1947 (86 boxes, 17 unboxed vols), incl Fabian Society papers (6 boxes); papers rel to the Board of Trade 1911-17 (2 vols); to East Africa 1929-31 (6 vols); working papers rel to trade unions c1814-1914 (298 vols), local government 1900-30 (350 vols), professional workers 1914-17 (20 vols) and the relief of distress 1914-15 (5 vols); misc papers, with those of his wife, 1885-1917, nd (9 vols, etc).
British Library of Political and Economic Science, London (Passfield Papers; Webb Local Government and Trade Union Collections; COLL MISC 43-352 passim). NRA 7533 (partial list); *Guide to archives and manuscripts in the University of London*, i, 1984, pp26–8.

[667] **WEBSTER, Richard Everard** (1842-1915), Baron Alverstone 1900, Viscount Alverstone 1913

MP Launceston 1885, Isle of Wight 1885-1900; attorney-general 1885-6, 1886-92, 1895-1900

Many of his papers are understood to have been destroyed (C Hazlehurst and C Woodland, *Guide to the papers of British cabinet ministers 1900-1951*, Royal Historical Society 1974, p148). Others were sold at Lawrence's of Crewkerne 14 Feb 1980, lots 430-61: the present location of some of these is unknown.

Corresp and papers (4 vols), comprising letters from AJ Balfour, Joseph Chamberlain and other politicians, judges, colonial governors and churchmen 1865-1915, and misc family corresp and papers 1795, 1827-74.
British Library (Add MSS 61737-40). Purchased at Lawrence's 14 Feb 1980, lots 434, 436-7, 450, 461.

Letters from HH Asquith 1892-1913 (21 items).
Bodleian Library, Oxford (MSS Eng. lett. e.159). Purchased at Lawrence's 14 Feb 1980, lot 431.

[668] **WELLESLEY, Richard** (1787-1831)

MP Queenborough 1810-11, East Grinstead 1812, Yarmouth 1812-17, Ennis 1820-6; a lord of the Treasury 1812

Political, family and general corresp and misc papers 1803-31 (21 bundles), incl letters from Stratford Canning 1808-28, Lord Grenville 1815-24, EJ Littleton c1815-30, Spencer Perceval 1811-12, Lord Wellesley 1807-30 and the Duke of Wellington 1819-29; political journal 1810-14 (1 vol); notebooks 1809-10, 1822 (2 vols).
Southampton University Library (A751: Carver MSS). Presented by Field Marshal Lord Carver 1987. NRA 30631.

WELLESLEY-POLE, see Pole-Tylney-Long-Wellesley.

[669] **WENTWORTH-FITZWILLIAM, Charles William** (1786-1857), 5th Earl Fitzwilliam 1833

MP Malton 1806-7, Yorkshire 1807-30, Peterborough 1830, Northamptonshire 1831-2, N Northamptonshire 1832-3

Corresp, canvass books, returns, accounts, etc rel to the Yorkshire elections 1806-12 (172 vols and bundles); election corresp and papers 1818-52 (13 bundles); political corresp and papers 1820-53 (9 bundles), incl letters from his father rel to the Queen's trial 1820, from the Duke of Bedford 1848-53 and from JE Denison 1846-52; general corresp 1807-57 (c800 items), incl letters from the 1st Baron Abinger, JN Fazakerley and the 4th Earl Spencer; letters from Sir Richard Bourke rel to publication of the corresp of Edmund Burke 1839-40, 1852 (2 bundles); misc corresp 1807-c1847 (10 bundles); family corresp 1801-55 (19 bundles); business and estate corresp and papers 1814-57, nd (44 bundles); letter book 1851-7; personal cash book 1855-7; diary 1857; commonplace book nd.
Sheffield Record Office (WWM/E, G). Deposited by the 9th Earl Fitzwilliam 1949. NRA 1083.

Corresp rel to Northamptonshire and Yorkshire politics and local affairs, estate business, family matters, etc c1806-57 (several thousand items).
Northamptonshire Record Office (Fitzwilliam (Milton) MSS). Deposited by WTG Wentworth-Fitzwilliam 1946.

[670] **WENTWORTH-FITZWILLIAM, William** (1839-1877), styled Viscount Milton

MP W Riding of Yorkshire (S division) 1865-72

Corresp and papers 1858-71 (21 vols and bundles), incl letters mainly from his agent rel to electoral matters 1866-9 (1 bundle), letters from constituents 1867-70 (1 bundle), private secretary's letter book 1869 (1 vol), lists of divisions with notes of pairing 1865-8 (1 bundle), and notes rel to the ballot, the Irish church, trade unions, etc (1 vol).
Sheffield Record Office (WWM/T51-71). Deposited by the 9th Earl Fitzwilliam 1949. NRA 1083.

[671] **WENTWORTH-FITZWILLIAM, William Thomas Spencer** (1815-1902), 6th Earl Fitzwilliam 1857

MP Malton 1837-41, 1846-7, co Wicklow 1847-57

Political and election corresp 1838-93 (1 vol, 5 bundles), incl letter book rel to the co Wicklow election 1857; papers as lord lieutenant of the West Riding 1857-92 (4 bundles); corresp and returns rel to the 1st West Riding Yeomanry Cavalry 1844-61, 1884-6 (1 vol, 8 bundles); personal and family corresp 1827-99 (11 bundles); hunting, racing and yachting corresp and papers 1839-91 (12 vols and bundles); legal and estate corresp 1840-98 (8 bundles).
Sheffield Record Office (WWM/T1-50). Deposited by the 9th Earl Fitzwilliam 1949. NRA 1083.

[672] **WESTENRA, Warner William** (1765-1842), 2nd Baron Rossmore 1801

MP co Monaghan 1800, 1801

Corresp and papers rel to King's County and co Monaghan politics 1801-58 (219 items), incl some of the 3rd Baron; corresp and papers rel to the Scottish and Irish representative peerage, his UK peerage, etc 1828-35 (93 items); misc political papers 1825-52 (92 items); corresp and papers on military matters c1786-1803 (43 items) and as lord lieutenant of co Monaghan 1831-5 (59 items); personal, family, estate, etc corresp and papers 1807-57 (1,033 items), incl letters from his eldest son and others rel to co Monaghan politics.
Public Record Office of Northern Ireland (T 2929). NRA 25191.

[673] **WHITBREAD, Samuel** (1764-1815)

MP Bedford 1790-1815

Political, local and family corresp and papers 1792-1815 (c7,000 items), incl letters from the 6th Duke of Bedford (55 items), HP Brougham (40 items), John Cartwright (22 items), Sir Willoughby Gordon (45 items), the 2nd Earl Grey and his family (c100 items), Samuel Whitbread junior (c135 items) and Christopher Wyvill (39 items), and papers rel to Bedfordshire militia and county affairs 1794-1815 (c420 items), Catholic emancipation 1807-15 (125 items), parliamentary elections 1807-12 (210 items), petitions to Parliament 1792-1814 (79 items), misc political matters 1797-1815 (192 items), the poor law 1807-15 (107 items) and the Princess of Wales 1806-15 (190 items); corresp and papers rel to the impeachment of Lord Melville 1805-6 (16 bundles).
Bedfordshire Record Office (Whitbread MSS). Deposited by the Whitbread family 1958-84. NRA 1123.

Misc political corresp 1798-1815 (1 bundle); family and personal corresp 1784-1815 (c5 bundles).
Earl Waldegrave (a descendant of Whitbread's eldest daughter). Access through the Historical Manuscripts Commission. NRA 28249.

Letters mainly from the 2nd Earl Grey 1802-10 (104 items).
Durham University Department of Palaeography and Diplomatic (Grey of Howick Collection). Deposited by the 5th Earl Grey 1955. NRA 6228.

Letters from William Lee Antonie, the Duke of Bedford and George Harrison 1804-10 (14 items).
Bedfordshire Record Office (UN 525-35, 546-7, 554). Deposited by Unilever Research Laboratory 1962. NRA 7125.

Cash books 1797, 1801-2 (3 vols).
Derbyshire Record Office (90M/E1-3). NRA 8918.

Cash book 1800 (1 vol).
Bedfordshire Record Office (Z 430). NRA 6970.

[674] **WHITELAW, Alexander** (1823-1879)

MP Glasgow 1874-9

Letter books 1863-79 (5 vols), incl letters rel to political, business and religious affairs.
Glasgow University Archives (UGD/101). Deposited by the Right Hon William Whitelaw. NRA 19052.

[675] **WHITMORE, William Wolryche** (1787-1858)

MP Bridgnorth 1826-32, Wolverhampton 1832-5

Election accounts and papers, Bridgnorth 1826, 1830, Wolverhampton 1832 (2 bundles); manuscript poll book, Bridgnorth 1826; letters from Sir Edward Ryan on Indian affairs 1829-30 (5 items); shrievalty corresp and accounts 1838-9 (2 bundles); travel journal 1814.
Shropshire Record Office. Deposited by his great-great-great-niece Lady Labouchere 1973. NRA 4482.

[676] **WHITWORTH, Charles** (1752-1825), Baron Whitworth 1800, Viscount Whitworth 1813, Earl Whitworth 1815

A member of the Board of Trade 1807-25; lord lieutenant of Ireland 1813-17

Corresp and papers as lord lieutenant 1813-17 (39 vols, 232 bundles and files, 54 items), comprising letters from Lord Sidmouth (3 files), general corresp incl many letters from CW Flint and Robert Peel (141 bundles), copies of letters to ministers (6 vols), general letter books (4 vols), statistics rel to the Irish civil establishment and pension list (4 vols), patronage corresp and papers (4 vols, 6 bundles), papers rel to civil defence (2 bundles), notes about Irish politicians (1 vol), engagement book (1 vol), audience books and indexes (5 vols), illuminated addresses (54 items), accounts, vouchers, dinner books and other papers rel to his household (14 vols, 57 bundles), and misc corresp and papers (23 bundles); accounts rel to the Kent election 1802 (2 bundles, 1 item); corresp and papers rel to his diplomatic career mainly 1798-1803 (5 vols, 18 bundles, 1,044 items); personal and

family corresp and papers 1778-1824 (2 vols, 6 bundles, *c*220 items).
Kent Archives Office (U 269/A263, A555, C341-6, L67, O195-253, O312-13). He married the widow of the 3rd Duke of Dorset, and his papers were deposited among those of the Sackville family by the 4th Baron Sackville 1950. NRA 8575.

See also *Diplomats.*

[677] **WICKHAM, William** (1761-1840)

MP Heytesbury 1802, Cashel 1802-6, Callington 1806-7; under-secretary for home affairs 1798-1801; chief secretary for Ireland 1802-4; a lord of the Treasury 1806-7

Irish corresp and papers mainly 1798-1804 (*c*130 bundles), incl corresp with Charles Abbot, Henry Addington, Lord Castlereagh, Lord Hardwicke, Sir Edward Littlehales, Alexander Marsden and other politicians and civil servants (31 bundles), general corresp 1802-4 (76 bundles), and papers rel to defence, sedition, ecclesiastical affairs, etc mainly 1799-1804 (*c*23 bundles); Treasury corresp, minutes and papers 1800-9 (3 vols, 9 bundles); corresp and papers rel to foreign affairs 1793-1802 (7 vols, 165 bundles), incl corresp with Lord Grenville, Lord Hawkesbury and the Duke of Portland; misc corresp and papers 1784-1840 (73 bundles and items), some rel to his public career, and incl personal corresp with Lord Grenville 1802-30.
Hampshire Record Office (38M49). Deposited by his great-great-granddaughter Lady Bonham Carter 1949-84, and converted into a gift 1986. NRA 550.

[678] **WILBERFORCE, William** (1759-1833)

MP Hull 1780-4, Yorkshire 1784-1812, Bramber 1812-25

Personal and family corresp 1771-1833 (*c*500 items), incl corresp with Thomas Babington 1807, 1826-32 (15 items), Lord Brougham 1804-31 (*c*24 items), Thomas Clarkson 1806-19 (25 items), Zachary Macaulay 1803-32 (*c*32 items) and James Stephen 1805-32 (27 items); copies of letters from him 1784-1826 made by his son Robert (1 vol); diaries, incl some copies, 1788-1833 (4 vols and loose papers); religious journals 1787-1826 (3 vols and loose papers); autobiography 1759-92 (1 vol); religious and misc papers 1779-1830 (1 bundle, 17 items).
Bodleian Library, Oxford. Purchased 1987 from the trustees of CE Wrangham, a descendant of his son Robert. NRA 7132.

Personal corresp 1776-c1830 (1 box, 5 vols), incl letters from Jeremy Bentham 1796-1812 (10 items), Lord Brougham 1806-20, nd (10 items) and George Canning 1811-26 (13 items), and corresp with Lord Muncaster 1788-1811 (19 items) and James Stephen 1794-1831, nd (25 items); family corresp 1814-33 (*c*3 boxes); misc papers, with those of his wife, 1772-1836, incl diary fragments 1787-1823, nd

(16ff), speech notes and papers rel to the slave trade.
Bodleian Library, Oxford (MSS Wilberforce c.1-4,30, d.9,13-17,20, f.5). Purchased from the executors of Dr Octavia Wilberforce 1965-6. NRA 7132.

Political and personal corresp 1782-1833 (585 items), incl letters from Lord Brougham, George Canning, Spencer Perceval, William Pitt and others rel to the abolition of the slave trade, Catholic emancipation, parliamentary reform, etc; bank account books 1829-33 (2 vols).
William R Perkins Library, Duke University, Durham, North Carolina. Acquired 1955-81. NRA 29600 (partial list); _Guide to the cataloged collections,_ 1980, p622.

Political and misc corresp 1788-1825 (41 items).
Kingston-upon-Hull City Record Office (DFW). Deposited by John Wilberforce. NRA 25933.

Diary rel to personal and social affairs 1814-23 (1 vol).
Wilberforce House Museum, Kingston-upon-Hull.

WILBRAHAM-BOOTLE, see Bootle-Wilbraham.

[679] **WILLIAMS, Arthur John** (1830-1911)

MP Glamorgan (S division) 1885-95

Political corresp with LH Courtney, Arnold Morley, John Morley, Lord Rendel and others 1879-1910 (c140 items); corresp and papers rel to the National Liberal Club 1883-1911 (c60 items); pocket diaries 1864-1911 (43 vols); misc personal, literary and legal corresp and papers late 19th-early 20th cent.
National Library of Wales (AJ Williams Papers). Purchased at Phillips's 26 June 1986, lot 158.

[680] **WILLIAMS WYNN, Herbert Watkin** (1822-1862)

MP Montgomeryshire 1850-62

Montgomeryshire election corresp and papers 1850-8 (90 items).
National Library of Wales (Wynnstay MSS L 1094-1246 _passim_). Deposited by Sir Herbert Williams-Wynn, Bt 1934. NRA 30545.

[681] **WILLIAMS WYNN, Sir Watkin** (1772-1840), 5th Bt

MP Beaumaris 1794-6, Denbighshire 1796-1840

Denbighshire election corresp and papers 1826-38 (c120 items); Montgomeryshire election bills and vouchers 1821 (1 bundle).
National Library of Wales (Wynnstay MSS L 868-1323 _passim_). Deposited by Sir Herbert Williams-Wynn, Bt 1934. NRA 30545.

Corresp and papers rel to Denbighshire and Merionethshire militia and yeomanry 1779-1813,

1827-8 (2 bundles); misc commissions 1796-1837 (6 items); voters' list, Merionethshire c1824.
Clwyd Record Office, Ruthin (DD/WY/6683-8, 6704-5, 6761). Deposited by Sir Watkin Williams-Wynn, Bt 1979. NRA 27821.

[682] **WILLIAMS WYNN, Sir Watkin** (1820-1885), 6th Bt

MP Denbighshire 1841-85

Corresp and papers rel to Denbighshire politics and elections 1840-59 (c100 items).
National Library of Wales (Wynnstay MSS L 922-1168 _passim_). Deposited by Sir Herbert Williams-Wynn, Bt 1934. NRA 30545.

Denbighshire political papers 1853, 1859 (2 items); corresp and papers rel to the Montgomeryshire yeomanry cavalry 1858-62 (1 bundle).
Clwyd Record Office, Ruthin (DD/WY/6707, 6763-4). Deposited by Sir Watkin Williams-Wynn, Bt 1979. NRA 27821.

[683] **WILMOT-HORTON** (formerly **WILMOT**), **Sir Robert John** (1784-1841), 3rd Bt

MP Newcastle-under-Lyme 1818-30; under-secretary for war and the colonies 1821-8

Corresp and papers c1806-37 (c445 vols), incl semi-official corresp and papers on colonial matters 1821-8 and as governor of Ceylon 1831-8, letters from political economists and other papers rel to the Poor Laws and emigration c1823-36, letters from abolitionists and other papers rel to slavery c1822-30, corresp and papers rel to Catholic emancipation 1825-9, general political corresp c1825-31, personal corresp with Bishop Heber and others 1806-27, and some estate and financial corresp and papers mainly 1830s; misc unbound letters and papers c1806-40 (c1,400 items), incl further political and semi-official corresp.
Derbyshire Record Office. Purchased from DWH Neilson 1987 (formerly deposited in Derby Central Library). NRA 27876.

Corresp and papers (some copies) rel to Lord Byron 1824-5, 1828-30 (8 vols).
In private possession. NRA 27876.

See also _Colonial Governors._

[684] **WILSHERE, William** (1804-1867)

MP Great Yarmouth 1837-47

Corresp and misc papers rel to political and constituency affairs 1838-41 (65 items).
Hertfordshire Record Office (D/EX 14). Presented by Mrs HL Hine 1951. NRA 13775.

Letters to him and petitions from constituents 1838-45 (22 items).
Norfolk Record Office (Great Yarmouth Borough Archives L15). NRA 9311.

[685] **WILSON, George** (1808-1870)

Chairman of the Anti-Corn Law League 1841-6; president of the National Reform Union 1864-70

Corresp of and rel to him 1827-85 (c5,000 items), incl letters from John Bright, Richard Cobden and WE Gladstone.
Manchester Central Library (M 20/1-41). Presented by GMT Wilson 1956.

[686] **WILSON, Henry Joseph** (1833-1914)

MP W Riding of Yorkshire (Holmfirth division) 1885-1912

Corresp and papers rel to the Sheffield Liberal Association, the Sheffield Reform Association and Liberal organisation in Sheffield 1873-1910 (35 bundles); to the Holmfirth constituency 1892-1912 (12 vols and bundles); to elections and candidates in Sheffield constituencies 1874-1911 (48 bundles); to Sheffield municipal politics, elections, etc 1871-1911 (32 bundles); to the Sheffield Liberal press 1872-1911 (20 bundles); to Ireland 1868-1902 (18 bundles); to contagious diseases 1870-1914 (22 vols and bundles); to South Africa 1880-1909 (25 vols and bundles); to the opium trade 1893-1912 (9 bundles); misc political and other corresp and papers 1851-1912 (c72 bundles); diaries 1892, 1900, 1909, 1914 (4 vols); travel journal and letters, Syria 1852 (2 vols).
Sheffield Record Office (HJ Wilson Papers). Presented at various dates by his children Gertrude Lenwood, Helen Wilson and RE Wilson. NRA 7902.

Corresp, papers and printed material rel to local and national politics and social reform 1859-1910 (2,105 items), incl letters from Joseph Chamberlain, Robert Leader and AJ Mundella, and papers rel to Sheffield Liberal organisation and general elections 1874-92; records of the Sheffield Nonconformist Committee 1872-7 (7 vols, 348 items).
Sheffield University Library (Wilson Papers). Deposited by RM Wilson 1961. NRA 7902.

Corresp and notes rel to the Sheffield Smelting Co Ltd and to political and family affairs 1851, 1867-1912 (26 vols and bundles).
Sheffield Record Office (SSC). Deposited 1960. NRA 489.

Corresp and papers 1872-1907 rel to the campaign for the repeal of the Contagious Diseases Act (c25 files).
Fawcett Library, London (Henry J Wilson Papers and Josephine Butler Papers). Deposited by the Josephine Butler Society, which had acquired them from his daughter Helen. NRA 20625.

Corresp rel to politics and social reform c1860-c1900, with some letters to his son AC Wilson (81 items).
Haverford College Library, Pennsylvania (Quaker Collection). Presented by SS Wilson 1977. *National union catalog*, MS 80-66.

[687] **WILSON, General Sir Robert Thomas** (1777-1849)

MP Southwark 1818-31

Letters from British and foreign politicians, army officers and others 1799-1848 (15 vols), incl Lord Brougham, John Cartwright, Lord Castlereagh, the 2nd Earl of Donoughmore, the 1st Earl of Durham, the 2nd Earl Grey, the 3rd Baron Holland and Sir Robert Peel; letters from him to Grey 1810-28 (7 vols); papers mainly rel to political affairs 1800-29 (1 vol), incl an account of the Manchester riots 1819 and notes of parliamentary debates 1829; journals, notebooks, memoranda, etc mainly rel to his military career and to foreign affairs 1800-41 (28 vols, 2 items).
British Library (Add MSS 30095-30144, 30147-8). Purchased from and presented by his son-in-law the Revd Herbert Randolph 1876.

Letters from Lord Grey 1814-26 (120 items).
Durham University Department of Palaeography and Diplomatic (Grey of Howick Collection). Deposited by the 5th Earl Grey 1955. NRA 6228.

[688] **WINN, Rowland** (1820-1893), 1st Baron St Oswald 1885

MP N Lincolnshire 1868-85; a lord of the Treasury and Conservative whip 1874-80

Political corresp 1873-88, incl letters from Sir William Hart Dyke, Sir Stafford Northcote, WH Smith and TE Taylor (2 vols); notebook as chairman of the Conservative central committee for the southern division of the West Riding 1868-80; misc corresp 1830-92 (c10 items); account book 1833-9; botanical notebook c1835.
West Yorkshire Archive Service, Leeds (St Oswald MSS A1.10, D3.8). Deposited by the 5th Baron St Oswald 1986. NRA 10409.

[689] **WOOD, Sir Francis Lindley** (1771-1846), 2nd Bt

Yorkshire politician

Corresp mainly rel to Yorkshire local affairs and estate business 1795-1845 (6 boxes), incl corresp with FH Fawkes and the 4th and 5th Earls Fitzwilliam and other papers rel to politics and elections 1807-44 (9 bundles); family and business corresp and misc papers 1783-1846 (7 boxes), incl letters from his son Charles rel to politics, etc; diaries 1803-34, 1842-6 (35 vols); accounts 1792-9, 1821-39 (2 vols).
Borthwick Institute, York University (Halifax Papers A2, A4, A7). Deposited 1980 by the 3rd Earl of Halifax. NRA 8128.

[690] **WRAXALL, Sir Nathaniel William** (1751-1831), 1st Bt

MP Hindon 1780-4, Ludgershall 1784-90, Wallingford 1790-4

Political memoirs 1784-9, published as *Posthumous memoirs of his own time* (1836) (4 vols).
British Library (Egerton MSS 2141-4). Purchased 1871.

Reminiscences, anecdotes and character sketches 1796-1811 (3 vols); travel journals 1777-9, 1815-16 (6 vols).
Beinecke Library, Yale University, New Haven, Connecticut (Osborn Collection MSS c23-9, c56, fc17). NRA 18661.

Scottish travel journal 1813 (1 vol).
National Library of Scotland (MS 3108). Purchased 1942.

[691] **WRIGHTSON, Sir Thomas** (1839-1921), 1st Bt

MP Stockton 1892-5, St Pancras (E division) 1899-1906

Political and personal letters from AJ Balfour, Joseph Chamberlain, the 6th Marquess of Londonderry, Lord Ullswater and others 1857-1920 (160 items); letter books mainly rel to business affairs 1878-96 (2 vols); family and trust papers 1873-1905 (1 bundle).
Sir Mark Wrightson, Bt. NRA 15949.

[692] **WRIGHTSON, William Battie** (1789-1879)

MP Hull 1830-1, Northallerton 1835-65

Corresp, notes, printed papers, etc mainly rel to Hull, Northallerton and Newcastle elections 1825-66 (4 bundles, 1 item); corresp, notes, etc rel to the Poor Law c1830 (1 bundle); misc corresp 1821-46 (1 bundle, 5 items).
West Yorkshire Archive Service, Leeds (BW/C, BW/P). Deposited 1952 by WL Pearse, trustee of the estate of Lady Isabella Battie-Wrightson. NRA 2622.

Letters, petitions, etc to him as MP for Hull 1830-1 (34 items).
Kingston-upon-Hull City Record Office (DMX 8). NRA 14004.

Business and estate corresp, accounts and papers 1827-77.
Doncaster Archives Department (DD BW).
Transferred from Doncaster Museum 1976. NRA 12415.

[693] **WYNDHAM, George** (1863-1913)

MP Dover 1889-1913; private secretary to AJ Balfour 1887-91; under-secretary for war 1898-1900; chief secretary for Ireland 1900-5

Corresp and papers, with those of his wife, incl his letters to her 1887-1913 (21 files), other family corresp, constituency papers (1 box), misc speech notes and annotated press cuttings mainly 1906, and literary papers.
In private possession. Access restricted. C Hazlehurst and C Woodland, *Guide to the papers of British cabinet ministers 1900-1951,* Royal Historical Society 1974, pp155-6; NRA 21227 (partial calendar).

Family and collected corresp.
In private possession. Hazlehurst and Woodland, *op cit,* p156.

[694] **WYNDHAM, George O'Brien** (1751-1837), 3rd Earl of Egremont 1763

Lord lieutenant of Sussex 1819-35

Royal, political, personal, family and estate corresp 1788-1837, incl letters rel to Sussex, Cumberland and co Clare politics; manuscript poll books, accounts and other papers rel to the Sussex elections of 1807 (11 bundles, 23 items), 1818 (6 vols, 2 items) and 1820 (7 vols, 36 bundles, 100 items); corresp and papers rel to the Sussex yeomanry and militia and as lord lieutenant 1795-1837; misc papers and accounts, incl grand tour accounts 1770 (1 vol, 6 items).
Lord Egremont. Access through West Sussex Record Office. *The Petworth House archives: a catalogue,* 2 vols 1968-79.

[695] **WYNDHAM, Henry** (1830-1901), 2nd Baron Leconfield 1869

MP W Sussex 1854-69

Corresp rel to Horsham divisional Constitutional Association 1890-3 (16 bundles); misc political papers 1880s (3 items); military papers 1868-71 (8 items); estate, sporting and family corresp and papers c1867-1900; accounts 1881-6 (5 items).
Lord Egremont. Access through West Sussex Record Office. *The Petworth House archives: a catalogue,* 2 vols 1968-79.

[696] **WYNDHAM-QUIN, Edwin Richard Wyndham** (1812-1871), 3rd Earl of Dunraven 1850

MP Glamorgan 1837-51

General corresp and papers, with those of his wife, 1826-71 (58 bundles), incl co Limerick election, political and patronage corresp, etc 1838-71, nd (5 bundles), and a parliamentary journal 1838 (1 vol); corresp and papers rel to Glamorgan politics and elections, with some of the 2nd Earl, 1837-8, c1849-50 (2 bundles); estate, railway, building, antiquarian and other corresp and papers mainly c1827-71 (51 bundles, 7 items).
Public Record Office of Northern Ireland (D 3196). Deposited by the 7th Earl of Dunraven 1976. NRA 26717.

Family corresp 1830-67 (4 envelopes).
The Earl of Meath (his great-grandson). NRA 4528.

[697] **WYNDHAM-QUIN, Windham Thomas**
(1841-1926), 4th Earl of Dunraven 1871

Under-secretary for the colonies 1885-6, 1886-7

Political and administrative corresp and papers
1868-1903 (52 items); copies of corresp and papers
rel to his election to Limerick County Council 1889
(1 vol); misc personal, business and estate corresp
and papers c1850-1908 (11 bundles); drafts and
copies of speeches 1885 (6 items); travel journal nd
(1 vol, 2 bundles); press cuttings 1862-1921 (7 vols,
3 bundles).
Public Record Office of Northern Ireland (D 3196).
Deposited by the 7th Earl of Dunraven 1976. NRA
26717.

Political corresp 1880-9 (1 bundle); misc royal
corresp 1884-1923 (1 bundle); misc corresp and
papers 1876-1924 (1 vol, 2 bundles, 1 envelope);
journals c1868-72 (5 vols); diaries 1908-25 (6 vols);
photographs and press cuttings (10 vols).
The Earl of Meath (his grandson). NRA 4528.

WYNN, see Williams Wynn.

[698] **WYSE, Sir Thomas** (1791-1862)

MP Tipperary 1830-1, Waterford 1835-47; a lord
of the Treasury 1839-41; joint secretary of the
Board of Control 1846-9

Political and other corresp and papers c1823-49
(c2,000 items), incl some rel to the Waterford
elections 1826, 1847 and the Tipperary election
1830; family corresp, especially with his brother
George 1810-61 (c500 items); journals 1830-57
(13 folders); misc diplomatic, financial, literary and
other papers.
National Library of Ireland (MSS 1434, 15019-44).
Deposited by WL Bonaparte Wyse 1951-2.
Manuscript sources for the history of Irish civilisation,
ed RJ Hayes, 1965, iv, 925 and *Supplement*, 1979,
i, 793-4.

Political diaries 1829-30, 1839-40, 1845, with other
diaries and notebooks and an essay on Irish politics.
In private possession. A microfilm is in the National
Library of Ireland (n.4984-5, p.5077-8).

Political memoranda 1826-8 (3 vols).
In private possession.

Letters to him and his family from politicians,
authors, members of the Bonaparte family and
others c1820-60.
Untraced. Sold at Sotheby's 17 Nov 1983, lots 223,
225-6, 230, 305-6, 10 May 1984, lots 236, 246 and
28 May 1985, lot 839.

[699] **WYVILL, Christopher** (1740-1822)

Chairman of the Yorkshire Association

Political corresp and papers 1779-1822 (259 vols
and bundles), mainly rel to the campaign for
parliamentary reform, incl minute books of the
Yorkshire Association 1779-84 (4 vols), and corresp

with and papers rel to John Cartwright 1797-1812
(5 bundles, 41 items), Sir George Cayley 1808-19
(56 items), Henry Duncombe c1780-1817 (2
bundles, 69 items), Walter Fawkes 1796-1812 (66
items), CJ Fox 1780-1805 (5 bundles, 19 items),
the 1st Marquess of Lansdowne 1794-1815 (1
bundle, 17 items), William Pitt 1783-96 (2 bundles,
11 items), Sir George Savile 1779-82, nd (4 bundles,
34 items), Lord Stanhope 1786-1812 (4 bundles,
51 items), Sir John Swinburne 1801-19 (1 bundle,
60 items), Samuel Whitbread 1809-15 (2 bundles,
21 items) and William Wrightson 1797-1817 (1
bundle, 112 items); misc family, financial and
estate corresp and papers 1787-1818, nd.
North Yorkshire County Record Office (ZFW).
Deposited by the executors of MF Wyvill
1957,1966. NRA 13480.

[700] **WYVILL, Marmaduke** (1815-1896)

MP Richmond 1847-65, 1866-8

Political corresp and papers, mainly Richmond
election papers, c1841-85 (c14 bundles); personal,
family and estate corresp and papers 1835-85 (c37
bundles); engagement diaries, incl accounts,
1865-85 (41 vols).
North Yorkshire County Record Office (ZFW).
Deposited by the executors of MF Wyvill 1957,
1966. NRA 13480.

[701] **WYVILL, Marmaduke D'Arcy** (1849-1918)

MP W Riding of Yorkshire (Otley division)
1895-1900

Political corresp and papers c1885-1915 (2 vols, c28
bundles), incl Bishop Auckland election papers
1885-6 (2 bundles) and Otley constituency and
election corresp 1886-1900 (11 bundles), notes for
political speeches 1891 (1 bundle) and scrapbook
1890-1915 (1 vol); family, personal, business and
estate corresp and papers 1879-1914 (3 vols, c29
bundles); Eton journal 1863-5 (1 vol); memoranda
1908, 1913 (2 vols).
North Yorkshire County Record Office (ZFW).
Deposited by the executors of MF Wyvill 1957,
1966. NRA 13480.

[702] **YONGE, Sir George** (1731-1812), 5th Bt

MP Honiton 1754-61, 1763-96, Old Sarum
1799-1801; secretary at war 1782-3, 1783-94;
master of the Mint 1794-9

Corresp, mainly as secretary at war, with the 4th
Duke of Grafton, Lord George Lennox, Sir David
Lindsay, Sir George Osborn and other politicians
and army officers 1750-c1812 (850 items).
Huntington Library, San Marino, California.
Purchased from G Michelmore and Co 1922. *Guide
to British historical manuscripts in the Huntington
Library,* 1982, pp365-6.

Letters to him and his deputy secretary Matthew Lewis from members of the Gordon family 1784-94 (18 items).
Aberdeen University Library (MS 2284). NRA 16127.

Letters from Lt-Colonel Jeffrey Amherst and related papers 1784-92 (23 items).
Kent Archives Office (U 2480/O15-37). Purchased at Sotheby's 17 Dec 1981, lot 112. NRA 15261.

Letters from Amherst 1786-92 (14 items).
Untraced. Sold at Sotheby's 22 July 1982, lot 191.

[703] **YORKE, Philip** (1757-1834), 3rd Earl of Hardwicke 1790

MP Cambridgeshire 1780-90; lord lieutenant of Ireland 1801-6

Corresp and papers as lord lieutenant of Ireland mainly 1801-6 (105 vols), comprising official corresp with ministers of state (4 vols), confidential corresp with his brother CP Yorke (6 vols), letters from chief secretaries and under-secretaries (14 vols), letters from Lord Cathcart (1 vol) and Lord Redesdale (2 vols), general Irish corresp (41 vols), letter books (11 vols), papers rel to civil and military establishments, etc (15 vols), and papers rel to audiences and patronage (11 vols); royal, political and general corresp 1778-1831 (12 vols, *c*350ff); corresp mainly rel to the corn laws 1795-1829 (1 vol); corresp and papers rel to Cambridge University, Cambridgeshire militia and local affairs, estate business, etc *c*1779-*c*1834 (*c*32 vols); family corresp 1770-1826 (17 vols); grand tour journals and notebook 1777-9 (3 vols).
British Library (Add MSS 35349-50 *passim*, 35377-35424 *passim*, 35641-35787 *passim*, 35919-34, 36258-60, 45031-2). Purchased from the 6th Earl of Hardwicke 1899, except for Add MSS 45031-2 presented by the 7th Viscount Clifden 1937.

Letters from his son-in-law Lord Caledon, Lord Grenville, Lord Moira, William Pitt and others

*c*1773-1834, with misc papers (140 items); historical and grand tour notebooks *c*1773-8 (3 vols).
Public Record Office of Northern Ireland. (D 2433/D5). Deposited by the trustees of the Caledon Estates 1969. NRA 13276.

Estate corresp 1778-98 (137 items); letter books 1810-20 (9 vols).
Hertfordshire Record Office (D/ECd/F86-94, Add E/4-11). Deposited by the trustees of the Caledon Estates 1972 and by the 6th Earl of Caledon 1976-8. NRA 19506.

Letters mainly from his agent William Paterson 1796-9 (31 items).
Bodleian Library, Oxford (Dep.c.408). Deposited by the Oxford University Institute of Agricultural Economics 1971. NRA 8117.

Letters mainly from Sir Robert Keith 1778-85 and Lord Balcarres 1790-1818 (28 items).
National Library of Scotland (Crawford Muniments 39). Transferred from the John Rylands University Library of Manchester 1988. *Hand-list of personal papers from the muniments of the Earl of Crawford and Balcarres*, 1976, p67.

[704] **YOUNG, George Frederick** (1791-1870)

MP Tynemouth and North Shields 1832-8, Scarborough 1851-2

Corresp 1832-64, mainly rel to his support for Protection (116ff); family corresp 1812-49, mainly letters from him to his wife (1 vol); letter book 1842-6; journal of his honeymoon 1814.
British Library (Add MSS 46712 ff68-183, 46713, 46715A-C). Presented by his grandson DHW Young 1948.

Letters to him from his wife 1852 (1 vol); a few letters from him to her nd, with other misc papers.
Museum of London Library (Young MSS). NRA 28408.

Index of peerage titles

Titles are given only when they differ from the family name

Sutherland, Duchess of (wife of 2nd Duke):
  Sutherland-Leveson-Gower, HEG
Sutherland, Duchess of (wife of 3rd Duke):
  Sutherland-Leveson-Gower, Anne
Sutherland, 1st Duke of: Leveson-Gower
Sutherland, 2nd Duke of: Sutherland-Leveson-
  Gower, GG
Swansea, 1st Baron: Vivian, HH

Talbot of Hensol, 2nd Earl: Chetwynd-Talbot
Tankerville, 4th Earl of: Bennet
Tweeddale, 8th Marquess of: Hay, George
  (1787-1876)

Walsingham, 2nd Baron: De Grey, Thomas
  (1748-1818)

Walsingham, 6th Baron: De Grey, Thomas
  (1843-1919)
Wantage, Baron: Loyd-Lindsay
Wemyss, 10th Earl of: Charteris
Westminster, 1st Duke of: Grosvenor, HL
Westminster, 1st Marquess of: Grosvenor, Robert
  (1767-1845)
Westminster, 2nd Marquess of: Grosvenor,
  Richard
Wharncliffe, 2nd Baron: Stuart-Wortley-
  Mackenzie
Winchilsea, 10th Earl of: Finch-Hatton

Zetland, 1st Marquess of: Dundas, Lawrence

Index of Repositories

The references are to entry numbers

ABERDEEN
University Library 23, 351, 702

ABERYSTWYTH
National Library of Wales 132, 157, 207, 208, 252, 303, 336, 343, 372, 373, 381, 387, 388, 449, 450, 461, 511, 531, 538, 540, 544, 634, 635, 656, 657, 662, 679, 680, 681, 682

AMSTERDAM
International Institute of Social History 137, 348, 451, 491

ANN ARBOR
William L Clements Library, University of Michigan 35, 148, 290, 363, 458, 537

AUSTIN
Humanities Research Center, University of Texas 165

AYLESBURY
Buckinghamshire Record Office 55, 241, 242, 327, 534, 578

BALTIMORE, Maryland
Milton S Eisenhower Library, Johns Hopkins University 428

BANGOR
University College of North Wales 181, 182, 303, 334, 382, 453

BEDFORD
Bedfordshire Record Office 140, 364, 545, 553, 673
Central Library 317

BELFAST
Public Record Office of Northern Ireland 2, 15, 23, 24, 35, 57, 69, 70, 144, 145, 184, 223, 234, 281, 282, 283, 294, 308, 309, 310, 345, 391, 392, 418, 424, 445, 480, 498, 520, 572, 577, 578, 580, 583, 609, 610, 632, 642, 643, 644, 672, 696, 697, 703
Queen's University Library 467

BIRMINGHAM
Central Libraries Archives Department 10, 389
University Library 494, 584

BLACKBURN
Museum and Art Gallery 29

BOLTON
Archive Service 29

BOSTON, Massachusetts
Public Library 148

BRADFORD
University Library 314
West Yorkshire Archive Service, Bradford 218, 527, 603, 604

BRIGHTON
Sussex University Library 49

BRISTOL
University Library 488, 515

BURY ST EDMUNDS
Suffolk Record Office 227, 306, 307, 311, 537

CAMARILLO, California
St John's Seminary Library 148

CAMBRIDGE
Churchill College 75, 90, 175, 401, 608
Fitzwilliam Museum 61, 125, 357, 451
Girton College 494
King's College 84, 577
Trinity College 401, 431
University Library 143, 201, 312, 537, 589, 637

CAMBRIDGE, Massachusetts
Houghton Library, Harvard University 67, 95, 577

CANBERRA
Australian War Memorial 454
National Library of Australia 454

CANTERBURY
Cathedral Library 340

CARDIFF
Glamorgan Archive Service 274, 468, 469, 634
South Glamorgan County Library 146

CARLISLE
Cumbria Record Office 393, 395

CARMARTHEN
Carmarthenshire Area Record Office 103, 380, 512, 539

CHELMSFORD
Essex Record Office 46, 47, 79, 551

WIGAN
Wigan Record Office 637

WINCHESTER
Hampshire Record Office 11, 134, 233, 484, 545,
574, 661, 677
Winchester College 585

WORCESTER
Hereford and Worcester Record Office 649

YORK
Borthwick Institute, York University 268, 689
Minster Library 573

Printed in the United Kingdom for Her Majesty's Stationery Office
Dd289370 6/89 C15 G443 10170